THE FATHERS OF THE CHURCH

MEDIAEVAL CONTINUATION

VOLUME 11

THE FATHERS OF THE CHURCH

MEDIAEVAL CONTINUATION

EDITORIAL BOARD

Gregory F. LaNave
The Catholic University of America Press
Editorial Director

Peter Casarella
DePaul University

Steven Marrone
Tufts University

John Cavadini
The University of Notre Dame

Barbara Newman
Northeastern University

Frank A. C. Mantello
The Catholic University of America

Jan Ziolkowski
Harvard University

David J. McGonagle
Director
The Catholic University of America Press

Carole Monica C. Burnett
Staff Editor

THOMAS AQUINAS
THE ACADEMIC SERMONS

Translated by
MARK-ROBIN HOOGLAND, C.P.

THE CATHOLIC UNIVERSITY OF AMERICA PRESS
Washington, D.C.

Copyright © 2010
THE CATHOLIC UNIVERSITY OF AMERICA PRESS
All rights reserved
Printed in the United States of America

The paper used in this publication meets the minimum
requirements of the American National Standards for
Information Science—Permanence of Paper for Printed
Library Materials, ANSI Z39.48 - 1984.
∞

LIBRARY OF CONGRESS CATALOGING-IN-PUBLICATION DATA
Thomas, Aquinas, Saint, 1225?–1274.
[Sermons. Selections. English]
The academic sermons / Thomas Aquinas ; translated by
Mark-Robin Hoogland.
p. cm. — (The Fathers of the Church,
mediaeval continuation ; v. 11)
Includes bibliographical references and indexes.
ISBN 978-0-8132-2819-8 (pbk.)
ISBN 978-0-8132-1728-4 (cloth : alk. paper) 1. Church year
sermons. 2. Catholic Church—Sermons. 3. Sermons, Latin
—Translations into English. 4. Church year sermons—Early
works to 1800. I. Hoogland, Mark-Robin.
II. Title.   III. Series.
BX1751.3.T4913 2010
252'.02—dc22
2009036243

To all who study God's Word carefully,
meditate on it attentively,
and proclaim the Good News
in word and deed
with a sincere heart

CONTENTS

Preface	ix
Abbreviations	xi
Select Bibliography	xiii

Introduction	3
The "Unknown" Thomas	3
Time and Place	7
The Composition	8
Some Characteristics	10
Main Themes	13
The Translation of the Texts	18

THE ACADEMIC SERMONS

SERMON 01: *Veniet desideratus*	23
SERMON 02: *Lauda et letare*	34
SERMON 03: *Abjiciamus opera*	44
SERMON 04: *Osanna filio David*	46
SERMON 05: *Ecce rex tuus*	62
SERMON 06: *Celum et terra transibunt*	79
SERMON 07: *Ecce ego mitto*	85
SERMON 08: *Puer Jesus*	87
SERMON 09: *Exiit qui seminat*	108
SERMON 10: *Petite et accipietis*	129
SERMON 11: *Emitte spiritum*	138
SERMON 12: *Seraphim stabant*	159
SERMON 13: *Homo quidam fecit cenam magnam*	171
SERMON 14: *Attendite a falsis*	195
SERMON 15: *Homo quidam erat dives*	214
SERMON 16: *Inveni David*	233
SERMON 17: *Lux orta*	242
SERMON 18: *Germinet terra*	259

CONTENTS

SERMON 19: *Beati qui habitant*   281
SERMON 20: *Beata gens*   295
SERMON 21: *Beatus vir*   313

Appendix: "Behind the Names"   329

INDICES

General Index   339
Index of Holy Scripture   345

PREFACE

One day, as I was preparing my lectures on St. Thomas Aquinas (1224/5–1274) as a theologian for today for the Summer Institute at the Catholic Theological Union of Chicago, I came across a reference to one of his sermons. It was quite a shock to realize that I had been studying the life and the works of this member of the Order of *Preachers* for years, but had never read or seen or even heard of a sermon of his—apart from the series on the Our Father, the Hail Mary, and the Ten Commandments. I found the sermon *Homo quidam fecit cenam magnam* (Sermon 13 in this collection), read it, and became totally fascinated with it. Hence, I translated the *Collatio in sero* (part 3) into English and read it together with my students. It was absolutely delightful to see the enthusiasm of the students; three hours were not enough to reflect on the text. This was the beginning of a search for all the sermons and the most reliable versions of the texts, in order to make their content available to a wider audience.

Professor Louis Bataillon, O.P., has been studying Thomas's academic sermons for years. He leads the project group of the *Commissio Leonina*, which is preparing the first critical and complete edition of the Latin texts. He has been most helpful: he provided me with the texts that I did not yet have, gave permission to publish the translations, and was always open to comments and willing to assist me with questions concerning the background of the sermons. For this I am very grateful to him.

Furthermore, I would also like to thank Dr. Antoon Johan Vermeulen for his helpful comments concerning the Latin.

This book has been compiled for my friends, Brethren, family, colleagues, students, and all who are interested in the spirituality and the theology of St. Thomas Aquinas and the meaning of it for today. I hope this publication will contribute to a deeper understanding and appreciation of him as well as a greater enthusiasm to study his writings, and, not in the last place, that at least some of the words he communicated to his audience may inspire us, so that we too may be strengthened in leading a life that is characterized by faith, hope, and love.

DR. MARK-ROBIN HOOGLAND, C.P.
Rome (Italy) / Haastrecht (Zuid-Holland, the Netherlands)
Sunday the 3d of June 2007, the canonization of Fr. Charles Houben, C.P.

Professor Louis Bataillon, O.P., died in the peace of Christ in Paris, on the 13th of February 2009.

ABBREVIATIONS

GENERAL ABBREVIATIONS

SCG	*Summa contra Gentiles*
SN (or In Sen.)	*Commentary on Peter Lombard's* Sententiae
ST	*Summa Theologiae*
Vg	Vulgate

BIBLICAL ABBREVIATIONS

The biblical references in this book are to the present-day numeration. References are made to the Vulgate text (by adding "Vg") in cases when the Vulgate text differs much from the critical source text.

Old Testament

Genesis	Gn		Ezra	Ezr
Exodus	Ex		Nehemiah	Neh
Leviticus	Lv		Tobit	Tb
Numbers	Nm		Judith	Jdt
Deuteronomy	Dt		Esther	Est
Joshua	Jos		1 Maccabees	1 Mc
Judges	Jgs		2 Maccabees	2 Mc
Ruth	Ru		Job	Jb
1 Samuel	1 Sm		Psalm(s)	Ps(s)
2 Samuel	2 Sm		Proverbs	Prv
1 Kings	1 Kgs		Ecclesiastes	Eccl
2 Kings	2 Kgs		Song of Songs	Song
1 Chronicles	1 Chr		Wisdom	Wis
2 Chronicles	2 Chr		Sirach	Sir

Isaiah	Is	Obadiah	Ob
Jeremiah	Jer	Jonah	Jon
Lamentations	Lam	Micah	Mi
Baruch	Bar	Nahum	Na
Ezekiel	Ezek	Habakkuk	Hab
Daniel	Dn	Zephaniah	Zep
Hosea	Hos	Haggai	Hg
Joel	Jl	Zechariah	Zec
Amos	Am	Malachi	Mal

New Testament

Matthew	Mt	1 Timothy	1 Tm
Mark	Mk	2 Timothy	2 Tm
Luke	Lk	Titus	Ti
John	Jn	Philemon	Phlm
Acts of the Apostles	Acts	Hebrews	Heb
Romans	Rom	James	Jas
1 Corinthians	1 Cor	1 Peter	1 Pt
2 Corinthians	2 Cor	2 Peter	2 Pt
Galatians	Gal	1 John	1 Jn
Ephesians	Eph	2 John	2 Jn
Philippians	Phil	3 John	3 Jn
Colossians	Col	Jude	Jude
1 Thessalonians	1 Thes	Revelation	Rv
2 Thessalonians	2 Thes		

SELECT BIBLIOGRAPHY

Bataillon, L.-J. "Les crises de l'université de Paris d'après les sermons universitaires." *Miscellanea Mediaevalia* 10 (1976): 155–69.
———. "L'emploi de la langue philosophique dans les sermons du treizième siècle." *Miscellanea Mediaevalia* 13/2 (1981): 983–91.
———. "Le sermon inédit de Saint Thomas *Homo quidam fecit cenam magnam.* Introduction et edition." *Revue des Sciences Philosophiques et Théologiques* 67 (1983): 353–68.
———. "Les sermons attribués à Saint Thomas. Questions d'authenticité." *Miscellanea Mediaevalia* 19 (1988): 325–41.
———. "Béatitudes et types de sainteté." *Revue Mabillon* n.s. 7 (1996): 79–104.
———. "Sermon pour les Rogations, *Petite et accipietis.* Préface." Unpublished.
Fatula, M. A. "*Contemplata aliis tradere:* Spirituality and Thomas Aquinas, the Preacher." *Spirituality Today* 43.1 (1991): 19–35.
Käppeli, Th. "Una raccolta di prediche attribuite a S. Tommaso d'Aquino." *Archivum Fratrum Praedicatorum* 13 (1943): 59–94.
Kwasniewski, P. A. "A tale of two wonderworkers: St. Nicolas of Myra in the writings and life of St. Thomas Aquinas." *Angelicum* 82 (2005): 19–53.
Leclercq, J. "Un sermon inédit de Saint Thomas sur la royauté du Christ." *Revue Thomiste* 46 (1946): 152–66.
Torrell, J.-P. "La pratique pastorale d'un théologien du XIIIe siècle, Thomas d'Aquin prédicateur." *Revue Thomiste* 82 (1982): 213–45.
———. "Le semeur est sorti pour semer: L'image du Christ pêcheur chez frère Thomas d'Aquin." *La vie spirituelle* 147 (1993): 657–70.
———. *Saint Thomas Aquinas, Volume 1: The Person and His Work.* Translated by Robert Royal. Washington, DC: The Catholic University of America Press, 1996. Especially pp. 69–74, 358–59.
———. *Saint Thomas Aquinas, Volume 2: Spiritual Master.* Translated by Robert Royal. Washington, DC: The Catholic University of America Press, 2003.
Tugwell, S., ed. *Albert & Thomas: Selected Writings.* Translated, edited, and introduced by Simon Tugwell. Preface by Leonard E. Boyle. New York: Paulist Press, 1988.

INTRODUCTION

INTRODUCTION

THE "UNKNOWN" THOMAS

The philosophical and theological works of St. Thomas Aquinas are held in universal esteem, and there is also an increasing attention to his commentaries on Scripture and the role of Scripture in his theological works. Over the years, however, Thomas's sermons have been widely neglected. The Latin texts of some of Thomas's occasional academic sermons are not even published and so not available yet.[1]

It is remarkable that in the past hardly any attention has been given to these occasional academic sermons.[2] After all, Thomas was a Dominican, a member of the *Ordo Praedicatorum*, the Order of Preachers. Preaching was and is their core business, so to speak. And although for *magistri*, professors at the universities like Thomas, the spreading of God's good news was also done by teaching and by giving the good example in everyday life,[3] preaching as such remained an important aspect of their

---

1. The Sermons 01 *Veniet desideratus*, 02 *Lauda et letare*, 04 *Osanna filio Dauid* (complete version), 06 *Celum et terra* in manuscript "P" (Paris), 11 *Emitte Spiritum*, 12 *Seraphim stabant*, and 16 *Inueni Dauid* are not yet published.

2. In the 19th century some sermons were published by P. A. Uccelli (Sermons 08, 14, 17, and 18) in 1869, by J. B. Raulx (Sermons 03, 06, 07, 08, 10 [attributed to Thomas], 14, 15, 17, 20, and 21) in 1881, and by B. Hauréau (two sermons attributed to Thomas: Sermon 10 and *Omnia parata sunt*, "All things are ready" [Mt 22:4]) in 1892. Note that none of the sermons in the collection *Sermones dominicales et Sermones festivi* (schemes or summaries of sermons, translated into English by John M. Ashley in London in 1873 and reissued in Washington in 1996) attributed to Thomas is his. In 1943 Th. Käppeli published his versions of Sermons 04, 09, and 19. Three years later J. Leclercq published Sermon 05. L. J. Bataillon published a part of Sermon 13 in 1974. He has been working on the critical Latin edition of all authentic occasional academic sermons by Thomas for the *Commissio Leonina*.

3. Cf. Thomas's golden rule, as it were, in Sermon 09 *Exiit qui seminat:* "It must

lives. For, not only was preaching part of Thomas's life as a Dominican friar, but it was also one of his three tasks as a *Magister in Sacra Pagina*. The task of a *Magister in Sacra Pagina* was described as *legere, disputare,* and *predicare. Legere* ("reading") means reading and explaining the Scriptures in class. It was done consecutively, verse by verse. His commentaries, for instance, on Job, on the Psalms, and on Paul's letter to the Christians of Rome, are a result of this, as are the *reportationes* (written by a secretary as he was teaching) on the Gospels according to Matthew and John. *Disputare* ("discussing") is a dialectical form of teaching, not on the basis of a text but on a certain topic. The *magister* examined arguments in order to come to the solution of a certain problem. The *Quaestiones disputatae De Veritate* (*On the Truth*) and *De Potentia* (*On Power*) are examples of the fruit of this type of teaching. Furthermore, twice a year, during Advent and Lent, discussions were organized at the university during which anyone present (other *magistri*, students, interested people) could pose a question on any topic. The *Quaestiones quodlibetales* (*On Whatever You Want: Various Subjects*) find their origin in these events. The third task of a *magister* was *predicare* ("preaching"). This third task was taken as seriously as the other two. In order to be appointed as a Bachelor, a theologian first had to deliver two sermons (that is, two S*ermones* or a *Sermo* and a *Collatio in sero;* see below), as a test. Yet, interestingly enough, the work that made Thomas famous, the *Summa Theologiae* (ST), a work in the style of the *quaestiones disputatae*, was not part of his duty as a *magister;* he wrote it in his spare time.

Why, then, were Thomas's sermons (almost) forgotten for such a long time? Because they are regarded as "only" a pastoral application of the theology he taught? At least one of the reasons seems to be that Thomas never bundled them himself; he never composed a collection of his occasional academic sermons. This fact also renders it more complicated to establish the authenticity of texts that are attributed to him.[4] Moreover,

---

not be so that a preacher preaches to others what he is not doing himself." According to his biographers Thomas put into practice what he preached.

4. In this book we follow L. J. Bataillon, O.P., *Les sermons attribués à Saint Thomas: questions d'authenticité,* in: *Miscellanea Mediaevalia* 19 (1988): 325–41. He finds 19 authentic sermons, which are also listed in J.-P. Torrell, O.P., *Saint Thomas*

these sermons do not form a complete whole like the sermons on the Our Father, the Hail Mary, the Creed, and the Ten Commandments. In the thirteenth century, a time when theologians sought to collect, order, and systematize knowledge, wisdom, and insights (which was done in a *summa*), the occasional academic sermons may, therefore, have been regarded as less interesting, even by Thomas himself. There is, insofar as we know, only one collection of Thomas's occasional academic sermons, a collection of eleven sermons attributed to him. In some cases their authenticity is probable, but not absolutely certain.[5]

The lack of interest in his occasional academic sermons in the past is at the same time favorable for us in a way. For by reason of this there are not as many versions of the text as there are, for instance, of the sermons on the Our Father and the Ten Commandments. As Thomas was preaching, one of his secretaries (such as Reginald of Piperno or Peter of Andria, for instance) took notes. These were copied, and so the text was disseminated. There neither is nor was a version in Thomas's own handwriting, nor was a version edited by him. Moreover, copyists sometimes "improved" (that is, clarified, changed, made additions to) the text, so that different versions may be quite divergent. Since there was not much interest in the occasional academic sermons, they were not copied as much. Hence there

---

Aquinas, Volume I: The Person and His Work, trans. R. Royal (Washington, DC: The Catholic University of America Press, 1996), 358–59. Later L .J. Bataillon, O.P., discovered *Inueni Dauid* (Sermon 16). There is no doubt that it is Thomas's, as also other scholars, such as P. A. Kwasniewski, have confirmed. Also *Petite et accipietis* is included (as Sermon 10), although it is in all probability not Thomas's. It has long been attributed to Thomas, but I find L. J. Bataillon's argumentation convincing that it is very unlikely that it is from his hand, on the ground of textual data (e.g., one of the two manuscripts does not carry Thomas's name at all) and the content (which does not quite match what Thomas says in the ST on prayer), and also in view of the style and the atmosphere that it breathes, which are quite different from those of the other occasional sermons. Bataillon decided to include it in the collection because two manuscripts have rubrics ascribing them to Thomas.

5. These manuscripts are known as *Salamanca* and *Sevilla*. They are found in the edition of Thomas's *Opera Omnia* (volume VI) produced by Robert Busa, S.J., and on the internet: www.corpusthomisticum.org/it and www.unav.es/filosofia/alarcon/amicis/ctcorpus.

are not as many versions of them: never more than four. Sometimes there is even only one manuscript, whereas there are around eighty of the serial sermons and even as many as one hundred and fifty manuscripts of the sermons on the Creed. Still, if there are only two manuscripts, they may diverge quite a bit, as is the case with Sermon 06 *Celum et terra.*

There are more aspects which make these occasional academic sermons interesting: they give us a better insight into the content and style of Thomas's preaching than do the serial sermons. After all, Thomas preached on the Our Father, the Hail Mary, and the Ten Commandments in the vernacular (*in vulgari*, Italian), and the secretaries translated them into Latin. The Latin text is the only form in which these sermons are handed down to us. Now, translation inevitably means a loss as well as interpretation. The occasional sermons, however, were given in Latin. When the translated Latin texts of the sermons are compared to ones that were given in Latin, we see some differences; for example, in the latter we meet a Thomas who is stylistically looser and livelier. Although he spoke his native tongue in the serial sermons, we find more colloquial language in the occasional Latin sermons: some sentences are grammatically challenged. On the other hand, the style of the texts of the translated sermons is more formal and streamlined; there we do not find formulations like "I say" (that is, "I interpret this as," which appears, for example, several times in Sermon 13 *Homo quidam fecit*) or "Because of the shortness of the time we say just something about . . ." (Sermon 20 *Beata gens,* at the beginning of the *Collatio in sero*). It is also eye-catching that in the occasional sermons we find examples from everyday life that are concrete, short, and to the point, but not in the serial sermons. Yet William of Tocco, Thomas's first biographer, speaks of Thomas's rapture as he preached *in illo suo vulgari* in Rome, moving his audience to tears as he preached on the Passion of Christ and made the people take part in the joy of the Resurrection.[6] In light of this it seems likely that the more formal style in the translated seri-

---

6. J.-P. Torrell, O.P., refers to this in his article "La pratique pastorale d'un théologien du XIIIe siècle Thomas d'Aquin prédicateur, " in *Revue Thomiste* 82 (1982): 217.

al sermons is due to the translation into Latin (and possibly the adaptation of the text) by a secretary. The same applies to the absence of examples; the secretary might have left them out for the sake of the clarity of the line of reasoning. But in the end we cannot be sure. Furthermore, at times we see a more passionate Thomas in the occasional sermons, such as Sermons 06 *Celum et terra* and 14 *Attendite a falsis,* where he addresses his audience with "My dearest brethren" ([*Fratres*] *karissimi*), and the same is true of Sermon 08 *Puer Iesus,* where he tries to persuade his audience by making an appeal not only to the intellect but also to the emotions in order to get his message across and to strengthen the listeners in a virtuous life with God.

TIME AND PLACE

Since Thomas did not list, collect, or order his occasional academic sermons, it is often very complicated, if not impossible, to establish when and where he gave them and even whether Thomas actually is the author.[7] The occasion of the sermon is never a problem, since it is always mentioned. The year, however, is never mentioned. When the exact date is certain or probable, it is mentioned in the notes.

In the course of the academic year, *magistri* and bachelors took turns preaching on the Sundays and feast days, some of which were observed only by the theological faculty. When this was the case the sermon was probably given at the house of the Dominicans or Franciscans.[8]

In Paris an occasional sermon usually consisted of three parts: *Prothema, Sermo,* and *Collatio in sero.* The *Prothema* and the *Sermo* were given in the morning, at Mass, after the Gospel reading. The *Collatio in sero* was given in the late afternoon, during the vespers. If a sermon does not have a *Collatio in sero* (Sermon 04 *Osanna filio Dauid* and Sermon 16 *Inueni Dauid*), it was probably given by another preacher.

7. See note 4.
8. This is according to the statutes of the university of 1335, but it may well have been the practice already before that year and when Thomas was in Paris (1252–1256 and 1268–1272); cf. the heading of Sermon 06 *Celum et terra.*

Most of the occasional sermons were given in Paris, *coram universitate*. It is very likely that a good number of them were given at St. James (Saint Jacques), the house of the Dominicans. We know that Sermon 03 *Abjiciamus opera* was given at Bologna and that Sermon 07 *Ecce ego mitto* was given at Milan, maybe one week later. But it is very unlikely that it was in December of the year 1268, as we long thought on the basis of P. Mandonnet's reconstruction of Thomas's journey from Rome to Paris.[9]

At any rate, therefore, for a good understanding of the occasional sermons—what is Thomas saying and why—it is important to realize that the audience addressed consisted mostly of other friars (Thomas's Dominican brethren and Franciscans), colleagues, and clerical students.

THE COMPOSITION

Eleven of the twenty[10] sermons are made up of three parts: a *Prothema*, a *Sermo* and a *Collatio in sero*. Two sermons have a *Prothema* and a *Sermo*, and four merely a *Sermo*. These four may well have been delivered in Italy. Three other sermons (03, 06, and 07) are known to us only in abridged versions; these are preserved in a collection of abridged sermons, nearly all by Bonaventure—a collection that was meant, it seems, as a source of ideas for Franciscan preachers. It is quite obvious that Sermon 06 *Celum et terra* is the summary of a sermon in three parts. Also, Sermon 03 *Abjiciamus opera* is preserved as a summary. It could well have been a sermon in three parts, too.[11] Of Sermon

---

9. In the Editio Leonina part XLV (i, pp. 286*–287*) R. A. Gauthier argues that P. Mandonnet's reconstruction of Thomas's journey from Rome to Paris over land in the winter of 1268–1269 cannot be correct. In the company of Nicolas Brunaccio, Thomas traveled to Paris earlier, most probably in August or September of 1268. Furthermore, it is most likely that the major part of the journey was by boat. Cf. Simon Tugwell, ed., *Albert & Thomas, Selected Writings* (New York: Paulist Press, 1988), 225, 317 (note 249).

10. In what follows we leave Sermon 10 aside, in view of what is said in note 4.

11. This seems plausible, for the first part of the text is in the form of a *Prothema*. Furthermore, since there is no *Sermo* that consists of two parts (all but one, the *Sermo* of Sermon 17, consist of three or four parts), and since the second part of the text concerns the first part of Rom 13.12, it is more likely that

INTRODUCTION   9

07 *Ecce ego* only a fragment is preserved, on the basis of which we cannot draw conclusions.[12]

The *Prothema* is the introduction of the sermon. It begins with the Scripture verse that is the subject of the sermon. Subsequently Thomas makes one or a few preliminary remarks. This is usually not the introduction of the theme of the sermon (although it is, for example, in Sermon 08), but rather the framework in which the sermon is given. Thomas underlines, for instance, how important the Holy Spirit is if we want to speak wisely (Sermon 11, on Pentecost) or that we need spiritual strength in order to live without deception (Sermon 14, on how to distinguish the true sheep from wolves in disguise). The *Prothema* usually ends in a prayer for divine help and inspiration: "that I may say something useful about 'the subject' to the honor of God," or something similar. Only in Sermons 06, 08, 18, and 20 is the full prayer written down by the secretary; in the other instances he contented himself after quoting a few words with "et cetera."

The *Sermo* and the *Collatio in sero* are two parts of the sermon in which the verse from Scripture is dissected and explained. The *Collatio in sero* is the continuation of the *Sermo*.[13] Mostly it focuses on the second half of the verse, highlighting one or a few other aspects of the same theme. The *Collatio in sero* is generally somewhat shorter than the *Sermo*.

At the beginning of the *Sermo* Thomas tells his audience which steps he is going to take. Usually he also does so in the *Collatio in sero*. At the beginning of the *Collatio in sero* he briefly refers to what he has said in the morning. Most of the time he follows precisely the plan announced, although an exception is found, for example, in Sermon 20 (see note 56 there).

The sermon (or sometimes the *Sermo* and the *Collatio in sero*

---

this part is a summary of the *Sermo*. Then the third part of the text, which concerns the second part of Rom 13.12, would be a summary of the *Collatio in sero*.

12. The first part of the text is probably the beginning of the *Sermo;* Thomas presents the three steps that he is going to take. Since the second part of the text speaks of angels, it may be an excerpt from Thomas's second step.

13. The term *collatio* is also used in other senses. In Thomas's *Collationes in decem preceptis* (*Sermons on the Ten Commandments*), for instance, it designates a sermon in a series, not necessarily given in the late afternoon or early evening.

individually) is usually divided into three or four parts, in accordance with the classical rhetorical rules. It is in that sense a very convenient arrangement. The first point Thomas makes is generally much more elaborate than the second point—sometimes the first point even takes the whole *Sermo*—and the second point is more elaborate than the third, and the third than the fourth. Each part is subdivided in most cases into three or four parts, and often a subdivision is broken down again. Because of this the structure of the text may not always be clear at first sight.[14] Therefore I have numbered the paragraphs in accordance with the structure as Thomas himself has indicated it.

SOME CHARACTERISTICS

Most of the sermons are based on a verse from the Gospels, especially the Gospel according to Matthew, or the Psalms.

Within the sermons the number of Scripture references stands out. Furthermore, besides the many quotations there are quite a few references to Scripture in Thomas's sermons that are not made explicit. In the text I refer to these by recognizing them in the notes or by "[cf. a certain text]." Thomas is not, however, simply quoting and referring to Scripture at random in order to gain authority and to get his point across. For Thomas, Scripture is the highest authority, and it is the directive for his line of reasoning. A clear example is found in the *Sermo* of Sermon 21 for the Feast of St. Martin, where the three steps he takes are based on what we read in Rom 8.30. Thus Thomas is explaining the Scriptures with the Scriptures, something he does also in his theological works.

Relatively many quotations are from the Psalms. This is no surprise since Thomas prayed them every day together with his brethren in the Liturgy of the Hours, except for the time when he had dispensation from communal prayer so that he could be more devoted to his theological work. He probably, however, still prayed them by himself. So he was very familiar with the Psalms. The same applies to the many quotations from Job, the

---

14. The *Sermo* of Sermon 13 is in this respect the most complicated text.

Prophet Isaiah (often referred to as "the Prophet"), the Gospel according to Matthew, and the Letters of Paul (generally called "the Apostle"): these are the books on which he lectured at the university.[15] Also Proverbs, Qohelet (Ecclesiastes), the Book of Wisdom, and Sirach are cited and referred to frequently; since these books contain many concrete, practical directions for a good, virtuous life, they suit sermons well.

For us the Christological reading of the Old Testament in Thomas's works is notable. In his time it was a common interpretation, regarded as part of the *sensus litteralis*.[16] The Christological interpretation of Old Testament texts is already found in the New Testament: words and sayings are read as (also) Christ's and referring to Christ: for example, Old Testament texts are applied to Christ's coming (as in Mt 2.6), life (as in Lk 4.18), and Passion (as in 1 Pt 2.24). Such exegesis was common among the Church Fathers and in the later tradition. The basis for reading the Old Testament in this way is the belief that the Old Testament is fulfilled in Christ, as we read in Jn 19.28 and Lk 24.25–27.

At times the references to Scripture are not explicit and the quotations not precise, and many are not complete—in some sermons more than others, probably because there were different secretaries and copyists. A verse may be referred to just by a few words followed by "etc." Even more, the pivotal word(s) or term(s) may not be in the text quoted. In that case the translation of the whole verse is found in the text, but the words omitted in the Latin text appear in parentheses.

The texts themselves seem to indicate that Thomas had the use of a concordance: he cites many less familiar Scripture texts, and, furthermore, several times he quotes Scripture texts

---

15. Thomas lectured on the Psalms only at the very end of his life, in 1272–1273. His commentary is unfinished: it covers Psalms 1 to 55.16 (Vg 54.16).

16. Thomas stands in the tradition that holds that the Scripture texts contain and reveal not only the truth about created things, but even the mystery of God. Therefore, a word, sentence, or narrative can have more than one meaning. Four levels are distinguished: the literal or historical sense, the allegorical sense, the moral sense, and the anagogic sense. See also ST I 1,10. This determines Thomas's approach, for instance, in Sermon 16 *Inueni Dauid*.

consecutively that have one word in common.[17] Concordances became more and more available in the 13th century.[18]

Other quotations in the text are mainly from Church Fathers, especially Augustine. Also Aristotle, "the Philosopher," is cited as an authority a few times. It is interesting to see how he is systematically ignored in one of the manuscripts of Sermon 06 *Celum et terra* (see the notes there). Apparently a secretary or copyist did not consider it appropriate to present a pagan philosopher (as an authority) in a Christian sermon, or, the other way round, someone has added Aristotle's sayings when copying the text. Yet another source from which Thomas drew was the liturgy, for instance, several times in Sermon 21 when, in regard to the life of St. Martin, he refers several times to the Dominican reading of that Feast.

It cannot come as a surprise that Thomas used his own theological works as he was preaching. In the footnotes I connect the sermons with texts from the *Summa Theologiae* (ST) or, if a certain theme in a sermon is not (or not clearly or extensively) reflected upon, from other theological works. These sermons are a typical example of the way in which the friars transmitted to others what they had been contemplating, in conformity with the Dominicans' device: *contemplari et contemplata aliis tradere*, that is, to contemplate and to pass what has been contemplated, the results of this contemplation, on to others.

---

17. E.g., *miles*, "soldier," in Sermon 12 (in paragraph 2.2.3) and *miser*, "wretched," in Sermon 13 (*Collatio in sero* paragraph 3.2).

18. The Dominicans compiled the first concordances. Hugo of Saint-Cher, assisted by 500 fellow Dominicans as it is reported, was the very first who completed one, in 1230: the concordance of Saint Jacques. Data on a given word were references only to the biblical book and chapter (according to the arrangement made a few years before, by Stephen Langton, Archbishop of Canterbury). Hugo divided the chapters into seven equal parts and indicated them with the letters *A* through *G*, in order to make the references more precise (only in 1545 were the verses numbered, as we know them, by Robert Estienne). In a few instances we find these letters in Thomas's texts. In the years 1250–1252 English Dominicans published an improved version: it contained not only references to the biblical locus, but it gave the whole sentence in which the word occurred, which was much more useful to the preachers and theologians.

INTRODUCTION 13

Now, it is significant to see that Thomas uses hardly any theological terms in his academic sermons. He could have done so, since the main part of his audience would have understood it. Yet Thomas's language in these sermons is strikingly plain and simple; he did not want to show off, it seems, as some of his contemporaries did. He may well have taken St. Paul's words to heart, that Christ sent him "to preach the Gospel, and not with the wisdom of human eloquence, so that the cross of Christ might not be emptied of its meaning" (1 Cor 1.17). Neither do we find any theatrical elements like jokes and elaborate anecdotes in his sermons. If he puns, he does it in a subtle way, as in Sermon 17, on the Feast of Mary's birth, concerning the words *virgo* (virgin) and *virga* (twig).

Not many people will overlook that in one of the sermons, Sermon 16 *Inueni Dauid*, Thomas speaks of women as naturally weak; a strong woman is a rare find. He is not very original when he says this; this explanation of Prv 31.10 ("A strong woman, who will find her?") echoes the way of thinking of that time.[19] Before drawing quick and easy conclusions it is good to see that, although he is a child of his time, in his further writings he is more distinguished than in this remark. Likewise, in the *Sermo* of Sermon 18 *Germinet terra*, Thomas juxtaposes the feeble, corrupted woman and the virtuous, strong woman through whom salvation came into the world, the Blessed Virgin Mary.

MAIN THEMES

Thomas's uncomplicated language in the occasional academic sermons suits the content. For these sermons are primarily practical, aimed at the edification of his audience. Beside the contemplation of God's love for us and our love for God as a response to it, there is a strong emphasis on active love of the neighbor, relatively more than in his theological works. He

19. In the text it is clear that Thomas touches common ground when he says this; he just uses it as an example to make something clear about what we commonly understand by the verb "to find."

clearly states that, for a Christian, knowledge and putting that knowledge into practice belong together: a believer, and especially a preacher, must live in accordance with what he or she knows (Sermon 09 *Exiit qui seminat*). This does not mean that the sermons are full of examples from everyday life; Thomas rather speaks of this love of others in the broader view of the neighbor's and his audience's well-being, spiritual and material.

In these sermons there is more emphasis on the spiritual, for eventually happiness is not found in anything earthly; the body is temporary, as are earthly glory, honor, and riches, too, whereas the soul does not die. Yet also the material aspect of human life is clearly brought to the listeners' attention. It is good to see this against the background of the growing poverty in the fairly new cities of the 13th century. In earlier, more rural times there had always been something to eat, so to speak. Primarily poverty had to do with not being able to do what you wanted to do. But in the new urban societies poverty was characterized more by a lack of money, food, and shelter, while there were many more rich people than ever before (because of a prospering trade). This situation of social injustice colors Thomas's preaching.

Not only are people to share what they have, but also what they know. Only in Sermon 08 *Puer Jesus* (*Collatio in sero*) does Thomas explicitly depict what the attitude of a scholar should be, but in fact Thomas himself makes a display of this attitude in all his works: it is an obligation that we share with others what we have learned. Even more, sharing wisdom, insights, and knowledge is *the* way for us to acquire these.

❖

Thomas's language suits the content of his sermons, and many of his themes are clearly geared to his audience. In quite a few sermons the religious life is a theme, as in Sermon 04 *Osanna filio Dauid* and Sermon 09 *Exiit qui seminat:* he brings up questions like "Does it make sense to take vows? What is the surplus value of it?" and "Should young people be led into religious life?" Why he does this is obvious against the background of the tensions between the regular and the secular *magistri* and bachelors at the University of Paris, which had already begun in the 20s of the 13th century and only deteriorated in the course of time, culminating in a most serious crisis in 1270–1271. Here we come to know Thomas as a zealous defender of the religious life: the religious life is most meaningful and valuable and it must be promoted, so that they who are called to it also choose to live it.

The same applies to the assessment of the relation between faith and philosophy, that is, the relation between what is a (supernatural) gift from God and (natural) human wisdom and knowledge. Debates between philosophers and theologians are reflected in the sermons where Thomas harps upon the primacy of faith over any human insight. Sermon 14 *Attendite a falsis* is illustrative in this respect, where he says that because of her faith an old (uneducated) woman knows and understands more than any of the great non-believing philosophers.

Thomas is an ardent preacher when it comes to defending the faith and religious life, but at the same time he is not rigorous. Thomas is reluctant to use violence towards sinners and even towards heretics; since the latter are a great danger for the unity of the Church and the salvation of the people, they must be converted: first by convincing them by means of words and signs, and only eventually by giving them a hard time (*Collatio in sero* of Sermon 13 *Homo quidam fecit*).

This attitude of his, which we also find in his theological works, is the expression of the virtuous life that he promotes. In all sermons Thomas urges his audience to lead a virtuous life. Three aspects stand out: first, the love of God and, in connection with this, the love of the neighbor; second, the great attention to the cardinal virtues,[20] the virtues that order our lives in such a way that we can live together in harmony and peace; third, virtues that he brings to the fore as important in religious life (after all, his audience consists mostly of religious): obedience, humility, prayer,[21] and fidelity to vows.

In twelve of the twenty sermons Thomas explicitly brings to

---

20. Prudence, justice, strength, and temperance, and the virtues connected with these; cf. the many references in the notes to ST II–II 47–170.

21. Thomas gives instructions on how and for whom we should pray, with explicit and implicit references to Matthew 6 and Luke 11 and 18.

our attention that we are created in the image of God,[22] the triune God (Sermon 12, on Trinity Sunday), but that in us this image is obscured to a greater or lesser extent through sin (Sermon 05). If we look at Christ, we see what is meant by being and living as the image of God. Hence, Christians are to follow (a) God (Sermon 13); (b) Christ, in everything (Sermon 08), even in his Passion (as Thomas fervently advocates at the end of Sermon 05); and (c) the renewal of the Holy Spirit (Sermon 11, on Pentecost). Such is the perfection of a Christian life. The holy ones go or have gone before us on the way (Sermon 20). Following the crowds (Sermon 08), the advice of sinners (Sermon 21), and your own thoughts (Sermon 14) and desires (Sermon 09), is at odds with such a virtuous way of life; God became like us so that we would become like him.[23]

An interesting consequence of this view is found in the *Sermo* of Sermon 15 (*Homo quidam erat dives*). Soiling a crucifix, an image of Christ in wood, is blasphemous; how much more, then, if someone damages a fellow human being, which is the image of God in the flesh, a much more excellent image?

❖

Three more themes arrest the attention because these are not discussed in other works by Thomas as they are here: the Holy Spirit, the Church, and Mary. Indeed, many of the points made in these sermons are found throughout the *Summa Theologiae* and in other theological works, but in these occasional sermons Thomas presents a more integral view of these themes. In the *Summa Theologiae* the Holy Spirit is contemplated in the context of the Trinity, the sending of the Son and the Holy Spirit, the moral life, the Incarnation, the miracles that Christ worked, the Passion, and the sacraments, whereas in Sermon 11, given on Pentecost, these and other aspects are presented in one very fine meditation on the mystery of the sending of the Holy Spirit to us and what this means for our lives as Christians. In particular the *Collatio in sero* of this sermon is a beautiful reflection of Thomas's spirituality.

---

22. Sermons 04, 05, 08, 09, 11 to 17, and 20.
23. Cf. Athanasius, *De incarnatione* 54.

In Thomas's theological works we do not find an exposition on the Church.[24] Yet in Sermons 13 and 19 we come across some noteworthy insights. In Sermon 19, given on the Feast of All Saints, Thomas depicts one community of God and believers on earth and in heaven: the community of the ones who are in community with Christ. Characteristic of this community is that the members share the same end—happiness—but also that they help one another to attain it; thus the saints who have reached that happiness (they are *comprehensores*) help us who are on the way (*viatores*) to attain it. Thus the Community of Faith is characterized by solidarity. In the *Collatio in sero* of Sermon 13 on Lk 14.16, "Someone gave a great dinner and invited many," Thomas speaks of the question of who is invited. The text shows that according to Thomas the Church is an inclusive community; for instance, referring to Ambrose, Thomas endorses that sinners must not be cut out, but rather must be invited in. Therefore the servant in the Gospel who was sent, and thus Thomas's audience, must go to great lengths to gather everybody in. Educating the ignorant is an obvious method for a Dominican.

In the *Summa Theologiae* we read very little about the Blessed Virgin Mary outside the context of the Incarnation. In some occasional academic sermons and, in particular, in Sermon 17 *Lux orta* and in the *Sermo* of Sermon 18 *Germinet terra*, both given on the Feast of the Birth of the Blessed Virgin Mary, we get an insight into Thomas's devotion to Mary.[25] As in the *Summa Theologiae* she is the one through whom our salvation became flesh and blood in the world. Furthermore, she is the one to call upon in distress (Sermon 15), a great example of meditation (Sermon 08), and the paragon of virtue in general (Sermons 17 and 18). Thomas presents her as so perfect that she becomes almost super-human. Here Thomas breathes the common culture and spirituality of his time.

---

24. Sermons 12 and 13 of the series on the Creed concerning "I believe in one, holy, catholic, and apostolic Church" are obviously dedicated to this theme.

25. The prayer *O beatissima et dulcissima virgo Maria*, ascribed to Thomas, is not his.

THE TRANSLATION OF THE TEXTS

The present volume contains a translation of the twenty occasional academic sermons that are deemed authentic by Louis-Jacques Bataillon, O.P. (see note 4, above), as well as the sermon *Petite et accipietis*, which was long considered Thomas's.

The considerable length of the sermons, their divisions and subdivisions, and the number of quotations from Scripture and the Church Fathers may be trying to the reader. In order to make the texts more accessible and to clarify the line of reasoning, the divisions and subdivisions of the texts are numbered, following Thomas's own indications. The translations in this volume have retained the format of the scriptural references as they appear in each of the Latin texts; these formats vary from text to text in regard to whether the references are bracketed or are simply embedded as an intrinsic part of the sermon.

As was said above, in the notes the reader finds in particular references to Thomas's theological works, especially the *Summa Theologiae* (ST) and the *Summa Contra Gentiles* (SCG). These show that his theology is the foundation of his sermons. In addition, the references may invite the reader to explore further the themes of interest in Thomas's theological works.

❖

The textual versions used for this book are listed below. The texts whose titles appear in italics are not yet available in the critical edition of the Commissio Leonina, but will be published by the commission in the near future; for the time being, they are available only through the first translation of these in this book. An earlier, available version of the unavailable Latin textual versions is referred to in notes 25 through 31. "Busa" refers to volume VI of Thomas Aquinas's *Opera Omnia*, edited by Roberto Busa, S.J. (Stuttgart-Bad Cannstatt, 1980).

01 *Veniet desideratus:* text by L. J. Bataillon (provisional Leonine text)
02 *Lauda et letare:* text by L. J. Bataillon (provisional Leonine text)
03 *Abjiciamus opera:* text Lutetia Parisiorum 1879, also in Busa, page 38a

INTRODUCTION 19

04 *Osanna filio Dauid:* complete text by L. J. Bataillon (provisional Leonine text)[26]
05 *Ecce rex tuus:* text by J. Leclercq, published in *Revue Thomiste* (1946), also in Busa, page 45a
06 *Celum et terra transibunt:* texts (manuscripts Milano and Paris) by L. J. Bataillon (provisional Leonine text)[27]
07 *Ecce ego mitto:* text Lutetia Parisiorum 1879, also in Busa, page 42a
08 *Puer Jesus:* text Cod. Lat. 15034 Bibl. Nat. Parisiorum, also in Busa, page 33a
09 *Exiit qui seminat:* text by Th. Käppeli in *Archivum Fratrum Praedicatorum* (1943), also in Busa, page 42b
10 *Petite et accipietis:* text by L. J. Bataillon (provisional Leonine text)[28]
11 *Emitte Spiritum:* text by L. J. Bataillon (provisional Leonine text)
12 *Seraphim stabant:* text by L. J. Bataillon (provisional Leonine text)
13 *Homo quidam fecit cenam magnam:* text by L. J. Bataillon, published in *Revue des Sciences Philosophiques et Théologiques* (1983)
14 *Attendite a falsis:* text by L. J. Bataillon (provisional Leonine text)[29]
15 *Homo quidam erat dives:* text by L. J. Bataillon (provisional Leonine text)[30]
16 *Inueni Dauid:* text by L. J. Bataillon (provisional Leonine text)
17 *Lux orta:* text Parma 1869, also in Busa, page 36b
18 *Germinet terra:* text by L. J. Bataillon (provisional Leonine text)[31]

26. Text published in part by Th. Käppeli in *Archivum Fratrum Praedicatorum* 13 (1943), also in Busa, page 42a.
27. Text Lutetia Parisiorum 1879 (of the manuscript Milano) in Busa, page 37c.
28. Text Lutetia Parisiorum, 1879, in Busa, page 582a.
29. Text Parma, 1869, in Busa, page 35a.
30. Text Lutetia Parisiorum, 1879, in Busa, page 38a.
31. Text by P. A. Uccelli published in *I Gigli a Maria* 12 (1874), also in Busa, page 38a.

19 *Beati qui habitant:* text by L. J. Bataillon (provisional Leonine text)[32]
20 *Beata gens:* text Lutetia Parisiorum, 1879, also in Busa, page 39c
21 *Beatus vir:* text Lutetia Parisiorum, 1879, also in Busa, page 41a

Since in only a few sermons do we know the exact year in which Thomas gave them, it is impossible to arrange them in a chronological order. Therefore, they are put in a liturgical order:[33] first, the sermons of the Sundays in the order of the liturgical calendar (01–15), and then, in the same way, the sermons on the feast days (16–21).

32. Text by Th. Käppeli in *Archivum Fratrum Praedicatorum* 13 (1943), also in Busa, page 44a.
33. Following the proposition of L. J. Bataillon, O.P. It is the order in which the Latin texts will be published by the Commissio Leonina.

THOMAS AQUINAS
THE ACADEMIC SERMONS

SERMON 01
VENIET DESIDERATUS

Sermon on the First Sunday of Advent

Haggai 2.7: *He who is desired by all the nations together will come, and he will fill this house with glory.*

Sermo

IT IS AS Augustine says to Optatus: "Nobody is freed from the damnation that came through Adam but through faith in Jesus Christ." This is sufficiently proven by the Apostle in Hebrews 11 [verse 6], where he shows that no one has ever been able to please God without faith. From this it follows that at all times after a lapse faith has been a necessity for recovery, for there is no other medicine for the weakness of original or actual sin.[1] And therefore all the saints always, from the beginning of the world, longed for and desired the coming of the Savior.[2]

And this is shown well and plainly in the saying mentioned in which the Prophet shows three things, in this order: (1) first, he shows God's Son himself who is coming down from the heavens: "he will come"; (2) second, he shows the one who mercifully fulfills the desires of the Fathers [Patriarchs]: "who is desired by all the nations together"; (3) third, he shows the one who freely bestows his pleasing benefit [upon us]: "and he will fill

---

1. Cf. ST I–II 109,7, 113,4, and 114,7, where Thomas underlines that this is not a matter of merit; faith is a gracious gift from God.

2. Hence Thomas employs a Christological reading of the Old Testament: Moses, the prophets, and the Psalmist speak already of the Christ, and he speaks through them.

this house with glory." In the first part the lowliness of the coming one or of the coming is shown in view of the way; in the second the necessity of the coming in view of the human race; in the third the utility of the coming in view of the gift offered. The first brings to the fore that we should prepare a warm welcome for him; the second, that we should focus our desire on him; the third, that we should receive the benefit offered.

❖

(1) So, first, he shows that the Son of God comes down humbly from the heavens when he says: "He will come." I interpret "He will come" as: insofar as it is absolutely necessary for us. Well, the coming of the Savior was necessary, for three reasons: first, because the world was imperfect in many ways; second, because man was cast down from his rightful honor in a foul way; and third, because God was offended by man in a wondrous way. Therefore, he came (1.1) in order to grant to the whole world the highest grade of dignity, (1.2) in order to lead man back to his proper human state, and (1.3) in order to take away the offense of man against God.[3]

(1.1) Now the grade of perfection in the world fell short in three respects: (1.1.2) one way of generation is more sublime than the others; (1.1.1) one grade of union is more wonderful[4] than the others; and (1.1.3) one way of perfection is more excellent than the others. Yet, when Christ came into this world, he accomplished a new union, he took on a new generation, and he brought along a new perfection.

(1.1.1) So in the world one grade of union was lacking, the one more wonderful than the others. For in our world there are four kinds of union: the first is the union of something corruptible with something corruptible, as in natural things. The

---

3. Thomas's order reflects the focus of his approach: the salvation of humankind. The same we see in the *Summa Theologiae*, especially in how he approaches the Incarnation (ST III 1,1–6, from the very beginning; cf. 1,1sc) and the Passion (ST III 46,1–4); see also his introduction to the *Tertia Pars*.

4. Thomas uses the same word here as for the offense against God: *mirabilis*. There it has the connotation of "mysterious" (for how can a temporal being hurt the Eternal One? ST I 9,1 esp. ad 3), whereas here the meaning tends more towards "perfect," "excellent," and therefore "evoking awe."

second is the union of something corruptible with something incorruptible, as in human beings.[5] The third is the union of something incorruptible with something incorruptible, as in spiritual things: a union of *essentia* and *potentia*.[6] The fourth, however, was lacking: the union of something temporal with something eternal. Well, this union was made when "the Word became flesh and dwelt among us," as it says in Jn 1.14; "when he emptied himself (and took on the form of a slave; made in the likeness of human beings he was, through his way of life, found a man)," as Phil 2.7 reads; that is "when the king of Israel disguised himself," as it is said in 1 Kgs 22.30; and Is 43.19 reads: "Behold, I make all things new."[7]

(1.1.2) Also, the one way of generation was lacking that is more wonderful than the others. For there are four kinds of generation in the broad sense of the word:[8] the first is from the Father without a mother, the generation that occurs eternally.[9] The second is without a father and without a mother, in the beginning, as with the first parents.[10] The third is from a father and a mother, the generation that occurs all around us. The fourth did not exist before, namely, the generation from a mother without a father in time. Well, this generation was made when the Virgin conceived, when, as we read in Isaiah 10, "the stone is hewn from the mountain without hands," which, according

---

5. In people the corruptible body and the incorruptible soul are united: ST I 75,4 and 6.

6. As in angels for instance: ST I 50.

7. Actually Thomas is quoting Rv 21.5: *ecce nova facio omnia*; Is 43.19 reads: *ecce ego facio nova* ("Behold, I make new things").

8. Thomas's order is as we come across the different generations in salvation history, which is preceded, so to speak, by the eternal forthcomings.

9. ST I 27,2, where he explains Ps 2.7: "You are my son; this day I have begotten you."

10. In Genesis Adam and Eve have no human parents, no father and mother in time. They come forth from the triune God—not only from the Father; the name Creator is appropriated to the Father (ST I 32,1 and 39,7–8)). Since Adam and Eve came forth from God, who created them (ST I 44 and also 65,4), he is their father, yet in an analogical way; he is their father. God's fatherhood for people is similar but not quite the same as the fatherhood of human beings (ST I 13,5), or rather the other way round: the human fatherhood is similar to God's: Eph 3.15; cf. ST I 13,6, 33,2,4, 45,5,1.

to Daniel 10 "became a great mountain and it filled the whole earth."[11] The stone hewn from the mountain [without hands] is Christ, born from the Virgin without a human action. Indeed, then "the Lord made a new thing upon the earth: (the woman will encompass the man)," as Jeremiah 21 [Jer 31.22] puts it.

(1.1.3) Also lacking was the one grade of perfection that is more excellent than the others, although anything that is connected with its end is perfect.[12] Hence, a creature is most perfect when it is united with its Creator.[13] Well, with a triple connection a creature is conjoined with its Creator: the first is a union in respect of strength, by reason of a dependency that is in all things. Hence "all things would fall into nothingness, unless they were kept by the hand of the Almighty," according to Gregory.[14] The second is in respect of the [human] species: through the grace that is in just people, since according to Dionysius love (*amor*) is a unifying force.[15] The third union concerns the thing itself, by essence. This did not exist before, but it came into being when the human nature was taken on by the Son of God in unity of supposit or person.[16] In taking on the human nature in a certain way the whole world was taken on, because, according to Gregory, "in a way every creature is a human being."[17]

11. The first part is a quotation from Dn 2.45, the second part from Dn 2.35.
12. ST I 6,3, and the other way round in III 44,3,3.
13. ST 6,2,2; cf. texts like Heb 2.10 and 1 Cor 8.6.
14. Cf. ST I 8,1, and in Scripture: Wis 11.25.
15. *Specialis*: it is special or concerns a species, namely, the human species. Through God's gracious gift of love we are united with him. Cf. Jn 14.23 and 15.9–10; cf. ST I 20,1,3 and Thomas's commentary on Dionysius's *On the Divine Names* (*De divinis nominibus*), c.4.
16. It is *unio realis;* it concerns the very essence of the *res*, of the thing itself. So although there were two natures in Christ, the divine and the human, he was one individual, one rational individual. For Thomas's exposition on the unity of Christ: ST III 2.
17. Thomas's terms in 1.1.3 are: *virtualis* (concerning *virtus*, "strength"), *specialis* ("special" or "concerning a species," i.e., the human species) and *realis* ("belonging to the *res*," the thing itself). Through the Incarnation the whole of creation became more valuable, since the Eternal One had entered it in a new way; cf. Wis 19.6, Rom 8.19–22. See also texts on God as *causa exemplaris*, esp. ST I 44,3.

(1.2) Second, he came to gather the scattered and to lead them back to the proper state of man or to the practice of the one religion [cf. Jn 4.20–23, Eph 1.10]. For the people were (1.2.1) subjected to different kings, (1.2.2) adopted different laws, and (1.2.3) were corrupted by different errors. We read in Judges 11: "In those days there was no king in Israel" [Jgs 17.6] and in Hosea 10: "Many days the children of Israel sat down, without a king or a ruler (as well as without sacrifice or altar, as without priestly garb or house gods)."[18]

(1.2.1) And therefore Christ came, in order to be the one reigning king of the whole world himself, whose dominion would be universal, whose empire universal, and whose reign eternal. And this is shown clearly in his birth, because then he manifested himself as the king of the people when kings adored him [Mt 2.11]; as the king of the angels playing on their stringed instruments as they rejoiced [Lk 2.13–14]; as king of the [Jews] awaiting him because the shepherds listened [Lk 2.15–16]; as king of the heavenly bodies because the stars knew him [Ps 148.3]. Thus it is said in Zec 9.9: "Behold, your king comes unto you (the just one and the savior himself)." This king has conjoined the scattered and made them one when he called Jews and gentiles to the faith. Ezek 37.22 reads: "There will be one reigning king for all and there will be two nations no more"; and in the same chapter: "They will be my people and I will be their God, and my servant David will be king over them and shepherd of all" [Ezek 37.23–24].

(1.2.2) Furthermore, he came so that there would be one law moving the people of the whole world forward. For the Law of Moses was specifically given to some since it did not oblige all people; its promises concerned the flesh since it promised things of the flesh; it was penal in its provisions since it inflicted punishments [cf. Rom 4.15]: "A tooth for a tooth, an eye for an eye,"[19] et cetera. Therefore, because there was an imper-

18. It is in fact Hos 3.4. In 1.2 Thomas follows the order of this verse.
19. Thomas has changed the order of these two sayings, which are found in Ex 21.24, Lv 24.20, Dt 19.21. They are taken up by Jesus in Mt 5.38. Thomas discusses these texts in ST I–II 105,2,10 (on the application of the precepts of the Old Testament), II–II 61,4 and 65,1 (on justice)

fect law, another legislator had to come whose task would be to give a general law for all, as we read in the last chapter of Mark [16.15]: "(Go into the whole world,) preach the Gospel to every creature," et cetera.

Moreover, a spiritual law is written in the hearts [of the people], as it says in Jeremiah 13: "I will put my law within them and I will write it in their hearts" [Jer 31.33].

Even more, the law of love (*amor*) which speaks of heavenly things: "Do penance; the Kingdom of heaven has drawn near," as Mt 3.2 reads, and Is 33.22: "The Lord, our king, the Lord, our lawgiver." And the Psalmist says: "Establish, O Lord, a legislator over them, so that they may know (that they are mere human beings)" [Ps 9.21].

(1.2.3) Furthermore, he came so that there would be one judge administering justice, who would have full authority, so that he could exercise every judgment.[20] He was such a judge, since "the Father has given every judgment to the Son," Jn 5.27. Who would be so profound that he could know all things? Indeed, this one is, whence Jer 29.23 reads: "I am the judge and the witness, (says the Lord)." Who would be so powerful that no one could resist him? Jas 4.12 says: "There is one legislator and judge, who can spare and set free." For in that judgment all hidden things will be made manifest, according to 1 Corinthians 3: "Do not judge before time."[21] Also, all things will be scrutinized. In the last chapter[22] of Ecclesiastes it reads: "God will lead to judgment all the things that happen," et cetera. Moreover, all things will be requited, as we read in Mt 25.46: "These will enter into punishment, yet the just into eternal life." 1 Sm 8.20 says: "Our king will judge us and will go before us and will fight our wars for us."

(1.3) Third, he came to take away the offense and establish peace between us and God. Since man had trespassed, he of-

---

20. ST III 56,1,3 and 58.

21. 1 Cor 4.5. It seems quite probable that Thomas quoted the whole verse, which continues: "until the Lord comes, who will bring to light the things hidden in the dark, and he will manifest the plans of the hearts, and then there will be praise for everyone from God."

22. It is in fact the chapter before last: Eccl 11.9.

fended God and had to die.[23] Thus a certain case, so to speak, was set in motion from the beginning of the world for the coming of the Lord. For truth required that man would die, because[24] it is written in Nm 15.30: "A soul that sins through pride will be cut off from his people." But mercy required that man would be set free. The Psalmist says: "Will God reject in eternity, (so that he would not remember) that he was more favorable until now, or will he until the end (abandon his grace)?" [Ps 77.8–9] Justice, however, requires in the end that he be condemned, because Genesis 1 reads: "On whatever day you will eat from it, you will die" [Gn 2.17].[25] And Deuteronomy 18: "A person who will be so proud as to disobey an order of the wise one will die by decree of the judge."[26] But peace requires that a settlement be arranged and the disposition be changed. The Psalmist says: "Will you be angry with us in eternity (or do you extend your wrath from generation to generation)?" [Ps 85.6] And therefore Isaiah asked: "Send out the lamb, Lord, the ruler of the earth." [Is 16.1 (Vg)] And Moses: "I beseech you, Lord, send the one whom you will send" [Ex 4.13]. But since God is good and merciful [cf. 2 Mc 1.24], he could "not deny himself" [2 Tm 2.13], but he answers through Jeremiah in Jer 31.20: "My inner parts are stirred up because of him; I will show him great mercy." And Hos 11.8: "My heart is turned within me; my penance has turned likewise."

Thus the Lord has sent someone to settle: not a human being, not an angel, but God's Son, who satisfied through mercy so that it did not fall short of justice in anything. And so it happened that there was in the same [man] justice to the full and infinite mercy,[27] and so "mercy and truth have met one another; (justice and peace have kissed one another)" [Ps 85.11].

---

23. Rom 5.2; cf. ST I–II 94,5,2, III 14,1, 52,5.

24. "Every truth is from God" (ST I 16,5), and "His word is truth" (Jn 17.17). So the Law which YHWH gave to Moses is truth.

25. Cf. ST III 50,1.

26. It is Dt 17.12, but Thomas left out a few words; the whole verse reads: "A person who will be so proud as to disobey an order of the priest who serves the Lord your God in that time, and the decree of the judge, that person will die."

27. As it is in God: ST I 21,1–2 and 21,3–4.

It was justice to the full in this respect, that he punished very harshly,[28] but infinite mercy because he bore the punishment in himself, as we read in Is 53.4: "Truly, our infirmities he took away himself and our pains he bore himself."

Thus he came to make peace between humankind and God [cf. Eph 2.15–16]. And for this he is the appropriate arbiter, since "he is himself our peace which makes both one," as we read in Eph 2.14. He came to battle against the devil, like a strong soldier, as it says in Jos 5.14: "(I am) the leader of the army of the Lord." He came to take away the contamination of sin, like a doctor. Mt 8.7 reads: "I will come and cure him." He came to be in our company, like a friend; it says in Baruch 5: "From the holy one my joy comes."[29]

Thus he received our way of life, he who had given his first.[30] He paid our debts who had not contracted any [cf. Ps 69.5; cf. Sir 4.8]. He redeemed the lost one whom he had created before [cf. Col 1.16]. Prv 13.12 says: "The wood of life is the desire that comes."[31]

(2) Second, the prophet shows that he is the one who fulfills the desire of the fathers in a merciful way, as he says: "who is desired by all the nations together." For man was (2.1) weak through an incurable wound, (2.2) oppressed by an unbearable tyrant, and (2.3) thirsty with an unquenchable thirst. And just as the weak desired the remedy of salvation, the oppressed desired a pleasing dominion, and the thirsty the basin of a fountain. In this way the human race desired the coming of the Savior.

(2.1) For man was weak through an incurable wound, since it had corrupted the whole human nature.[32] Is 1.6: "From the foot-sole till the top of his head there is no health in him." Jer-

---

28. See how Thomas explains in which respects Christ's Passion was the greatest suffering, in ST III 46,6.

29. Bar 4.22. This verse continues: "over the mercy that will come to you from our eternal salvation." In SCG IV 54 Thomas mentions God's friendship with us as a motive for the Incarnation. Also: ST III 1,5,1.

30. 1 Cor 8.6, Col 1.15–16, 3.4, 2 Tm 1.9, 1 Jn 3.16, 5.11–12.

31. Or: "the desired one that comes"; the desire is going to be fulfilled; cf. Hg 2.7.

32. ST III 1,2, esp. ad 2.

emiah 3 reads: "Why is my pain made everlasting and why does my hopeless wound refuse to be cured?" [Jer 15.18] And therefore he had a strong desire for the remedy of salvation. Is 53.2 reads: "We have seen him," and it continues: "we have desired him, a despised man, the last of men, a sorrowful man who knew weakness."

(2.2) Furthermore, he was oppressed by an unbearable tyrant,[33] for just like an unjust person he was handed over to enemies. We read in Hos 8.3: "Israel has thrown away the good; the enemy pursues him." And in Is 14.3: "When you will be freed from hard slavery in which you served before." And therefore they desired a pleasing dominion, as we read in Song 5.15: "His face is like Lebanon and his neck is sweet and the whole of him is desirable." And in the last chapter of Micah [7.17]: "They will desire your Lord and fear you."

(2.3) Furthermore, he was thirsty with an unquenchable thirst, because he had withered by reason of the lack of sacramental grace. Job reads: "Can rushes live without moisture, or can grass grow without water?" [Jb 8.11] This signifies the people who had no water in the desert. And therefore they desired the basin of a fountain, as the Psalmist says: "Like the deer that longs (for fountains of water, so my soul thirsts for you, O God)" [Ps 42.2].

So, they desired him; deep sighs show this. The Psalmist says: "Lord, bend down the heavens and come down" [Ps 144.5]. Is 64 says: "O may you rend your heavens and come down" [Is 63.19], and he also says in chapter 28: "My soul desired you in the night" [Is 26.9]. Moreover, they asked for him, which the frequency of the prayers shows; the Psalmist says: "Evoke your power and come" [Ps 80.3]. They also awaited him, which the striking signs of the divine revelation show. Is 26.8 reads: "On the path of your judgments we have awaited you; the memory of you is in the desire of our soul," and he also says: "I will expect God my Savior" [Mi 7.7]. Even more, they loved (*amo*) him, which the excellence of their praise shows, in Micah 2: "And you, Bethlehem, land of Judah, (you are certainly not the least

---

33. ST III 1,1sc.

among the rulers of Judah, for from you a leader will come forth who will reign over my people Israel)."³⁴

(3) Third, the prophet shows [to us] the one who in a wondrous way bestows gracious gifts [upon us]: "He will fill this house with glory."

(3.1) The unique house is the Virgin Mary, which the providence of the Father has built, as we read in Proverbs 8: "Wisdom has built a house for herself."³⁵ The wisdom of the Son dwells in it; Kings 7 says: "I dwell in a house of cedar" [1 Chr 17.1]. The grace of the Holy Spirit has prepared it, as we read in 1 Chr 29.1: "This great work is not built as a dwelling-place for man, but for God."

(3.2) The special house is the Church Militant. Christ has built this house from living stones [cf. 1 Pt 2.5]. It is said in 2 Chr 2.4: "The house that I wish to build is large." He has consecrated it with the gifts of grace.³⁶ Isaiah 64 reads: "My house will be called a house of prayer."³⁷ It says in Zec 12.10: "I will pour out over the house of David a spirit of grace"; he has established it at his own expense; we read in Zec 4.9: "The hands of Zerubbabel have established this house."³⁸

(3.3) The general house is the heavenly homeland. As for love³⁹ (*caritas*), this house is the greatest, as we read in Baruch 4:

---

34. Thomas cites Mt 2.6 here, which is based on Mi 5.1.
35. It is Prv 9.1. Thomas explains this verse in ST III 32,1,3.
36. Here Thomas refers to the gifts of the Holy Spirit (ST I–II 109–114; II–II 45,5, 171 intr., 172,2,2), as will be clear further on in the text, under "ad 3.2."
37. Thomas seems to quote from Mt 21.13 where the last words of the verse are missing: *cunctis populis*, "for all the peoples together" (or he may be quoting from Mk 11.17 where it says: *omnis gentibus*). Cf. Is 56.7.
38. This verse continues: "and his hands will finish it; then you will know that the Lord of hosts has sent me to you."
39. In his writings Thomas uses four terms from Scripture which we usually translate as "love." He interprets them as follows: (1) *Amor*: the collective term. (2) *Dilectio*: love as the result of a well-considered choice; it is etymologically connected with *eligere* and *electio*: "choosing carefully." The object of *dilectio* is consciously willed. God's love, therefore, is always *dilectio*. (3) *Caritas*: love for someone or something of great value; it is etymologically connected with *carus*: "precious," "dear" (cf. Italian *caro*; French *cher*). In Scripture and in the Christian tradition this term is used for perfect love (cf. 1 Cor 12.31–13.13), in

"O Israel, how great is the house of God" [Bar 3.24]. As for preciousness, it is the most noble, since "glory and riches are in his house," it says in the Psalm [Ps 112.3]. As for its eternity, it is the strongest; 2 Cor 5.1 reads: "For we know that when of this dwelling-place our earthly house is demolished, we have a building from God, a house not made by hand but eternal in heaven."

(ad 3.1) He filled the first house with the glory of divinity in the Incarnation, as we read in Hg 2.9: "Great is the glory of this newest house, more than of the first"; and Ezek 10.3 reads: "The house is filled with a cloud[40] and the atrium is filled with splendor through the glory of the Lord."

(ad 3.2) The second house was full of joy in the mission of the Holy Spirit, because of the grace of languages [Acts 2.4], gracious gifts [Gal 5.22], and works of miracles [Acts 2.43]. Is 33.5: "He has filled Zion with justice and right judgment."

(ad 3.3) The third house was full of the grace of happiness in the Ascension. For then the splendor of brightness appeared by reason of the shining of Christ's body, the praise of the divine goodness by reason of the clear manifestation of this work, and the taste of an intimate alliance by reason of the double joyfulness. We read in 2 Chr 6.4: "He has fulfilled (in deed what he had said to David, my father)." In 1 Kgs 8.11 it says: "He filled the house of the Lord with the glory of the Lord." Ezek 43.5 reads: "The house was full of the glory of the Lord." And Zechariah 9: "Glory has entered the temple of the Lord" [Ezek 43.4].

---

particular, love between two Christians as well as love of and for God. (4) *Amicitia:* mutual love, friendship (see also Thomas's commentary on Dionysius's *On the Divine Names,* c.4 *lectio* 9, and ST I–II 26,3).

40. In Ex 16.10 and elsewhere, the cloud refers to God's hidden presence; cf. SCG III 49 (where Thomas cites Ex 20.21) and 50 (where he cites Sir 24.7 [Vg] = Sir 24.4).

SERMON 02

LAUDA ET LETARE

Another Sermon on Advent

Zechariah 2.14: *"Sing praise and be glad, daughter of Zion,*
for behold,
I come and I will dwell in your midst," says the Lord.

Sermo

It is as St. Bernard says: "While I often think of the burning desire of the fathers who expected Christ's coming, I feel shame in myself." For someone who considers the sighs of those who were imploring, the desires of those who were expectant, and the joy of those who announced the coming of the Savior, can well become aware of his own tepidity in respect of the benefit already received that proceeds from his coming [cf. Rv 1.7, 3.16]. Isaiah implored this coming with a frequent sigh, in Is 16.1 [Vg]: "Send out the lamb, Lord, (the ruler of the world)," and elsewhere: "O may you rend your heavens (and come down)" [Is 63.19]. Jeremiah expected him with great desire: "The Lord will make something new upon the earth: (a woman will encompass a man)" [Jer 31.22]. Zechariah preached with tremendous joy, as is clear from the saying mentioned at the beginning.

Here the Prophet does three things: (1) First, he shows the affection of the holy fathers who preceded the coming of the Savior, continually persisting in their praises of him, where he says: "Sing praise and be glad, daughter of Zion." (2) Second, the Son of God himself coming down from the heavens: "Behold, I come." (3) Third, him humbly appearing in human flesh: "And I will dwell in your midst."

(1) So, first the joyfulness of the coming is presented, which is shown by a double and perfect gladness [cf. Jn 15.11]. Note, in view of this, that three things are required for a perfect gladness. (1.1) First, that the mind is elevated to a divine benefit; this is mentioned where it says: "Daughter of Zion." (1.2) Second, that the affection is enlarged by spiritual joy, which is mentioned where it says: "Be glad." (1.3) Third, that the tongue is excited to the favorable gift of the divine praise, where it says: "Sing praise." For if you carefully consider the divine benefits, then you will be a daughter of Zion; if you sing of the divine announcements in exultation, and praise them in thanksgiving with delight, your joy will be perfect;[1] if spiritual gladness is born from this consideration, you will rejoice, daughter of Zion. And this is what the Prophet taught, saying: "Sing praise and be glad, daughter of Zion."

(1.1) So, first, for perfect gladness it is required that the mind be elevated to a divine benefit, which is mentioned when it is said: "Daughter of Zion." Zion, after all, is interpreted as "watchtower" [cf. Is 21.8], and, understood in a spiritual way, she always signifies the soul of someone who is contemplating [cf. Ps 130.6]. For a man <. . .>[2] came in order to announce the coming of his Lord by means of preaching, as we read in Is 52.7: "How beautiful (upon the mountains) the feet of the ones who announce and preach peace;" and then: "of the one who says to Zion: '(The Lord) your God will reign.'" For such a person deserves to hear the divine preaching who does not want but to become conversant "from Christ and with Christ"[3] [cf. 1 Jn 1.3]. Therefore the Lord says in Mt 21.5 and Zec 9.9: "Say to the daughter of Zion," that is, to the soul that tends towards contemplating the benefits of God through meditation: "Your king is coming for you." I interpret this as: Tell that person who desires to hear the joy of his coming because

---

1. Because the object of our joy is something perfect and present: Thomas's Commentary on John 15.11 (c.15 *lectio* 2 n.5) and ST II–II 28,3.

2. In the original Latin text a word is missing.

3. *De Christo et cum Christo:* the inverted commas are in the Latin text, but where this quotation is from is not exactly clear; it could be that Thomas refers to the last words of the Eucharistic prayer: *per ipso, cum ipso et in ipso:* "through him, with him, and in him."

of the consolation it brings.[4] Isaiah says: "Rejoice and be glad," [Lam 4.21] "Zion, because your Savior will come" [Isaiah 62.11] from "the midst of the nations" [Ezek 5.5]. For, according to what St. Bernard says: "The divine consolation is enlarged, but it is not given to those who admit someone else's consolation."[5]

Such are the daughters of Zion, and therefore the sight of his coming through contemplation is announced and promised to them. Zechariah 9.9 says: "Exult greatly, daughter of Zion." And Song 3.11 reads: "Go out, daughters of Zion, and see (King Solomon; look upon the crown with which his mother has crowned him)." "Go out," from the rags of vices [cf. Eph 4.21-31], and be "daughters of Zion," through contemplation of the things that are above,[6] and thus you will be able to see "King Solomon," meaning the Lord of the angels [cf. Heb 1.5], in "the crown with which his mother has crowned him," that is, according to a gloss, in the humanity [cf. Ps 8.6] assumed from Judah's posterity [Heb 7.14, 8.8].

(1.2) Second, for perfect gladness it is required that

(1.2.1) the affection be enlarged by a spiritual joy, which is mentioned where it says: "Be glad." Well, justly a faithful soul ought to exult, indeed the whole human nature ought to overflow with a richness of spiritual joys, as it sees itself united[7] with the divine partner. For she who was once "a wilderness and impassable" [Ps 63.2, Is 35.1] because of the aridity in regard to the heavenly grace, is now made flourishing and sprouting, because she is assumed by the Son of God in the unity of supposit.[8] Is 35.1 reads: "The wilderness and the impassable will be glad, and the desert will exult and flourish like a lily, produce abundantly, and exult full of gladness and singing praise."

---

4. Knowing about his coming makes us rejoice; cf. ST II–II 9,4 (cf. Jb 15.11 and 2 Thes 2.16–17).

5. The consolation of this world is not compatible with the consolation from the Lord, e.g., Lk 6.24; cf. ST I–II 69,2.

6. Cf. Gal 4.26, Col 3.1, Heb 12.22.

7. Thomas uses the word *copulatum*, referring to the union of two spouses. This image is continued in what follows.

8. Cf. 2 Cor 2.17, 12.19. "She" is the human nature. With the expression "unity of supposit" Thomas refers to what Christians understand by Incarnation: that Christ is one "supposit," one person, yet in two natures: ST III 2,2–3.

And he proceeds: "The glory of Lebanon is given to her" [Is 35.2]. And elsewhere it is said, in Is 2: "You will not be called 'the abandoned' any more" [Is 62.4].

(1.2.2) Furthermore, at the same time she experiences that she is placed in the community of the holy ones.[9] For the soul that was counted once upon a time among the company of the ones from hell [cf. 2 Pt 2.4], is now reckoned among the company of the angels [Eph 2.19]. Thus it says in the last chapter of Hab [3.18]: "Yet I will rejoice in God and I will exult (in God my Jesus)."[10] Now the people enter Zion singing praise, as it was foretold in Is 35.10: "Everlasting gladness upon their heads."[11] And the Psalmist says: "I am glad because of these things that are said to me: ('we will enter the house of the Lord')" [Ps 122.1].

(1.2.3) Furthermore, at the same time she experiences the strength of the heavenly help. Once there was a sadness in the whole human nature because of a lack of grace, because the door was closed [cf. Acts 14.27], because of the oppression of the ancient captivity [cf. Acts 10.38, Lk 4.18]. But now the divine grace is poured out, since "all are filled with the Holy Spirit," as we read in Acts 2.4 and 4.31. The heavenly door is opened, as it is said in Rv 4.1: "I have seen the gate opened in heaven." The power of the devil is repelled, as it is said in Jn 12.31: "The ruler of this world is thrown out." And Rv 12.10: "(Now the salvation, the strength, and the reign of our God has come and the authority of his Christ, because) the accuser of our brothers is cast out (who accused them before our God day and night)," and further on [verse 12]: "Rejoice, heavens and you who dwell in them." This was foreseen, as we read in Isaiah 9.3: "They will rejoice before you as those who rejoice in harvest time, (as those who exult when they divide the booty)."

---

9. Being made part of the *collegium sanctorum* is a description of *sanctificatio*, an effect of the sending, the gift of the Holy Spirit to us: ST I 43,3; cf. I 27.

10. The Vulgate text reads *Iesu meo*, which could also be translated as "who saves me"; cf. Mt 1.21.

11. The whole verse reads: "And the ones redeemed by the Lord will be converted and will come to Zion with praise and everlasting gladness upon their head; they will obtain joy and gladness, and pain and sighing will flee."

(1.3) Third, for perfect gladness our tongue must be excited to the proclamation of the divine praise, which is mentioned where it says: "Sing praise." For, if there is a graceful knowledge of God in our intellect and an intimate exultation in our affection, the consequence is that it cannot be otherwise than that there is a song of praise in our mind.[12] Therefore, he says: "Sing praise." For a faithful soul is satisfied. Because of this she gives praises to her Redeemer in return, for, as it is said in Philippians 3: "The peace of God, which surpasses all understanding, will guard our heart and our intellect" [Phil 4.7]. Therefore it says in Sirach 43.29: "Exult when you bless God as much as you can, because he is greater than every praise."

(1.3.1) Yes, we ought to praise the power of the One who battles for us [Is 63.1], who has led us out, away from dangers [2 Mc 1.11, 2 Cor 1.10]. Quite a big danger is serving the devil and sin, for this is the slavery of Pharaoh. "But now we," because "freed from sin, we have yet become slaves for God" [Rom 6.22], "sing to the Lord: 'Gloriously (he is magnified, for the horse and his rider, he cast them down in the sea)'" [Ex 15.1]. And it follows: "My strength and my praise are the Lord" [verse 2]. In the last chapter of Sirach [51.11]: "My soul will praise the Lord till death," [verse 12:] "because you sustain those who await you and you deliver them from the hands" of those who oppress.

(1.3.2) Furthermore, [we ought to praise] the justice of the Redeemer, since "by dying he destroyed our death."[13] For it was proper to justice that death would be paid for death. But that it was paid by Christ, was proper to mercy, for he paid "what he had not robbed" [Ps 69.5][14]—and this together with justice is to the highest extent praiseworthy. In Proverbs it says: It is proper to justice "that the praise of God will stand straight" [Sir 15.10 (Vg)]. And Is 61.11 says: "The Lord will make justice and praise arise for all the nations."

---

12. ST I–II 101,2.

13. These words, derived from 2 Tm 1.10, are used in the Eucharist as an acclamation after the consecration.

14. It is a central verse in the interpretation of Christ's death on the cross as satisfaction (Anselm, Thomas) and justice (Thomas): ST III 46,4, 47,2,1, and 48,2. What Thomas understands by justice: ST II–II 57–122.

(1.3.3) Furthermore, the benevolence of the Savior, because he has led us back to eternal life; just as the Apostle says in Col 1.11–13: "With joy" we ought to "give thanks to God the Father" "who wrested us away from the power of darkness and brought us over into the" beloved (*dilectus*) "kingdom of his Son." Hence it is said in Isaiah 43: "Praise the Lord, you heavens, because he has worked mercy" [Is 44.23].

(2) Second, in the saying above, it is stated that the coming is at hand, which is shown by the short distance where it says: "Behold, I come."

(2.1) I interpret "I come" as a coming in a visible way, in the form of humanity, whereby a novelty unheard-of is shown: he says, "Behold."[15]

(2.1.1) By speaking in this way he excites our tepidity, that we may go to meet him [cf. Mt 25.6, Eph 4.13], as we read in Isaiah 36: "Behold our God; we awaited him, and he will save us" [Is 25.9]. Zec 9.9: "Behold, your king comes."[16]

(2.1.2) Furthermore, he demonstrates the newness of it, that we may be attentive and stand in awe. And thus the spouse speaks in Song 2.8: "Behold, he comes, leaping on the mountains." And in Isaiah it says: "Behold, I make all things new, and now he appears."[17]

(2.1.3) Furthermore, he makes known that it is at hand, so that we may organize a place where he is welcome to stay. In Mal 3.1 it says: "Behold, he will come to his holy temple." And we read in Daniel 2: "Behold, the Son of man will come on the clouds of heaven" [Dn 7.13].

So, by saying: "Behold," the Son of God made himself known as visible in the form of humanity.[18]

(2.2) In a personal way he also comes in the substance of di-

---

15. The word *ecce*, "behold," implies that there is something to see. For the invisible mission of the Son see ST I 43,5.

16. In fact Thomas quotes Mt 21.5 or Jn 12.15 here; the verb in Zec 9.9 is in the future tense: "Your king will come."

17. The first part of the quotation is in fact from Rv 21.5; Is 43.19 reads: "Behold, I make new things and now they [plural] appear."

18. Phil 2.7; cf. ST III 2,5, 5,1.

vinity, in which an infinite sublimity is shown. And this is mentioned where it says, "I."[19]

For this is the person who has spoken through the mouth of all the prophets.[20] Isaiah says: "I who have spoken: 'behold, I am here'" [Is 52.6]. What he speaks is the redemption of all sinners, as we read in Isaiah 36: "I speak justice" [Is 63.1].[21] What he speaks is the judgment at the end of all times, according to the Psalmist: "When the time will have come, I will administer justice" [Ps 75.3]. Moreover: "His tongue will speak justice" [cf. Ps 35.28].

And justly so,

(2.2.1) for he has eternal being and thus precedes all things, as it is said in Ex 3.14: "I am who am." After all, he comes forth from God consubstantially and thus eternally, as we read in Jn 8.42: "I have come forth from the Father and I have come."[22]

(2.2.2) Furthermore, he has an immense power,[23] and thus he has brought forth all things. It says in Isaiah: "I am God and there is no other who formed the light and created the darkness, (who made peace and created evil; I, the Lord, made all these)" [Is 45.7]. For, since the Son is God, the origin from the origin, he has with him the same being and power.[24]

(2.2.3) Furthermore, he has a perfect knowledge, and thus he governs all things.[25] Sir 24.3: "I have come forth from the mouth of the Most High [Sir 24.5 (Vg)]: the firstborn, before

---

19. The personal pronoun "I" refers to Christ's divinity also in the "I am" sayings in the Gospel according to John, e.g., 6.35–51, 10.11, and 14.6. See also Thomas's Commentary on the Gospel according to John, c.1 *lectio* 1 (where he cites Ex 3.14).

20. Cf. ST II–II 178,1,1.

21. This quotation makes sense in view of what follows: "and I am a battler for them in order to save."

22. This verse is explained by Thomas in ST I 27,1.

23. Thomas uses the infinitive *posse* ("can," "be able to," from which *potentia*, "power," is derived): Thomas refers to the properties of the Son of God using verbs (being, being powerful, and knowing, etc.); this usage underlines that the One coming is active and dynamic.

24. ST III 13,2,1 and Thomas's commentary on Mt 28.18 ("All power is given unto me").

25. Cf. ST I 108,6.

every creature." Since he is himself "light from light,"[26] just as the Father has infinite power, so also the Son. Jn 8.12 reads: "I am the light of the world."

(2.3) Still, "although I am so sublime and of such great dignity, 'behold, I come' as a friend, bringing what is useful for you."[27]

"I come," as if he says: "I do not send an angel, not a spirit, not a deputy, but I myself come in person," in which the greatest love (*maxima caritas*) is shown [cf. Jn 3.16]. I interpret "I come" as meaning "invited by the holy fathers." For it is he whom all the holy people had invited from the beginning of the world, although their person was brought forth by the spouse.[28] It says in Song of Songs 2: "My beloved (*dilectus*) will come into his place."[29] And in the last chapter of Revelation [22.20]: "Come, Lord Jesus." And likewise Isaiah, Jeremiah, and the rest of the prophets have spoken.

Furthermore, "I come" is a movement and a push of piety that touch the inner parts; Luke 2 reads: "Through the heartfelt mercy of our God in which (the daybreak from on high has visited us)" [Lk 1.78]. Elsewhere he had shown his power and wisdom; here he showed his mercy, as Bernard says.[30]

(2.3.1) Furthermore, he underwent our weaknesses with us.[31] Mt 8.7 reads: "I will come and cure him," and in Lk 19.10:

---

26. Thomas says *lux de luce et lumen de lumine*, using two words for light: *lux* and *lumen*; the first in view of the Scripture text that he is going to quote, which reads *lux*, and the second in view of the Creed, in which Christians profess that Christ is "Light from Light": *Lumen de Lumine*.

27. This is what Thomas calls the *amicitia utilis*, in ST II–II 23,5.

28. Thomas points to the mystery that the One to whose coming the fathers were looking forward was in fact before them; they were brought forth by him.

29. It is in fact Song 5.1. Thomas reads *ortum* instead of *hortum*: "He will enter his garden."

30. What this mercy contains is explained in the next steps: it is not just *compassio*, a "suffering with" or "undergoing with," but it includes curing, saving, restoring honor, reuniting us with God's love, and giving us light again.

31. The word used is *compassus*; *misericordia* includes a movement towards the neighbor in order to alleviate his/her suffering, as in the subsequent quotation from Mt 8.7. The term *misericordia*, therefore, is closer to our word "compassion"—as in "I am moved with compassion"—than the term *compassio*.

"The Son of man has come to seek and to save what had perished." And it says in John 12: The Son of man has come "into the world not to judge the world but in order to save the world through him" [Jn 3.17].[32] For, since we were stripped of all honor, therefore he has come as a leader with an infinite dignity. In Jos 5.14 it is said: "I am the ruler of the army of the Lord, and now I come."

(2.3.2) Furthermore, since we were separated from the divine love (*divinus amor*), therefore he has come, as the peace of a love (*caritas*) never heard of [1 Cor 2.9]. As we read in Ephesians 5: "He himself is our peace, who has made both one" [Eph 2.14] and: "coming he brought the good news of peace unto you who were far off" [Eph 2.17]. And it was not only the love (*caritas*) of the coming Son, but also of the Father who sent him, as we read in Jn 5.43: "I have come in the name of my Father."

(2.3.3) Furthermore, since we were deprived of light or splendor [cf. Is 59.9], he came as light of an infinite clarity; Jn 12.46: "I am the light that has come into the world."

(3) Third, in the saying above, the humility of his coming is shown, where it says: "And I will dwell in your midst," as if he is saying: "I will be your companion on the pilgrimage."[33]

(3.1) Therefore he says: "I will dwell." Well, he dwelt with us in three ways:

(3.1.1) with all people, in a general way, through the substance of the flesh, as we read in Jn 1.14: "The Word became flesh and has dwelt among us." And Bar 3.38: "Since then he was seen on earth and lived with the people."

(3.1.2) Furthermore, with the holy people, in a special way, through infused grace,[34] as we read in 2 Cor 5.16: "I will dwell among them and I will be their God."

(3.1.3) Furthermore, with the good people, in a familiar way

---

32. For the motive of the Incarnation: ST III 1, esp. 2–3.

33. Our life is a pilgrimage on the way (*via*) to the City of God, i.e., the heavenly fatherland or homeland (*patria*); we are *in via*, not yet *in patria* (as the saints are).

34. As in Jn 14.23, etc.; cf. ST I 43,5–6.

[cf. Jgs 19.4], by being present before their eyes, as the Psalmist says: "Forever they will exult and you will dwell among them" [Ps 5.12]. Bernard says: "For this he came (into the world), that he might dwell among the people and in them, and that he might enlighten the darkness for people, lighten their labor, and ward off dangers."

(3.2) Furthermore, he was like the middle person in reconciliation [1 Tm 2.5, Heb 9.15]: "in your midst,"[35] as it is said in Luke 22: "I am in their midst."[36]

(3.2.1) Now, he was in our midst in order to reconcile God and man [cf. Rom 5.10, 2 Cor 5.19, Eph 2.16]. John 2 reads: "In the midst of you he has stood whom you do not know" [Jn 1.26]. And it says in Deuteronomy: "I was the middle person and the intermediary between you and God" [Dt 5.5].

(3.2.2) Furthermore, in order to bring along the fullness of joy,[37] as it is said in John 20.19: "Jesus stood in the midst of his disciples and said: 'Peace be with you,'" and it continues: "The disciples rejoiced" [verse 20]. And we read in Is 12.6: "Exult and sing praise, inhabitants of Zion, because great in your midst is the Holy One of Israel."

(3.3) Furthermore, he was with us as the Lord in distributing favorable gifts: "says the Lord." And it is clear from here.

Continue as you want.[38]

---

35. *In medio tui:* this phrase in Zec 2.10 occurs 29 more times in Scripture and in this salvific way in Dt 7.21, Ps 116.19, Is 12.6, Zep 3.15, 17.

36. *Ego autem in medio eorum sum.* It is not really clear to which verse Thomas is referring here; if it is from the Gospel according to Luke, it is probably Lk 24.36: "Yet (*autem*) while they were saying these things, Jesus stood in their midst (*in medio eorum*) and said to them: 'Peace be with you. It is I (*ego sum*); fear not.'" In view of what follows, however, it seems more likely that Thomas refers here to Mt 18.20: "For where two or three are gathered in my name, I am in their midst" (*sum in medio eorum*).

37. Cf. ST II–II 28,3.

38. *Et patet de hoc. Procede ut uis.*

SERMON 03

ABJICIAMUS OPERA

Sermon on the First Sunday of Advent[1]

Romans 13.12: *Let us throw off the works of the darkness and put on the arms of the light.*

SUMMARY

"LET US THROW off the works of the darkness and put on the arms of the light" [Rom 13.12]. The Apostle, teacher of the Christians and leader in faith and truth, formulates this in this time of the gracious coming of our Lord with these words, or in these words, for two reasons: in order to stir up (1) a liberating abhorrence of all worldly stains and vices as well as (2) an honorable love (*amor*) or pursuit of heavenly virtues. The first thing he does when he says: "Let us throw off the works of the darkness"; the second, when he adds: "and let us put on the arms of the light."

(1) Concerning the first thing, note that the works and the vices of the world are called "dark," and that therefore they must be thrown off. (1.1) For there is in them an obvious lack of the wisdom that is needed in order to arrive at the truth which we are to know. Jn 1.5 reads: "The light shines in the darkness and the darkness did not recognize[2] it." (1.2) Furthermore, in darkness there is an obvious lack of foresight, which is need-

---

1. Thomas gave this homily on December 2, 1268, at Bologna, according to L. J. Bataillon, O.P.

2. Or "comprehend."

ed for preventing evil. Wis 17.3 reads: "They are scattered by a dark veil of forgetfulness."[3]

(2) Concerning the second point, note that the works of the Gospel and the spiritual gifts of the Holy Spirit are for us the arms against the world, the flesh, and the devil, and that they make us stand firm in the light. (2.1) Because through the effect of enlightening grace, which is like a light, they cause us to recognize the divine secret.[4] In 2 Cor 4.6 it says: "Yet God, who has said that light will shine from the darkness, (has shone his light in our hearts in order to bring to light the knowledge of the glory of God which is on the face of Jesus Christ)." (2.2) Because by the effect of reconciling grace, which is like a light, these [spiritual gifts] make peace when we wage war among ourselves [cf. Gal 5.22–23]. Prv 6.23 says: "The commandment is a lamp and the law a light," et cetera. (2.3) Because through the effect of the grace of honesty, which is like a light, they make us beautiful,[5] and, in us, the whole universe. Jn 5.35 reads: "He was a burning and light-giving lamp."

---

3. Forgetfulness opposes prudence: in ST II–II 47,16, Thomas speaks of *praevidentia;* in ST II–II 49,6, of *providentia.*

4. Thomas describes the movement of *conversio:* turning away from what distracts us from the ultimate end and turning towards God and what is God's, that is, turning to Jesus Christ. By citing 2 Cor 4.6 Thomas indicates that the initiative is with God; cf. ST II–II 45,5, where Thomas refers to 1 Cor 12.11.

5. Cf. ST II–II 145,2.

SERMON 04
OSANNA FILIO DAVID
Another Sermon on Advent[1]

Matthew 21.9: *Hosanna to the Son of David. Blessed is he who comes in the name of the Lord.*

PART 1: *Prothema*

"HOSANNA TO the Son of David. Blessed is he who comes in the name of the Lord" [Mt 21.9]. These words are spoken by the crowds praising Christ. These crowds clung to Christ. And so, please God, let us ask the Lord at the beginning to make us cling to him, so that we may understand his teaching.

PART 2: *Sermo*

"Hosanna" [Mt 21.9], et cetera. In these words we can consider three things to the praise of our Savior: (1) first, the task of our Savior; (2) second, the privilege of his origin; and (3) third, the highest point of his power.

(1) First, I say that the task of our Savior is mentioned where it says: "Hosanna." The proper task of the Savior is that he is a savior; indeed, for this he came into the world, "to seek and save what was lost" [Lk 19.10]. Is 45.15 reads: "Truly, you are a hidden God, God of Israel, Savior." And it is therefore that his name signifies salvation. Hence we read in Mt 1.21: "His name shall be called Jesus, for he will save (his people from

---

1. This sermon was given on the first Sunday of Advent, December 1, 1269.

their sins)."[2] And this task of savior is mentioned because it says: "Hosanna," which is compounded from the corrupted and the pure. For "hosanna" is the same as "hosyanna," which means: "Save, I beseech." For they would have implored salvation from him in vain unless they had believed in him as savior.[3]

Well, note that the human race was in need of salvation for three reasons: (1.1) first, because of the perversity of sin; (1.2) second, because of the oppression by enemies; and (1.3) third, because of the rejection of the glory of the world.

(1.1) First, I say: the human race was in need of salvation because of the perversity of sin. For when people who are ill are cured from their illness, they are called "saved." Therefore, the Lord says: "Your faith has saved you" [Mt 9.22]. Sin is a spiritual illness;[4] thus sinners are in need of salvation. The Psalmist says: "Salvation is far away from sinners" [Ps 119.155]. For example, someone is sick to death; the doctor will say that the person who is ill is far from salvation.[5] Anyone who is in the state of mortal sin[6] is sick to death, and sinners cannot reach salvation by themselves.[7] Therefore, salvation, that is, Jesus Christ [cf. Ex 15.2], has drawn near to them—he who became like us in all things [cf. Heb 2.17] "emptied himself, taking on the form of a slave, was made in the likeness of the people, and through his condition was found a man" [Phil 2.6–7], who accepted the human nature, and underwent suffering.[8] The Apostle is teaching

---

2. This verse is also cited in ST III intr.; salvation history is the framework in which Thomas speaks of Christ, the sacraments, and the last things. See also ST III 37,2.

3. Thus linguistically "Hosanna" is a corruption, whereas the person who utters this corruption is pure.

4. Cf. ST II–II 15; III 44,1. In ST III 1,3–4 Thomas speaks in the context of Incarnation and sin in terms of *remedium*, medicine. Elsewhere, he even calls sin the death of the soul, in ST I–II 102,5,4.

5. The Latin text reads: *longe a salute;* in Latin and also in, for instance, Spanish (*salud*) and Italian (*salute*), "salvation" and "health" are the same or etymologically connected.

6. ST I–II 72,5, 88.

7. ST I–II 68,2, 79,4; II–II 2,3 and 2,7–8; III 46,1,1.

8. Undergoing something (*passio*) distinguishes the human nature from the divine nature; cf. ST III 46,12. Jesus Christ's *passio* tells us that he was truly

that we are to rejoice because of this, saying: "Rejoice in the Lord always. I say it again: Rejoice, for the Lord is near" [Phil 4.4], namely, in our nature and in our heart. And this is meant where it says in the Gospel: "When Jesus had drawn near" [Mt 21.9].

See to whom Jesus is drawing near, three kinds of people: (1.1.1) to those who make peace with him, (1.1.2) to those who are devoted to God, and (1.1.3) to those who are kind (*pius*) to their neighbors.

(1.1.1) First, I say that he draws near to those who make peace with him. For God is the One who brings about peace [1 Cor 14.33]; and where else should peace dwell than in peace? The Apostle writes to the Corinthians: "Have peace, and the God of peace and love (*dilectio*) will be with you" [2 Cor 13.11]. How should we have peace with God? By not acting against his precepts.[9] And with yourself? By not doing anything against your conscience.[10] And with your neighbor? By not insulting him and by serving justice; "a work of justice" equals "about peace" [Is 32.17; cf. Bar 5.4].[11] So serve peace, and you will obtain salvation. Thus we read in Is 60.1: "Stand up, be radiant," Jerusalem, the city that is interpreted as the "vision of peace" [cf. Ps 122.6–8]. The Prophet continues: "Salvation will take possession of (your walls, and praise) your gates" [Is 60.18]. If you are in Jerusalem, you will have salvation. And this is indicated in the words: "Jesus drew near to Jerusalem" [Mt 21.1].

(1.1.2) Second, Jesus, that is to say, salvation, has drawn near to those who are devoted to God [cf. Jas 4.8]. It is a fact that "the Lord is in his holy temple" [Ps 11.5]. The mind that is dedicated to the divine worship is a temple of God. So when our mind is dedicated to God, God dwells in it [cf. 1 Cor 3.16] and gives salvation to it. As the Psalmist says: "God is near to all who call upon him (in truth. He fulfills the desire of all who fear him.

---

human (ST III 46,5–7). The suffering he underwent was salutary for us: ST III 46,1 and 3; 49,1–5.

9. Obedience is a virtue, coming forth from love: ST II–II 104,3–4.

10. ST II–II 75,1,3. Thomas's general view of our conscience is found in ST I 79,13 and I–II 19,5–6.

11. E.g., ST I–II 69,3, 73,4,1, 100,2, and II–II 29,3,3.

He also hears their cry) and he saves them" [Ps 145.18–19]. And this is pointed out because it says: "He had come to Bethphage" [Mt 21.1], which is interpreted as "jaw" or "house of the cheek"; it signifies the divine praise that comes forth from the devotion of the heart.

(1.1.3) Third, Jesus, that is, salvation, draws near to those who are merciful. For birds gather with birds that are alike [cf. Sir 27.9]. Now, God is merciful, since "his acts of mercy are above all his works" [Ps 145.9].[12] And when he sees someone like him, namely, someone merciful, he goes to him. So if you see someone who is in need, have at the least a kind affection towards him [cf. Lk 10.33]. Thus we read in the Gospel: "Be merciful (just as your Father is merciful)" [Lk 6.36].[13] And the Apostle says: "He saves us according to his mercy" [Ti 3.5]. And this is signified because he went "to the Mount of Olives" [Mt 21.1], for an olive signifies mercy [cf. Ps 52.10].

Hence the human race is in need of salvation because of the perversity of sin.

(1.2) Second, it is in need of salvation because of the oppression by enemies. It is a law in the world and with God that "someone is a slave of someone or something else by whom he has been overpowered" [2 Pt 2.19; cf. Jn 8.34]. The world was overpowered by the devil through sin, and the devil scourged his slave cruelly. So the world was in need of salvation, insofar as it seemed hardly possible that it could be saved. For we read in Is 49.24: "Will booty be taken from the strong one, and will what has been seized by the powerful be saved?" Indeed, someone who has been taken prisoner will be taken away by a strong man, namely, when the stronger man overpowers him; he will disarm him [cf. Mk 3.27] and "what has been seized by the powerful[14] will be saved." And therefore Christ wanted to be

---

12. According to ST I 25,3,3 God's mercy is the greatest expression of his almightiness.

13. In ST II–II 30,4,3 (and III 84,10) Thomas focuses more on the consequences for our relationship with God; the neighbor is certainly not absent, but, overall, the neighbor is more in view in his sermons than in his more theocentric, theological works.

14. Jesus Christ, the Savior, as in Prv 24.5.

called king, so that his authority would be designated by which he would set the world free. Hence it says: "Behold, your king comes" [Zec 9.9, Mt 21.5]. And the Psalmist says: "Lift up your gates, you princes," et cetera, and he continues: "and the king of glory will come in" [Ps 24.7, 9].

Usually kings have their servants. Thus Christ had servants or messengers whom he sent to save the people. These servants are the apostles who received from the Lord the task of preaching and bringing salvation [cf. Mk 16.15–16]. Hence it is said in Obadiah 17: "The saviors will go up from Mount Zion." These glorious apostles, who received the task of savior or salvation from Christ, are sent in twos [cf. Lk 10.1], by which it is signified that the whole choir of preachers ought to be led by two precepts: the love (*dilectio*) of God and of the neighbor [cf. Lk 10.27]. Or[15] it points to the active and the contemplative life,[16] which they ought to have, because they must draw by contemplation what they pour out by preaching, as Gregory says.[17]

See that in these messengers we can consider three characteristics: (1.2.1) their courage, (1.2.2) their power, and (1.2.3) their justice.

(1.2.1) First, I say that in the apostles we can admire their courage,[18] because, although they were poor and illiterate, they had such a confidence that they invaded the whole world and "conquered kingdoms by faith" [Heb 11.33].[19] We read in Jb

---

15. When Thomas explains Scripture he often shows multiple interpretations, different layers of the mystery revealed through what is written; cf. ST I 1,10: the four senses of the Scripture texts.

16. ST II–II 188,2. Since Thomas was a Dominican friar, he promotes in his sermons and in his theology a so-called *vita mixta*: a form of religious life that is contemplative (monks, like the Benedictines and Cistercians, are living a purely contemplative life) and active as well: ST II–II 186–189.

17. The device of the Dominican order is *Contemplata aliis tradere*, "Passing the outcomes of contemplation on to other people" (whence Thomas's formulation in ST I intr.: *Propositum nostrae intentionis in hoc opere est, ea quae ad Christianam religionem pertinent, eo modo tradere*, etc.).

18. *Audacia* is a passion which belongs to the virtue of strength (*fortitudo*) and can become a vice if it becomes too ardent and so out of control: ST I–II 45, 60,4–5; II–II 123,3, 127, 129,6,2.

19. The next thing Heb 11.33 mentions is that they administered justice, which Thomas mentions further on, in 1.2.3.

39.21: "He rejoices courageously; armed, he goes out to an encounter." This courage is also mentioned where it says: "Go into the fortress that is opposite to you" [Mt 21.2]. The world and the worldly life were opposed to them. Hence the Lord says: "I have chosen you from the world; therefore, the world hates you" [Jn 15.19b]. "If you were from the world, (the world would love [*diligo*] you as its own)" [Jn 15.19a]. "Do not be surprised if the world hates you" [1 Jn 3.13; cf. Jn 15.18].

(1.2.2) Secondly, their power must be admired, for although they were earthly people, the Lord gave them the power to cast out demons, to cure the sick, and to raise the dead [Mt 10.8, Mk 16.20, Lk 10.17, *et alibi*]. He even gave them the power to forgive sins [Jn 20.23] and to absolve from punishments or sins, which is proper to God [Mk 2.7].[20] Hence the Lord said to Peter: "Whatever you bind on earth (will also be bound in heaven, and what you loose on earth will be loosed in heaven)" [Mt 16.19]. And this is indicated where it says: "You will find a donkey tied (and a colt with it)." And he continues: "Untie them and bring them to me" [Mt 21.2]. The tied donkey is the synagogue that was subdued under the Law; the young animal that was not subdued is the people of the gentiles who until then had not received the Law. The Apostle says: "All of us, Greeks and gentiles,[21] are brought under the power of sin" [Rom 3.9]. He also says: "Indeed, all have sinned and lack the glory of God" [Rom 3.23]. Or[22] we must say that the donkey signifies the greater ones and the young animal the smaller ones, who all were subject to sin. As we read in Is 1.6: "From the sole of the foot to the top, there is no soundness in him."

(1.2.3)[23] Third, we can admire in the apostles their justice. Justice is giving back to everyone what is his.[24] And the apostles were just, because they gave God back what was his, name-

---

20. Thus people become children of God, according to Hilary, quoted by Thomas in his commentary on Mt 9.8 (c.9 *lectio* 1). Still, they are not almighty; cf. ST III 13,1.
21. The Scripture text reads: "Jews and Greeks."
22. See note 15.
23. Here starts Th. Käppeli's text. It ends just before section 1.3; see note 40.
24. One of the cardinal virtues: ST II–II 57–122; also I 21,1.

ly, glory. [Scripture] says: "I will not give my glory to someone else" [Is 42.8].

The apostles have converted the whole world. Did they subject them[25] to themselves? Did they seek dominion or temporal profit? No, they sought nothing else than that they would be subjected to Christ. Hence they could say this: "I will not hold dominion over you, nor will my son hold dominion among you, but the Lord will rule over you" [Jgs 8.23]. The Apostle says: "not seeking glory from the people" [1 Thes 2.6]. The apostles did not keep the colt for themselves, but they brought it to Christ and let him sit on it [Mt 21.7], to designate that the converted people is subject to Christ. Someone who converts someone else, and seeks to subject him to himself, is not a guardian, but a thief and a robber.[26]

How are people led to Christ? Certainly through faith, since it "is necessary that someone who draws near to Christ believes" [Heb 11.6]. They are led to him through love (*caritas*) and the observance of the precepts and counsels.[27] Take a look at this: "If someone says something, tell him that the Lord (needs it)" [Mt 21.3]. Bede comments on this that "erring *magistri* hinder the apostles in leading the colt to Christ."

But who are the ones who hinder in our time? For instance, those who say that people should not be led to Christ in religious life unless they have been instructed in the precepts.[28] In a gloss on Ps 131.2: "As a weaning child on his mother's lap," we read: "Many overthrow this order, which is from the easier things to the higher, like the heretics and the schismatics; they want to be separated from the mother's milk before their time, and die thereupon.[29] Yet if one of them still holds that he keeps

25. I.e., the people who inhabit the whole world.
26. We belong to Christ (Rom 14.8). Therefore, placing yourself in the center, his place, is theft; cf. Jn 10.1, 10.
27. In other words: following Christ in faith is a matter of learning by doing.
28. ST II–II 189,1. In this part of the sermon the conflict between the seculars and the regulars, both teaching at the University of Paris, clearly resounds.
29. Thomas argues that people who are too radical should not be admitted into a religious order; they must first learn the method of proceeding on the way to perfection, in religious life (cf. ST II–II 186,2) and theological knowledge: step by step, like a child; otherwise, it leads to a spiritual death, killing the

this order, he binds himself to a curse," as if he said: "May it be done unto me as unto someone who reclines on his mother's lap and, not yet well grown, is not given any milk." The gloss continues: "I have not only been humble among other people, since I learned in a humble way, but I was also humble in respect to the knowledge itself; I was first fed with the milk that the Word had become flesh [Jn 1.14], whereas later on I grew on the angels' food, which is 'in the beginning the Word was with God'" [Jn 1.1].

Yet do easier things always come before more difficult ones? I say they do not. The abstinence of virginity is more difficult than abstinence in marriage; should therefore the abstinence in marriage precede the abstinence of virginity? Definitely not. But I say that in the state in which we are[30] we must proceed from easier to more difficult things. Should someone who wants to proceed to the perfection of a state first go towards an easier state? He does not have to. But who [rightly] overthrow this order? Those who conceive through the spirit and have finished with the flesh[31] [cf. Gal 3.3].

Some say that preachers who prefer to convert rich people rather than the poor and make distinctions between people in this way must be refuted. I say that if they do this in order to become rich, they act in an evil way. But can converting rich people come to pass with a good inclination? Yes. Thus Augustine says in *Confessions:* "The ones with authority who are well known to many, lead many to salvation and are an example for many to follow. Therefore, the holy men rejoice more in them."

---

true faith in a person. It is clear that, besides Psalm 131, Thomas's imagery is derived from 1 Cor 3.1–2, Heb 5.12, and 1 Pt 2.2.

In what follows, Thomas identifies "milk" as the teachings on Christ's humanity (cf. Jn 1.14), and "angels' food" as the teachings concerning the divinity of Christ (cf. Jn 1.1).

30. Thomas distinguishes between a life in the world, which can be living single or as a married person or as a secular priest, and a life fully dedicated to the Lord as a vowed religious. The latter is valued much more highly by Thomas. Sometimes he mentions living as a bishop distinctly, e.g., in Sermon 21 *Beatus vir;* cf. ST II–II 185.

31. After all, some could have received the grace that makes this possible for them.

Someone who converts a poor person does well, but someone who converts a rich person well known to many does better, because others are edified.[32]

But is this making a distinction between people? No. Hence Augustine says: "It should not be that in your tent rich persons would be received before the poor." Thus it can be that someone does this with a good inclination, says also Augustine: "Concerning these things that can be done with a good and a bad inclination, they ought to be interpreted with the benefit of the doubt." So does this mean for you that you should interpret it negatively?[33] If people who think so had lived in the time of Christ, they would have refuted Christ, because he invited himself to the house of the rich Zacchaeus; he converted him who was a high person among the tax collectors, whereas there were still many poor people there [cf. Lk 19.2–10]. Such people would have said: "You go to him so as to be filled with meat and drink."[34]

Others say: "Those who live well in the world are more praiseworthy than those in religious life."[35] They give an example and say that a soldier who keeps guard well over a dilapidated castle for a king is more praiseworthy than a soldier who keeps guard over a strong castle. You are deceived; you think that serving God would be in exterior acts only and not in interior acts of virtue. Yet the principal acts are the interior virtues,

---

32. So those who prefer to convert the rich cannot for that fact be counted among those who hinder what the apostles began or who err. From the outside one cannot know what someone's intention is, whereas this is essential for establishing whether an action is good or evil. Thomas explains in what follows that favoring the rich over the poor is not the right thing to do for a Christian. But someone who *seems* to do so must be treated with the benefit of the doubt (*in melius interpretari*). The story of the conversion of Zacchaeus (Lk 19.1–10) seems to be a basis for Thomas's exposition.

33. Since Augustine is the highest authority for Thomas after Scripture, the implied answer is obviously "no."

34. Reference to Mt 11.19. Thus Thomas underlines the risk of this way of thinking. In Scripture people who reason like this are depicted as people who do not believe in Christ. Note that faith is the very subject of this section of the text: the point of departure is the statement that people are led to Christ through faith.

35. ST II–II 184,5–8. See note 28.

like wisdom and prudence.[36] When someone preserves chastity in religious life, that is the stronger castle. You will say that the one who shuns occasions for sinning[37] has lesser chastity and prudence? This is certainly not true, because the Apostle says: "Everyone who trains for a match abstains from all things" [1 Cor 9.25]. Someone who places the treasure of a king in a dilapidated castle, even though he would be very eager to watch over it, still would not be as praiseworthy as someone who would watch over it in a strong castle, because he should be rebuked for his negligence. But if it almost cannot be in another way, then the one who watches over it in a dilapidated castle should be praised more. We have the example of St. Agnes, who preserved her chastity in prostitution. Must, therefore, people leave the monastery to preserve their chastity and will they be more praiseworthy? Certainly not, but if there is a necessity for you to leave because you must be in the world, and if you preserve your chastity there, it will be more praiseworthy.

I am amazed about some things: once it was said that it was an evil that heresies were preached in Lombardy, but nowadays they are preached in this very house![38] There are two counsels given by Christ: that of chastity and the one of poverty. About chastity the Lord says: "Let him who can grasp it grasp it" [Mt 19.12]. And the Apostle says: "I do not have a precept about the virgins, but I give a counsel as someone who pursues mercy" [1 Cor 7.25]. And about poverty the Lord says: "Someone who wants to be perfect should come and sell everything he possesses and follow me" [Mt 19.21]. In the early Church there were Jovinian and Vigilantius. Jovinian has said that abstinence within marriage must be considered equal to virginity; this is what he preached. Vigilantius preached that the state of the rich who give alms must be considered equal to

---

36. Wisdom is one of God's gracious gifts which corresponds with the greatest theological virtue, love: ST II–II 45. Prudence is the first of the cardinal virtues: ST II–II 47–56.

37. That is, the person who withdraws from "the world" by entering a religious order.

38. A third issue in the conflict (notes 28, 35) at the university is addressed by Thomas.

poverty,[39] which is at odds with what Jerome says: "It is good to expend your means for the poor with stewardship, but it is better to give your means at once with the intention of following Christ, suffering want with Christ."[40] Against all these things we have what the Lord says: "If someone might say anything to you, tell him that the Lord needs these things" [Mt 21.3].

(1.3) Furthermore, the human race was in need of salvation, so that it would reject worldly glory. Well, you should know now that someone who looks for salvation where it is not [cf. Ps 146.3, Acts 4.12], is very much in need of it. Some look for salvation in the things of the world, whereas there is no salvation in those. The Psalmist says: "A king is not saved by a great strength, nor will a warrior be saved in the greatness of his strength" [Ps 33.16]. So in order to show that this is not the proper way of salvation, the Lord showed us another way of salvation: the way of humility.[41] As the Psalmist says: "He will save the humble in spirit" [Ps 34.19]. He showed this humility when he rode on the donkey [Mt 21.7];[42] he showed complete humility by willing to carry the cross-beam of the cross [cf. Heb 12.2]. As the Apostle says: "He humbled himself" [Phil 2.8], et cetera. But for what did he will humility but for teaching us humility? [Cf. Phil 2.5, 1 Pt 2.21] Hence he says in Mt 11.29: "Learn from me that I am meek and humble (of heart, and you will find rest for your souls)." Hence he wanted to maintain humility in order to teach us to humble ourselves.

Now see that a human being ought to humble himself in three ways: (1.3.1) he ought to humble his mind, (1.3.2) his body, and (1.3.3) his affection.

(1.3.1) I say, to begin with, he ought to humble his mind. We recognize a proud man by his mind: him who is "puffed up by his carnal mind," as it is said in Col 2.18. Against them the Apostle says in Rom 12.16: "(Associate with humble people,)

---

39. So these heretics were of a different kind than the ones mentioned before; the former were too radical, but these do not go far enough.

40. Here ends Th. Käppeli's text.

41. ST II–II 161. See also Thomas's praise of this virtue in Sermon 18 *Germinet terra*, on the Feast of the Birth of the Blessed Virgin Mary.

42. Instead of a horse: Est 6.6–11, Eccles 10.7a.

do not be the prudent among yourselves." And in Prv 3.5 we read: "(Have confidence in God with all your heart,) so that you do not lean on your own prudence." Let us follow the life and the deeds of the great people. The crowds that followed Christ have shown a sign of this humility. Christ has shown humility because he rode on a donkey; the crowds have shown a sign of this humility when they cut off the branches of trees and laid them down on the way [cf. Mt 21.8]. For Gregory says that cutting branches is accepting the authorities and examples of the saints and placing them on the way of one's moral life. Therefore a man first ought to humble his mind.

(1.3.2) Second, he ought to humble his body by fasting and vigils. The Psalmist says: "I humbled my soul in fasting" [Ps 35.13]. If someone had a slave and he gave him delicate food to eat in the beginning instead of in the end [cf. Lk 17.7–8], he would find him haughty. So it is with our body. Because of this we should humble our body with fasting and vigils. The crowds offer an image of this humility by spreading out their garments on the road [cf. Mt 21.8], which stands for throwing the body to the ground. In Rv 3.4 it says: I have "a few names in Sardis who did not defile their garments."

(1.3.3) Third, a man ought to weaken his affection in such a way that he gives it completely over to God [cf. Phil 3.10]. When you love (*diligo*) something that is yours which you do not link to God, you are not perfectly humble. It is said in Jdt 8.17: "Let us humble our souls and serve him with a contrite and humble spirit" [cf. Lk 16.13]. See that the crowds humbled their affection in this way: that they yearned[43] for salvation from Christ, saying: "Hosanna," et cetera.

These things are sufficient about the task of the Savior.

(2) Let us take a look at his origin. You should know that in the Old Testament salvation was promised in two ways: first, by someone who would be born from the stem of David, where it says: "In those days I will save Judah and I will raise for David a just shoot" [Jer 23.5]. And elsewhere salvation is promised

---

43. Thomas uses the verb *affecto*.

to them in the coming of the Lord, as it says in Is 35.4: "The Lord himself will come, and he will save you." Thus the crowds smartly connected these two: that he who will be from the seed of David will save us and that the Lord will save us in his coming. (2.1) As they were calling him "Son of David" [Mt 21.9], they called to mind his humanity; (2.2) they called to mind his divinity as they were saying: "Blessed is he who comes in the name of the Lord" [Mt 21. 9].[44]

(2.1) See that David bears the image of Christ in three respects:[45] (2.1.1) first, as for the royal sovereignty; (2.1.2) second, as for the victory of wars; (2.1.3) third, as for grace.

(2.1.1) As for the royal sovereignty, David bears the image of Christ. Know that David was the first accepted king of God in Israel [cf. 1 Sm 16]; and concerning Christ it is said: "The Lord will give him the throne of David, his father" [Lk 1.32].

(2.1.2) Second, David bears the image of Christ as for the victory of wars, because he was victorious in war. Hence it says in Ps 144.1: "Blessed is the Lord my God, who schools my hands for the battle (and my fingers for war)." And [Christ] was especially victorious because he completely conquered the powers of the air[46] and led "the defeated out of the lake in which there is no water" [Zec 9.11].

(2.1.3) Third, David bears the image of Christ as for grace. Thus says the Lord about David: "I have found a man after my heart" [1 Sm 13.14, Ps 89.21]; whereas the Lord says about Christ: "This is my beloved (*dilectus*) Son (in whom I am well pleased)."[47] Moreover, we find that David had love (*caritas*), whence it says: "I made peace with those who hated peace (when I spoke to them; they pursued me without reason)" [Ps 119.7 (Vg)]. Furthermore: "If I have given what is due to those who repaid me with evil things" [Ps 7.5]. Hence he was mild, in accordance with this: "Remember, Lord, David and all his mild-

---

44. Cf. Thomas's commentary on Is 6.3 (*lectio* 1).

45. King David is the prefiguration of Christ the King: a Christological reading of the Old Testament.

46. The devil and his demons; cf. Eph 2.2.

47. Mt 3.17, 17.5, a quotation from Ps 2.7 (although this Psalm is not explicitly ascribed to David).

ness" [Ps 132.1]. He had humility as well. Hence he said: "Lord, my heart is not proud" [Ps 131.1]. Also Christ was mild and humble. Thus he said to his disciples in Mt 11.29: "Learn from me, for I am meek and humble of heart." So, by calling to mind the humility of Christ, the crowds said: "To the Son of David."

(2.2) Next, as for the recognition of his divinity, it says: "Blessed is he who comes in the name of the Lord." Well, see that Christ comes in the name of the Lord in a threefold manner:

(2.2.1) First, in the truth of the divine name.[48] For when a generation is perfect, what is generated receives the nature and the name of the one who generates. So, because the generation of Christ was perfect, therefore Christ received the nature of the divinity from the Father as well as the name. Hence the Apostle says: "He has given him a name that is above every name" [Phil 2.9], the name of the divinity, that is. So, he comes first in the truth of the divine name.

(2.2.2) Second, he comes in the strength of the divine name. Hence we read in Prv 18.10: "A very strong tower is the name of the Lord; (the just runs to him and will be exalted)." In natural things the strength of a cause does not have an effect unless it is applied [cf. Jn 15.4]; in this way, everything that the saints have done is entirely done in the strength of the name of the Lord [cf. Is 26.12, Phil 2.13].

(2.2.3) Furthermore, he comes, thirdly, in the manifestation of the divine name. Therefore he says: "Father, I have manifested your name to the people" [Jn 17.6].

Now the task of the Savior and his origin are clear.

❖

(3) Let us look at the highest point of his power, because it says "Hosanna," meaning "save," "in the highest" [Mk 11.10].[49] Some who are in hell are saved; the Psalmist says: "The Lord will save people and beasts of burden" [Ps 36.7; cf. Jon 3.8], so that people are saved and undamaged. Salvation "in the highest" is salvation in God. Thus we read in Hos 1.7: "I will save

---

48. ST I 16,5.
49. Mt 21.9 reads *Osanna in altissimis*, whereas Lk 19.38 reads *Gloria in excelsis*. Mark's text is used in the liturgy of Palm Sunday.

them in their God," that is, in the participation in divine glory. Also, elsewhere this is said <. . .>.[50] Such people say: "Hosanna in the highest," meaning: "I implore, Lord; let your salvation be in the highest."

But behold: although there is one God, it says "in the highest," plural. The reason is that he[51] willed to distinguish the distinctions of the Persons, so that we might consider which things are attributed to the Persons. Thus Hilary says that "eternity is attributed to the Father; appearance," or beauty, "to the Image; and use," or delight, "to the Gift."[52] To the Father, who is the beginning, eternity is attributed; to the Son, who is called "Image" [cf. Col 1.15], beauty is attributed; to the Holy Spirit, who is the Gift, use or enjoyment is attributed. Hence[53] our salvation consists (3.1) in the stability of eternity, (3.2) in the beauty of the light, and (3.3) in the enjoyment of delight.

(3.1) First, I say that our salvation consists in the stability of eternity.[54] A ship is saved when it is on its way to a stable harbor [cf. Ps 107.30]; in the same way a human being is not saved during his life on earth (*in via*), but in the heavenly homeland (*in patria*). Hence Is 45.17 says: "Israel is saved in the Lord through an eternal salvation." Errors perish and cease to be when people get to know the truth.

(3.2) Second, it consists in the beauty of the divine light. People in this world are in a certain way saved, as the Psalmist says: "Show us your face, and we will be saved" [Ps 80.4, 8, 20]. Yet then they will be saved in a perfect way, as the Psalmist indicates, at the sight of the face in which every good finds its existence, according to that saying in Ex 33.19: "I will show you every good."[55]

(3.3) Third, [our salvation consists] in the enjoyment of the di-

50. Some words are missing in the original text. Thomas may have referred to Hos 14.4: "Assyria will not save us, nor shall we have horses to mount."

51. It seems that God is the subject here: he has put the words in the mouths of the people; cf. Is 51.16.

52. ST I 39,8.

53. The way in which our salvation takes place in time reflects who the eternal God is; cf. Rom 1.20; ST I 32 and III 1,1sc.

54. Eternity implies no change: ST I 9,1–2, 10,1–4.

55. Cf. Jn 12.46–47 and Jn 14.9; Col 1.15.

vine delight, as the Psalmist says: "Your houses will be drenched with abundance" [Ps 36.9a]. A man who is drunk is beside himself; in the same way the saints in the heavenly homeland (*in patria*) will be; "and from the stream of your pleasure you will give them drink" [Ps 36.9b], namely, when they will say: "My heart has exulted in being saved"[56] [1 Sm 2.1, Lk 1.47],[57] et cetera.

We will ask the Lord, et cetera.

56. The words used in this subparagraph refer to ecstasy (ST I–II 28,3) as well as contemplation (ST II–II 180,7).

57. In Lk 1.46–55 we find quite a few themes that play an important role in this sermon, such as humility, handmaid/servant, the power and mercy of God, God's holy name, et cetera; it seems that the *Magnificat* has been a directive for the content of this sermon.

SERMON 05
ECCE REX TUUS

Sermon on the First Sunday of Advent[1]

Matthew 21.5: *Behold, your king comes unto you, mild.*

PART 1: *Prothema*

"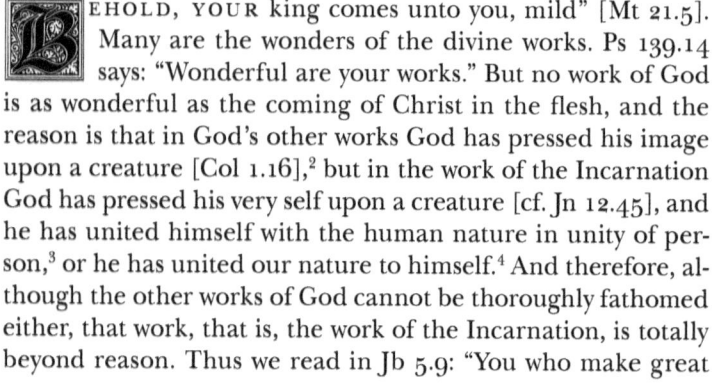EHOLD, YOUR king comes unto you, mild" [Mt 21.5]. Many are the wonders of the divine works. Ps 139.14 says: "Wonderful are your works." But no work of God is as wonderful as the coming of Christ in the flesh, and the reason is that in God's other works God has pressed his image upon a creature [Col 1.16],[2] but in the work of the Incarnation God has pressed his very self upon a creature [cf. Jn 12.45], and he has united himself with the human nature in unity of person,[3] or he has united our nature to himself.[4] And therefore, although the other works of God cannot be thoroughly fathomed either, that work, that is, the work of the Incarnation, is totally beyond reason. Thus we read in Jb 5.9: "You who make great

---

1. This sermon was very probably delivered on the 29th of November 1271, since in the *Collatio in sero* at the Vespers Thomas refers to Saint Andrew, whose feast day is the 30th of November.

2. In ST I 47,1 Thomas speaks of the representation of God's goodness in the multitude and diversity of the creatures; cf. Rom 1.20. And this is in particular true for the human being: Gn 1.26, Wis 2.23; cf. ST I 93,6 (esp. 93,6,1 and 4).

3. Here Thomas uses the term *persona* in the theological sense; later on he does not: see note 24.

4. A typical approach of a mystery of faith: since we do not fathom it, we do not have the exact words to formulate it; approaching it from different angles, we need many words; cf. ST III 2–4.

and wonderful things and countless things that cannot be fathomed."

This is one work that I cannot see: "If he comes to me, I will not see him" [Jb 9.11].[5] And in Mal 2.3 we read: "Behold, the Lord of hosts comes, and who could imagine the day of his coming?" As if he says that this exceeds human thinking. But the Apostle teaches us who could imagine the day of his coming, when he says: "We are not able to think of something by ourselves as if it came from ourselves, but every ability of ours comes from God" [2 Cor 3.5]. Thus we will ask the Lord at the beginning that he may give me something to say, et cetera.[6]

PART 2: *Sermo*

"Behold, your king" [Mt 21.5], et cetera. These words are taken from the Gospel that is read among us today. They are taken from Zec 9.9, although they are read in a slightly different wording there. Anyway, in these words the coming of Christ is clearly announced to us. In order to avoid talking about something uncertain, you should know that we speak of the coming of Christ in a fourfold way: (0.1) The first is the way in which he comes in the flesh. (0.2) His second coming is the way in which he enters the mind. (0.3) The third coming of Christ is the way in which he comes in the death of the just ones. (0.4) But the fourth coming of Christ is the way in which he comes to judge.

(0.1) First I say that the coming of Christ is into the flesh. And we must not understand this as if he came into the flesh by changing place, because he says in Jer 23.24: "I make heaven and earth full." So how did he come into the flesh? I say that he has come into the flesh descending from heaven, not by leaving heaven, but by assuming our nature. Thus it says in Jn 1.11: "He

---

5. ST I 12,1–11. Seeing and knowing are almost synonymous, as in English: "I see" means "I know/understand"; in Greek οἶδα means "I have seen" and therefore "I know." Cf. ST I 84–89.

6. Thomas is aware that we need God's help if we want to speak meaningfully of the mysteries of God which we do not fully understand and yet believe and are called to proclaim: ST I 12,12–13.

came into his own." And how do I say that he was in the world? When I say: "The Word has become flesh" [Jn 1.14].[7]

(0.2) And see that this coming leads to another coming of Christ, which is in the mind. That Christ has come into the flesh would not have been to our benefit at all if with this coming he had not entered our mind as well, namely, by sanctifying us.[8] Hence it says in Jn 14.23: "If someone loves (*diligo*) me, he will keep my words, and my Father will love (*diligo*) him, and we will come to him and make our home with him."

(0.3) In the first coming only the Son comes. In the second coming the Son comes with the Father to inhabit the soul [Jn 14.23]. By this latter coming, which is by means of justifying grace, the soul is freed from guilt—not from every punishment—because grace is brought in, but not yet glory. And because of this the third coming of Christ is necessary: when he receives them to himself. Thus he says in Jn 14.3: "When I will have departed," in the Passion, and "will have prepared a place for you," by taking away the obstacle, "I will come unto you again," that is, in death, "and I will take you to myself," namely, in glory, "so that where I am there you also will be."[9] Likewise, he says in Jn 10.10: "I have come so that they may have life," meaning his presence in our souls [cf. Jn 14.23], "and that they may have it more abundantly," that is, through the participation in glory.

---

7. Descending from heaven is the One who is in heaven. So here Thomas is speaking about the descent of the divine Son. God is not a body (Jn 4.24: "God is spirit"; cf. ST I 3,1); he *assumed* a body, a human body: Incarnation. This body was like any human body (ST III 31,4) confined to place (and time), whereas, insofar as he is God, Christ is not confined to place (and time). In other words, the divine Son is everywhere in his ubiquity, *omnipraesentia* (ST I 8,2). Therefore, "coming down" and similar formulations must be understood in an analogous way, not in terms of leaving one place in order to arrive at another. According to the Christian faith it was not the Son's presence among us that was new, but *the way in which* he became present among us was new: through the Incarnation God was with us as a man (cf. SCG IV 30, ST I 43,1).

8. ST I 43,5. Sanctification is the gracious gift of God himself by which sins are taken away and virtues are infused and strengthened. Thus people become happier and (more) dedicated to God, while God makes himself a home in them.

9. Thomas interprets this text as concerning our soul; the human soul does not die: ST I 75,6.

(0.4) The fourth coming of Christ will be for judging, namely, when the Lord will come to judge,[10] and then the glory of the saints will overflow all the way to the bodies, and the dead will rise [cf. 1 Cor 15.52]. Therefore, he says in Jn 5.25: "The hour has come, and now is the time when all who are in graves will hear the voice of the Son of God and those who have done good things will go forth into the resurrection of life." And because of these four comings of Christ the Church expressly celebrates the four Sundays previous to Christ's coming.[11]

❖

Now on this Sunday the Church celebrates the first coming of Christ, and we can see four things in the verse mentioned above: (1) first, the demonstration of the coming of Christ, where it says: "Behold"; (2) second, who the one is that is coming, where it says: "your king"; (3) third, the benefit of his coming: "comes unto you";[12] (4) fourth, the way of his coming, where it says: "mild."

❖

(1) First, I say, we can see the demonstration of the coming of Christ, where it says: "Behold." And we must note that by "behold" we usually understand four things: (1.1) first, the certification of a thing: we say "behold" regarding things that are certain for us; (1.2) second, we understand by "behold" a demarcation of the time; (1.3) third, the manifestation of the thing; and (1.4) fourth, the comfort of people.

(1.1) First, I say that by "behold" we usually understand the certification of a thing. When someone wants to certify, he says "behold." Thus the Lord says in Gn 9.13: "Behold, I will establish my bond with you and with your seed after you. I will place my arch between me and you," namely, in the sign of peace. By this arch[13] God's Son is signified, because, as the arch is brought forth by the reverberation of the sun onto a cloud of

10. ST III 59.
11. Advent is in this way presented not only as a time of preparation for Christmas, but as a time to meditate upon the whole of the history of salvation.
12. In Latin it says *tibi:* he is coming "to you for your benefit."
13. The rainbow.

water vapor, so Christ is brought forth from the Word of God[14] and from the human nature, which is as the cloud;[15] and just as soul and flesh form one human being, so God and a human being form one Christ.[16] And about Christ it is said that he ascended upon a light cloud [Acts 1.9], meaning upon human nature, by uniting it to himself.[17]

Christ has come unto us as the sign of peace, and it was necessary that it would happen in this way, since nowadays there are some who doubt the second coming of Christ. Thus we read in what the Apostle writes: "In the last days indeed mocking people will come who leave the faith, who walk after their own desires, and say: 'Where is now his promise and his coming?'" [2 Pt 3.3–4; cf. Jude 18] Such people will even say that there will not be a soul after the body has died.[18] And because of this the Prophet says to certify the coming of Christ: "Behold" [Zec 9.9], et cetera. And in Hab 2.3 we read: "The Lord will appear in the end, and he will not lie." And in Isaiah: "The Lord of hosts will come" [Zec 5.4].

(1.2) Second, we usually understand "behold" as a demarcation of time. As for Christ's coming to the judgment the time is not marked out for us. Hence Jb 32.22 (Vg) says: "I do not know how long I will remain and when my Maker will take me." Also in Lk 17.20 we read: "The reign of God will come unnoticed." But why has the time not been marked out for us as for this coming? Maybe because the Lord wanted us to be watchful always.[19] But as for Christ's coming into the flesh, the time was

---

14. Which is like the sun, e.g., in Ps 84.12.

15. Jb 7.9, 37.15; elsewhere in Scripture the cloud usually signifies YHWH's hidden presence.

16. It is remarkable that Thomas is making this comparison, since Thomas endorses in his theology how different the union of God and human being in Christ is in many ways, when compared to other unions in creation (ST III 2–5). But what Thomas is referring to in this sermon is the oneness itself and "the union of the Incarnation means the greatest unity" (ST III 2,9: *unio incarnationis importat maximam unitatem*).

17. ST III 2,8, 3,1–7.

18. See note 9.

19. No wild speculation, but a tentative answer ("maybe") on the basis of Scripture: Lk 12.35–48, Mt 24.42.

marked out for us. Thus [the Lord says] in Jer 23.5: "Behold, the days will come, and I will give rise to the just offspring of David, and he will reign and be wise."

(1.3) Third, by "behold" we usually understand the manifestation of a thing. One of God's comings unto us is hidden, namely, the coming by which he enters the mind; it cannot be known through certification.[20] Thus we read in Jb 9.11: "I will not see him if he comes to me, and I will not understand if he leaves." But in the coming in the flesh the manifest and visible Christ has come. Therefore it says in Is 52.6: "Because of this my people will understand my name, since I myself am the One who said: 'Behold, I am present.'" And John the Baptist has pointed him out with his finger as present, saying: "Behold the Lamb of God" [Jn 1.29]. Zechariah has truly pointed him out as the One to come in the future by saying "behold" [Zec 9.9].[21]

(1.4) Fourth, by "behold" we usually understand the comforting of people, and this consists in two things. If someone suffers from the troubles caused by his enemies, and his enemies are made subject to him, he says: "Behold." Thus we read in Lam 2.16: "My enemies have opened their mouth, and the day that I desired has come." In a similar way someone says "behold" when he obtains something. Thus it says in Ps 133.1: "Behold how good and how pleasant it is that brothers live together," et cetera. These two things we obtain in the coming of Christ: the human being is freed from the insults of demons[22] and rejoices in the hope he gained.[23] It says in Is 35.4: "Say to the petty-hearted: 'Take comfort; fear not; behold, your God will bring revenge over your enemies; he himself will come and save you.'"

---

20. ST I 43,3.
21. Thus this invisible coming must be pointed out to us explicitly, which is done by God himself as well as by someone sent by God (a prophet, an angel, an apostle, a preacher).
22. This is completed through the Passion, by which we are freed from the power of the devil: ST III 49,2.
23. ST II–II 1,7,1, also 7,1,2, 17,2 and 7.

(2) Let us now look at who the one is that is coming. The coming of a person[24] requires that he be expected or announced with festivity because of the greatness of the person—if it is a king or a legate of the lord Pope—or because of friendship and affection. And this one who is coming is a king as well as our neighbor and friend.[25] Because of this we ought to expect him with festivity. You know that a king rules with the authority of dominion [cf. Rom 13.1, etc.], but not everyone who has the authority of dominion is called a king; (2.1) four characteristics are required for calling someone a king, and if one of the four is lacking, he is not called king. For a king ought to be (2.1.1), first, the only king; (2.1.2) second, he ought to have full power (2.1.3); third, full jurisdiction; and (2.1.4) fourth, the equity of justice [cf. Prv 2.9].

(2.1.1) First I say that a king ought to be the only king, because if there are in a kingdom many rulers and the dominion does not belong to one, he is not called a king. In this sense the Kingdom is like a monarchy, and Christ is the only King. Therefore, it says in Ezek 37.22: "There will be one king over all of us." It says "one king" to signify that there is no other, no other lord, for the Son with the Father will be one Lord, our King.[26] Hence Christ says: "I and the Father are one" [Jn 10.30], which is contrary to what Arius has said, that the Father would be another one than the Son. The Apostle says: "Also if there are many gods and many lords, we have one God and Lord" [1 Cor 8.5–6].[27]

(2.1.2) Second, "king" means fullness of power.[28] Someone who does not rule with the fullness of power, but in accordance

---

24. (Cf. note 3.) Here Thomas does not use the word *persona* in the theological sense, but as we usually understand it: a human person, someone. From here on, this term is used in this sense; cf. the beginning of the *Collatio in sero* (see also note 39).

25. The theme of Jesus Christ as a close friend is not elaborated any further here. See for this Sermon 13 *Homo quidam fecit*, part 2: *Sermo*.

26. In this sense Christ is called the Most High (e.g., in the *Gloria*): ST III 57,4–5, 58.

27. Cf. ST I 11,3–4, 39,8, 47,2,2.

28. Thomas refers to the situation in which the legislative, executive, and judiciary power were united in the person of the monarch; cf. ST I–II 98,5,1.

with laws imposed upon him, is not called a king, but a magistrate or a man in power. It had to happen, however, that, when Christ came, the Law from God would be changed as for the ceremonial laws.[29] Thus Christ himself is the One who can establish the Law. Therefore, he says: "It is said to our ancestors: 'You shall not kill.' Yet I say," as if he says, "I have the power and I can establish laws."[30] Hence we read in Is 33.22: "The Lord our judge, our lawgiver, he himself will come and save us." We read that "the Father has given every judgment to the Son" [Jn 5.22] and that the Lord is our lawgiver, and by consequence he is our king. Thus we read in Est 13.9 (Vg): "Lord, almighty King, all things together are placed under your dominion." Hence the Son says: "All power is given unto me in heaven and on earth" [Mt 28.18].[31]

(2.1.3) Third, "king" implies the fullness of jurisdiction. The *paterfamilias* has the fullness of power in his house, but still he is not called "king." In a similar way someone who has one house in the country is not called a king because of this. But someone who has dominion over many territories and over a big population, such a man is called a king. We see that characteristic in this man who comes to us, since every creature is subject to him, because "God[32] is King over all the earth" [Ps 47.8]. And it had to be that such a man came who had such power, since once the Law was only given to the Jews and the Jews were called God's own people; but it had to come to pass that all would be led to salvation [cf. 1 Tm 2.4], so it was necessary that he would be the king of all things so that he would be able to save all

---

29. The ceremonial laws are the precepts of the Old Covenant concerning worship (see ST I–II 101,1, 103,3).

30. Mt 5.21–22. Nowadays we know that this was a common formulation of teaching rabbis. They were by doing so not changing the Law, but giving their interpretation. For more nuances of how Thomas taught on the relation between the Old and the New Law/Covenant, see ST I–II 107, where he considers this in view of Mt 5.17: "Do not think that I have come to abolish the Law or the Prophets. I have come not to abolish, but in order to fulfill."

31. On the power of Christ: ST I 42,6 (as for his divinity) and III 13 (as for his humanity).

32. Because of the Incarnation we speak of Christ as a man and as God; cf. ST III 16.

people.³³ Such was this One who comes to us. Therefore, Ps 2.8 says: "Ask me, and I will give unto you the gentiles as your inheritance, and the ends of the earth as your possession."³⁴

(2.1.4) Fourth, a king must be equitable, because otherwise he would be a tyrant. For a tyrant turns everything that is in his kingdom to his own benefit, whereas a king organizes his kingdom in view of the common good. Thus we read in Prv 29.4: "A just king raises up the land; a greedy man destroys it."³⁵ But this One does not come to seek after his own benefit, but after yours, because "the Son of man has not come to be served but to serve" [Mt 20.28].³⁶ And he who has come to serve surely came to give his life for the redemption of many [ibid.], and to lead the redeemed to eternal glory,

to which he may also lead us, et cetera.

PART 3: *Collatio in sero*

"Behold, your king comes" [Mt 21.5], et cetera. We said that in these words we can see a demonstration of his coming because it says³⁷ "behold." Second, the benefit of his coming, where it says "he comes." Third and fourth, the way in which he is coming, where it says "mild."³⁸ We also said that (1) we usually understand four things by this word "behold": first, the certi-

---

33. So this necessity is not absolute; it is not the result of blind fate or a lack of any other way (for God). It had to come to pass only because it was God's will (cf. ST III 46,1), as Thomas endorses here with an implicit reference to 1 Tm 2.4.

34. The preceding verse reads: "You are my Son; this day I have begotten you."

35. Cf. ST I–II 105,1,5. Since for Thomas "king" is not a neutral term, "a just king" is in his view a pleonasm. See also Sermon 19 *Beati qui habitant* section 2.2.1 and 2.2.2..

36. In brief: a king in the true sense of the word looks like God, our King (Ps 93.1 etc.). Note that in ST I–II 105,1,2 Thomas warns in this context against corruption (absolute power may well corrupt) in view of 1 Samuel 8: King Saul.

37. *Cum dicit*, usually conceived as a temporal construction (*cum temporale*) and thus translated as "when" (or "where," as synonymous with *ibi*, as also Thomas uses it) "it/he says." In some cases (e.g., in Sermons 05, 08, 09, 12, 15, 20, and 21) it could be interpreted as a *cum explicativum*: "because (of the fact that)."

38. This is a different layout from the one given at the beginning of the *Sermo*. Maybe the secretary lost Thomas here for a moment? After all, the text follows the original plan.

fication of a thing; second, a determination of the time; third, the manifestation of the thing; and fourth, comfort. (2.1) We also spoke about who the one is that is coming, which is mentioned where it says "your king": we said that someone's coming requires that he be expected or announced with festivity because of his greatness if he is a king or a legate or because of the friendship and the affinity with the person[39]—and [all] these things apply to this One who comes.

⁂

(2.2) Well, we must consider that the same One is the king of the whole of creation. Thus we read in Jdt 9.12: "Creator of the waters and king of the whole of creation." Yet in a special way he is called "your king," that is, the king of humankind, for four reasons: (2.2.1) first, because of the likeness of his image; (2.2.2) second, because of a special love (*dilectio*); (2.2.3) third, because of a special care and concern; and (2.2.4) fourth, because of his fellowship with the human nature.[40]

(2.2.1) First, I say that Christ is called "your king," that is, the king of humankind, because of the likeness of his image. You know that we say that those who wear the decorations of the king belong to the king in a special way, as if they bear his image. And although every creature is God's, still we say more specifically that there is only one creature of God that bears God's image, and this is the human being. Thus we read in Gn 1.26: "Let us make the human being to[41] our image and likeness." In what does this likeness consist? I say it does not apply to a physical likeness,[42] but to the intelligible light of the mind: in God is the originality of the intelligible light, and we have the sign of this light.[43] Thus we read in Ps 4.7: "The light of your face, O

---

39. See note 24.

40. In 2.1 Thomas has mentioned the highness of Christ; now he is going to emphasize how much he is with us.

41. In the Latin text we find the preposition *ad*, which indicated an approaching movement, or growth; we are on our way to becoming more and more like God (as he was in Jesus Christ: Col 1.15); cf. ST I 4,3; I–II 3,2,4.

42. Jn 4.24 ("God is Spirit"), cited in ST I 3,1. This text has so great an authority because it is Christ himself who says this, plainly.

43. *Signum:* sign or image, as on a seal-ring. ST III 5,4,2; cf. ST I 14,1, 16,5,3, 79,4, and 103,5,3 (also 115,4,2).

Lord, is imprinted (*signatus*) upon us"; humankind bears the seal (*sigillum*) of this light. Hence this image is created in man.

But it happens that it is diminished and obscured through sin. Ps 73.20 reads: "And you will bring their images back to nothing."[44] Because of this, God has sent his Son, in order to reform this image that is deformed by sin.[45] Thus we apply ourselves to be reformed in accordance with the Apostle who says: "As you lay aside the old man, put on the new man, which is created according to God and which is renewed in the image of him who created him" [Eph 4.24]. And how are we renewed? Surely, when we follow Christ. This image, which is deformed in us, is perfect in Christ [cf. Eph 4.13]. Thus we ought to bear the image of Christ, as we read in the Apostle's Letter to the Corinthians: "Just as we have borne an image of the earthly, let us bear the image of the Heavenly" [1 Cor 15.49] and in today's Epistle reading: "Put on Christ" [Rom 13.14], which means "act like Christ"; the perfection of the Christian life consists in this.

(2.2.2) Second, Christ is called "your king," meaning the king of humankind, because of a special love (*amor*).[46] Usually in a group of clerics a bishop who loves (*diligo*) some in a more special way than the others, is called "their" bishop. God loves (*diligo*) everything that is, but he loves (*diligo*) humankind in a more special way. Thus we read in Is 63.15: "Where is your [that is, God's] zeal and your strength, the multitude of your tenderness upon me?"[47]

See that God loves (*diligo*) the human nature in a special way. For we find different ranks of nature, but we do not find that God raises an inferior nature to a higher nature, for instance, a star to the rank of the sun,[48] or lower angels to the rank of higher angels. But God has raised the human being up

---

44. ST I–II 85.
45. ST III 1,2. The fullness of what Thomas says here is expounded further on by him, in III 46,3 and 49.
46. For Thomas's use of the different terms for "love" see Sermon 01 *Veniet desideratus*, note 39.
47. Verse 16 proceeds: "For you are *our* Father" (italics added).
48. The sun was considered the greatest heavenly body, on the basis of Scripture (and experience).

to the rank and equality of the angels.[49] Thus we read in Lk 20.36: "The children of the resurrection," the holy ones, "will be equal to angels." So God has loved (*diligo*) human beings in a special way. Hence we should not be ungrateful for such a great love (*dilectio*), but we ought to direct our love (*amor*) entirely to him. If a king loves (*diligo*) a poor person, that poor person would consider himself miserable if he did not recompense the king for his love (*amor*) as much as he can. Out of the infinity of his love (*amor*) the Lord has said to humankind: "Being with the children of humankind is my delight" [Prv 8.31]. Hence we ought to recompense him for this love (*amor*).[50]

(2.2.3) Third, Christ is called "your king," that is, the king of humankind, because of a unique care and concern. It is true that God cares for all things. As we read in Wis 12.13: "He cares for all things." There is not a thing so small that it is withdrawn from divine providence, since just as the thing is from God, so also the order is from God, and providence is the same as this order.[51] Yet human beings are subject to divine providence in a special way. Hence Ps 36.7–8 says: "You will save the people and the yoked animals, Lord," namely, through the salvation of the body, "the children of humankind will hope in the protection of your wings." And how do they hope? I say that not only spiritual goods, but indeed even eternal goods are prepared for them by God who leads them to eternal life [cf. 1 Cor 2.9]; God's care for other creatures does not go this far. Thus the Apostle says: "God's care does not concern cattle" [1 Cor 9.9]. God does not leave an action of a man unexamined.[52] Thus we read in Wis 12.18: "Yet, as the master, you judge sins with great calmness."

(2.2.4) Fourth, Christ is called "your king," meaning, "the king of humankind," because of the fellowship with the human nature. Thence we read in Dt 17.15: "You will not be able to make someone of another nation king if he is not your broth-

---

49. Cf. ST I 108,8. 50. ST II–II 27,8.
51. ST I 22,1–2.
52. ST I–II 105,1,1: Thomas underlines that God's love is beyond measure and that his care is about our well-being: it is special care or intensive care, so to speak; cf. Ps 139, Mt 10.28–31.

er." In this prophecy about Christ, the Lord determined that he would appoint a king for the people. He did not will that he would be of another nation, that is, of another nature, for then he would not have been our brother. Hence the Apostle says about Christ: "He has never made the angels his own, but the seed of Abraham" [Heb 2.16]; in these words it becomes clear that humankind is privileged over the angels. Christ is king of the angels and yet he is a man, not an angel.[53] Angels even serve humankind.[54] Thus the Apostle says: "All are helpers of the Spirit" [Heb 1.14]. It was even necessary for Christ to be a man in view of his saving work, as the Apostle says in Heb 2.11: "The One who sanctifies and the one who is sanctified are taken from one and the same." By reason of this it necessarily follows that we are [his] brothers and sisters, where he says: "I will make my name known to my brothers and sisters" [Heb 2.12].

❖

(3) The manifestation of the coming and the identity of the coming One are clear now. Next we will look at the benefit of his coming, which is mentioned by the words: "He comes unto you." For his coming was not required for his own benefit, but for ours. Well, he has come for four reasons: (3.1) first, he has come to make the divine majesty known; (3.2) second, to reconcile us to God; (3.3) third, to free us from sin; and (3.4) fourth, to give us eternal life.

(3.1) First, I say that Christ came to make the divine majesty known to us.[55] A human being desires to the highest extent to have knowledge of the truth,[56] and truth is especially considered as regards God.[57] The people, however, were in such a great ignorance that they did not know what God was. Some

---

53. ST III 8,4, where Thomas cites Col 2.10 (and other texts from Scripture).

54. The angels are sent by God to serve and protect us: ST I 112–113.

55. Namely, by being born as a poor and weak boy in a poor country and city: ST III 35,7,3.

56. Which is also God's will, according to 1 Tm 2.4, although people can hate the truth, too: ST I–II 29,5,2.

57. For God is in himself the truth as well as the first and highest truth: ST I 16,5.

said he would be a body; others have said that he did not care for individual people.[58] And therefore the Son of God came to teach us the truth. Thus he says: "For this I was born, for this I have come into the world, that I may bear witness to the truth" [Jn 18.37]. And in John we read: "No one has ever seen God" [1 Jn 4.12], and because of this the Son of God has come, so that you may come to know the truth [cf. Lk 1.4, Jn 8.32]. Our ancestors were erring so much that they did not know divine truth [cf. Gal 4.8, 2 Pt 2.12]. But by means of the coming of the Son of God we are led back to the truth of the faith.

(3.2) Second, Christ has come to reconcile us to God. You could say: "God was an enemy for me because of sin; so it was better for me not to know him than getting to know him." Because of this, Christ came not only to make the divine majesty known to us, but also in order to reconcile us to God.[59] Therefore, the Apostle says in Eph 2.17: "And as he is coming he will bring the good news of peace to those nearby and to those far away." And elsewhere the Apostle says: "We are reconciled to God by the death of his Son" [Rom 5.10], and because of this the angels sang at the birth of Christ: "Glory to God in the highest" [Lk 2.14]. And after the Resurrection the Lord brought peace to his disciples, saying: "Peace be with you" [Jn 20.19, 21, 26].[60]

(3.3) Third, he is coming in order to free us from the slavery of sin.[61] Hence the Apostle says: "Jesus Christ has come into the world to save sinners" [1 Tm 1.15]. "One who sins is a slave of sin" [Jn 8.34], and therefore we need what is said: "If the Son sets you free, you will be truly free" [Jn 8.36]. And: "The Son of man has come to seek and save what was lost" [Lk 19.10].[62]

---

58. These issues are discussed in ST I 3,1 resp. 22,2,4, 105,5, and SCG III 113.

59. ST III 49,4, 61,1,3.

60. This reference to John 20 is plausible only in the light of the second part of Lk 2.14, which Thomas does not quote here: "and peace on earth to the people of good will."

61. Through the Passion of Christ (ST III 48,4), for which the Incarnation is a prerequisite.

62. Cf. ST III 1,3.

(3.4) Fourth, Christ is coming to give us a life of grace[63] in the present and in the future a life of glory. Thus we read in Jn 10.10: "I have come, so that they may have life," namely, a life of grace in the present; and since "a just person lives from faith" [Gal 3.11], [he adds:] "and that they may have it more abundantly," namely, a life of glory in the future through love (*caritas*).[64] Hence it says in John: "We know that we are transferred from death to life, because we love (*diligo*) our brothers and sisters" [1 Jn 3.14], so let us live through good works. Likewise, we read in Jn 17.3: "This is eternal life, that they know you, the true God, and him whom you have sent, Jesus Christ."

Now also the benefit of the One who is coming is clear.

(4) But how does he come? I say that he has come as someone mild or tamed, the meaning of which is manifold. As we read in Prv 19.12: "The anger of the king will be as the roaring of a lion, and his gaiety will be as the dew over vegetation." Mildness is anger that is mitigated.[65] God is coming with mildness now, but in the future[66] he will come with anger. Therefore, Is 30.27 says: "Behold, the name of the Lord will come from afar, as if it were his burning rage." But Jb 35.15 reads: "Now he does not bring rage along nor is he zealous to punish very heavily." For now Christ is coming with mildness, and we ought to receive him with mildness. Thus it is said by St. James in 1.21: "Receive with mildness the word sown in [you] that can save your souls."[67]

See that we can consider the mildness of Christ in four aspects: (4.1) first, in his way of life; (4.2) second, in his correc-

---

63. See note 8.

64. Love is a unifying force (ST I 20,1,3); it aims at unifying the lover with the beloved. The object of love (*caritas*) is the ultimate end (ST I–II 19,10) or the eternal good (II–II 83,15), i.e., God.

65. Attributing mildness to God in this sense can, therefore, only be understood as a metaphor: ST I 1,9 and 21,1,1.

66. Again, Thomas is placing Advent, the beginning of a new era, in the broader context of the history of salvation (i.e., the end, the Last Judgment). Also in ST III 36,1,3.

67. Cf. ST II–II 157,4,1.

SERMON 05   77

tion; (4.3) third, in his gracious reception of people; and (4.4) fourth, in his Passion.

(4.1) First, I say, we can see the mildness of Christ in his way of life, because his whole way of life was pacific [cf. Jas 3.17]; he has not sought issues for disputes, but he has shunned all the things that could lead to a quarrel. Therefore, he has said: "Learn from me, because I am meek and humble of heart" [Mt 11.29]. And in this we ought to imitate him.[68] As Christ goes up to Jerusalem he is sitting on a colt, which is a mild animal—not on a horse[69]—and he has been a subjugated son.[70] Thus we ought to be mild. Therefore, it says in Sir 3.19: "Son, make your works perfect in mildness and you will spread your glory among the people."

(4.2) Likewise, the mildness of Christ appears in his correction. He has borne many abusive words from his persecutors; still he did not respond with anger or agitation to them [cf. Is 53.7]. About this it says: "(Ride on triumphant) for the sake of truth and mildness" [Ps 45.5].[71] Augustine says in an exposition of this text that "as Christ spoke, truth was acknowledged; as he answered his enemies patiently, mildness was praised." Ps 89.10 (Vg) reads: "Mildness comes over us, and we will be admonished." And in Is 42.2 it says: "Neither did he raise his voice nor did he shout."

(4.3) Third, the mildness of Christ appears in his gracious reception of people. Some people do not know how to receive with mildness. But Christ received sinners benignly and ate with them; he allowed them to his banquets or went to theirs, so that the Pharisees were amazed and said: "Why does your master eat

68. Mildness is mentioned as one of the twelve fruits of the Holy Spirit in Gal 5.22–23; cf. ST I–II 70,3, also 69,3,3; it moves us with reverence towards God.

69. In biblical times as well as in the 13th century, horses were used by soldiers (see Ex 14.23, Prv 21.31), and only the rich could afford them (see 1 Kgs 5.6; cf. Eccles 10.6–7).

70. Cf. Lk 2.51. In the text Thomas quotes Mt 21.5: *filius subjugalis*, where these words refer to the young animal on which Jesus rode.

71. Still in verses 4 to 6 the Psalmist speaks warlike language. Yet a Psalm is a sacred text; it contains a deeper, spiritual meaning. E.g., in his commentary on Psalm 45 (44) Thomas explains, referring to Eph 6.17, that the sword mentioned in verse 4 is the sword of the Spirit, the word of God.

with tax collectors?" [Mt 9.11] So he was mild.[72] Therefore, the Church can say about him what is written in 2 Sm 22.36: "Your mildness has made me many."[73]

(4.4) Fourth, the mildness of Christ appears in his Passion, because "as a lamb he has gone to the Passion" [cf. Is 53.7, Acts 8.32] and "although he was cursed, he did not curse" [1 Pt 2.23]. Yet he could have delivered all to death.[74] Hence he says in Jer 11.19: "I am as a lamb that is carried to the block." St. Andrew[75] has imitated him truly well in mildness, for when he was nailed to a cross and the people wanted to take him down from the cross, he continued to pray and asked them not to take him down from the cross, but to follow him in the Passion. Thus it is fulfilled in him that "this most meek man has appeared among the people."[76] Mildness enables us to inherit a happy world. Therefore, we read in Mt 5.5: "Happy the meek, for they shall inherit the earth."

May we be deemed worthy that this may be fulfilled for us by the One who with the Father and the Holy Spirit, et cetera.

---

72. Thus Thomas is advocating for a mild approach to sinners in pastoral work; his audience consists of preachers-to-be. Also in Sermon 14 *Attendite a falsis*, in the *Collatio in sero*.

73. Mildness is attractive; a mild Church will attract people, will grow (cf. note 68).

74. Thomas does not mention this among the ways in which Christ could have foiled his crucifixion in ST III 47,1.

75. See note 1.

76. Responsory verse 2, in the third Nocturne of the Feast of St. Andrew: *Vir iste mitissimus in populo apparuit: sanctitate autem et gratia plenus.*

SERMON 06

CELUM ET TERRA TRANSIBUNT

Sermon on the First Sunday of Advent[1]

*Another Sermon of Brother Thomas of Aquino
Given on the Same Sunday in the House of the Preachers
at Paris before the University of Paris*

Luke 21.33: *Heaven and earth will pass.*

SUMMARY

Prothema

"HEAVEN AND earth will pass" [Lk 21.33]. Dearest brethren, how great the delight, how great the pleasure, how great the sweetness that is in the heavenly words of wisdom! This is even obvious in the words of the natural philosopher,[2] who writes in Book 10 of *Ethics* about created knowledge: "All delights are at some point cut off. The greatest, however, is the delight that is in accordance with the operation of wisdom, and the most delightful operation is the one that is in accord-

---

1. This sermon dates from the first Parisian period (1252–1256). Only summaries of this sermon have been preserved. The point of departure for this translation is the "M" text, Milano Ambrosiana A11 sup. (which consists of a *Prothema*, parts I and II). Text version "P," Paris BnF lat 14595 (no *Prothema*, parts I, II, and III), is referred to in the notes and in the text where indicated.

2. Thomas usually refers to Aristotle as *Philosophus*, "the Philosopher." In other words, it is not a specifically Jewish or Christian, but a universal insight: every right-thinking person, even a (wise) pagan, can know it. This principle is worked out by Thomas in Part I where he first cites Aristotle and concludes with Scripture.

ance with the operation of wisdom." Also the theological philosopher[3] writes in Wis 7.8 that he "loved (*diligo*) it more than gold and outward appearance"; "it" is the heavenly wisdom about which we speak.

Because of this we will ask, at the beginning of this homily, our Lord Jesus Christ, the fountain of all wisdom [cf. Sir 1.5], who is, according to St. Dionysius[4] in Book 6 part c of *The Hierarchy of the Angels,* the principal instructor of all heavenly spirits and devout souls, to illumine our understanding, to kindle our hearts, and to make my mouth eloquent for the honor of his name in accordance with the Gospel teaching and the edification of our souls.

PART I

"Heaven and earth will pass" [Lk 21.33], et cetera. In these words[5] the situation of the just and the unjust is described according to a spiritual knowledge. Our most providential and meek Savior commended these words[6]—out of care for his sheep's salvation in faith [cf. Jn 10.13]—to his disciples and in them to all believers for serious attention to the Last Judgment, without mentioning the term, because it is clear. (1) By the noun "heaven" the marvelous loftiness of the heavenly man is mentioned, and (2) by the noun "earth" the deserved lowliness of the worldly person is mentioned, and (3) by the verb "will pass" he carefully refers to a distinctive quality of each.[7]

---

3. Only here does Thomas refer to the writer of Wisdom, allegedly Solomon, as *philosophus theologicus,* as distinct from the *philosophus naturalis.*

4. I.e., not St. Dionysius "the Great" of Alexandria (c. 200–c. 265), Pope St. Dionysius (†268), or St. Denis, patron saint of France (†258), but someone whom we call Pseudo-Dionysius: for a long time people thought that this author from the late 5th century who called himself Dionysius the Areopagite was the same person as the Dionysius in Acts 17.34. This identification contributed to the great spread and authority of his works.

5. P adds: "the beautiful but deformed variety of"; it seems that it is beautiful because the just and the unjust are where they deserve to be (as Thomas says in Part II), and yet it is deformed since God made all people to be just [cf. Rom 3.26].

6. P adds: "like a most merciful shepherd."

7. In Thomas's time as a *magister* there was a vehement controversy about the

(1) So, as he describes the marvelous loftiness and the worthy eminence of the heavenly man, he calls him "heaven." Yet we must consider that the heavenly man is signified by the noun "heaven" for four reasons:

(1.1) Heaven is of a great brightness,[8] as the Philosopher demonstrates in Book 2 of *On Heaven and Earth*. Thus it is shown that the just man ought to be full of light by heavenly wisdom, as we read in Sir 24.4: "I have made (my home) in heaven, so that perfect light may rise."[9]

(1.2) It has a splendid appearance, as the Philosopher demonstrates in Book 2 of *On Heaven and Earth*. Thus it is shown that the just man ought to be like a circle by a wide mercy, or like an orbit by a broad devotion and perfect love (*caritas perfecta*).[10] "I alone have gone round the canopy of heaven,"[11] says eternal Wisdom in Sir 24.5.[12]

---

question of whether the world would be eternal due to the Averroist interpretation of Aristotle's position on this, which was taken on by philosophers in Paris. Thomas, reasoning as a theologian, responded that creatures cannot be from eternity (only God is *ab aeterno*, according to Scripture) and yet that as soon as they are made they remain forever (*in aeternum*) in a way (*secundum aliquid*), namely, insofar as God has made them as such. Thomas cites Eccl 3.14 among others in this context (cf. ST I 46, 65,1,1, 104,4).

8. P continues: "Thus the heavenly man is very bright by reason of Gospel wisdom radiating from God, as we read in Sir 24.4: 'I have made my home in heaven, so that perfect light may rise.' 'In heaven,' that is, in holy men; in them the eternal Spirit of the Father kindled the spiritual 'light' of wisdom."

Also, in what follows, P has left out any (explicit) reference to Aristotle.

9. P reads "the heavens" (*in celis*), plural, and adds: "'In the heavens'; this means: the eternal Wisdom of the Father has kindled the spiritual light of wisdom in holy men (*in sanctis viris*)."

10. The vault of heaven is circular. The mercy and the devotion of the just must be like a circle: perfect and spreading as wide as possible. P speaks likewise, leaving out the reference to Aristotle, and, instead of "a wide mercy," it reads, "a wide compassion (*compassio*) and a devout mercy (*misericordia*)."

Wisdom (section 1) corresponds to love (*caritas*, ST II–II 45 intr.), and love is the first movement of the will toward what is good (ST I 20,1). Mercy is a virtue, closely connected with love and justice (ST II–II 30,3; cf. ST I 20–21).

11. P ends instead with: "– add: 'I, the Wisdom of the Father,' by dwelling with him through grace."

12. Section 1.2 echoes Ps 19.7 (cf. Thomas's commentary on Vulgate-Psalm 18 nn.1–3), Ps 45.5, and Dn 12.3.

(1.3) It sets in motion,[13] as the Philosopher shows in Book 8 of *Physics*. Thus it is shown that the just man ought to be moved always by a spiritual carefulness.[14] Jb 38.37 reads: "Who will narrate the heavens' thoughts, and who will put to sleep what they contain?"[15]

(1.4) It is high[16] in location, as the sight and the effect of it prove. By this it is pointed out that the just man ought to excel in holiness[17] by eminence. Because, as we read in Sir 43.1: "The firmament of highness"—that is, the highness of the firmament—"is his beauty, (the sight of heaven in a vision of glory)."[18]

PART II

(2) The worldly man is absolutely not comparable to him; he is compared to the earth,[19] [as follows:]

(2.1) On the ground of his capacity of understanding, as we read in Gn 1.2: "Darkness was over the face of the abyss. The earth was void and empty."[20]

(2.2) On the ground of the weakness of avarice,[21] as we read in Col 3.2: "Taste the things that are above, not those upon

---

13. P adds (*ordinatissimum*): "and orders to the highest extent" or: "and puts all things in order, precisely." P continues: "Thus we always find the just man moved by carefulness and ordered by honesty."

14. The virtue of *diligentia* implies caring, being thoughtful, attentive, considerate, precise, and solicitous; cf. ST II–II 54,1,1.

15. P adds: "And furthermore in the same place we read: 'Do you know the arrangement (*ordo*) of heaven?'" [Jb 38.33].

16. P reads: "the highest."

17. Holiness in human beings is serving God in everything: ST II–II 81,8, which Christ did to the full. Therefore, he became the source of salvation (cf. ST III 72,4,2) and of holiness for the whole Church: ST III 83,3,2. For God's holiness see ST I 36,1,1: *in divinis* the word "holy" signifies the purity of the divine goodness.

18. P quotes another verse instead, namely, Jb 35.5 (not verse 25 as the Latin text reads): "Look up to heaven; it is higher than you."

19. P leaves out the first sentence. It reads: "After the wondrous loftiness of the heavenly man thus described briefly by the word 'heaven,' the little value of worldly man follows by the word 'earth.' Now, we must know that the unjust man is compared to the earth."

20. Cf. also ST II–II 4,2sc and 4,4,1 and 171,4,2, with reference to 1 Cor 13.10–12: we will understand as the perfect comes.

21. *Avaritia*, one of the seven capital sins: ST I–II 84,3–4; II–II 118.

the earth" and Ps 44.25 says: "Our stomach is stuck to the ground."[22]

(2.3) On the ground of the aridity of wickedness [cf. Jn 4.10–15],[23] as we read in Gn 1.10: "And God called the arid land 'earth.'"

(2.4) On the ground of the immutability of the soul, or of the life,[24] or opinion, as we find it in Eccl 1.4: "The earth truly stands forever." And this is preceded by: "The generation" of the good ones "passes, and the generation" of the just ones "arrives" [ibid.].[25] Why? Because an evil person is not led in the right direction, nor is he changed.[26]

※

(3)[27] Well, now that the most deserved disdain toward the worldly man and the marvelous loftiness of the just have been described, the quality of the way of life of each of them must be distinguished, in view of the verb "to pass (*transire*)." Indeed, we must note that passing is said (3.1) of the just in a different way than (3.2) of the unjust.

(3.1) For the just passes on,

(3.1.1) firstly, from sin to justice,[28] as it says in Is 45.14: "Lofty men" and proud sinners "will pass over to you, and they will be yours."

(3.1.2) He passes, secondly, by advancing from virtue to vir-

---

22. P omits Ps 44.25.

23. P adds: "For such people are barren and arid." Malice is one of the causes of sin (ST I–II 78) as well as a consequence of sin (ST I–II 85,3: one of the four wounds, as Bede says) and leading to more sinning. On malice as such: ST I–II 18–21.

24. The soul is the life-giving principle in the human body (cf. ST I 70,3,2, 76,1 and 8).

25. Without Thomas's interpretative additions the Scripture text says: "Generations go and come."

26. P gives a shorter version here: "Fourthly, by reason of the immutability of his resolution. For such people are not moved towards penance, as we read in Eccl 1:4: 'The earth stands forever.'"

On stubbornness (*pertinacia*), the opposite of the virtue of steadfastness/perseverance: ST II–II 132,5 and 138,2.

27. This last part of the homily is preserved only in P.

28. On the cardinal virtue of justice: ST II–II 57–122. God's justice: ST I 21,1–2.

tue,²⁹ as it says in Sir 29.26: "Pass, stranger; prepare the table," meaning, "prepare your conscience for the heavenly spouse" [cf. Prv 9.1–6].³⁰

(3.1.3) He passes, thirdly, from labor in the present to the eternal refreshment, as it says in Ps 66.12: "We have come through fire and water, and you have led us out into refreshment."³¹

(3.2) Yet the unjust passes,

(3.2.1) first of all, from innocence to guilt,³² as Sirach 28 reads: "He passes from justice to sin" [Sir 26.19 or 26.28].

(3.2.2) He passes, secondly, from guilt into guilt,³³ as Prv 14.16 has it: "A wise man fears and turns away from evil; (a foolish man passes on and is self-confident)."³⁴

(3.2.3) He passes, thirdly, from guilt into eternal punishment, as Jb 36.12 reads: "If they will not listen, they will pass through the sword," namely, through eternal punishment.³⁵

❖

So in view of the short description of the marvelous loftiness of the heavenly man in the noun "heaven," also in view of the very well deserved disdain toward the worldly man in the noun "earth," and in view of the difference of the life of these two in respect of the verb "to pass," let us apply ourselves to renouncing earthly things and to loving (*amo*) heavenly things [cf. Col 3.1], in such a way that we disdain the worldly life and embrace the heavenly life, that we may pass over from labor to rest [cf. Heb 4.10], from the world to glory,

which may he grant us, et cetera.

29. ST I–II 63,2–4.
30. The image of a laid or clean table as a reflection of a person's readiness to receive someone is also found in 2 Chr 13.11 and Ezek 23.41.
31. Latin: *refrigerium.* Cf. Wis 4.7, Is 28.12, Jer 6.16, Acts 3.20.
32. A consequence of voluntarily turning away from God; cf. ST I 48,5; I–II 21,2; II–II 34,2.
33. ST I–II 75,4 and 84,1–2; cf. also note 23.
34. Thomas cites this verse twice in the ST: when he discusses the question whether an accused person may defend himself with cunning and guile (I–II 69,2) and when he distinguishes between the vice of fearlessness and the virtue of strength (II–II 126: the quotation is in 126,1,2).
35. Since the ST is not finished, there is not a section on the last things. For the distinctions of punishments see SCG III 141–145.

SERMON 07
ECCE EGO MITTO

Sermon on the Second Sunday of Advent[1]

Matthew 11.10: *Behold, I send my angel before your face.*

FRAGMENT

"EHOLD, I send my angel before your face" [Mt 11.10]. These words are taken from the last chapter of Malachi [3.1]. In these words three aspects of the gracious arrival of the Savior are described: (1) the marvelous estimation of God the Father, (2) the obliging ardor of the precursor, and (3) the marvelous kindness (*benignitas*) of the Savior. The first, where it says: "Behold, I send"; the second, where it says: "my angel"; the third, where it says: "before your face."

So note, regarding all these things, that, just as the Savior was sent,[2] so also the precursor was sent to us by the Father through the commission of an angel, not through nature.[3] For they have truly been our angels who were sent to us in the name of God, in order to prepare the ways[4] that lead to the heavenly dwelling places. Gn 28.12 reads: "Jacob saw the ladder and God's angels ascending and descending on it." This was [as follows:] (a) In order to disclose the secrets of the decrees of the divine will, "the Law was issued by the angels at the hand of a mediator," as it says in Gal 3.19. (b) In order to fulfill their duty

---

1. Probably given on the 9th of December 1268, at Milan.
2. Lk 1.26–38; cf. ST III 30.
3. John the Baptist: his coming was through a gracious act of God: Lk 1.10–20, 24–25; cf. ST III 27,1 and 6.
4. Is 40.3, Mk 1.2–3. On icons and in other art John the Baptist himself is sometimes depicted with wings of an angel; he is pre-eminently the messenger (*angelos*) of God; cf. ST III 38,1–2.

concerning the divine things coming down from heaven, "angels came to him and served him," as Mt 4.11 reads.[5] (c) In order to render examples and proofs of spiritual perfection, "the angels of God had gone to meet Jacob, and when he had seen them, he said: 'These are the encampments of God'"; Gn 32, 33.12.[6]

---

5. The mission of the angels was completed as Christ began to reveal himself; mediators were not needed anymore. What had been announced by angels and prophets and expected by the people for ages (cf. Mt 13.16–17) now became true (cf. ST I–II 98,3; II–II 172,2).

6. The words quoted are from Gn 32.1–3.

SERMON 08
PUER JESUS

Sermon on the First Sunday after Epiphany[1]

Luke 2.52: *The boy Jesus advanced in age and wisdom and in grace with God and the people.*

PART 1: *Prothema*

"THE BOY JESUS advanced in age and wisdom and in grace with God and the people" [Lk 2.52]. All the things together that the Lord has done or undergone in the flesh are salutary lessons and examples. Hence we read this in Jn 13.15: "I have given you an example, that whatever I have done you may do likewise."[2] And because there is not any age from which the way of salvation is absent—and to the highest extent this applies to the years in which one comes to discernment—the adolescence of Christ is made an example for adolescents.[3] Growth and progress are proper to adolescents. Therefore, the progress of Christ is made an example for adolescents.

---

1. Since we find many texts from the Catena Aurea in this sermon, we presume that it was given in the second period in which Thomas taught in Paris (1268–1272).

2. Cf. ST II–II 174,6 (last sentence of the *corpus*); III 37,1,2 and 46,3 (referring to 1 Pt 2.21). Also SCG IV 36 (*Nihil . . . aut nobis imitandum fuit*; quoting Mt 11.29 and Jn 13.15) and 54 (*. . . necessarium fuit homini . . . a Deo humanato et doctrinam et exempla virtutis acciperet:* Jn 13.15). Whereas the examples which Aristotle gives in his logical works should not be given much attention: ST I 67,2,2.

3. Thomas's audience consists, for the major part, of students. He presents the boy Jesus as the example for their lives: following him in everything is the road that leads to salvation.

But, to begin, let us ask God to enable us to say something about the progress of Christ for the honor of God and for the salvation of our souls.

PART 2: *Sermo*

"The boy Jesus," et cetera. If we want to consider these words carefully, we will find in them four progresses of Christ, namely, (1) the progress of age in regard to the body, (2) the progress of wisdom in regard to the intellect, (3) the progress of grace with God, and (4) the progress also of grace in view of his living together with the people.

❖

(0) Truly, all these progresses are amazing, yes, even full of astonishment and amazement. (0.1) For we must be amazed that eternity advances in age, for the Son of God is eternity[4] and from eternity. Psalm 117 and Psalm 119: "In eternity, Lord, your truth remains" [Ps 119.90, 160; cf. 117.2].

(0.2) Likewise, we must be amazed that the truth advances in wisdom, because the progress of wisdom is knowledge of the truth, whereas Christ is himself the truth, as we read in Jn 14.6: "I am the way, the truth, and the life."[5] (0.3) Likewise we must be amazed that the One from whom grace originates advances in grace; Christ is the One who renders grace. Thus we read in Jn 1.17: "Grace and truth came through Christ."[6] (0.4) Likewise we must be amazed that the One who exceeds all people advances with the people. Even more, the people ought to advance in grace with him. Ps 113.4 says: "The Highest is he above all the nations."

How, then, would Christ advance in these respects? I say

---

4. Insofar as Christ is God, what is said in ST I 3 applies to him. Since God is perfectly one, he is what he has (ST I 3,4 and 6): God is good and goodness, eternal and eternity, et cetera.

5. Also Jn 18.37–38; cf. the quotation from Psalm 119 in 0.1. By reason of the hypostatic union, the man Jesus Christ shared in God's omniscience (ST III 10,2, 11,1).

6. ST I 73,1,1; III 2,11, 27,5 (*Christus autem est principium gratiae, secundum divinitatem quidem auctoritative, secundum humanitatem vero instrumentaliter*), 38,3.

that if we want to consider this properly, immediately the reason regarding his progress in age comes to our mind: (ad 0.1) the eternal Son of God willed to become temporal, so that he could advance in age. Is 9.5 says: "A little child is born unto us." If he is born as a little child, why then would he not have grown as a little child does?[7]

(ad 0.2–4) The other progresses of Christ contain a greater difficulty. Christ took on the full human nature: according to the flesh he was born as a little child, but not according to the soul. For, from the beginning of his conception, his most blessed soul was full of every grace and truth, because it was connected with God. Thus we read in Jn 1.14: "We have seen his glory, the glory as of the only-begotten Son of the Father, full of grace and truth." He was full of every grace and truth because he was the only-begotten Son of God. Well, from the beginning of the conception he was the only-begotten Son. Hence from the very beginning he was full of grace and truth and perfect in virtue.[8] Jer 31.22: "A woman will encompass a man"; not in age, but as for the perfection of the mind.

But in what is meant by advancing in wisdom and grace? We must say that someone is said to advance in wisdom, not only when he acquires a greater wisdom, but also when the wisdom in him is more evident. It is true that Christ from the beginning of his conception was full of wisdom and grace, but he has not shown it from the beginning, but at an age when others usually show it. In that case we speak of advancing in wisdom, not in the absolute sense of the word, but in view of the effect through which he advanced amidst other people.[9]

---

7. Thomas emphasizes that Christ had a real human body. And since he is living in this world as a true man (*homo*), he is aging as time goes by. Within the framework of the mystery of the Incarnation, this consequence is as such not that amazing; cf. ST III 5,1–2.

8. ST III 7,12.

9. Concerning Jesus we say "advancing in wisdom" not because he advances in wisdom as such (through the Incarnation he is already full of it from the very beginning), but because the wisdom that was already present in him is revealed to us in his works as time goes by more and more, which looks, from the outside, like a progression, growth; cf. ST III 7,12,3.

If he had willed to show his wisdom when he was seven years of age, people could have doubted the truth of the assumed human nature.[10] And because of this, Christ wanted to be similar to others. Thus the Apostle says in Phil 2.7: "He has emptied himself, taking the form of a slave, being made in the likeness of men." Christ has made himself little by taking on our littleness, in order to show that he truly was little: "He was made in the likeness of men." Bar 3.38 reads: "He is seen on earth, and he has lived with the people." At the time when a sign of wisdom normally appears for the first time in a human being, Christ manifested his wisdom for the first time, namely, when he was twelve years of age: thus little by little. He did not will to show his [full] wisdom, so that the truth of the human nature in him would be acknowledged and in order to give us an example of advancing in wisdom.[11]

❖

So, fourfold, as was said, is Christ's progress, namely, of (1) age, (2) wisdom, (3) grace, and (4) the human life.

❖

(1) Let us first take a look at the progress of Christ's age, which is physical. It is set as an example for us so that we may advance in the age of body and mind as he did, because the progress of age in the body is empty if there is no progress in the soul as well. Therefore, we discuss the progress of Christ's age and of his wisdom and of his grace in one and the same sermon. Because if someone does not advance through a progress of the mind together with the progress of the body, four improper things would follow: (1.1) it would be monstrous, (1.2) damaging, (1.3) burdensome or troublesome, and (1.4) dangerous.

(1.1) First, I say, advancing in age of the body and not of the mind is monstrous.[12] A human being is composed of a soul and

10. If Jesus had shown the fullness of his wisdom from the beginning, he would have seemed super-human or not human at all, only divine (ST III 40,3). Cf., e.g., also the reactions of the Lycaonian crowds to the healing of a crippled man by the Apostle Paul, in Acts 14.10–13.

11. Cf. ST III 24,3: insofar as Jesus Christ was God, he cannot be an example for human beings as for their growth in wisdom.

12. The Latin term is *monstruosus*. That it is not good is not a moral judgment here (as in I–II 21,1,1), but a biological qualification.

a body, just as the body is composed of various members. But imagine that a body would grow in one member and would be little in the other members. This is monstrous. Likewise, when someone is a man according to the body and not according to the mind. Because of this the Apostle says in 1 Cor 13.11: "When I was a little child, I understood as a little child, I spoke as a little child; but now that I have become a man, I have left the things that belong to a little child." Little children think of playing and the like.[13]

It is true that the Lord ordered that we be like little children, saying, in Mt 18.3: "Unless you will be converted and become like little children, you will not enter into the Kingdom of the heavens." There is something in little children that we ought to preserve, because little children are not wicked and they are humble. But there is another thing in little children that we should get rid of: the lack of wisdom.[14] Because of this the Apostle says in 1 Cor 14.20: "Do not become little children with your mind, but be little children in respect of wickedness." We ought to think with the mind of the perfect man [Col 1.28, Eph 4.13],[15] so that insofar as we advance in the age of the body we advance in the age of the mind. If only one of the feet of a man is growing and not the other one, he focuses all his attention on a doctor, so that the other foot may grow in the same way. Likewise should you, whose body grows in age, focus all your attention in such a way that also your mind grows in age.[16]

(1.2) Furthermore, growing in age of the body and not of the mind is damaging. Someone who had the time to acquire

13. Thomas implies that students in his audience must not behave like little children, but apply themselves to their studies. He comes back to this explicitly in 1.3 and 1.4.

14. Also, e.g., intemperance or excess; cf. ST II–II 142,2,1.

15. Which is a human being led by wisdom and love (*caritas*): ST II–II 184,1; III 39,3 (cit. Col 1.28; cf. Eph 4.13).

16. As the body grows without extra effort, we must focus our attention on *Christus medicus*, who makes us healthy in body and especially in the soul. People, however, tend to focus their attention on the less important parts of the body; cf. 1 Cor 12.23 in ST II–II 145,2. Elsewhere Thomas underlines that the well-being of the soul is connected with the well-being of the body (ST I 75,3, 76), and that, therefore, we should *also* take good care of our body; see esp. II–II 25,5.

a great thing and wasted it, doing nothing [cf. Lk 19.16], would consider this a great damage. It is with a market vendor in the time of trading, who believes that then much profit can be gained, as with a student who believes that listening to a lecture is useful: if he lets that time pass by, he believes that he has damaged himself a lot.

Time is given to you, that you may not gain those cheap things, but God and heavenly goods, which no one can grasp. Hence the Apostle says in 1 Cor 2.9: "eye has not seen, and ear has not heard, neither did it come up in the heart of a man, what" you, "God," have "prepared for those who love (*diligo*)" you.[17] And because of this, Sir 14.14 says: "Let even a small piece of the good gift not escape you," that is: a part of the good time.

And Solomon says in Prv 5.9–10: "that you may not give your honor to others and your years to the cruel one; that foreigners may not take their fill of your strength, and that your labors may not be in a strange house."

(a) "That you may not give your honor to others." Honor is given to a man in war, when it is given to him because he triumphs over his enemies. Such honor is given to you, namely, if you triumph over the world [1 Jn 5.4], the flesh [2 Cor 10.3–5], and the devil [Jas 4.7; cf. 2 Tm 4.7–8]. But when you give your natural strength for service to the devil, although it is given that you may triumph over him, then you give your honor to a stranger.

(b) Solomon continues: "that you may not give the years" of your youth "to the cruel one," that is, the devil; he is cruel, because he will not give you rest[18] no matter how well you serve him. Thus we read in Jer 16.13: "You will serve strange gods, who will not give you rest."

(c) "And that your labors may not be in a stranger's house." Maybe you do good works, in which you have labored. If you are converted to the Lord, those labors will be in your house. Yet if you are not converted to the Lord, your labors, that is, your

17. ST I–II 5,5, and II–II 28,3.
18. Thomas alludes to Mt 11.28–30 ("Learn from me and I will give you rest") and Jas 4.1 and Rom 6.19–20, et cetera: following your own desires results in wanting always more; cf. Jn 8.34.

good works, will be in a stranger's house, because the saints in the heavenly homeland (*patria*) will rejoice in your good works, but not you.[19] Hence it says in Rv 3.11: "Hold on to what you have, that someone else may not take your crown."[20]

(1.3)[21] Furthermore, growing in age of the body and not in mind is troublesome. But you may say: "I am a young man; I want to play in my youth; when I am an old man, I will convert myself to the Lord." Surely, thus you commit yourself to great labor. Doing something is easy for someone if he is accustomed to it from his youth.[22] And this is clear, because it is easy for a farmer to work on the land, because he accustomed himself to it, whereas it is difficult for you. If you accustom yourself to doing your will and live in sins, either you despair about eternal life[23] or you preserve yourself with great labor. Therefore, Solomon says: "The adolescent will walk on his path, and when he gets older, he will not turn away from it" [Prv 22.6].[24] And Jeremiah says: "It is good for a man when he carries the yoke of the Lord from his adolescence" [Lam 3.27],[25] because such a man can raise himself above himself from what is easy. And therefore Christ has given us the example of working well from a young age, because when he was twelve years of age, he grew in wisdom [Lk 2.42].

19. The saints in heaven rejoice in every good work, but the one addressed will not rejoice in his own good works, because he will not benefit from them; they are not done in the right context, i.e., for the right master. What Thomas calls "your house" is God's house in view of Eph 2.19.

20. See Thomas's explanation of this text in ST I 23,6,1, where he distinguishes between divine predestination and merit.

21. Throughout the *Sermo*, but especially in this part we hear the echo of Sir 51.13–31: relentlessly seeking wisdom, from the very beginning of the (life) journey, and the benefits of it, the Temple, joy, praise to the teacher/Teacher, et cetera.

22. "What's learnt in the cradle lasts till the tomb"; in Latin: *in teneris consuescere multum est*.

23. Despairing about eternal life is something we should never do in view of our faith in the Almighty and Merciful: ST II–II 14,3,1; cf. I–II 62,3,2 (where Thomas refers to the Crucified through 1 Cor 1.25).

24. In the ST Thomas cites this verse in the consideration of baptism of infants: ST III 68,9.

25. Cited in ST II–II 189,5, on the question whether boys should be admitted to religious life.

(1.4) Moreover, it is dangerous when someone grows in age of body if he does not grow in age of mind. The Lord demands from all people an account. Thus we read in the Gospel, in Mt 18.23: "The Kingdom of the heavens is like a man who demanded an account from his household."

God has given you time, that you may serve him. But it is said in Jb 24.23: "He has given him time, and he abuses it in pride." The Lord will require an account from you regarding how you spent your time. In Is 49.4 we read: "And I said: 'Without a reason and in vain I have consumed my strength.'" He consumes his strength in vain and without a reason who passes his time doing useless things. And therefore Is 49.4 continues: "Hence my judgment is with the Lord." And Solomon says in Eccl 11.9: "Rejoice, young man, because of your adolescence. Know that for these things the Lord will lead you to judgment." But is that judgment not light? No! Because Is 65.20 says: "A boy of a hundred years of age," that is, a sinner, "will be cursed." Hence we read in Bar 3.11: "You have grown old in a strange land; you are counted among these who go down into hell." But, although you deserve it [hell], do not despair about God's mercy.[26]

❖

So the first point of attention is this: that we may grow in mind as we grow in age. But how does a human being grow in mind? Certainly when he grows "in wisdom and grace." And although in the verse that is the point of departure for this homily, wisdom is mentioned before grace, we will nevertheless speak about grace first, since "the beginning of wisdom is the fear of the Lord,"[27] according to Sir 1.14.

(2) Grace is something hidden, because it is in the soul. Hidden causes are not known except through manifest effects. Well, among all the effects none is as manifest as peace.[28] Hence the Apostle always connects peace with grace: "The fruits of the Spirit are joy, love (*caritas*), peace" [Gal 5.22]. And when someone has peace, it is a sign that he has grace, because "there is

26. See note 23. Also Thomas's interpretation of Heb 4.16 in ST III 59,2.
27. Cf. ST II–II 19,7. And fear of the Lord is a gracious gift of the Lord: ST II–II 19,9, referring to Is 11.2.
28. Cf. Thomas on peace in ST II–II 29.

no peace for unbelievers, says the Lord" in Is 48.22. And this is what God has signified in the progress of grace [in Christ]: when he was twelve years of age, he went to the city of peace, Jerusalem, which is interpreted as "the idea of peace (*visio pacis*)" [cf. Ps 122.7, Sir 24.11]. Hence, when we have the age of discretion, we ought to attempt to attain peace.

But many are deceived, because, while they believe they have peace, they do not have it. Thus the false prophets have said: "'Peace, peace,' but there was no peace," as we read in Jer 6.14. In order to know true peace, we must see that peace must have four characteristics: (2.1) it should be high, (2.2) customary, (2.3) persevering and constant, and (2.4) cautious.

(2.1) First, the peace that comes from grace should be high. A human being is constituted between two, and in accordance with this there can be a twofold peace. In one respect he is constituted between flesh and spirit. These are at war with one another, because "the flesh desires (*concupisco*) against the spirit and the spirit against the flesh" [Gal 5.17]. The spirit is high,[29] and the flesh is low.

According to this a human being can make peace in two ways: if he makes peace in such a way that the spirit consents with the flesh, this is neither a high peace, nor is it true peace; rather, it is low and false. Hence we read in Wis 14.22: "Those who live in a great war of ignorance regard so many and great evils which they undergo as peace." Such people are in a great war, because they fight against ignorance[30] and are tormented by their conscience.[31]

---

29. Thomas speaks of the higher part and the lower part of the soul; the higher part is directed towards what is (from) God, the Most High, the lower part towards earthly things: ST III 9,4,2.

30. Ignorance is a lack of knowledge in our intellect—especially about God, as Wis 14.22 says. Our knowledge directs the human actions, and the more perfect it is, the more it makes us avoid sin. Cf. ST I-II 76, 85,3.

31. No matter how sinful someone is, deep down he/she "knows" what is right and wrong (ST I 79,13). The peace between the spirit and the flesh is during our earthly life never true peace; at the most it is *concordia*, i.e., two different wills brought together in one. Since the spirit and the flesh do not always will the same, due to ignorance, the one must be surrendered to the other in order to have a oneness. Thus during our life on earth there will always be a tension

The other peace is when the flesh consents with the spirit. And how does this peace come to pass? Surely, when the flesh is subjected to the spirit by means of wearing out the flesh. Someone will say: "I want to make peace in such a way that the spirit consents somehow to the flesh and thus there will be peace; and then later on the flesh will be subjugated under the spirit." This cannot come to pass, since the flesh has a servile nature, and the more one indulges a slave, the more brazen he becomes. Thus we read in Prv 29.21: "The one who gives his slave something delicate to eat will find him stubborn." And the Philosopher says: "The appetite for what is delightful cannot be satisfied, and from all sides the operation of concupiscence increases the urge for the unwise." If you satisfy the delight of the flesh, it is not calmed down because of this; the urge rather increases, because "someone who drinks from this water will be thirsty again" [Jn 4.13].[32]

This true peace, how must it be brought about? Certainly, by wearing out the flesh.[33] Therefore, it says in Is 27.5: "In the fight I walk over it, and this will bring about peace for me." Because of this we read that the Lord went to Jerusalem, not that he descended to it. Thus it is said: "As they went up into Jerusalem,"[34] he went with them, Lk 2.42.

(2.2) Some practice abstinence when they want to bring about peace of the spirit with the flesh, but they do not comply with what is customary. They want to distinguish themselves

---

between the two, for the spirit naturally longs for what is good in the right order. Peace means, above *concordia,* a union even in the will of the two. So for peace the full knowledge is required that the aim of our life and our happiness are found in God. The fight that Thomas depicts here takes place in the context of our quest for happiness and peace, for which all people strive (ST I 2,1,1; II–II 29,1–2).

32. Cf. ST I–II 2,1,3, 30,4 and 33,2.

33. Thomas reckons it with the virtue of temperance, the fourth cardinal virtue. Abstinence, fasting, sobriety, chastity, and virginity are virtues that wear out the flesh (ST II–II 146–147, 149, 151–152). In ST I–II 64,1 Thomas endorses that in this we should not fall into extremes, as the Cathari and all kinds of penitential groups did.

34. *Ascendentibus*: Jerusalem is built on Mount Zion; the city, the place of peace is high.

from others, contrary to the command of the Lord in the Gospel: "When you fast," he says, "do not become sad as the hypocrites; (they neglect their appearance, so that they may appear to others to be fasting)" [Mt 6.16]. A man ought to do good works in secret [cf. Mt 6.1–4, 18] and in public he ought to be like others. Hence we read in Sir 32.1: "Amidst them he must be like one of them." When Augustine came to Milan, the people there did not fast, whereas the Romans and the Carthaginians fasted. His mother was very troubled: should she fast or not? So Augustine, then a catechumen, asked Ambrose whether she ought to fast or not. And Ambrose said: "To whatever church you go, comply with its manners if you do not want to be scandalized or scandalize others."[35] Hence Jesus went up "according to the custom" [Lk 2.42]. Do not distinguish yourself, because God really seems to abhor attracting attention to yourself.

But note what is said: "for the feast day" [Lk 2.42]. If companions want something contrary to virtue, as for that you ought not to be as they are.[36] Therefore, it says in Ex 23.2: "Do not follow the crowd doing evil." And Jer 6.16: "Inquire about the ancient paths, and see which is the good way and walk in it." That pertains to peace. Ps 122.3: "Jerusalem, which is built as a city whose union through fellowship is in itself." "In itself" meaning: "according to the concord of rules and other manners."

(2.3) Furthermore, that peace ought to be constant, because it is not enough to have it for a time; it is necessary that a man be persevering in it.[37] Thus we read in Jb 27.6: "Until I depart, I will not recede from my innocence; the justification which I began to have I will not abandon." He says two things. First he says: "Until I depart," meaning: "to my death," and: "from my innocence I will not recede."

A human being recedes from his innocence by sinning. Hence we read in Sir 26.28: "Who passes over from justice to in-

---

35. See Augustine, *Letter* 54.2.3.
36. Thomas maps out a very delicate distinction: we should not distinguish ourselves in order to draw attention to ourselves, but we must dissociate ourselves from sinful actions and customs.
37. Thomas speaks of a *habitus:* ST I–II 49.

iquity, God has prepared him for the *rhomphaia*," that is, for the sharpened sword.³⁸

It is not enough that someone would not sin. But if you have accustomed yourself to doing good, you ought not to abandon the good works.³⁹ Thus it says: "that I may not abandon the justification which I began to have." And therefore we read in Rv 2.4: "I hold against you that you have left behind your first love (*caritas*)."⁴⁰ This is also signified in the Gospel today, in Lk 2.43: "(When) the feast days (were over), Jesus remained in the Temple." Some may well abstain from sin during a feast, but after the feast they return to sin. Truly, man ought to remain in justice and in his innocence, which is designated in 1 Kgs 2.36–37, where Solomon says to Shimei, who is regarded as obedient: "Build yourself a house in Jerusalem, and live there; and do not leave it hither or thither; if one day you would leave, know that you must die." This means that this peace should be constant.

(2.4) Fourth, it ought to be cautious. You want to make peace with the spirit against the flesh? If you want to make peace with someone else and subject him to you, watch out for his friends. You want to make peace with the spirit against the flesh? You ought to watch out for the friends of the flesh.⁴¹ Hence Jer 9.3 says: "Let everyone watch out for his neighbor," that is, the carnal neighbor, "and let him not put his trust in any of his brothers," that is, the flesh. For it says in Mi 7.6: "The enemies of man are the ones who live in his house." And this is signified in today's Gospel, when the Lord wanted to remain in Jerusalem: "His parents did not know" [Lk 2.43]. Those who apply themselves to the perfection of the peace of the spirit ought to watch out for the friends of the flesh and for familiarity with the flesh.

---

38. A reference to the Last Judgment (Rv 2.12) and/or to a consequence in daily life, a judgment in time (e.g., Sir 21.3, 40.9); cf. ST I–II 85,3–5.

39. Doing good is not a matter of unconnected acts, but should become a habit: the habit of doing good all the time becomes a disposition; it makes someone do good spontaneously (ST I–II 49,1).

40. Even after receiving the Sacrament of Penance someone can sin again: ST III 88, SCG IV 70.

41. Characteristic of friendship is willing and not willing the same thing, according to Thomas in ST I–II 28,2 and II–II 29,3.

Ps 45.11 reads: "Forget your people and the house of your father, and the king will desire (*concupisco*) your beauty," namely, in the present by carrying you, and in the future by leading you, to glory.

May he deem it worthy to bestow this upon us, who lives and reigns, et cetera.

PART 3: *Collatio in sero*

"Jesus advanced" [Lk 2.52], et cetera. Today we have spoken about the double progress of Christ, that is, about (1) the progress of age and (2) that of grace. So it remains that we must speak about the other two progresses, namely, about (3) the progress of wisdom and (4) his life with the people.

❖

(3) And just as the progress of grace is shown in peace, so the progress of wisdom is shown in contemplation.[42] Therefore, Solomon says in Eccl 1.16: "I have surpassed all who were before me in Jerusalem"; and he adds why: "My mind has contemplated many things wisely."

Someone who contemplates many things wisely advances in wisdom. Behold: a building is called a temple by reason of the contemplating that takes place in it, or we speak of contemplation by reason of the fact that it takes place in a temple. So, since the Lord is found in the Temple, he shows us the application to contemplation and that by the Temple contemplation is signified. Ps 27.4 reads: "One thing I have asked from the Lord, this I will seek: that I may live in the house of the Lord all the days of my life and may go and see his holy Temple." He truly goes and sees the Temple, who goes to it not for foolish and trivial things, but in order to contemplate God's will.[43]

Let us see what Christ has done in the Temple; and on the basis of these things we can know whether someone advances

---

42. Pain and sadness are mitigated through the contemplation of the truth: ST I–II 38,4; cf. 35,5.

43. Cf. Thomas on prayer, in ST II–II 83,1,2 and 83,14,2. In this part of the sermon Thomas etymologically connects *templum* and *contemplatio*.

in the Temple. Now four things are necessary for man in order to advance in wisdom: (3.1) that he listens open-heartedly, (3.2) inquires diligently, (3.3) answers prudently, and (3.4) meditates attentively.

(3.1) First, I say that it is necessary for a man who advances in wisdom that he listen open-heartedly, because wisdom is so profound that no one is by himself sufficient to contemplate it.[44] So it is in itself necessary that he listen. Hence it says in Sir 6.33: "If you love (*diligo*) to listen, you will be wise."[45] You will say: "I am wise enough; I do not want to listen." Because of this it is said in addition: "A wise man who listens to wisdom will be wiser," in Prv 1.5. No one is so wise that he would not learn anything by listening. Thus his parents found Jesus as he was listening [Lk 2.46].

But how should you listen? Surely, with perseverance.[46] Some want to listen, in passing, to just one lecture in one academic field. Their heart is not there. In contrast: after three days they found that Jesus had been [in the Temple] constantly. Thus you, too, ought to listen constantly. Hence it says in Prv 8.34: "Happy the one who listens to me and keeps watch over my gates daily."[47]

Furthermore, we should not just open our ears to one teacher only, but to many, because the Apostle says in 1 Cor 12.4 that "there are different graces." One man has not advanced in all fields. St. Gregory knew the morals very well; St. Augustine was very good at finding solutions to problems; and St. Ambrose was very good at giving the allegorical meaning of sacred texts. What you do not learn from one, you learn from someone else. Thus we read in Sir 6.34: "Stand in the midst of prudent elders, and dwell in the wisdom of their hearts, so that you may be able

---

44. Cf. ST II–II 9,2, where Thomas distinguishes between wisdom and knowledge, *sapientia* and *scientia*.

45. Cf. ST II–II 157,4,1: humility and obedience as a way to wisdom; also II–II 162,3,1.

46. On perseverance, categorized under the cardinal virtue of strength: ST II–II 137.

47. In order to enter as they open or to welcome the Wisdom that comes forward through them (cf. Prv 8.35–36).

to hear what God is telling." And what one does not tell is told by another. I am not saying that I believe that it is useful that those who just begin to study (*audio*) a certain academic field, open their ears (*audio*) to different teachers. They should rather study (*audio*) with one until they are well-grounded; and when they are well-grounded, let them study with different teachers, so that they can "pick the flowers" from different teachers, that is to say: learn from different teachers the things that are useful [cf. Song 2.5 (Vg)].

Moreover, Jesus is found listening to many while he is standing in their midst. This is proper to a just judge. The office of judge is entrusted to someone who listens, because in a just way he ought to form a judgment about the things he hears.[48] Jb 12.11: "Does the ear not assess words?" A just judge should be a listener. Now some follow the opinion of *magistri*, because they attend their lectures (*audio*).[49] No one, however, ought to have a friend in truth; we ought to cling only to the truth, because the Philosopher says that disagreement in opinions is not incompatible with friendship.[50] Christ was in the midst, because it says in Sir 15.5: "He has opened his mouth in the midst of the Church, and the Lord has filled him with the Spirit of wisdom and understanding."

(3.2) Second, for progress in wisdom it is required that someone inquire diligently, because wisdom is more precious than all things that can be desired (*desidero*). Therefore, it says in Prv 3.15: "Wisdom is more precious than all jewels together; and all the things that people desire (*desidero*) do not have value compared to it."[51] And in Wis 7.8: "I have preferred it to thrones and kingdoms."

---

48. Cf. ST II–II 60,3. Jesus Christ will be our final judge (Mt 25.31–46). He listens to the just who call upon him (Mt 25.1–13, Lk 18.1–9; cf. Ps 7, 34.7, 58).

49. Cf. ST I 106,4 (last sentence of the *corpus*).

50. In other words, friendship is about love that goes beyond disagreement, in settings that include the Church and a religious order. We must adhere to the truth for the sake of the truth and not abandon it or our friends when we disagree with the latter; cf. also ST II–II 29,3,2.

51. Cf. ST II–II 100,1–2.

Take a look: for those who cannot do without a [certain] temporal thing, waiting until it is offered to them is not satisfying; they seek it diligently. In this way we ought to seek wisdom diligently. Hence Solomon says in Prv 2.4: "If you seek it as if it were money, you will find it." Some travel over mountains and seas in order to acquire money. In this way you too ought to labor for wisdom [cf. Eccl 1.13]. Thus they also found Jesus in the Temple as he put questions and sought wisdom, so as to give us an example of seeking wisdom.

But where ought we to seek wisdom and from whom? Surely from three:

(3.2.1) First, from a *magister* or from people who are wiser [than you are]. Hence it says in Dt 32.7: "Ask your father," that is, a *magister*. Because, as a father has brought you forth physically, a *magister* brings you forth spiritually;[52] "and he will tell you; ask the greater ones," that is, the wise, "and they will tell you" [ibid.].

Besides, you should not be satisfied inquiring only of the ones present, but you ought to inquire also of the old ones who are not with us any more. If you do not have an abundance of people, you still have an abundance of texts. When you see texts of Augustine and Ambrose, examine these. Jb 8.8: "Examine the former generation, and inquire diligently what we remember of the fathers,"[53] that is, the texts which they left for you to keep in mind.

(3.2.2) Furthermore, it is not only enough that you inquire of people or even these texts, but you ought to seek in the contemplation of creatures as well, for it says in Sir 1.9: "God has poured out his wisdom over all his works." God's works are his judgments of wisdom.[54] In the same way we can conjecture in a piece of art a lot[55] about the wisdom of the artist. Thus we read

---

52. ST I 117,1.

53. I.e., the Church Fathers, the Doctors of the Church. At this time no woman had been declared Doctor of the Church yet.

54. Wisdom itself is eternal. What God eventually does and makes in time is based on and comes forth from this eternal Wisdom; cf. ST I 1,6 22,1,2 (and 22,3).

55. *Multa,* but not all (*omnia*): the goodness and the order that we see in

SERMON 08   103

in Jb 12.7: "Examine the yoked animals, and they will teach you; the winged animals of the sky will also tell you."

(3.2.3) Furthermore, man ought to acquire wisdom by sharing with other people.[56] Hence the Wise says: "I have learned without delusion, and I share without envy," in Wis 7.13.[57] Everyone can perceive that no one can advance in knowledge so well as when he shares with others what he knows himself. This is even an obligation (*debitum*): that someone tells others in return about the thing he got to know. Thus it says in Prv 22.21: "(I have given insightful advice to you,) that I may show you the firmness and words of truth, so that you may give answers on the basis of these to the people who sent you."

(3.3) Christ gave answers, and "all were amazed at his prudence[58] and his responses" [Lk 2.47]. In an answer prudence is required in three ways:

(3.3.1) First, that the answer be in proportion with the one who gives the answer.[59] If someone asked from you what is beyond your knowledge and strength, you should not consider yourself obliged to respond. Therefore: "If you have the knowledge, answer your neighbor. If not, place your hand over your mouth, that you may not be captured in a foolish word and be confounded," as Sir 5.12 puts it.

(3.3.2) Furthermore, prudence in an answer requires that it be in proportion with the listener. Not just everybody must be answered, because maybe someone seeks something from you in order to attack or to accuse you [cf. Jn 19.9–10]. Hence it says

---

creation do not coincide with God's wisdom; they are coming forth from it (cf. Rom 1.20, in ST I 2,2); cf. the difference between God's absolute and ordained power, in ST I 25,5.

56. *Contemplari et contemplata aliis tradere* is the adage of the Dominican order; cf. II–II 186,6 and 7; III 40,1,2 and 40,2,3.

57. As also Christ did: ST III 42,3; cf. Sir 20.30, 41.14, and the scriptural references there. Again, Thomas's audience consists of the university's teachers and students.

58. The first of the four cardinal virtues: ST II–II 47–56. Prudence is a necessary virtue for a good life; cf. ST I–II 57,5.

59. Cf. also ST I 12,1,4: hence we can speak of God only insofar as we know him, i.e., insofar as he has revealed himself to us and insofar as we have understood what he has revealed.

in Prv 26.4: "Do not answer a fool with the same foolishness, in order to avoid your becoming like him." But what is a sign that someone is a fool? Certainly when he asks with insolent words, as we read in Prv 20.3: "The questions of a fool come with insolent words." But you ought to respond to a fool "with the same foolishness, so that you may not seem unknowing in his eyes," as Solomon says in Prv 26.5.[60] Christ has done this well; when some people asked him with which power he worked miracles, he replied to them by asking them another question in return [Mt 21.23–27].

(3.3.3) Furthermore, there ought to be prudence in an answer so that it is in proportion with the question, not with elegant epithets of words, but to the point. Otherwise the answer would be full of wind. Thus it is said in Jb 15.2: "Will the wise answer in the wind?" Christ responded prudently: "All were amazed at his prudence and his responses," in Lk 2.47.

(3.4) The fourth thing that makes prudence complete is that someone meditates with attention.[61] Ps 19.15: "The meditation of my heart is always directed towards you."

We have an example in the blessed Virgin; she "kept all these words with her in her heart," Lk 2.51 reads. In an explanation of this verse, a certain Graecus says quite remarkably: "Consider Mary, the most prudent woman and the mother of true wisdom, how she was made the mother of a scholarly boy: already she was focused on him, neither as a boy, nor as a man, but as God. And just as she had conceived the Word itself in her womb, she then conceived all his deeds and words in her heart." Take a look at three things concerning the meditation of the Blessed Virgin Mary:

(3.4.1) First, that it was fruitful. What is the fruit of meditation? I say that meditation is the key to the memory of someone who can read and listen to many things, but cannot keep it unless he meditates.[62] Ps 119.99: "I have understood more than all who taught me, because your testimonies are my meditation."

---

60. So one should neither become a fool nor make a fool of someone else even though one may consider the questioner foolish.

61. SCG III 37.

62. Cf. ST I–II 56,5,3.

For, just as food does not nourish unless it is first chewed, so you cannot advance in knowledge except by chewing, through frequent meditation, the things that you have heard.

(3.4.2) Furthermore, the meditation of the blessed Virgin was complete, because "she kept *all* the words." A man ought to meditate on all the things he has heard.

(3.4.3) Furthermore, the meditation of the blessed Virgin was profound. Some only want to meditate superficially. If you cannot meditate on all things at once, you may meditate another time. Mary "kept all the words with her in her heart." Ps 77.7: "I have meditated at night in my heart, and I trained my spirit and kept it focused."

There is no doubt that someone who listens open-heartedly, responds prudently, inquires diligently, and meditates with attention will advance much in wisdom. This is the way to advance in wisdom.

(4) Now it remains to speak about the progress of his living together with the people. It is true that on the basis of this Gospel passage someone who wishes to do so could well conceive this living together as with subservient people as well as with highly placed people. And since there are few highly placed people here and very many subservient people, we will speak about the subservient people.[63]

And we must note that if you want to advance in living together with people, you ought to have four characteristics: (4.1) devotion, (4.2) purity, (4.3) humility, and (4.4) discretion.

(4.1) First, I say that if you want to advance in living together with people, you ought to have devotion. Some are only devoted to themselves, that they may live in peace and advance in wisdom, but do not want to reach out to others. Such people can advance in grace with God, but not with people. But Jesus advanced in grace and wisdom "with God and the people" [Lk 2.52]. This is signified in his coming down [to be] with them: Jesus remained in Jerusalem during his time, but he came down

---

63. In tune with what Thomas just said in 3.3.2: his words are in proportion with the listener.

when he wanted.⁶⁴ Hence it says in Song 6.2: "My beloved (*dilectus*) has come down into his garden," that is, the garden of delights. And on the ladder that Jacob saw, he saw "the angels of God going up and down"; Gn 28.12. Thus we also should go up by a spiritual progress and go down by devotion to our neighbor.⁶⁵

(4.2) Some reach out to others, but too much, even to the point of sinning.⁶⁶ That is the reason why Christ came down to Nazareth, which means "flower," which stands for purity [cf. Sir 50.8].⁶⁷ Therefore, it says in Song 1.14: "Our couch is made of flowers." Happy the one whose conscience is free of what stinks or what is scandalous, but holds only the odor of a good name. Thus we read in Sir 24.17: "My flowers are the fruits of honor and honesty": fruits, namely, in merit. Therefore, the Apostle says in Rom 6.22: "You have fruit in sanctification." The flowers are in the future homeland (*patria*) [cf. Song 2.10b–13].

(4.3) Third, we ought to have humility.⁶⁸ As Augustine says: "Let the proud man blush with shame, because God has become humble."⁶⁹ Christ was subservient to the people, so that you may be subservient to highly placed people. Gregory says: "He never loses whatever by his progress advances obedience" [cf. Phil 2.8].⁷⁰

Before someone arrives at progress in living with people, it is necessary that he be obedient, since obedience leads to what is good [cf. Rom 16.19]. And Christ had the ultimate obedience [cf. Heb 5.8–9]. Some obey well in light things, yet not in great

---

64. Jesus never did anything against his will; cf. ST III 18 and 19,1–2.

65. On loving your neighbor: ST II–II 26,2 and 4–12.

66. ST II–II 26,4.

67. Thomas did not know Hebrew; he relies on explanations by Jerome and other Church Fathers. The Hebrew verb *nzr* means devoting oneself to fasting. A *nazir* was a man devoted to God who did not shave his hair, did not eat unclean food, and did not drink alcohol (cf. Samson in Jgs 13.4–5), whence he was considered pure. A Hebrew word for flower is *nitsah*, which occurs in Sir 50.8, where it is connected with purity.

68. See note 45. On humility, categorized under the cardinal virtue of temperance (ST II–II 143): ST II–II 161.

69. A similar line of reasoning is found in the corpus of ST III 46,3.

70. Cf. ST III 47,2.

things, but Christ was obedient in great things [too].[71] Hence a gloss on "He was obedient to them," [Lk 2.51] says [about his parents]: "They were righteous and honest people, though poor and in need of necessary things, as is witnessed for instance by the manger of the child to be adored [cf. Lk 2.7]; they sought the physical necessities of life by continual labor, and Christ toiled with them," as Ps 88.16 reads: "I am poor and in labor from my youth."[72] Many come to study, many want to advance in wisdom, but they do not make an effort to go down, [to reach out,] but only to go up. They are not in Nazareth, but in the foulness of sin. For they do so not in order to become subservient people, but highly placed people.[73] But Christ "went down to Nazareth," where "he was subservient to them."

(4.4) The fourth necessary characteristic is discretion, which is discretion in being obedient. For certain we ought to be obedient to our superiors in those things that do not lead us away from God. Thus St. Peter says in Acts 5.29: "We must obey God more than people."[74] Christ had this discretion; in the things that did not lead him away from God he was subservient to them: "Did you not know," he says in Lk 2.49, "that I had to be in these places that are my Father's?" And Ps 73.28 says: "It is good for me to cling to God," namely, in the present through grace[75] and in the future through glory,

which for us and for you, et cetera.

---

71. Obedience is a very important virtue, not only for a religious. It should not, however, make someone refrain from thinking and taking responsibility: ST II–II 104,3–5.

72. Also 2 Cor 8.9; cf. ST III 40,3. Voluntary poverty belongs to religious life: ST II–II 186,3, referring to Mt 19.21.

73. High ranks in the Church are not to be sought-after; cf. ST II–II 185,1. See also Sermon 21 *Beatus vir*, section 3.2.1; cf. ST II–II 185,1.

74. ST II–II 104,5.

75. ST I–II 4,7: so external goods are not *necessary* for our *happiness;* cf. ST II–II 23,7 and 82,3.

SERMON 09
EXIIT QUI SEMINAT

Sermon on the last-but-one Sunday before Lent, "Sexagesima"

Luke 8.5: *A sower went out to sow his seed.*

PART 1: *Prothema*

"A SOWER went out to sow his seed," Lk 8.5. Because our sermon is about a spiritual sowing, let us call upon the one who sows, our Lord Jesus Christ, who makes trustworthy people servants of this sowing; let us call upon him, so that he may give me something to say, et cetera.

PART 2: *Sermo*

"A sower went out," et cetera. Holy Mother the Church is a vineyard and a field, for the spiritual fruits of the Church, which are the works of justice, are wine as well as bread.[1] Wine, because these fruits make joyful: "for wine makes joyful," as Ps 104.15 reads and in Prv 13.9 it says: "The light of the just ones makes joyful." They are bread, because they make us strong; Ps 104.15: "and bread strengthens a man's heart." And in Prv 12.12 we read: "the root of the just ones will not be shaken."

There is one winegrower, one farmer of this vineyard and field, namely, Christ. "I am the true vine," he says insofar as he is a man, "and my Father is the winegrower" [Jn 15.1]; and inso-

---

1. In ST II–II 80 Thomas enumerates the virtues that are connected with justice, among which is *eucharistia*. The *Sermo* is preached at morning Mass.

SERMON 09   109

far as I am God, I am the winegrower with him;[2] that is to say, as Augustine says: "This winegrower is the whole of the Trinity who plants this vineyard and this field."[3] Thus it says in Jer 2.21: "I have planted you as a chosen vineyard, every seed."

Bernard says: "Let us sow an example for the people through good works, out in the open, as we read [in Mt 5.16]: 'Thus may your light shine before the people, that they may see your good works (and praise your Father in heaven).' For, on account of the hidden sighs and the like which are only known to them, the joy of God's angels is great over one sinner who repents, et cetera, as Lk 15.17 [that is, 15.10] says. Because of this the Apostle said in Rom 12.17 (Vg): 'caring for doing good things not only before God but also before the people.' He said 'before God,' meaning: before the ones who serve in the sight of God.[4] For it pleases them to the highest extent when they see us pray in secret or go over a certain Psalm again and again or do something like that. You too, sow! Because many before you have sown. O descendants of Adam, how many have sowed in you and how precious the seed; how disastrously will you perish, and how justly, if so great a seed perishes in you together with the effort of the sowing. You will be handed over to this destruction by the farmer [cf. Mt 3.10, Jn 15.2], if these seeds perish in you altogether [cf. Lk 8.5b–7]. The whole Trin-

   2. For, insofar as Christ is God, he is equal to the Father; cf. ST I 39,2 and 42.
   3. *Ad extra:* i.e., in creation, God is acting as one: the three Persons of the Trinity do not act independently from one another in creation; that "God" creates, loves, and heals is understood as that the triune God creates, loves, and heals; cf. ST I 45,6; III 23,2. Hence, calling the Father the Creator is not giving an exclusive name to the Father as if only the Father is the Creator and not also the Son and the Spirit. The name Creator is appropriated to the Father, because the word "father" is more associated by us with "source," or "beginning," than is "son" or "spirit"; cf. ST I 39,7–8. Likewise, "love" is a name of God which signifies the essence of the triune God; this name is usually appropriated to the Spirit, because love is as elusive as the wind. "Healer" is appropriated to the Son as well as to the Spirit, depending on how the healing takes place: if the person to be cured is touched, it is said to be the work of the Son, but if the cure is formulated as a healing flow, it is appropriated to the Spirit (cf. ST I 39,8,3, on Lk 6.19: "a power went out from him"). The basis of appropriation is Scripture.
   4. The angels; cf. Jb 1.6, Dn 7.10; cf. ST I 112,2,4.

ity has sown on our earth, the angels have sown in like manner, and the apostles, the martyrs and the confessors, and the virgins have sown. The Father has sown peace from heaven; the Son, truth; and the Holy Spirit, love (*caritas*).[5] The angels have also sown, because they have stood by others who were falling [cf. 1 Kgs 19.5, 7–8]. It is obvious that the martyrs have sown strength; the confessors, the justice which they have followed during their whole life; and the virgins, temperance, because they have scorned lust."

Now there are three things that must be considered here: (1) first, this seed; (2) second, who the sower is; and (3) third, the sowing, what and of what nature it is.[6]

(1) So first we must pay attention to the question what that seed is. Well, we cannot say that this seed is anything else than what the Lord says: "The seed is the word of God" [Lk 8.11]. Note that [Jesus] distinctly says: "*his* seed," that is, the seed of the Son of God. This is good seed. The seed that is not his, is bad seed, of which Is 17.10 speaks: "tares," as it is called in the Gospel [Mt 13.25–30]. We must carefully consider what that seed is because it saves us from sin. Thus we read in 1 Jn 3.9: "Everyone who is born from God does not sin, because the seed of God is in him."

But how can we know whether it is [God's] seed? I say in the same way as we know that a certain seed is a seed of a particular herb. Well, we know this in three ways: (1.1) first, because

---

5. See also note 3. Since the name "sower" does not signify God's essence, these attributions are not called appropriations; it is an attribution according to figurative speech. The basis for the attributions here is found in Scripture: respectively, Rom 1.7 (among others), Jn 14.6, and Gal 5.22. Note that such attributions are not strict: on the basis of Rom 1.7 and other texts, Jesus Christ can be called the sower of our peace as well; because of Jn 16.13 ("the Spirit of truth"), the Spirit can be called the sower of truth (as in ST I-II 106,4,2; II-II 1,9sc); in Jn 3.16 the motive for sending the Son is called love, which links "sowing love" also with the Father.

6. Thus the method is this: from (1) the effects to (2) the author—which is also the order in the *Prima Pars* of the ST, e.g., I 2,3—and then (3) what this means for our task of collaborating with him.

that seed is coming from that herb; (1.2) second, because the seed is borne in it; (1.3) third, because it brings forth such an herb. Hence the seed of Christ is from Christ, which has also appeared in Christ and makes someone similar to Christ, or which leads to Christ. Therefore, the seed of Christ is the seed that is from him as well as in him as well as leading towards him.

(1.1) Let us look at the first. I say that the seed of a certain herb is the seed that comes from it. Thus we read in Gn 1.11: "Let the earth put forth the green plant which produces its seed according to its own kind." But what seed is coming from the Lord Jesus Christ? I say that the word of wisdom is coming from him. Hence it says in Sir 1.5 (Vg): "The fountain of wisdom is God's Word in the highest."[7] Hence whatever pertains to the heavenly wisdom that is in the highest, is a word of wisdom or a seed of God.

But St. James says in 3.15 that there is a wisdom that is not from above; it is earthly, beastly, diabolic.[8] Earthly wisdom is the wisdom that is totally occupied with acquiring earthly things. So if you are confronted with a word that stimulates you to acquire earthly things, it is not a seed of God. Furthermore, beastly wisdom is totally focused on pursuing the pleasure of the body. So, if you are confronted with such a doctrine, you know that it is not a seed of God and that you should not believe it. It is said in Mal 2.15: "What does one look for, but where the seed of God is?" And which is the diabolic knowledge? Jb 41.26 reads, "It is king over all the children of pride." So the wisdom that is totally focused on being proud is diabolic.[9] So if someone confronts you with such a doctrine, it is not a seed of Christ. Hence the Apostle says: "My words and my preaching do not come from error or uncleanness" [2 Thes 2.3].

Of what kind, then, is the wisdom that is in the highest, whose fountain of wisdom is the Word of God in the highest?

---

7. Also 1 Cor 1.23–24, where (the crucified) Christ is called "the wisdom of God." Cf. ST III 3,8, 10,4.

8. Cf. ST II–II 45,1,1.

9. Thomas indicates pride as the beginning of every sin on the basis of Sir 10.15 (ST I–II 84,2) and Genesis 3 (frequently quoted in ST II–II 162–165).

St. James says in 3.17: "The wisdom that is from above is first of all modest. Next, it is peaceful; it does not bring about disagreements." Hence whatever brings about disagreements and is against peace and wisdom from above, is not a seed of God. And it is certain that whenever a teaching leads to rectitude of the virtues,[10] it is a teaching of Christ, whereas if it leads towards the corruption of the good, it is not a teaching of Christ. Therefore, it says in Prv 8.8: "(All my words are just, and) nothing (in them is crooked or) perverted."[11]

So, first, a seed of something is what comes from it.

(1.2) Second, a seed of something is what is in it. Hence it says in Gn 1.11: "Let the earth put forth the green plant which produces its fruit whose seed is in itself." So any teaching that is in Christ is the seed of God. Ps 109.3 (Vg): "In the splendor of the saints I brought you forth from the womb before daybreak."[12] The splendors of the saints are the radiance of the virtues. Well, every radiance of the virtues is derived from the Son of God, just as an example is from the exemplar, "for in him all treasures of wisdom and knowledge are hidden" [Col 2.3], et cetera.[13]

But you could say: "This does not apply to me, for I cannot see the Word in its eternity." Therefore, it is sufficiently provided for us: that Word has become man, and this [Word that has become man] shows us the example of each teaching of his, whence we read in Jn 1.14: "The Word has become flesh (and dwelt among us)." Augustine comments on this: "God's wisdom itself is made an example in a man whom it has taken on: an example for the people of returning up above and abiding with the angels."[14] So if someone came and confronted you with a doctrine whose exemplar is not in Christ, it is not a seed of God.

---

10. ST II–II 45,6,3: therefore, people who have received the gift of wisdom and live in accordance with it are called "children of God," in accordance with the seventh Beatitude.

11. Cf. ST II–II 34,3,1, where Thomas explains this verse by saying that hate towards a neighbor is a perversion, citing 1 Jn 2.9 and 3.15.

12. Thomas's text reads *Lucifer*, the Vulgate text *lucifer*, that is, "the carrier of (the) light."

13. ST I–II 68,1; III 7,2.

14. Thus Thomas says at the beginning of the *Summa Theologiae* that Christ,

Jovinian came to Rome and preached that being married must be regarded as equal to virginity, although Christ wanted to have a virginal mother and chose her, and although he loved (*diligo*) the virginal disciple to the highest extent.[15] The heretic Vigilantius preached in France that the state of the rich who give alms is equal to poverty. This teaching is [also] not in Christ, who became very poor for our sake [cf. 2 Cor 8.9]. Augustine says in the book *The Christian Struggle*: "Someone who contemplates the things Christ said and did does not miss this perversion; he loves (*diligo*)[16] and thoroughly examines the things said and done by that man, in whom the Son of God offers himself as the example for our life. Thus all men and women, every age and dignity have run to the hope of eternal life: some have run to the divine things, as they do not care about temporal things. Others proceed by their virtues: they practice them and praise what they cannot fulfill. A few, however, murmur and are tormented by too much envy: either they seek after things for themselves in the Church, although they seem to be Catholics, or they are heretics who seek honor in the very name of Christ." Also St. Gregory says: "There are several people in the Church who not only do not do good things, but even counteract the good things in others and detest the things in others which they themselves neglect to do. Their actions do not come from weakness or ignorance, but they do this because they are determined to do so; when done with determination, it is a sin against the Holy Spirit."[17]

(1.3) Third, we know whose seed it is when it leads to the same thing. The seed of a tree has the strength to produce a similar tree. Hence it says in Gn 1.11: "Let the earth put forth

---

insofar as he is a man, is for us the way into God (ST I 2,1 intr.), an implicit reference to Jn 14.6, where Jesus Christ says that he is the way.

15. The virginal disciple is John. Especially to religious who take the vow of chastity, this John was presented as a great example: ST II–II 186,4,1 and III 45,3,4.

16. For Thomas's terminology of love, see Sermon 01 *Veniet desideratus*, note 39.

17. Cf. Mt 12.31; ST II–II 14,1; i.e., rejecting out of contempt the gifts of the Holy Spirit, which prevent us from sinning.

the green plant which produces its seed according to its own kind." The strength of a species to bring forth is located in the seed,[18] whence it says in Jn 10.35: "He has called them gods to whom God's words were spoken." When you hear God's words with your ear and you love (*diligo*) them with your heart and actually fulfill them with works, then God's words were spoken to you [cf. Mt 13.23. Lk 8.15]. But it is true that the life of the saints is slandered, as we read in Wis 5.4–5: "We, foolish, considered their lives madness and their end without good. But behold how they are reckoned among the children of God." It proceeds: "Hence, *we* have strayed from the way of truth" [Wis 5.6]. I come to the conclusion: therefore you ought to imitate Jesus Christ, so that you may become like him [cf. Song 1.8 (Vg)].

Hence Augustine says, in *The Christian Struggle:* "If you have a high opinion of yourself, may you not scorn imitating him who will be called Son of the Most High. If you think little of yourself, dare to imitate the fishermen and the tax-collectors who have imitated Christ."[19] So the first point is clear, the one about the seed.

❖

(2) Now it remains to speak about the second thing, namely, the sower, because it is said that "a sower went out." Who is the one who went out? With certain authority it is Christ, in whose service all teachers are. Is 32.20 says about them: "Happy are you who sow beside the waters."[20]

This sower, Christ, went out because he wanted to sow. Thus other preachers must go out. There is, however, a difference between Christ and these preachers: For Christ went out in one single movement in order to teach thereupon, whereas a preacher ought to go out time and again. Christ went out from the hidden bosom of the Father. He says: "I have gone out from the Father," not because he had left the Father behind, but be-

---

18. ST I 78,2,2, 92,3,2, 118,2,3; I–II 17,9,3, 81,1,4 and 81,4, 114,3,3; III 32,1,1; cf. III 31,5,3 (*semen feminae*).

19. So if you think imitation of Christ is aiming too high, you can still follow him by imitating the poor sinners who followed him. Cf. Thomas's explanation of Jesus' call "Follow me" (Lk 5.27), in ST II–II 184,3,1.

20. Cf. Ps 1.3 and 23.2, and Ezek 47.12.

cause he was made visible, "and I have come into the world" [Jn 16.28], although he was there already, but now he appeared as visible.[21] But when? Early in the morning.[22] Hence it says in the Gospel that the *paterfamilias* went out early in the morning, at the first hour, to hire workers for his vineyard [Mt 20.1].

Now for a preacher it is necessary to go out in a twofold way:

(2.1) in the first way, by leaving the state of guilt, because it must not be so that a preacher preaches to others what he is not doing himself.[23] Ps 50.16 reads: "Yet, to the sinner God has said: 'Why do you speak of my justice?'" et cetera. Why do you preach that we must not steal, if you are stealing yourself, and that we must not commit adultery, if you are committing adultery? Therefore, we ought to leave the state of guilt, as the Apostle says: "Go out from their midst and separate yourself from their situation and do not touch anything unclean" [2 Cor 6.17].[24]

But whither should we go out when we leave sin? Certainly to Christ, that is, to the Passion of Christ. As the Apostle says: "Let us go out to him outside the camp, bearing his reproach" [Heb 13.13], that is, his cross.[25] The Apostle says that "the old man is crucified with him, so that the body of sin may be destroyed" [Rom 6.6].

When should we go out? Early in the morning. Therefore, it is said, "In time of trouble, rise early in the morning" [e.g., 1 Sm 29.10], and elsewhere: "Do not hesitate to be converted to the Lord, and do not delay it (day after day)" [Sir 5.7], and in Sir 21.1: "Have you sinned? Do not turn to it again."

(2.2) The other going out that is necessary for a preacher is leaving the world.[26] And this is signified in Jn 4.28–29, where

21. See Sermon 05 *Ecce rex tuus*, note 7.
22. Thomas explains this further on, in section 2.2.
23. A golden rule for preaching; otherwise, he denies his own preaching: 1 Tm 4.12, Ti 2.7b, as in Lk 11.39–52; cf. ST II–II 97,1,3, 100,3,2, 187,5,5; III 40,3, 41,3,1
24. Cf. ST 102,5,4.
25. The desire to be united with the suffering Christ through our own sufferings. This union is desirable, since his suffering is redemptive; we share in his sufferings so that we may share in his glory; cf. Gal 2.19–20 and Col 1.24. The stigmata are a most extraordinary form of such a participation in the Passion.
26. *Exitus de mundo* or *Fuga mundi* (cf. ST I–II 39,3). This is the image tradi-

it says that the woman left her water jar and went to announce Christ. Augustine expounds this, saying that someone who wants to preach ought to leave the water jar behind, meaning the cupidity of the world, at least the affections that accompany it, so that he does not love (*diligo*) the cupidity either because of the affection or because of its effect. About this going out, the Lord says in Gn 12.1 to Abraham: "Leave your land and your kindred and your father's house," meaning: let go of whatever is earthly and can be loved (*amo*), "and come into the land that I will show unto you." It is remarkable that he says this, for the Law does not lead anyone to perfection [cf. Heb 7.19], and the way of the counsels had not yet been shown. Therefore, the Lord has said to someone who had observed the Commandments: "One thing is missing for you; if you want to be perfect, go (and sell everything you have and give to the poor, and you will have a treasure in heaven. Then come, follow me)" [Mt 19.21]. "Come into the land" [Gn 12.1]: certainly that is the land of vision or contemplation, which is characteristic of the religious life.

But when should we come into that land? Early in the morning, that is, in our youth. Ps 5.4: "Early in the morning I will stand before you and I will see you," et cetera. Jerome's translation from the Hebrew text reads: "and I will contemplate you."[27] Is 50.4–5: "Early in the morning he excites my ear, that I may hear him as my *magister*. The Lord has opened my ear, and I have not talked back." Now because a lord has the authority and a *magister* wisdom, he has opened my ear as he came to my ear.

You will say: "I may not do what is said to me, for someone might call me an unlucky, senseless boy." Against this Is 51.7 says: "Fear not the people's reproaches or their blasphemies." Augustine says: "Let the boys who vowed modesty rejoice."

---

tionally used for entering religious life, also for Dominicans and other mendicants who left their monasteries regularly to preach in the city or in the country.

27. St. Jerome translated Scripture from the original Hebrew and Greek into Latin. The version of the Psalms usually cited by Thomas is the Vulgate *iuxta LXX* (not the *iuxta Hebraica*), a translation from the Greek text of the Old Testament, the Septuagint, which was also used in the liturgy.

You will say: "I only have a word, but I need an example."[28] May the holy boy Benedict come to mind then, who, after leaving his parents behind and temporal goods as well as his nurse, wisely retreated and took up a remote hermitage. If this is not enough for you, let the saintlier boy John the Baptist come to your mind, of whom it says in Lk 1.80: "The boy John grew and became strong, and he lived in deserted places until the day of his public appearance."[29] If even that is not enough for you, let the holiest boy Jesus come to your mind, who, when he was twelve years of age, stayed behind [in Jerusalem] unbeknownst to his parents, and was found in the midst of teachers [Lk 2.41–43, 46].

But you will say: "Three things warn me that I should not leave the world in my youth:[30]

(2.2.1) "The first is that one must gradually come to perfection, for no one becomes the best at once." But, my dearest,[31] you have less to do to come to perfection in your old age. The Apostle says: "May we be brought to the perfect One" [cf. Eph 4.13 and Heb 7.19]. Some want to become soldiers, others house-builders, et cetera. But there is no one who eagerly desires a certain state without eagerly desiring it in his youth, if he wants to be perfect in that state. Hence may you from the beginning of your age start with leaving the world, because no matter how much a person makes progress, he always grows. Besides, it is easy to do the things that have become a habit for us from our youth. Because of this it says in Lam 3.27: "It would be good for a man, if he carried (the yoke from his adolescence)," and in Prv 22.6: "(Train) an adolescent along his way; (even when he is old, he will not recede from it.)"

But you will say "Adolescence and pleasure," as it is said in

---

28. After all, examples are more convincing than words: ST I–II 34,1.

29. In the same context, ST II–II 188,8.

30. Issues concerned with entering religious life (when, how) are also treated in ST II–II 189, the last *quaestio* of the *Secunda Pars*.

31. *"Karissime."* This interjection seems to indicate that the secretary gives a very precise account of what Thomas said. Furthermore, it seems to be a sign that he was a vivid preacher. The word also shows Thomas's sympathy with his audience.

Eccl 11.10 (Vg), ("are empty"). I say that that book is written by way of conclusion, and it has two conclusions: one of the wise and one of the foolish. The conclusion of the foolish is: "Rejoice, young man, in your adolescence (and let your heart be glad in the days of your youth. Walk in the ways of your heart and in the sight of your eyes)" [Eccl 11.9]. The other conclusion leads to this advice: "Do not go after your lusts; if you give in to the lusts of your soul, those will hand you over to the joy of your enemies" [Sir 18.30–31]. This other conclusion is the one of the wise people: "Remember your Creator in your youth" [Eccl 12.1].[32]

(2.2.2) But you will say: "Another thing reminds me why I do not want to leave the world from my youth on: I do not know whether it is from the Holy Spirit,[33] because the saint is usually not brought out in boys." Well, the Holy Spirit has the freedom from the Father and the Son to blow where he will [cf. Jn 3.8], and you want to block his paths? Ambrose says: "This Spirit is not bent back by ages, nor limited by death, and it is not excluded from the womb."[34] Gregory: "I want to consider how this Holy Spirit is a master artist, and I fail in my very consideration, because he fulfills a boy who plays the cither and makes a Psalmist, he fulfills a shepherd of herds who picks mulberries and makes a prophet, he fulfills a boy who fasts," et cetera,[35] things which he mentioned in a homily for Pentecost and which you have heard before in a sermon on the Holy Spirit.

You will say: "It is not through the Holy Spirit that boys leave the world behind, because many boys are converted, yet do not persevere in religious life; but if it had been from God, they would have stayed in the order." Be careful, because if you understand this in a perverted way, you give way to the Manichaeans. Mani says that God is not the author of corruptible things

---

32. Thus Thomas gives an instruction on how to read Scripture: one cannot just quote verses haphazardly in order to sustain one's own opinion; the context and the structure of a text are important for a correct understanding of what it says.

33. Cf. ST II–II 189,9,1.

34. Cf. 1 Sm 3, Is 49.1, Jer 1.5–6, Ezek 37.1–14, Lk 1.15, Gal 1.15.

35. Through Gregory, Thomas refers to David.

and that what comes from God is not destroyed. This heretic also says that grace once possessed cannot be lost. In answer to these things we must explain: God's works are thoroughly corruptible; it also happens that someone receives the grace of entering religious life, but that the Lord does not give him the gift to persevere—but this does not alter the fact that it comes from God. It is true that the plan of God is not destroyed; it remains forever [cf. Ps 33.11].[36]

(2.2.3) But you will say: "Another thing reminds me why I do not want to leave the world behind in my youth: I am a boy, so I cannot carry arms." The arms of religious life are not the arms of Saul [cf. 1 Sm 26.7–8, 31.9–10], but the arms of David [cf. 1 Sm 17.45; cf. Ps 35.1–3, Wis 5], that is, the arms of Christ [cf. Rom 13.12, 2 Cor 10.4–5]. The arms of Saul are the observances of the Old Law, which are heavy arms. Hence St. Peter says: "This is a burden that neither we nor our fathers could carry" [Acts 15.10]. The observances of the New Law[37] and religious life[38] are light arms, whence the Lord says: "My yoke is sweet and my burden is light" [Mt 11.30].

Therefore, early in the morning we ought to leave the world behind and come to Christ. But what will be our fruit? Certainly, attainment of the kingdom of heaven. Thus the Lord says in the Gospel: "Allow the little ones to come to me, for of such people is the Kingdom of heaven" [Mt 19.14].[39]

---

36. Thomas distinguishes between, on the one hand, what is God and in God, for instance, his eternal, unchangeable plan, and, on the other hand, what is not-God, outside God, for instance, how things come to pass in time. The former is perfect as only God can be; it remains forever. Creation, including created grace, comes forth from God's perfection, but is not God; it is imperfect, unfinished; it grows towards perfection, fulfillment, but can also be corrupted. Cf. how Thomas speaks of God's eternal will and the execution of it in time in ST I 19,4–9.

37. ST I–II 107,4.

38. ST II–II 189,10,3.

39. Also cited in the context of entering religious life: ST II–II 189,5sc.

PART 3: *Collatio in sero*

(2.3) "A sower went out" [Lk 8.5], et cetera. Today we spoke about the seed and about the sower's double way of going out. It remains now to speak about the sower's third way of going out,[40] that is, preaching, because a preacher ought to go out from hidden contemplation and go to the public [field] of preaching, for a preacher first ought to draw in contemplation what he will pour out later on in preaching.[41] Hence it says in Is 12.3–4: "With joy you shall draw water," that is, with the joy of contemplation,[42] "from the fountains of the Savior,"—that is, from divine wisdom [cf. Wis 1.5 (Vg)]—"and then you will say on that day," after you have drawn: "Give thanks to the Lord" [e.g., Ps 33.2, 106.1], et cetera. This going out is very similar to the Savior's going out from the secret dwelling place of the Father to the public area of what is visible.[43] Therefore, it says in Song 7.11: "I am (here) for my beloved (*dilectus*), and he is turned towards me," namely, in the hidden realm of contemplation.

There are two things that can turn the soul towards God: devout prayer and contemplation;[44] and through internal speech God is turned to the soul.[45] Hence the soul says: "My beloved (*dilectus*) is mine, and I am his" [Song 2.16]. But will we not always be here? No.[46] Therefore, he says: "Come, my beloved (*di-*

---

40. N.B.: This point was not announced by Thomas at the beginning of the *Sermo*.

41. *Contemplari et contemplata aliis tradere* (ST II–II 188,6, III 40,2,3): the adage of the *Ordo Praedicatorum*, the Dominicans.

42. Contemplation of the divine things is most delightful: ST I–II 3,5.

43. Thus Jesus Christ coming into this world is presented as the model for preachers who contemplate before going out.

44. Thomas's theology on prayer in a nutshell in ST II–II 83; on contemplation: I–II 35,5 and II–II 82,3.

45. Cf. Ps 6.5. As in Ps 53.7 it is an image that God is listening and that he is favorably disposed towards us, because we have turned wholeheartedly towards him. Cf. Thomas's exposition of Ps 90.1 (Ps 89.1 [Vg]) in ST I 13,7,2.

46. That is, in prayer and contemplation. The answer is "no"; Dominican friars are not contemplative monks. He advocates for what is called a *vita mixta:* a religious life which is characterized by a balanced combination of action in the world and a rhythm of prayer and contemplation every day. Cf. ST II–II 182.

lectus), let us go out in the field" [Song 2.10], meaning: the public field of the preaching; "let us remain," when we preach, "in the country houses" [Song 7.11], that is, with the people who are open to the preaching [cf. Lk 10.5–9]. Note that when he says "let *us* remain," a particular familiarity of God with the preacher is indicated; "Let *us* go out": I by inspiring you, and you by preaching.[47]

When shall we go out? Let us go out early in the morning to the vineyards; in the same way Christ went out early in the morning, as we read in the Gospel: "He went out most early in the morning to hire workers for his vineyard" [Mt 20.1]. We read that Christ went out at three hours, namely, at the third hour early in the morning, at the sixth hour, and at the ninth hour. And Gregory says that the fact that he hired workers early in the morning signifies that he converts boys in the first period of life. It is said in Eccl 11.6: "Sow your seed early in the morning and let your hand not be inactive in the evening." By "early in the morning," a young age is signified; by "in the evening," old age. Some say that boys must not preach. Against them it says: "Sow your seed early in the morning." Others say that old men must not preach, because they are hardened. Against them it says: "Let your hand not be inactive in the evening." Boys as well as old men must preach, because "you do not know whether the latter or the former [seed] comes up, and if both come up it is even better" [Eccl 11.6].

You will say: "You must not summon such people nor lead them to religious life, according to a sentence passed by the Lord, who says: "You have gone round sea and dry land to make one proselyte" [Mt 23.15], et cetera. May you see that the meaning of this is that some go round sea and dry land to convert others. This is praiseworthy. Thus the Lord says: "Go into the whole world, preach the Gospel to every creature" [Mk 16.15]. This was already announced beforehand by Isaiah, who says in 27.6: "And they will enter from Jacob with force and fill the face of the earth with seed."[48]

---

47. As in Mk 16.20; cf. ST II–II 171,1.
48. That is, the seed of God's word: Lk 8.11.

What is meant by what follows: "and you make him a son of Gehenna, twice as bad as yourselves" [Mt 23.15]? Concerning whom do we understand this? It is explained by the saints[49] in two ways. First, concerning the Jews and the scribes. Chrysostom says that it is understood concerning the Jews and the scribes who keep the statutes of the Old Law. And why do they make [the newly converted proselyte] a son of Gehenna twice as bad as themselves? This is not because they have sinned by converting others, but because they led others to sinning by bad examples.[50] And why does it say "twice as bad as yourselves"? Chrysostom says that a disciple sins more carelessly when he sees a teacher sinning, and, just as a preacher who gives an example of a bad life is to be condemned, so is the one who gives an example of a good life to be praised. Another interpretation with authority is the explanation by Jerome, who says that these words concern the Pharisees and scribes who, being under the Old Law, converted others to circumcision: these sin in a double way, because they let go of the Law of Christ [cf. Gal 6.2, 15] and because they want to be circumcised.

You will say: "It is good for boys to preach, so that they let go of the secular world and come to Christ in religious life, but it is not good to attract or allure them with temporal benefits, because Scripture says that the Jews are not attracted to the faith by threats, terrors, and benefits. But Scripture does not say that they cannot be allured by flattery" [cf. Prv 29.5]. Twofold is the Covenant, namely, Old and New: under the Old Covenant God promised temporal things, promises which we make to little children who are allured by benefits. Thus he said: "If you are willing and listen to me, you will eat the goods of the earth" [Is 1.19]. Still some among the people were spiritual, like Dav-

---

49. These saints are the Doctors of the Church who are believed to be in heaven now. See also ST II–II 189,9,2.

50. This explanation is clear in the context of Mt 23.15, where Jesus criticizes the scribes' and Pharisees' behavior. Jerome's exposition, in the following text, is also found in ST II–II 189,9,2, but the emphasis in this homily is on Chrysostom's interpretation: as a preacher one must give the good example; you have a great responsibility, for people will do as the preacher does (cf. ST I–II 34,1; II–II 33,1 and 3, 187,2).

id, who clung to God because of God, whence he said: "Yet for me it is good to cling to God" [Ps 73.28],[51] et cetera. Likewise, he said: "One thing I have asked from the Lord, for this I long: (that I may live in the house of the Lord all the days of my life)" [Ps 27.4].

Likewise, under the New Covenant there are some perfect people who do not want to be allured by temporal things. Others are imperfect men who are allured also by temporal things.[52] Therefore, regulations are given in the Church, so that they would be led by the hand to come to the liturgy of the hours. Let it not be so that they go [and pray] because of these [temporal] things, but that they become more kind-hearted and lead a happier life.[53]

You will say: "It is allowed to attract boys to religious life, but not to let them take vows."[54] Why not? You will say: "Because many who had taken vows returned [into the world]." I then will say what the Apostle says: "Will the unbelief of those make the faith empty?" [Rom 3.3] He says in so many words: No. If someone gives up the religious life, others are not to be bound any less to the religious life. Christ called many disciples, and many returned [into the world] [cf. Jn 6.66]. Philip the apostle called Simon the magician, and yet he left and went back [Acts 8.9–24].

The net is twofold: the one is that through which some are brought to eternal life, about which we read in Jn 21.11: "The net was full of great fishes." The other one is that through which some are brought to religious life; in this one good and evil people are brought together, the ones who are known beforehand and the ones who are predestined [cf. Mt 20.14]. There is a place in the Gospel where we read about this: "The Kingdom

---

51. This Psalm is in fact not attributed to David, but to Asaph.

52. So Thomas is not saying that the Jews were focused on temporal goods and Christians are not; he rather points at something generally human. After Christ it still is not an exception for people to be attracted by temporal gain. That is why we need to translate Christ's wisdom into rules and regulations.

53. A regular prayer life leads to insight; see, e.g., Psalm 49. Thomas presents here very briefly the purpose of religious life; cf. ST II–II 189,1.

54. Cf. ST II–II 189,5.

of heaven is like a dragnet thrown in the sea and gathering fish of every kind" [Mt 13.47], et cetera.

You will say: "Many have entered and left and remained in the world and became good bishops and good archdeacons." It cannot be that someone who did not fulfill his vow would be a good bishop. The bishop of Geneva had made a vow about joining religious life, and the Pope says that he cannot have a sound conscience unless he resigns the episcopate and enters religious life.[55]

Hence it is allowed that preachers call boys and bring them to religious life and let them take vows.

❖

(3) It is clear what has been said about the seed and the going-out of the sower. It remains that we look at the sowing itself, about which we must say two things: (3.1) the first is what hinders the sowing; (3.2) the second is about the fruit of the sowing.

(3.1) Concerning the first we must note that there is a triple hindrance for the sowing on behalf of those for whom the seed is sown: (3.1.1) the first is emptiness of the affection; (3.1.2) the second, hardness of the heart; and (3.1.3) the third, fierce concupiscence or cupidity.

(3.1.1) I say the first hindrance for sowing is emptiness (or the vanity) of the affection. Some have a heart so empty and so ready to sin that they immediately consent to sin when it is proposed to them. And about these it says in Ps 4.3: "Sons of men, till how long do you, with a heavy heart, (love [*diligo*] emptiness and do you seek after lies)?" They are empty and worldly, because they promise things that they cannot fulfill. Such people surrender their seducible heart to every sin. These are signified by the road, where the seed does not bear fruit [Lk 8.5]. Is 51.23 reads: "You have lain down on the ground, as if your body were a road for travelers." On this road seed cannot bear fruit nor can it prosper. Hence it says in Ezek 33.31–32: "They hear your words, but do not do them, since they turn them into the

---

55. ST II–II 185,4; cf. 189,2–3 (esp. 189,3,1). If, however, someone is a religious and is created a bishop, he remains a religious: ST II–II 185,8.

song of their own mouth, for they say: 'This one blesses, that one curses,' and their heart follows avarice,[56] and you are for them like a musical song that is sung with a pleasing and sweet sound; they hear your words, but do not do them."

Twofold is the danger when seed is sown on the road, because it is trampled upon and eaten by the birds [Lk 8.5]. In this way the seed of God's word is trampled upon by the bad examples of people who are your companions, and it is eaten up by the evil plans of demons and so the fruit is lost. Thus it says in Ps 89.42: "All who passed him on the way have plundered him," et cetera.

(3.1.2) The second hindrance is on account of the fact that seed does not bear fruit when it is sown over rock. Rocks are hard and solid things, which are held together on their own terms. Who has no love (*amor*) but for himself, has a hard heart, and "a hard heart will behave badly in a very young person" [Sir 3.27].[57] If it is sown in a hard place, the seed does not take root deeply. Thus some take up a good plan, but have a hard heart, and therefore it does not stay with them long. Therefore, the Apostle says: "But in accordance with your hardness and your impenitent heart you store up the wrath for yourself for the day of the revelation of the just Judgment" [Rom 2.5].

(3.1.3) The third hindrance that does not allow the seed to bear fruit is concupiscence or cupidity. Someone hears God's word, places it in his heart, lets it take deep root, and then concupiscence or cupidity of having a thing overpowers it: it puts down whatever man considers good. These sow over thorns [Lk 8.7]. Against them the Lord says in Jer 4.3: "Renew your fallow land, and do not sow over thorns." Those who want to sow remove thorns, and so you ought to remove every concupiscence or cupidity, as the Apostle did, who says: "I chastise my body, and I bring it back to servitude" [1 Cor 9.27]. Passions of the soul are called thorns [cf. 2 Cor 12.7], because, as thorns mutilate the body, so the passions of cupidity mutilate the soul. In Gn 3.17–18 it says: "Cursed is the land in view of your work. It

---

56. On the capital sin of avarice: ST II–II 118. It is even considered the root of all evils; cf. ST II–II 119,2,1.

57. For God's role in this: ST I–II 79,3.

will bring forth thorns and thistles for you." This is because of the sin of the first parent.

These are the hindrances for the fruit-bearing of the seed.[58]

(3.2) It comes to pass [in Lk 8.8], however, that the earth in which it is sown is good—and then it produces a triple crop: (3.2.1) thirty-fold, (3.2.2) sixty-fold, and (3.2.3) hundred-fold. When does it produce a hundred-fold crop?

(3.2.1) I say that when people hear God's word, it produces a triple crop. Some are converted, so that they pursue the fruit that [converted people] necessarily bring forth. This is the thirty-fold crop. Now the number thirty comes from multiplying three by ten: you have faith in the Trinity and the Ten Commandments of the Law,[59] as Mt 19.17 says: "If you want to enter into life, follow the Commandments." Thus you have produced a thirty-fold crop. And in order to show that the thirty-fold fruit is necessary for salvation, the Lord wanted to be baptized[60] in his thirtieth year,[61] and there the whole Trinity appeared: the Father in the voice, the Son in the flesh, and the Holy Spirit in the form of a dove, as Luke records in 3.21–22.

(3.2.2) Others go further and convert to the highest state of perfection through a way of penitence[62] after having committed sins, and thus produce a sixty-fold crop. The number of sixty comes from multiplying six by ten. Six is a perfect number. The six counsels[63] must be added to the Ten Commandments, and then you will produce a sixty-fold crop.

---

58. It is for these reasons that a preacher must have left "the world" before he starts preaching; cf. ST III 40,3,2, 41,3,1: the preacher must be a good listener, he must have a loving heart, and he must not be swept away by his passions.

59. These two elements are basics of the Christian faith: ST I–II 100,8; II–II 1,1 and 1,5.

60. Cf. ST III 68,7, where Thomas refers to Rom 6.4. Note also that Thomas explains that not being baptized does not necessarily imply that someone is not saved: the disposition of the soul is decisive (ST III 68,2). In the same way, faith is not required for baptism: it is good to be prepared for it, but, after all, faith is God's gracious gift that comes with the sacrament (ST III 68,8). Since faith can be kindled by the word preached, the preacher has a great responsibility.

61. ST III 39,3.

62. ST I–II 35,8 and II–II 152,3,3. Religious life is the place of penance *par excellence:* II–II 186,1,4.

63. Christ's interpretation of the Law in Mt 5.21–48. The evangelical coun-

(3.2.3) But what's more, some produce an even greater crop: they are not so much converted through a way of penitence, but to the state of perfection through a way of innocence,[64] and they produce a hundred-fold crop. By experience they know that they count to one hundred with the left hand, but with their right hand they already count one hundred. By the left hand the temporal things are understood, by the right hand the spiritual things [cf. Prv 3.16]. Therefore, it is said that the ones that are at the right hand only know spiritual things and nothing about temporal things [cf. Col 3.1–17]. They produce a hundred-fold crop. We read in Gn 26.12 that Isaac sowed in the earth that year and found a hundred-fold.

(ad 3.2.1) In Matthew 4[65] it says: "Thus they make one (*unum*) bear fruit thirty times." A gloss between the lines explains: "faith in the Trinity in the hearts of the chosen ones"; and concerning "one bears fruit sixty times," a gloss between the lines says: "the perfection of a good operation, because the ornamentation of the world is completed in six days"; and about "one bears fruit a hundred times," it says: "a perpetual benediction, because the hundred-fold fruit is transferred from the left hand to the right hand one by one.[66] Likewise it is written in a gloss on Mt 13.8: "thirty refers to marriage; sixty to widows; hundred is someone who is in the right hand already, and the right hand refers to virginity." And it continues: "Or the good earth of the martyrs brings forth a hundred-fold crop, either by their abundance of life or their contempt of death;[67] the good earth of the virgins, a sixty-fold crop, because of the peacefulness of their way,"[68] since they do not fight against the habits of

---

sels are not aimed at destroying, but at fulfilling, the Law, including the Commandments (cf. Mt 5.17); they are aimed at a perfect Christian life; cf. ST I 19,12; I–II 100,2; II–II 44,4,3, and thus they are focused upon in religious life; cf. ST II–II 189,1,5.

64. The innocent is regarded as more perfect than the penitent sinner: ST I 20,4,4.

65. It is in fact Mk 4.20.

66. Thus he/she becomes a spiritual person.

67. Martyrs do not despise their lives; cf. ST II–II 124.

68. So these interpretations of 30, 60, and 100 are not absolute: in one, virginity refers to 100; in another one, to 60.

the flesh, for after service in the army usually peace is given to sexagenarians; "of the ones who are married a thirty-fold crop," because this is the age of the ones who fight. This is a greater combat, for it is fought in order to avoid being overwhelmed by lust.[69]

(ad 3.2.2) Counsels are not given in order to hinder the Commandments; a precept of the Law is for instance that you do not commit perjury [Lv 19.12]. Thus Christ, who advises you not to take an oath [Mt 5.34], causes you to be further away from the possibility of committing perjury.[70] And the same applies to the other ones. Thus the Counsels are safeguards to make sure that the Commandments are kept.

(ad 3.2.3) So, accordingly, someone who is in the state of innocence and pursues the state of perfection, has a hundred-fold fruit. Hence we read in the Gospel according to Matthew 19.29: "Everyone who left behind father or mother," et cetera, "will receive a hundred-fold"—that is, a pile of spiritual goods in the present—"and in the future he will possess eternal life."

May he guide us to this, et cetera.

---

69. In Thomas's view someone who lives in marriage has a greater chance to be swept away by feelings of lust (*libido*) than someone who lives as a religious; for the latter, abstaining from sexual activity becomes a *habitus*, whereas the former is tempted more seriously, because what starts out as making love can end in pure lust (cf. ST I–II 72,2; II–II 154, 170,1,2; also III 27,3).

70. Taking an oath is discussed in ST II–II 89, perjury in II–II 98.

SERMON 10
PETITE ET ACCIPIETIS

*Sermon on the Sunday before the Feast of the Ascension
(authenticity uncertain)*[1]

John 16.24: *Ask, and you will receive, so that your joy may be complete.*

PART 1: *Prothema*

"ASK, AND YOU will receive, so that your joy may be complete" [Jn 16.24]. St. Jerome says that the Lord's Prayer ought to precede all our works, and the working of the graces ought to follow. Hence he says in a letter of his to Paula: "Pray the Lord's Prayer at the beginning of any work of yours and press the sign of the Holy Cross upon your forehead." Likewise: "Just as it does not befit a soldier to go to war without arms, so it does not befit a soldier of Christ to go to war against a demon unless he would be protected by these arms: the Lord's Cross and the Lord's Prayer." And I add to this: the angel's greeting.[2] And hence we will first say an Our Father and a Hail Mary beforehand, et cetera.

---

1. Since there is no parallel either between themes in this sermon and Thomas's commentary on the Gospel according to John or between this sermon and his exegesis of the parallel text Mt 7.7, the *Catena Aurea*, or passages in Thomas's theological works where he speaks about prayer (e.g., ST II–II 83), and since one of the two *reportationes* of this sermon mentions a certain William Brito as the author, it is not very likely that this sermon is Thomas's.

2. The Hail Mary, *Ave Maria;* the second part of the prayer, "Holy Mary, Mother of God, . . . our death," was not part of the prayer in the 13th century; it is a later addition. Cf. Thomas's *Collationes* on the Hail Mary: *Expositio Salutationis angelicae*; and on the Our Father: *In orationem dominicam* and ST II–II 83,9.

PART 2: *Sermo*

"Ask," et cetera. [Jn 16.24]. The Apostle says in Rom 12.12 that quite often we do not know what we ought to ask. Therefore, our Advocate, Jesus Christ, of whom John says in his letter [1 Jn 2:1–2] that "we have an advocate with the Father, Jesus Christ, and he is the atonement for our sins," this Advocate invites us today to pray, and he promises to give to us, yes, he even swears to give to us, provided that we ask in the name of the Savior the things that are necessary for our salvation. Thus at the beginning of today's Gospel this Advocate of ours invites us to ask and teaches us to formulate our petition, saying: "Very truly, I tell you, if you ask the Father for something in my name, he will give (it) to you" [Jn 16.23].[3]

Accordingly he touches in these words upon three things. (1) First, the Lord invites us to pray: "Ask." (2) Second, he assures us about our obtaining: "and you will receive." (3) And third, so that we may rightly ask, he underlines what is necessary for us to have, when he adds: "So that your joy may be complete." For elsewhere it is said: "To every one who has, it will be given, abundantly even" [Mt 25.29]; and elsewhere, in Lk 11.9:[4] "Ask and you will receive, seek and you will find, knock and it will be opened for you." "Ask" with confidence; "and you will receive" the gift of prosperity by which the body is upheld; "seek" carefully; and "you will find" the good of grace by which the soul is refreshed; "knock" ceaselessly, and the door of paradise "will be opened" for you, so that your heart may be filled with "joy."

❖

(1) So first, the Lord invites us in these words to ask; in this we see the highest courtesy of him who so courteously invites us to ask. There are four things that really ought to move us to ask: (1.1) first, our poverty and want; (1.2) second, the greatest generosity of Christ; (1.3) third, the favorable time for asking; (1.4) fourth, the surety of obtaining.

1.1 I say that the first thing that ought to move us to ask is

---

3. Cf. Thomas's discussion of this verse in ST II–II 83,7,2.
4. Cf. Thomas's discussion of Mt 7.7 in ST II–II 83,3,2.

our poverty and want. For we have nothing good from ourselves, but from God. The Apostle says in Romans: "What do you have," that is, what good do you have, "that you have not received? If you received, why do you boast as if you did not receive it?" [1 Cor 4.7] A sinner has nothing from himself but his sin, and someone who is in the state of mortal sin loses everything good that he has done, because, as Jas 2.10 says: "If someone has served the whole Law, yet offends against one, he has become the transgressor against all." Someone who offends God by transgressing a mandate of his will be condemned for this one sin as he would be condemned for all sins; yet he will not be punished as he would be punished for very many sins. Or, someone who offends against one, the distributor of all goods, Christ, is made the transgressor against all, meaning: he will undergo the suffering for all evils. Or someone who offends against one thing, namely, the precept of love (*caritas*), is made the transgressor against all other virtues, because love (*caritas*) is the mother of all virtues; just as someone who offends the *paterfamilias* consequently offends the whole family. Hence, a sinner who lies down in many mortal sins is in a great misery, because he does not know his defects. John says this plainly in Rv 3.17 in respect of a sinner: "You say: 'I am rich and wealthy, and I do not lack anything,' but you do not know that you are wretched: miserable as well as poor and blind and nude." "You say: 'I am rich'" in knowledge, "'wealthy'" in riches; "'I do not lack anything,'" for I am healthy and strong; "but you do not know that you are wretched" because you commit sins, "miserable" because you have been robbed of the virtues, "poor" because you lost the grace of God, "blind" because you do not know, "naked" because of a bad reputation. Mortal sin causes all these evils, for "sin makes peoples wretched" [Prv 14.34]. Hence, first our poverty and want should move us to ask. These are so big, because we do not have anything good from ourselves. Indeed, we only have our sins and defects of ourselves, and each and every good that we have we have from God.

(1.2) The second thing that ought to move us to ask is the greatest generosity of Christ. For he himself is the most bountiful distributor of all goods. He is prefigured as such by King

Ahasuerus, who has said to Queen Esther: "What is your petition, Esther? If you asked me for half my kingdom, I would give it to you" [Est 5.3]. Yet he does not give a part of his kingdom to his friends, but the whole of his kingdom [cf. Mt 5.3, 25.34]. The former reigned over 120 provinces, the latter reigns over the whole world. Therefore, more than Ahasuerus, he is someone who gives (a) with courtesy, (b) to all people, (c) abundantly. These three characteristics are also mentioned by James in his letter: "He gives to all abundantly and does not reproach" [Jas 1.5]. He does not sell; "he gives": behold courtesy. "To all": behold abundance. "And he does not reproach": behold his generosity.

His gift is not the gift of a fool, about which we read in Proverbs: "The gift of a fool will not be useful for you; he will give to you and reproach you" [Sir 20.14]. This popular dictum has no place there: "*à bon demandeur, bon refuseur*,"[5] but rather: a good requester finds a bountiful giver.[6] For, "every very good present and every perfect gift" [Jas 1.17] is from him. A good present is the good of prosperity like riches; a better gift is a gift of nature, like physical strength or health; the best is the gift of grace, like the virtues; the perfect gift is the gift of glory. He gives all these gifts.

He is more ready to give than we are to receive. And so, because his generosity is so great, a complaint is made about those who do not want to ask, because it is St. Gregory who says: "He does not deny that he himself is a debtor who goes to meet those who ask him to give a lot, knowing that we need a lot." He also says: "Human laziness blushes with shame, because God is more willing to give than we are to receive; he is more willing to show mercy than we are to be liberated from misery."[7]

(1.3) The third thing which ought to move us to ask is the favorable time [cf. 2 Cor 6.2]. Someone who has to do something in the palace of a prince serves in a favorable time when the

---

5. *A bon demandeeur, bon escondeeur:* "You may well ask; it may well be refused." Or in Dutch: *Kinderen die vragen worden overgeslagen;* i.e., "Children who ask will not receive."

6. *Ad bonum petitorem largissimum datorem.*

7. Thomas's view of misery (*miseria*): ST I 21,4 and II–II 30,1.

lord is joyful and the family is joyful. Likewise, the time to ask is favorable now, since our Lord Jesus Christ goes to the heavenly palace with the representation of our flesh, [to ask the Father on our behalf]. So, now are the *dies Rogationum*, ["the days for asking,"] during which the Lord wants us to ask him, because, after he has ascended into heaven, the angelic citizens and all the heavenly nobles rejoice. And so, since the time is favorable now, because on Thursday Christ enters heaven to ask the Father on our behalf, let us ask him now. Let us neither anticipate with the gourmand, who was late asking for a drop of water and who did not obtain it [cf. Lk 16.24], nor let us anticipate with the foolish virgins for whom the door was closed [Mt 25.10–11], but let us in the name of Christ the Savior ask the things that are necessary for our salvation, and we will obtain it. Hence it says in today's Gospel: "Until now you have not asked anything in my name. Ask and you will receive" [Jn 16.24].

(1.4) The fourth thing is the surety of obtaining it, and this follows from three things mentioned before: by reason of our great poverty and want, God's greatest generosity, and the favorable time for asking, we can be sure that we will obtain it. Thus John says in his letter: "And this is the trust we have in the Father, that whenever we ask, he will hear us" [cf. 1 Jn 3.22]. This is true if we ask for the things that are necessary for our salvation.

It is true that nowadays people are lazy with respect to asking God and praying; therefore, two things in particular ought to move us to pray: (1.4.1) the preciousness of prayer and (1.4.2) our necessity.

(1.4.2) Its preciousness, because, although these three, fasting, almsgiving, and prayer, ordain us to have eternal life, prayer is the most worthy one, since fasting and almsgiving have to do with what is next to us, whereas prayer has to do with what is above us. So it is more worthy, because a person[8] approaches God as someone familiar, and there he fulfills the command, where the flesh cannot arrive.

(1.4.2) The necessity to pray is clear because of three reasons why people cry out: fire, water, and robbers. The fire of lust-

8. Cf. Sermon 05 *Ecce rex tuus*, note 3.

fulness attacks us; the water of avarice troubles us; the infernal robber and his henchmen disquiet us. And therefore, because in the present we have so many assailants, we ought to direct prayers to God more often, so that he may hear us in the present by his grace, and in the future grant us eternal life.

PART 3: *Collatio in sero*

"Ask, and you will receive" [Jn 16.24]. In the first sermon it was mentioned what those things are that move us to pray, for, as was said, there are four: our necessity, Christ's generosity, the favorable time, and the surety of obtaining it.[9]

It is true that there are many hindrances because of which our prayer is frustrated. Therefore, we can put forward seven hindrances in this homily, by reason of which our asking is frustrated and our prayer is not heard by God.[10] The first hindrance is due to the indiscretion of the asking; the second is due to the doubt of the one who asks; the third is due to the uncleanness and the unworthiness of the petitioner; the fourth is due to hypocrisy and feigning; the fifth is due to hatred and rancor; the sixth is due to harshness towards the neighbor; and the seventh is due to contempt of the divine law and disobedience.

(1) So the first hindrance is due to the indiscretion of the asking. James says about this: "You ask but do not receive, because you ask in an evil way" [Jas 4.3],[11] that is, indiscreetly, as the mother of John and James did: she asked God that one of her sons would sit at his right hand and the other at his left hand in his Kingdom. To them the Lord responds: "You do not know what you are asking. Can you drink the cup that I will drink?" [Mt 20.22], meaning: suffer a passion similar to that which I will undergo. "We can," they said. And the Lord: "You will drink my cup, yet sitting at my right or left is not mine to give you"

---

9. This is the only connection with the *Sermo*; the steps announced there are not taken in the *Collatio in sero*. It seems that a completely different *Collatio in sero* is added to the *Sermo*.

10. Some of these are also discussed by Thomas, in SCG III 95–96, but there in the context of the friendship between God and us (*amicitia*).

11. Cf. in contrast Thomas's discussion of this verse in ST II–II 83,5,1.

[Mt 20.22–23; Mk 10.40]. A gloss adds: "without preceding merits." Augustine speaks against those who ask for worldly honor as follows: "When you ask for the things that God praises and promises to give, ask him with confidence, because God grants those things to us. Yet if you ask for temporal things,[12] ask with discretion, for God knows better than man whether things are good or bad for us." Still, many ask God more freely for temporal than for eternal goods. All such people ask in an indiscreet way, because it does not befit God to give such a small gift, just as it does not befit the king of France to give a dime. Or God prefers not to listen to such people, because what they ask for is not salutary for them, just as he did not listen to Paul [asking to be delivered from] the stimulus of the flesh [cf. 2 Cor 12.7], and just as he does not listen to boys in schools asking that they not be flogged, because it is of no avail to them.

(2) The second hindrance why someone is not heard is his doubt. Against them James says: "Let him ask in faith, not hesitant about anything. For someone who hesitates is like a wave of the sea that is moved by the wind" [Jas 1.6].[13] And he adds: "Therefore, that person should not think that he receives anything from God" [Jas 1.7]. Gregory says: "Someone is made unworthy of a heavenly blessing who asks the Lord in doubt to bring about something." And this is what John says in his letter: "All things, whatever you may ask" in faith, "believe that you receive them" [Mk 11.24].

(3) The third hindrance is the unworthiness of the one who asks and his uncleanness. About this, Is 1.15 says: "When you have multiplied your prayers, I will not hear you." Then he gives the reason: "for your hands," that is, your works, "are full of blood" [ibid.], meaning: sins. And in Lam 3.42 we read: "We have acted unjustly and have brought about your rage; for that reason you are inexorable." Against such people it says in Ps 66.18: "If" I have "iniquity in my heart, the Lord will not hear." A gloss there says: "Purity of prayer is heard by God." A prayer is pure which is not disturbed by worries of worldly things, by love (*amor*) of the flesh. The mind is far away from God when it

12. Cf. ST II–II 83,6.
13. Cf. Thomas's discussion of this verse in ST II–II 83,15,3.

is occupied with worldly worries and dedicated to the desires of the flesh. Therefore, the mind must first be purified from the worldly worries and separated from the desires of the flesh first, so that the attention of the mind may be directed to God. This is clear through a visible example: the Bishop of Paris would not give the allowances (*prebendae*) of his church to unclean people, villains, and those who openly charge interest [cf. Lv 25.36–37]; likewise, the heavenly High Priest will not give the allowances of his glory to such people.

(4) The fourth hindrance why someone's asking is frustrated is hypocrisy and feigning. For a hypocrite shouts with his mouth, but is silent in his heart. Is 29.13[14] says, referring to such a person: "This people praises me with the lips, but their heart is far from me." Gregory says: "If we seek eternal life with our mouth but do not desire it with our heart, we are silent as we shout." Hence, aiming at a hypocrite the commonly known saying goes: "A hypocrite cries out when the tribulation of temporal things frightens him; God does not hear him in this favorable time, because he has not heard the cry of the Lord in the time of peace."[15]

(5) The fifth hindrance[16] is due to hatred of the heart and rancor. In Sir 28.3 we read: "A man maintains anger against another man and asks help from God." No one receives a favor from God unless he lets go of his rancor against his brother or his neighbor. We find in the Gospel the example of a wretched slave to whom his lord says: "'Wretched slave, I have forgiven you every debt, because you asked me; should you then not have had mercy upon your fellow slave, just as I have had mercy upon you?' And he ordered that he would be handed over to be tortured, until he would have paid back the entire debt." And the Evangelist concludes: "In the same way my Father in heaven will do with you, if each one of you does not forgive from your hearts" [Mt 18.32–35]. This is the bond that the Lord has made with us: "Forgive, and you will be forgiven" [Mt 6.14]; otherwise, he will

---

14. Cf. Thomas's discussion of this verse in ST II–II 91,1,1.
15. St. Gregory: *Moralia in Job* 18,8,15.
16. Cf. ST II–II 83,16 (esp. arg./ad 3, where he discusses Sir 28.2 and Mt 6.12).

not forgive you. Thus one says in vain in the Lord's Prayer: "Forgive us (our debts as we forgive our debtors)" [Mt 6.12].

(6) The sixth hindrance is due to the harshness towards the neighbor: there are many rich people who have so many of the goods of this world but do not want to come to the aid of the poor of Christ at all. Because such people do not practice mercy for the poor, they will not find mercy from God in the future, just like the rich gourmand in hell who did not obtain one drop of water, because he had denied one crumb of bread to the poor Lazarus [Lk 16.19–26].

(7) The seventh and last hindrance is due to contempt of the divine Law and disobedience. In Sirach we read: "Someone who closes his ear in order not to hear the Law, his prayer will be detestable" [Prv 28.9],[17] meaning: it will not be heard in the chapel of the heavenly court, just as a servant of someone who is excommunicated may not be heard in the court of one or another worldly judge.

On top of these seven, note that in order to obtain, it is important for man above all to remember how fragile he is himself and to consider how good God is. Thus Isidore says: "When we stand before God to pray, we ought to mourn and shed tears, calling to mind how many and serious the sins are that we have committed, how cruel the tortures of hell are that we fear, and how incomparable the joys in heaven are to which we look forward." Robbers and plague-sufferers teach us how to pray.[18] The robber who saw what he had done and the torture that was prepared for him asked in between these two with many tears for mercy [Lk 23.42]. Plague-sufferers show the weaker and unsightly members of their body to others and hide the healthy ones, in order to move others to compassionate devotion and the giving of alms.

Likewise, let us show to God in the present our weaknesses and our sins, so that he may hear us in the present through his grace and bring us eternal life in the future. Amen.

17. Cf. ST II–II 83,16 (esp. arg./ad 1).
18. These examples are from William of Alvernia's *Rhetorica divina*, chapter 32.

SERMON 11
EMITTE SPIRITUM

Sermon on Pentecost

Psalm 104.30: *Send out your Spirit, and they will be created, and you will renew the face of the earth.*

PART 1: *Prothema*

"SEND OUT your Spirit, and they will be created, and you will renew the face of the earth" [Ps 104.30]. On this Psalm. We must speak about him without whom no one can speak what is right and who can make or makes everyone speak abundantly. Indeed, without him we cannot correctly speak. So it is not surprising that it is said in Wis 9.17: "Who could have known the sense," of God's truth, "unless he had sent his Spirit from on high?" Without a sense of the truth no one could speak what is true.[1] Again, the Holy Spirit enables all to speak abundantly [cf. 1 Cor 12.3]. Therefore, Gregory says: "He makes wise those whom he has filled." Today this is evident, as the apostles "were filled with the Holy Spirit and began to speak in various tongues" [Acts 2.4]. Therefore, we will ask this One, who even makes the mute speak abundantly [cf. Is 35.6; Mt 9.32–33], that he may give me to speak, et cetera.

PART 2: *Sermo*

"Send out your Spirit, and they will be created" [Ps 104.30], et cetera. Today Holy Mother Church solemnly celebrates

1. In order to know the truth concerning natural things, grace is not necessary, but it is concerning things that exceed nature: ST I–II 109,1.

the mission of the Holy Spirit that occurred among the apostles, the mission that was besought in a prophetic spirit by the Prophet, saying: "Send out your Spirit, and they will be created," et cetera. We can consider four things in these words, namely, (1) the property of the Holy Spirit, (2) his mission, (3) the strength of the One sent, and (4) the receptive *materia* of this strength. For it says: "Send out"—behold, the mission (2); "your Spirit"—see, the Person sent (1); "and they will be created, and you will renew"—lo, the effect of the One sent (3); "the face of the earth"—see, the receptive *materia* of this effect (4).[2]

(1.) First, I say, the property of the Holy Spirit is mentioned when he says: "your Spirit." Here we must notice that the name "spirit" seems to imply four things: (1.1) the fineness of substance, (1.2) the perfection of life, (1.3) the incitement of a movement, and (1.4) his hidden origin.

(1.1) First, I say that the name "spirit" seems to imply the fineness of substance.[3] For we usually call substances without a body "spirits." Likewise, we call fine bodies, like air and fire, "spirits." Hence [the risen Christ] says, in the last chapter of Luke: "Touch and see," because "a spirit does not have flesh and bones" [Lk 24.39].[4] And in this way a spirit is distinct from things that have a coarse *materia*, those that are composed of flesh and a body.

(1.2) Second, the name "spirit" seems to imply the perfection of life. Because as long as animated creatures have a spirit, they live, but when their spirit recedes, they perish.[5] As the Psalmist says: "You will take away their spirit, and they will cease to be" [Ps 146.4], et cetera. And in Genesis: he called forth "the spirit of life (in) all the flesh."[6]

---

2. Thus the structure of the sermon is that of Aristotle's four causes: respectively, the formal (who the Spirit is), the final (why he acts), the effective (that he acts), and the material (the object).

3. Or: the word "spirit" signifies an essential fineness; cf. ST I 3,5,1; also *On the Metaphysica of Aristotle*, Book VII, *lectio* II (nn.1270–1305).

4. The resurrected Christ had a true body: ST III 54,1.

5. The *anima* is the life-giving principle of the body: ST I 18,3,2, 70,3,2.

6. This quotation is from a liturgical book called *Historia de Noe*, "The History of Noah," from the section on Gn 7.4–8.

(1.3) Third, the name "spirit" seems to imply the incitement of a movement.[7] In this way we call the winds "spirits" [cf. Acts 2.2]. And concerning this it is said in Ps 107.25: "He spoke, and a spirit of a storm came about"; [Ps 10.7 (Vg)] "a spirit of storms (will be) the portion of their cup." We also say that people act in a spirit when they do something impulsively, as Is 25.4 does: "The spirit of the strong is like a hurricane that pushes over a wall."[8]

(1.4) Fourth, the name "spirit" usually means a hidden origin, just as it is attributed to a spirit when someone is disturbed but does not know what is disturbing him. Thus we read in Jn 3.8: "The Spirit (is like the wind: it) blows where it wills and you hear its sound, but you do not know (where it is coming from)."

Let us inquire, with regard to these four [implications of his name], about the properties of the Holy Spirit, in reverse order: he is called Holy Spirit because of his hidden origin, the incitement of the movement, the holiness of life, and the fineness of substance.

⁂

(ad 1.4) First, I say that a property of the Holy Spirit is his hidden origin. Faith teaches and reason argues that all visible and changeable things have a hidden cause [cf. Col 1.15–16, Heb 11.3]. What is that cause? That cause is God. Thus the Apostle says: "The one who has created all things is God" [Eph 3.9]. It is certain that everything that is not God is created by God.[9]

But how has God created all things? I say that he did not do it by reason of a natural necessity, just as fire completely consumes, but that he has brought forth all things of his own free will, as the Psalmist says: "All things he has made, whatever he willed" [Ps 115.3].[10] A house-builder builds a house because he wants to and yet at the same time because necessity or utility urges him, for instance, in order to make money or to live in

---

7. Cf. ST I 27,4, 36,1.
8. As in English: "He burst in," and, "In a burst of anger she told him what was bothering her/she hit him," etc.
9. ST I 44: God is the first cause of all that is.
10. Cf. Rv 4.11; there is no necessity in God: ST I 19,3.

the house. God truly did not make the world because he wanted to gain something, since he is not in need of our goods.[11] Why then did he make the world? Certainly out of his loving will, not out of cupidity. We have an example of this: a housebuilder who would know how to design a house while he does not stand in need of it but loves (*amo*)[12] the beauty of a house—that love (*amor*) of the house-builder would bring the house into being.

But what, then, is the cause and the root of bringing forth hidden things? For sure, it is love (*amor*). Thus it says in Wis 11.24: "You love (*diligo*) all things that are, and you hate nothing of the things which you have made." And St. Dionysius says that "divine love (*amor*) has not sent forth itself in order to be without offspring." Love (*amor*) is the Holy Spirit.[13] Hence it is said at the beginning of creation in Genesis that "the Spirit of the Lord glided over the waters" [Gn 1.2], namely, in order to make the *materia* and to bring things forth into being.

We celebrate now the feast of the Holy Spirit, and the Spirit is the principle of being in all things. Thus the Spirit has a hidden origin, the property of which is love (*amor*).

(ad 1.3) Second, "Holy Spirit" implies the incitement of a movement. For we see in the world different movements, natural and voluntary ones, in people and in angels. Where do these different movements come from? They must come from one first mover,[14] evidently from God. The Psalmist says: "You will change them, and they will be changed" [Ps 102.27]. And God moves by his will.

But what is the first movement of the will? For certain it is love (*amor*).[15] And what is the operation of love (*amor*)? I say: someone who is moved by love (*amor*) rejoices through the love (*amor*) for a loved (*amatus*) thing and is saddened about what

---

11. *Deus uero fecit mundum non uoluntate cupiditatis quia bonis nostris non eget*: Ex 9.29, 19.5; Dt 10.14 (in ST I 61,4); 2 Sm 7.5, 11; Jb 41.2, Vg (in SCG II 28); Ps 50.8–13, 89.12; 1 Cor 10.26.

12. For Thomas's terminology, see Sermon 01 *Veniet desideratus*, note 39.

13. Love is the proper name of the Spirit (appropriation): ST I 37,1; also 74,3,3; I–II 70,3; II–II 14,1.

14. Because no thing moves by itself: ST I 2,3 (*prima via*).

15. In God as well as in creatures: ST I 20,1; I–II 25,2.

is contrary to it. Thus we read in the prophet Ezekiel, the first chapter: "Where the incitement of the Spirit was," that is, the inclination of divine love (*amor*), "that is whither they will be brought" [Ezek 1.12]. Yes, in a just way all things that are in the world are moved by the Holy Spirit, which is indicated by Est 13.9 (Vg), where it says: "There is no one who could resist (his) will."[16] This Holy Spirit, whose feast we celebrate now, is the principle of the movement of all things.[17]

Nevertheless, some things are moved in the world by themselves, and others by others. They who have life are moved by themselves, whereas the things that lack life are moved by others. The principle of the movement of all things is alive. Even more: it *is* life.[18] Hence, the Holy Spirit is life, insofar as he is the principle of the movement of all things. As the Psalmist says: "With you is the fountain of life" [Ps 36.10]. And since he is life, he is, therefore, the Giver of life.[19]

Great is the Holy Spirit, therefore, by whom all things that exist are moved and live. Thus we read in Acts 17.28: "In him we live and move and are." So all things have their movement and being from the Holy Spirit.

(ad 1.1) Third, if we consider, concerning the Holy Spirit, the fineness (*subtilitas*) of substance, we will see that the Holy Spirit is love (*amor*). And whose? It is the love of God and of the One who loves (*diligo*) God.[20] On the basis of this understanding of love (*amor*), the Holy Spirit has a fineness of substance.

And from the angle of the beloved, he is the love through which God loves God and the Father loves the Son.[21] Hence we read in Wis 7.22: "For in her," that is, God's wisdom, "is the spirit of understanding," which makes people understand.[22]

---

16. Not because we are forced, but because we are inspired: ST II–II 24,2; our natural inclination towards what is good is strengthened by (the movement of) the Spirit: ST I 83,1 and the Scriptural references there; also I 105,4; I–II 9,6.

17. ST I–II 109,9,2; II–II 1,8,5.

18. ST I 10,1 and 18,3–4.

19. As we profess in the Creed: *vivificantem*, the Giver of life; cf. the quotation from Ps 143.10–11, just before section (2).

20. An obvious circumscription of Jesus Christ; cf. Jn 14.31.

21. *Amatus, amor, amo*; on the relations *in divinis*: ST I 28.

22. Cf. ST I 14,4. Just as love is appropriated to the Spirit, knowledge and

In Greek the word "holy" [Wis 7.22] signifies cleanness.[23] It is true that the love (*amor*) through which a person loves (*diligo*) corporeal things is unclean or foul: for through love (*amor*) the lover (*amans*) is united with the beloved thing (*amatus*), and the more the lover is mingled with the beloved thing, the more he collects foulness. Just as silver, if it is mixed with something impure, collects foulness [cf. Prv 25.4], so your mind [is defiled] if it is mixed with love (*amor*) for lower things. But when it is connected with the highest thing, it is called holy love.[24]

There are some who want to be dedicated to God and who pay no heed to the salvation of their neighbors.[25] But the Holy Spirit is not like that [Wis 7.23]. The Apostle Paul was seriously concerned about the salvation of his neighbors, whence he said: "I have been made all things for all people in order to enlighten all" [1 Cor 9.22].

Furthermore, some others are many-sided yet deceitful. The Holy Spirit is not like that. He is multiple [Jb 11.6, Wis 7.22] in such a way that he who is one [Wis 7.22] shows himself to different people.

Furthermore, he is fine[26] [Wis 7.22], because he makes a person draw back from coarse things and cling to God, as the Psalmist says: "One thing I have desired of the Lord" [Ps 27.4] and elsewhere: "Yet clinging to God is my good" [Ps 73.28].

(ad 1.2) Fourth, this Holy Spirit not only gives us that we are, live, and move, but even more: he makes us holy [Wis 7.24–27]. Therefore, the Apostle says in Rom 1.4: "God has predestined in strength according to the Spirit of sanctification." No one is holy unless the Holy Spirit sanctifies him.[27]

---

understanding are appropriated to the Son: ST I 34,1,2, 39,7; the Spirit proceeds from the Father and the Son: ST I 36,2.

23. ἅγιος [*hagios*]: consecrated, cleansed, clean, holy, reverent, etc.

24. *Amor sanctus*. Thus this love is called "holy" in an analogical way: ST I 13,5–6; the highest thing is the Holy One.

25. Cf. ST II–II 167,2,3; The love for our neighbors is founded in God; Thomas underlines the necessity for those who love God of being in solidarity with their fellow human beings: ST II–II 19,6, 32,3, 44,2, 105,2 (cf. Mt 22.39), and 18.43.

26. Or "subtle"; Lat., *subtilis*.

27. ST I 36,1,1, 43,3; III 2,10, 62,6,2.

And how does he sanctify? I say that he makes every single thing mentioned appear in those whom he sanctifies,[28] because he turns the ones he sanctifies into refined people and makes them despise temporal things. Thus it says in John: "Do not love (*diligo*) the world nor the things that are in the world. If someone loves (*diligo*) the world, the love (*caritas*) of the Father is not in him" [1 Jn 2.15].

Furthermore, he bestows the spiritual life on the ones whom he sanctifies. Thus we read in Ezek 37.5: "Behold, I will send the Spirit into you and you will live." Spiritual life is life through the Holy Spirit.[29] The Apostle [impresses on us]: "If you live by the Spirit, walk also by the Spirit" [Gal 5.25].

Again, the Holy Spirit moves those whom he sanctifies through his incitement to do good.[30] Isaiah testifies: "Because he comes like a wild river, driven by the Spirit of the Lord [Is 59.19].

Others are lazy;[31] they do not seem to be set in motion by the Holy Spirit. Thus a gloss on Acts 2.2: "Suddenly a sound came from heaven," et cetera, says: "The grace of the Holy Spirit does not know late undertakings."

And the Holy Spirit sanctifies you: he leads us back to the hidden origin, that we may be united with God. Therefore, Isaiah says: "The Spirit of the Lord will carry you off to a place you do not know,"[32] meaning: to the heavenly inheritance. The Psalmist says: "Your good Spirit will lead me away (in a land with straight paths; because of your name you will give me life; in your justice you will lead me away from my fear)" [Ps 143.10–11].

Now it is clear that this is the property of the Holy Spirit and that he is the origin of living, being, and moving [cf. Acts 17.28].

---

28. Gal 5.22–23: the fruits of the Spirit; ST I–II 70, esp. 70,3,1.

29. SCG IV 20–22.

30. By inspiration, not by coercion: ST I 83,1,3.

31. Which is a kind of fear that paralyzes, ST I–II 44,4,3 (cf. the quotation of Ps 143.10–11 at the end of this section of the text); Thomas connects it with the attitude of negligence in II–II 54,2,1.

32. It is in fact King Ahab's vizier Obadiah who speaks these words to the prophet Elijah, in 1 Kgs 18.12.

SERMON 11

(2) Let us look at the second aspect: the mission of the Holy Spirit, which is wondrous and unknown to us, because the Holy Spirit is sent (2.1) without a need for his part, (2.2) without a change in him, (2.3) without subjection, and (2.4) without separation.

(2.1) First, I say: the Holy Spirit was sent while there was no necessity for him [to be sent]. When someone is sent to a certain place so that some things happen which cannot happen unless he is sent, it is a mission out of necessity. But there is no necessity in the mission of the Holy Spirit, as we read in Wis 7.23: "He has every strength, oversees all things."

What then is the reason for the mission of the Holy Spirit? I say: *our* want.[33] The necessity of this want is partly because of the dignity of our human nature and partly because of the defect of it. For the rational creature surpasses the other creatures because it can stretch out to the enjoyment of God, something no other creature is capable of.[34] Thus we read in Lam 3.24: "'My portion,' he has said, 'is the Lord of my soul.'" Some seek their portion in the world, like honors, esteem. But the Psalmist says: "Clinging to God is my good" [Ps 73.28].

You should realize that it is necessary that all things that are moved to a certain end have something that moves them to that end. The things that are moved to a natural end are moved by something in nature, whereas things that are moved to a supernatural end, namely, the enjoyment of God, must have a supernatural mover.[35] Well, nothing can lead us to this but two, for by these two things a person is led to this end: by knowledge and by love.[36]

Such a knowledge is supernatural. Thus we read in 1 Cor 2.9: "Eye has not seen, ear has not heard, nor did it come up in the heart of man (what God has prepared for those who love [*diligo*] him)."[37] And in Is 64.3: "Never have they heard, neither did

---

33. Cf. ST I 43,3 and I–II 111,1; also 113.
34. Cf. ST I–II 1,2ff.   35. Cf. ST I–II 5,5 and 112,1.
36. *Amor;* see note 21.
37. St. Paul says this in the context of the mystery of Christ's life and death (1 Cor 1.18–2.8); he continues saying that it is revealed to us through the Spirit (1 Cor 2.10–13); cf. ST I 12,13 and II–II 45.

they perceive it with their ears, nor has an eye seen without you, God, the things you have prepared for those who awaited (them)."[38] Everything man knows he knows either because he finds out or because he learns it. For sight serves the finding, and hearing serves the learning. Because of this it is said that "eye has not seen and ear has not heard," by showing that it transcends human knowledge. It even exceeds the human desire, and that is why it is said: "Nor did it come up in the heart of man."[39]

So how is man led into the knowledge of him? It could not be otherwise than that the heavenly secrets were made known to man, that is, that the Holy Spirit would be sent visibly[40] in order to move our affections so as to direct them toward those [heavenly secrets]. Therefore, it says: "Eye has not seen." So, how do we know? "God has revealed them to us through his Spirit. For the Spirit examines everything thoroughly, even the profound things of God" [1 Cor 2.10]. Hence we read in Wis 9.17: "Who will be able to know your thoughts unless you gave wisdom and sent the Holy Spirit from the highest heavens?"

Thus the Holy Spirit is not sent because of necessity on his part, but for our benefit.

(2.2) Furthermore, this mission happens without a change in him.[41] When a messenger is sent from place to place, it is with a change. But the Holy Spirit is sent without a change of place, since he is the true God and unchangeable.[42] Thus it is said in Wis 7.27: "Remaining in himself, he renews all things."

How, then, is he sent? He draws us to himself, and this is called being sent only in the sense in which we say that the sun is sent to someone when that person stands in the sunlight.

---

38. Hence it is necessary to have another doctrine than philosophy for the sake of our salvation: ST I 1,1.

39. We cannot desire what we do not know at all: ST I 27,3,3, 36,2, 75,6; I–II 27,4,2 (cf. I 20,1); quoting Augustine: *Nihil amatum nisi cognitum*, in: ST I 60,1; I–II 3,4,4, 27,2; II–II 27,4,1.

40. *Visibiliter* (Kwasniewski, however, reads *inuisibiliter:* "in an invisible way"); this happens when Christ is baptized: Mt 3.16 (cf. ST I 43,7); and at Pentecost: Acts 2.3 (ST III 66,3,1).

41. ST I 43,1.

42. ST I 9, because God is one (ST I 3) and eternal (ST I 10,1–4).

Thus it is with the Holy Spirit.[43] So it is said concerning uncreated wisdom, in Wis 9.10: "Send her out from the heavens and from the throne of your greatness, so that she may be with me (and work with me and so that I may know what is pleasing to you)." Likewise, in Gal 4.6: "He sent his Spirit, who calls: 'Abba, Father.'"

These missions spread throughout all nations and enter holy souls [cf. Wis 7.27]. When the fullness of time had come, the Son of God was sent into the flesh,[44] and thus it was right that also the Holy Spirit would be sent visibly, not, however, that he would be received in the unity of a person[45] as the Son in the human nature.

(2.3) Furthermore, the Holy Spirit is sent although he is not subjected.[46] Slaves and servants are sent by their masters, since they are subjected to them. Hence some heretics believed that the Son and the Holy Spirit would be lesser than the Father, since they are sent by the Father. This, however, is not true. The Holy Spirit sets people free [cf. Gal 4.5]; hence he is not a servant; he is sent out by reason of his own decision, for "the Spirit blows where he wills" [Jn 3.8]; and the term "being sent" is used merely because the Father is the originator (*auctoritas*).[47]

We find places where it says that the Holy Spirit is sent by the Father, while elsewhere it says that he is sent by the Son. But the Greeks[48] oppose strongly in this matter, for they hold that the Holy Spirit proceeds from the Father only, not from the Son, and they argue in an unrefined way. Unrefined, for where the Son speaks about the mission of the Holy Spirit, he connects the Son with the Father or the Father with the Son: for instance, in John 15, he says: "The Paraclete, whom the Fa-

---

43. ST I 9,1,2. Hence we share, participate, in it, but do not have it to the full, as the one who has it by essence: I 44,1, 84,4,1.

44. As Paul says in Gal 4.4; cf. ST I 43,5 (on the invisible mission of the Son).

45. But in our heart: cf. Gal 4.6.

46. ST I 43,1,1; cf. SCG IV 16–18 and 24–25.

47. The word "father" implies origin; therefore, we never read that the Father was sent; cf. ST I 43,4.

48. Thomas refers to the Orthodox Church: this issue (the *Filioque* controversy) was a reason for the Eastern Schism in the year 1054.

ther will send in my name" [Jn 14.26] and in another place: "When the Paraclete comes, whom I will send to you from the Father" [Jn 15.26]. Thus the origination of the source comes from the Father.[49]

(2.4) Furthermore, the Holy Spirit is sent without separation,[50] since the Spirit of unity is [naturally] opposed to separation. Hence the Apostle says: "Exert yourselves to serve the unity of the Spirit in a bond of peace" [Eph 4.3]. The Holy Spirit gathers together according to Ephesians 4. Thus also Jn 17.22 says: "That they may be one" in us, through the unity of the Holy Spirit, "just as we, too, are one."[51]

This union is begun in our time through grace, and will be completed in the future through glory,

to which may he lead us, et cetera.

PART 3: *Collatio in sero*

"Send out your Spirit" [Ps 104.30], et cetera. Early in the morning today we have said some things in keeping with the measure of our understanding about the property of the Holy Spirit and his mission. Now it remains to speak about (3) the effects of the Holy Spirit and (4) whom or what it befits to receive these effects.

(3) In the words cited above we are given to understand the twofold effect of the Holy Spirit, namely, (3.1) creation and (3.2) renewal, where it says, "and they will be created and you will renew."

(3.1) If we truly want to accept these words in the sense that creation means bringing forth things into the existence of nature,[52] the Spirit is indeed the Creator of all things, in keeping with what is touched upon in Jdt 16.14: "You sent your Spirit, and they were created."

---

49. For Thomas Scripture is the key to a solution in this matter. The Son is the *origo de origine* (cf. the Creed: *Deum de Deo, Lumen de Lumine, Deum verum de Deo vero*); cf. ST I 32,3, 33,1, 36,2–4.
50. ST I 43,1,2.   51. ST II–II 183,2,3.
52. ST I 45, 46,2,2.

SERMON 11

Let us speak now of another creation. It is commonly understood nowadays that those who are promoted to a higher state, such as the episcopate or another dignity, are said to be "created."[53] In the same way all those who are promoted and made sons and daughters of God are said to be created, as if they were promoted, as St. James says: "(By his free will he brought us forth,) so that we may be the beginning of his creation" [Jas 1.18]. The Lord willed to establish a new creation, as we also read in Wis 1.14: God "created so that all things would be," namely, in the existence of nature; and he willed to re-create them, namely, so that they would be in the existence of grace. The apostles were the first-fruits of this re-creation. We read about this creation in Gal 6.15: In Christ Jesus "neither circumcision nor the foreskin is of value, but the new creation." What does this saying mean? Previously there were gentiles, and with reference to this it says "foreskin." Later on the Jews were circumcised. Still this situation of being circumcised was of no value unless they would be re-created through the grace of Christ.[54] This re-creation is an effect of the Holy Spirit.

You should know that this re-creation consists in phases: (3.1.1) first, concerning the grace of love (*caritas*); (3.1.2) second, it is extended as far as the wisdom of knowledge; (3.1.3) third, peaceful harmony; and (3.1.4) fourth, the constancy of strength (*firmitas*).

(3.1.1) Just as when you see that, when people are brought into being or existence, the first thing they obtain is that they live, so it should be when we are in grace. But what is it that makes a man live when he is in grace? Certainly it is love (*caritas*).[55] Thus John says: "We know that we are brought over from death to life, because we love (*diligo*) our brothers and sisters" [1 Jn 3.14]. Whoever does not love (*diligo*) his brother and sister—whatever good works he may do—he is dead [cf. 1 Cor 13.1–3]. Love (*caritas*) gives life to the soul, for just as the body lives through the soul, so the soul lives through God, and God

---

53. Also in English: "He was created a bishop" means that he became a bishop.
54. In view of the sacrament of baptism: ST III 70,1.
55. ST I 43,5,2; II–II 1,8,5; cf. II–II 23,2,2.

dwells in us through love (*caritas*). Hence John says: "Someone who remains in love (*caritas*) remains in God" [1 Jn 4.16], et cetera. And in today's Gospel [we heard]: "If someone loves (*diligo*) me, (he will keep my word, and my Father will love [*diligo*] him, and we will come, and) we will make (our dwelling in him) [Jn 14.23].[56] Now, someone who does not do the will of God does not love (*diligo*) him [cf. Jn 14.24] in a perfect way, for "it is proper to friends that their willing and disdaining correspond."[57]

Gregory says in a homily on Pentecost: "Proof of love (*dilectio*) is the production of the work."[58] But you will say: "I cannot fulfill the commandments of God." I say that you cannot fulfill them through your own strength, but that you can do it well by means of the grace of God.[59] Hence [Christ] adds: "My Father will love (*diligo*) him," so he will not fail him, "and we will come to him" [Jn 14.23], meaning: We will be with him and give him the strength (*vires*) to fulfill the commandments of God. Concerning this love (*caritas*) for fulfilling God's commandments, it is said in Eph 2.10: "We are his makings, created in Christ Jesus for good works."

From where is this love (*caritas*) in us? From the Holy Spirit, as the Apostle says: "The love (*caritas*) of God is spread in our hearts through the Holy Spirit, who is given to us" [Rom 5.5].[60] Someone who imparts light has it from the sun. Likewise someone who has love (*caritas*) has it from the Holy Spirit. Therefore, "send out your Spirit and they will be created," namely, into the existence of a life of grace through love (*caritas*).

(3.1.2) You see that when people are made more loving (*dilectio*), they get to know the will of God better. Thus we read in Proverbs: "It is proper to friends to be of one heart."[61] Well,

---

56. The Latin text refers to this verse as follows: *Si quis diligit me, etc., usque ibi: faciemus.*
57. From St. Jerome: "Concord of will is proper to friends, whose willing and disdaining correspond," cited also in SCG III 95.
58. Cf. ST I–II 105,2,1 (answer is found in the *corpus*).
59. Cf. ST I–II 109,4 and 10.
60. Cf. ST I 43,3,2; I–II 109,3,1; II–II 24,2sc.
61. This saying is not from Scripture. It seems to be based on what for in-

God reveals his secrets to his friends [cf. 1 Jn 3.2]. And this is the second stage of the creation that is from the Holy Spirit: that through Wisdom they get to know God. Thus we read in Jn 15.15: "Yet I have called you friends, because everything I have heard (from my Father I have made known to you)." Hence also the understanding of the truth is from the Holy Spirit.[62]

In the Gospel [Christ says]: "The Paraclete, the Holy Spirit, whom the Father will send (in my name, he will teach you everything)" [Jn 14.26]. Yet no matter how much a person may teach outwardly, it is no good unless the grace of the Holy Spirit is within him. Thus it is said in the Gospel: "The anointing will teach you about all things" [1 Jn 2.27].

And he does not only teach, but together with this he reminds us [Jn 14.26]. I can teach you, but you do not believe it or do not want to put it into practice. Now the one who makes you believe and put into practice what you hear, that is the one who reminds (you). This is what the Holy Spirit does, for he bends the heart, so that it agrees and follows what it hears.[63] Therefore, the Lord says: "Everyone who will have heard and will have learned from the Father will come to me" [Jn 6.37; cf. Mt 11.25, 28].

(3.1.3) The third stage of the creation is directed towards a peaceful harmony. James distinguishes in his letter between earthly wisdom and wisdom from above, and, as he discusses the property of the wisdom from above, he says: "The wisdom that is from above is indeed first of all chaste, then peacemaking, modest, gentle" [Jas 3.17], et cetera.

Yet earthly wisdom is not chaste, for it corrupts the affection through love (*amor*) of earthly things. Thus we also read in a

---

stance Aristotle says in VIII *Ethics*: "It is proper to friendship that it is made through concord." In his commentary (*reportatio*) on Paul's letter to Philemon, pr. (*proemium*), he writes similarly: "For this is proper to friends, that they are one in soul as for what they do not want and want," upon which he quotes Acts 4.32.

62. Without grace we can know natural things: ST I–II 109,1; but supernatural truth, like God himself (ST I 16,5), can be known only through grace: ST I 12,13.

63. Phil 2.13; cf. ST I 83,1,3, 105,4.

Letter [of the New Testament]: "They are corrupted in all the things that they know" [Jude 10]. Furthermore, it makes people divided and full of strife, whereas the wisdom from above consists in attracting us to God, for it is "peace-making, modest," et cetera. Quarrels arise from three things: first, when someone is not modest. Hence it says in Prv 28.25: "Someone who boasts in himself and aggrandizes himself" before others "stirs up quarrels."[64] Furthermore, some are stubborn in their manner of thinking, so that they do not allow anything to persuade them but stay with what they have in their head.[65] Yet this wisdom [from above] is "amenable." Furthermore, the wisdom of the world does not allow its wise to agree with others, whereas this wisdom is agreeing with good people and hence "peace-making."

But who makes the peace? The Holy Spirit, "for he is not the God of dissension, but of peace" [1 Cor 14.33].[66] Thus we read in Eph 4.3: "Exert yourselves to preserve the unity of the Spirit in a bond of peace." The Lord exhorts us to preserve this peace in today's Gospel, saying: "Peace I leave you; my peace I give to you; not as the world gives, I give it to you" [Jn 14.27].

Peace is twofold: one is in the present, in which we live peacefully, in such a way, however, that we still struggle against vices. This peace is left to us by God [cf. Jn 14.27a, 20.21, 26]. The other one is the peace which we will have in the future, without struggle. And about this peace he says: "Not as the world gives, I give it to you" [Jn 14.27b]. Some want peace in order to enjoy goods, whence Wis 14.22 says: "Although they live in a great war of ignorance, they consider so many and such great evils peace."[67]

Which peace, then, is true peace? Augustine says: "Peace is security of mind, quietness of soul,[68] simplicity of heart, a bond of love (*amor*), and the company of love (*caritas*)." True peace is

---

64. *Iurgia* is a serious sin: ST II–II 112,2,1.
65. Which is opposite to the virtue of perseverance: ST II–II 138,2.
66. Peace is an effect of love (*caritas*): ST II–II 29,3.
67. Some pursue what they consider peace but is not peace: ST II–II 29,2, esp. 29,2,3.
68. The term used is *animus* (not *anima*): the power of feeling, the sensibility, the heart, the feelings, inclination, passions.

threefold: in relation to yourself, to your neighbor, and to God. As for peace with yourself, it is required that your reason not be infected by errors or obscured by passions. And in view of this he says: "Peace is security of mind." There also needs to be quietness in one's affection, and in view of this he says: "quietness of soul." Furthermore, there ought to be simplicity in one's intention, and in view of this he says: "simplicity of heart." Peace with your neighbor is "a bond of love (*amor*)," and the peace through which we have a bond with God is "the company of love (*caritas*)."[69]

Is peace, then, very necessary for us? It certainly is. The Lord gave witness of peace, and those who do not want to preserve this testimony cannot receive the inheritance; in the same way, those who do not want to preserve peace cannot arrive at the heavenly inheritance. Now, someone will say: "I want to have peace with God but not with my neighbor." This, however, cannot be,[70] as a certain saint has said: "No one can have peace with Christ who is at odds with a Christian."[71]

Hence, the third stage of the creation is being of one heart in peace, as Isaiah puts it: "I have created peace as the fruit of my lips" [Is 57.19].

(3.1.4) The fourth stage is the constancy of strength,[72] and this comes from the Holy Spirit. Thus the Apostle writes in Eph 3.16: "May he give you strength through the Holy Spirit to make you strong," et cetera. And in Ezek 2.2 we read: "The Spirit entered me, and I stood on my feet." And in the Gospel: "Let not your heart be disturbed, and do not be frightened" [Jn 14.27c], et cetera. And in Wis 2.23 we read: "God has created humankind imperishable."

Therefore, the first effect of the Holy Spirit is that he creates.

(3.2) The second effect is renewal, which consists in four things: in accordance with (3.2.1) cleansing grace, with (3.2.2)

---

69. Cf. ST II–II 29,1.

70. 1 Jn 4.20; cf. ST II–II 26,2,1, 44,7.

71. Augustine (in conformity with Mt 5.24). Thomas cites this text in the *Catena Aurea* on John 14, at the end of *lectio* 7.

72. The virtue of constancy is connected with the virtue of perseverance, which is reckoned as a part of strength: ST II–II 137,3; strength, *firmitas* or *fortitudo*, is the third cardinal virtue: ST II–II 123–140.

progressing justice, with (3.2.3) illuminating wisdom, and with (3.2.4) the glory that makes complete.

(3.2.1) First, I say that the renewal through the Holy Spirit consists in cleansing grace. Sin is something that has been in the soul for a long time,[73] and man [*homo;* humankind] is not liberated from it but by justifying grace, through which man is removed from sin.[74] Thus the Apostle says: "Just as Christ rose from the dead, so let us, too, walk in the newness of life" [Rom 6.4]. From where does this newness come? From the Holy Spirit, as the Apostle says in Ti 3.5: "He has saved us not by reason of the works of justice that we did but according to his mercy through the bath of regeneration and renewal (through the Holy Spirit)."[75] Through this bath all sins are forgiven, and in this way man is renewed.

(3.2.2) Second, this renewal consists in progressing justice.[76] If someone walks and gets tired and becomes weak [and subsequently rests], his strength seems to be renewed. And when a person works with a great concentration, he is renewed when his strength is deployed in work of a different kind. Jb 29.20 says about this renewal: "My glory will be renewed, and the bow in my hand will be restored." The glory of the saints is the testimony of conscience. A person is renewed when he is prepared to struggle against vices. Is 40.31 says: "(Those who hope in the Lord renew their strength); they will take wings like wings of an eagle; they will fly and not cease,"[77] meaning: they will not cease to run "on the way of God's commandments" [Ps 119.32]. But who causes them to run? The Holy Spirit, as we read in Is 63.13–14: "He has led us through the depths like a horse in the

---

73. Original sin: ST I–II 81–83; the sin of the first human being: ST II–II 163–165.

74. ST I–II 113,1–2, referring to Rom 8.30 and 3.24.

75. The sacraments are important in this new, spiritual life: ST III 62,1, 65,1, esp. baptism, 69,4sc, and confession, 84,10,1.

76. Not only justice towards the neighbor, but also towards God, which consists of religiosity: devotion, prayer, adoration, sacrifices, praise, etc.; ST II–II 81–91.

77. In the last *articulus* of ST II–II, i.e., 189,10, Thomas uses this image for the one who enters religious life without extensive deliberation, trusting in God's help instead of his own strength/virtue.

desert that does not stumble; the Spirit of the Lord led him."

(3.2.3) Third, the renewal comes by means of illuminating wisdom. When a person from the beginning gets to know more about the goods of God, he is renewed. In Colossians 3 it is said about this renewal: "Clothe yourselves with the new man who is created according to God" [Eph 4.24]. Christ is called the "new man," for his conception is new: "not from the seed of a man" [cf. Jn 1.13, 1 Pt 1.23], et cetera. Also, his birth is new, since his mother remained a virgin after birth.[78] It is a new suffering, since it is without guilt.[79] It is a new resurrection, since it is quick and renewing: quick, because he also rose in glory.[80] It is a new ascension, since he went up by his own strength, not by someone else's like Enoch and Elijah.[81] Thus it says in Sir 36.6: "Renew the signs and change the wondrous deeds."[82] And because through Christ all things are renewed, we use new vestments on solemn feast days in the Church, so that we "sing a new song to the Lord"[83]—as if we say that someone who puts on a new garment by means of an exterior cleanness renews the mind internally through grace. The Apostle says in Col 3.9b–10: "Take off the old man," that is, the habit of the sinners with their deeds, "and clothe yourselves with" the habit of virtue which is not without deeds,[84] "the new man," a rational mind, that is. This new man "is renewed in the knowledge of God," et cetera. He continues: "Clothe yourselves with the new man" [Col 3.12], as I said above. In Rom 13.14 we read: "Be clothed with the Lord Jesus Christ."

And from where is this wisdom? From the Holy Spirit. Jb

---

78. ST III 28,2–3.

79. Our suffering is a consequence of guilt: cf. ST I 95,2; I–II 79,3,3; not Christ's: cf. ST III 47.

80. ST III 54,2.

81. ST III 57,3. See Gn 5.24 and 2 Kgs 2.

82. And yet it is not *totally* new; the whole of salvation history is already prefigured in the six days of creation; cf. ST I 73,1,3.

83. Ps 96.1, 98.1, 149.1. These Psalms are sung on solemn feasts during the Eucharist, and during evening and morning prayer.

84. These virtues are mentioned in Col 3.12–17 (cf. ST II–II 4,7,4, 30,4sc, 161,5sc), which lead to a perfect life if they come from love (*caritas*): ST II–II 184,1.

32.8: "As I see it, the Spirit is in people, and the inspiration of the Almighty gives (understanding)."[85]

(3.2.4) Fourth, the renewal is through glory that makes complete, namely, when the body will be renewed, away from the old punishment and the old guilt. In Is 65.17 it says about this: "Behold, I create new heavens and a new earth."[86] And from where does this renewal come? From the Holy Spirit; he himself is the pledge of our inheritance,[87] and he leads us to the heavenly inheritance.

Someone who longs to be created and renewed will obtain it from the Holy Spirit.

❖

(4) But who receives that renewal? "The face of the earth" [Ps 104.30], that is, the whole world, which once was full of idolatry. But on this day the Lord has bestowed the gifts of the "charismata" [cf. 1 Cor 12.31] on the apostles. Is 27.6 (Vg) says about this: "Those who enter with incitement," of the Holy Spirit, "will fill the face of the earth with the seed from Jacob." The face of the earth is also the human mind, for just as we see with our face in a corporeal way, so we see with the mind in a spiritual way. Hence it says in Gn 2.7: "God created man from the clay of the earth and blew the breath of life into his face."[88]

Well, in order to receive this renewal, the human mind ought to have four [characteristics]: it should be (4.1) clean, (4.2) uncovered, (4.3) directed, and (4.4) stable and firm.

(4.1) In Mt 6.17 it says about the first: "When you fast, however, anoint your head and wash your face," meaning: with tears of a moved heart,[89] and then you will be able to receive the renewal of the Holy Spirit. The Psalmist says: "Create a clean heart in me, God, (renew my spirit; make it righteous within me)" [Ps 51.12].

---

85. Cf. ST II–II 171,1,4 on prophecy.
86. See SCG IV 83; cf. 79–85.
87. Eph 1.13–14. "Pledge" (*pignus*) means either that one day it must be given back, or, as in this case, that one day it will be made complete, full, fulfilled.
88. Cf. ST I 94,2.
89. The term *compunctio cordis* is a medieval term that signifies a heart deeply touched or moved. It could be brought on by beauty in appearance, music, or poetry, but here it is used in terms of contrition. Cf. Acts 2.37; also ST I–II 79,4,3.

(4.2) Second, the face of the mind ought to be unveiled and uncovered. The Prophet says: "Thickness has concealed his face" [Jb 15.27]. Some have the face of their mind covered by a mist of ignorance. Jb 23.17 reads: "Mist has not concealed my face." And the Apostle says: "Yet we who behold the glory of God with an unveiled face"—meaning: free from attraction to earthly things—"are transformed into the same image from clarity (into clarity, as through the Spirit of the Lord)" [2 Cor 3.18].[90]

(4.3) Third, the face of the mind ought to be directed towards God. Thus we read in Tb 3.12: "Now I turn my face to you, and I direct my eyes to you." How do we turn our face to God? Through an upright intention, and thus we obtain the renewal of the Holy Spirit,[91] whence it is said in the Gospel according to Luke 11.13: "He will give the good Spirit to those who beseech him."[92]

Furthermore, if you are converted through obedience,[93] he will give the Holy Spirit to those who obey him [cf. Acts 5.32].

Furthermore, we ought to turn our face to our neighbor as well, as we read in Tb 4.7: "Do not turn away your face from your neighbor (for then, likewise, the face of the Lord will not be turned away from you)." Therefore, the apostles received the Holy Spirit while they were together [cf. Acts 2.1].

(4.4) Fourth, the face of the mind ought to be firm. We read about Anna, the mother of Samuel: "She did not look in different directions any more" [1 Sm 1.18; cf. Ps 121.1]. And therefore she received the Holy Spirit [cf. 1 Sm 1.19, 2.1–10]. Jb 11.15 reads: "Then you will be able to lift up your face." To those people the Holy Spirit is given, as we read in the Gospel: "While meeting with them, he instructed them not to leave Jerusalem, but to await the promise (of the Father 'about which you have heard through my mouth; for John baptized with water, yet you

---

90. Therefore, there could not have been ignorance in Christ: ST III 15,3.
91. Through grace we know and love God and turn to him again: ST I 8,3,4, 43,5,2; I–II 113,8.
92. For this beseeching we need God's help; cf. ST I–II 109,6 esp. ad 2.
93. A central Christian virtue, esp. in religious life: ST II–II 104, respectively, 186,5–8.

will be baptized with the Holy Spirit')" [Acts 1.4–5]. If they had left, they would not have received the Holy Spirit. Thus we read in Mt 24.13: "Someone who perseveres (till the end) will be saved."[94]

We will ask the Lord, et cetera.

---

94. As if Thomas is saying to his audience: "Keep your vows"; cf. ST II–II 88,3, 189,3.

SERMON 12
SERAPHIM STABANT

Sermon on the Feast of the Trinity[1]

Isaiah 6.2–3: *Seraphim stood over it:
the one had six wings and the other had six wings;
with two they covered their face and with two their feet
and with two they flew and they cried to one another:
"Holy, holy, holy Lord God of the hosts; and the whole
earth is full of his glory."*

Sermo

AMONG ALL religions and sects the Christian faith rejoices in this privilege that it contains very much that surpasses the natural and the rational, that is, what is beyond reason, more than other religions. The reason for this is that in this faith some most excellent things have been promised which exceed not only our understanding, but even the very desire of a rational creature. Hence the Apostle says that "eye has not seen, and ear has not heard, neither did it come up in the heart of a man, (what God has prepared for those who love [*diligo*] him)" [1 Cor 2.9].[2] And therefore, in accordance with the fitness of what has been promised, the excellence of the things to be believed is in the Christian faith.

Whereas in the Old Law earthly and carnal things are promised, as we read in Is 1.19: "If you are willing and listen to me, (you will eat the goods of the earth)." And because of this it was not necessary that in the Old Law the revelation of things

---

1. Probably from the first Parisian period (1252–1256).
2. Cf. ST I–II 5,5 (happiness) and 62,3 (theological virtues of faith, hope, and love), 114,2 (eternal life).

that exceed the reason be revealed explicitly, although implicitly and in a certain hidden way many things that exceed the reason were handed down in it.³ And this is what the Lord says in today's Gospel: "When I spoke to you about earthly things, you have not believed me, how then (would you believe me) if I spoke to you (about heavenly things)?" [Jn 3.12] Hence, if they do not believe Christ when he spoke to them about earthly things through the prophets—because he himself is the Word by which every word spoken to the prophets is said⁴—how can they believe him if he spoke of heavenly things? Yet we cannot know those things that are above the reason, but we are to believe them, for knowing is proper to reason, whereas believing is proper to the will.⁵ And so it was becoming that the authority of the ones who reveal and of the things that are revealed would be above all others, and in particular about the things that belong to the Holy Trinity.⁶

(1) Now, the Prophet makes the authority of those revealing the mystery of the Holy Trinity known for our day and age based on three things: (1.1) the task, (1.2) the dignity, and (1.3) the unanimity.

(1.1) So, based on the task, because he says "seraphim," that is, those who glow and set on fire,⁷ by whom the order of the apostles is implied. For, just as seraphs⁸ excel among all the orders of the heavenly spirits, so also the apostles are exalted above all the other saints in grace as well as in glory.⁹ 2 Thes

---

3. Even the Incarnation; cf. ST I 73,1,3.

4. Cf. Ps 68.11. The triune God speaks his Word through the prophets: ST I 43,3 and 5; I–II 102,2.

5. Cf. ST I–II 62,2 (citing Augustine); I–II 110,3,1.

6. Seraphim are characterized by an excellent love: ST I 108,5,5. Love is, just like the other theological virtues of faith and hope, connected with the will (note 4). We can know about the Trinity only through our faith: ST II–II 2,8, 171,3. Prophets excel through the grace they received: ST I–II 111,4; cf. II–II 171,4 and 6 and Isaiah in particular because he had a vision; cf. ST II–II 174,2.

7. ST I 108,5,5: Thomas explains the name "seraph" etymologically as fire/glow/heat (*ardor*) setting on fire (*incendo*), for instance, the lips of the prophet Isaiah: Is 6.7; cf. ST I 112,2,2.

8. *Seraphim* is Hebrew plural and used as such by Thomas; *seraphin* is Latin plural and therefore translated as "seraphs."

9. ST I 43,7,6; I–II 106,4; III 72,2,1.

2.13 reads: "God has chosen" us "as the first fruits for salvation, for the sanctification of the Spirit and belief in the truth." For they are the ones who have the first fruits of the Holy Spirit, as the Apostle says to the Romans [Rom 8.23]. Thus the apostles, set on fire by the fire of the Holy Spirit [Acts 2.3], were the right and suitable[10] ones to hand down the mystery of the Holy Trinity.[11]

Well, since it is becoming that something that comes from something else makes known the thing from which it comes, the Son, who comes from the Father, makes the Father known. Thus we read in Jn 17.6: Father, "I have made your name known." [Likewise,] the Holy Spirit, who comes from the Father and the Son makes known the Father and the Son, as it is said in Jn 16.14: "He will proclaim me, (for he will receive from what is mine and announce it to you)."

Therefore, it was becoming that the mystery of the Trinity was revealed to us by seraphim, that is, through the apostles, who were taught by the Son and set on fire by the Holy Spirit.[12] The Apostle says: "Yet to us (God) has revealed it (by means of his Spirit, for his Spirit fathoms all things, even the profundities of God)" [1 Cor 2.10]. And it is for this reason that after the feast of the Holy Spirit the feast of the Trinity is celebrated.

(1.2) Based on the dignity, for they were "above it," meaning: above the temple. By this their primacy and the source of their authority are made known. The Psalmist says: "You will appoint them as princes" [Ps 45.17].[13] But concerning this we must notice that it is said of the seraphim that "with two wings they covered their head, and with two wings they covered their feet, and they flew with two wings." By this their authority obtained from God is expressed, for it is granted to them to reveal some things and to keep other things hidden for the people. Just as the Apostle says that he has heard "secret things that no people ought to

---

10. They received the graces of the Holy Spirit, so that they could do the work of the Holy Spirit: ST III 42,1,2.

11. Which the prophets before them could not do; cf. ST I 57,5,3; I–II 106,4,2; II–II 176,1,1.

12. ST II–II 2,8,2.

13. Therefore, only bishops and priests can administer the sacraments; cf. ST III 67,2,2.

speak of" [2 Cor 12.4], as he also says somewhere else: "As with little children in Christ, I gave you milk as food, not solid food" [1 Cor 3.1–2]; for he is "the debtor to the wise and to the ignorant" [Rom 1.14]. Thus they flew by teaching, but by hiding they covered the head, since the first principle of all things itself cannot be examined; and since the very principle is also the end, as it is said in Rv 1.8 and 22.13, they covered their feet as well. The things in the middle were indeed not covered, because the things that are from the beginning to the end, namely, the divine effects, are manifest to us.[14] And therefore it is said in the Gospel: "The Spirit blows where it wills, and you hear its sound, but you do not know where it is coming from or where it is going to" [Jn 3.8]. So we only hear its sound, that is, the effects of the Spirit of the Lord, but they are known insofar as it is possible to know them; but we do not know "where it is coming from," and this is the meaning of them covering their head, "or where it is going to," to which the covering of the feet refers.[15]

(1.3) Third, the source of the authority of the apostles is called to mind on the ground of their unanimity, since all, and not one or two or three, have handed down unanimously, explicitly, and clearly the mystery of the Trinity. The Apostle says: "Whether I or they, that is not the point; (this is what we preach and this is what you have believed)" [1 Cor 15.11]. And therefore it is said about the seraphim that they "cried to one another."

Thus the source of the authority of the ones who reveal the mystery of the Trinity is clear.

(2) Now it remains to look at what they revealed when they said: "Holy, holy, holy," et cetera. In these words they make known three things to us: (2.1) first, the mystery of the sacred Trinity; (2.2) second, the image of the Trinity itself impressed upon rational creatures; (2.3) third, a trace of the same Trinity that is reflected in all other creatures.[16]

---

14. Cf. Rom 1.20; cf. ST I 2,2.
15. Cf. ST I 1,6,2: we receive knowledge through natural things (ST I 14,8,3, 16,2); therefore, we cannot know by our own effort our principle and our end itself, i.e., the triune God, who is of the highest dignity (ST I 42,4,2).
16. Cf. ST III 83,4 and *Rigans montes,* Thomas's inaugural lecture, where he

(2.1) So they make the mystery of the Trinity manifest to us, when they say: "Holy, holy, holy."[17] Concerning this we must know that, as Dionysius says, no way is as successful for getting to know God as the way of removal.[18] For then God is perfectly known, when we know that he is above every thing that can be thought of. Hence we read about Moses, who was very familiar with God according to what is granted to a human being in this life, that he approached God in a cloud and a thick mist, meaning: by getting to know what God is not, he arrived at knowledge of God.[19] Well, this way of removal is understood by the term "holiness," for, in general, according to all teachers, "holy" is the same as what is pure, and "pure" is what is separated from other things.[20]

For the evidence of this we must know that we find in creatures three most excellent things: (2.1.1) essence, (2.1.2) knowledge, and (2.1.3) affection.[21] But still they differ a lot; yes, they can in no way touch upon purity in the way that these are in God.

(2.1.1) Now, in the essences of created things we find a threefold defect that keeps them completely remote from God.[22]

(a) The first defect is the weakness of corruption, and this is

---

explains these words, used in the Eucharistic prayer, as referring to the divinity of Christ. He interprets "Blessed is he who comes in the name of the Lord" as referring to Christ's humanity.

17. This manifestation is a prophetic act: ST II–II 171,3.
18. *Via remotionis*—which is a part of the *via negativa*—i.e., saying what God is not, rather than what he is; cf. ST I 13,2: the things that do not belong to God are removed, like a body, imperfection, change, ignorance, powerlessness, and all things incompatible with divinity (cf. ST I 3–11). This method is applied by Thomas in this section of the sermon, 2.1.
19. ST I 12,11; I–II 98,3,2. In II–II 174,5,1, however, Thomas says that Moses did see the divine essence, although posthaste and by way of a passion, not remaining and by way of happiness.
20. Cf. ST II–II 81,8: in people holiness is also being directed towards the Holy One and so *in humanis* holiness is a synonym for religiosity.
21. These three correspond with respectively the Father, the Son, and the Holy Spirit.
22. God and God alone is essentially perfect: ST I 4. God's perfections are perfect as such, whereas they are in us as created; cf. Thomas on analogy in ST I 13,5–6.

found in all corruptible creatures.[23] Is 24.4 reads: "The earth has slid down and is weakened."

(b) The second defect is the defect of composition. This defect is in heavenly bodies, which, although they are free from corruption and from transitoriness,[24] nevertheless still do not come near the purity of the divine essence at all, because they are composite.[25] It is said in Jb 15.15: "(Behold, among his saints no one is immutable, and) even the heavens are not clean before him."

(c) The third defect is mutability. This defect is in the angels, who, although they are free from corruption[26] and free of composition,[27] are still found changeable, as we read in Jb 4.18: "Behold, the ones who serve him are not steadfast." And the reason for this is that "in his angels he has found badness" [ibid.].[28] And if some are found immutable, this is not because of their nature, but because of the grace of God.[29]

Hence the first principle is above this: incorruptible, simple, and immovable.[30] And this holiness is the holiness of God the Father, who is the principle of the whole Divinity.[31] The Psalmist says: "Let them acknowledge your (great) name (for it is terrifying and holy)" [Ps 99.3].

And therefore, three names are attributed to the Father, in

23. Hence God is not corruptible (ST I 9,2). Also angels and the human soul cannot be corrupted: ST I 50,5 and 76,6. Yet the human body is corruptible: ST I 102,2.

24. The *materia* in celestial bodies is without *potentia passiva*. The only change in them is of place: ST I 66,2.

25. Composition does not refer to different material parts made one (physical level), but to the ten categories of Aristotle: on a meta-physical level all creatures are composed of substance (e.g., man) and quality (e.g., black), relations (e.g., taller than someone else) and quantity (e.g., weight), time (e.g., now) and place (e.g., here), position (e.g., standing), state (e.g., dressed, drunk), *potentia* (e.g., being touched, moved) and *actus*, (e.g., to touch, to move). Only God is not composed; his being is his essence, etc.; cf. ST I 3,2–8.

26. ST I 50,5.   27. ST I 50,2.
28. ST I 63.

29. Angels do not have bliss (*beatitudo*) from the beginning: ST I 62,1. When God grants angels this ultimate happiness, they cannot sin any more: ST I 62,8.

30. Respectively, ST I 4, 3 and 9.

31. ST I 27,1, 42,3.

order to exclude the defects mentioned: (ad a) Power, in order to exclude the weakness of corruption; the Psalmist says: "Lord, you are powerful" [Ps 89.9].³² (ad b) Unity, a name given by Augustine, in order to exclude composition excluded.³³ (ad c) Eternity, a name given by Hilary, in order to exclude mutability; the Psalmist says: "You yourself, however, are the same (and your years do not decrease)" [Ps 102.28].³⁴

(2.1.2) Also, in knowledge we find a threefold defect, according to which the knowledge of creatures falls short in three ways.

(a) The first defect is of the knowledge of material and singular things. This is the knowledge through touching and being touched. In the senseless creatures this is the only knowledge.³⁵

(b) The second defect of knowledge is the one that we have through appearances. For, although we have knowledge of general things, it is still obscure, because "now we see in a mirror, (enigmatically)" [1 Cor 13.12]—and we know insofar as sensible things appear to us.³⁶

(c) The third defect of knowledge is insofar as it is diminished. This defect is in the angels; although they have a clear knowledge since they do not receive knowledge through senses—and as a sign of this they appeared before prophets with sparkling eyes [cf. Dn 12.3]—still their knowledge is diminished, because on the basis of their natural powers they cannot see God in his essence, for no created intellect can see the essence of God unless through grace.³⁷ The Apostle says: "God's grace is eternal life" [Rom 6.23].³⁸ What's more, it is diminished because, although they see the essence of God through grace, they do not understand it, nevertheless.³⁹ Therefore, it

---

32. ST I 25, 32,1,1; cf. 39,8,3 (with a reference to Augustine): the name "Powerful" signifies God as cause.
33. ST I 11; cf. ST 39,8,2: this name signifies God as for his unity.
34. ST I 10; cf. 39,8,1: this name signifies God as such.
35. Someone knows in accordance with his/her nature; cf. ST I 12,11.
36. ST I 1,9, 12,12. This defect is in all human beings.
37. ST I 56,3.   38. Cf. ST I 18,1–3.
39. ST I 62,2 and 56,3,1.

is said that, when the voice sounded in the firmament, the angels "lowered their wings" [Ezek 1.25]. Chrysostom says about this that even these heavenly essences could never see God's essence as it is.

So above the knowledge of these [three] is the knowledge of the Word of God; it contains all things, knows all things [Wis 1.7]. And so the Arians, who separated the Word from God, were foolish, because, if they had been right, God would not have known himself.[40] And therefore is this holiness the holiness of God's Word. The Psalmist says: "Yet you dwell in the Holy One, Praise of Israel" [Ps 22.4],[41] for this is the praise of the ones who see God, that they may dwell in the Holy One, meaning: participate in the knowledge of God's Word.

And since the Word of God is clear of these defects, three things are attributed to him: (ad a) wisdom, to exclude singular knowledge;[42] (ad b) Hilary attributes beauty to him, namely, splendor,[43] to exclude obscure knowledge; (ad c) Augustine attributes equality to him, in order to exclude diminishment.[44]

(2.1.3) In the affection we find in a similar way a threefold defect of holiness.

(a) The first defect is when our affection is deprived. For, a nature degenerates when it makes itself equal to an inferior nature. Well, other creatures, those without reason, have an affection aimed at one single good: the preservation of themselves. And thus, when someone has a deprived affection, he falls away from his honor. The Apostle says: "All who seek their own interest (do not belong to Christ Jesus)" [Phil 2.21].[45]

---

40. ST I 14,2 and 34,2 ("Word" signifies an efflux of the intellect).

41. "You," "the Praise of Israel," is identified as the eternal Word of God: a Christological reading of the Psalms.

42. In ST I 39,8,3 (with reference to Augustine): this name signifies God as cause. "Wisdom" includes all knowledge, knowledge as such; it is not about knowledge of this and that.

43. ST I 39,8,1: this name signifies God as such.

44. ST I 39,8,2; also 47,2,2 and III 58,2,3. This name signifies God as for his unity.

45. Someone who becomes like an inferior, irrational creature by becoming self-centered is not a disciple and/or a friend of Jesus Christ. Self-preservation is not the highest good; Thomas even considers it illicit to kill someone who attacks you in order to defend yourself; cf. ST II–II 64,7.

(b) The second defect is when our affection is held back and closed. This is caused by the first defect. For it is for this reason that people do not share their goods: because they love (*diligo*)[46] themselves. These people are rebuked by St. John: "Someone who sees his brother in need (and closes his heart against him—how can the love (*caritas*) of God remain in him?)" [1 Jn 3.17].[47]

(c) The third defect is when our affection is disquieted, and this occurs when the affection is not at peace in view of the ultimate end.[48] Augustine says [in *Confessions*]: "Disquieted is our heart until it finds peace in you."

So holy affection is above these affections; it is the divine love (*amor divinus*) that is not deprived since it loves (*diligo*) "all things that are," as it is said in Wis 11.25, "and (you hate) nothing (of the things you made)." It is not closed, because "when you open your hand (everything will be filled with goodness)," as the Psalmist says [Ps 104.28]. It is not disquieted, since it is the love (*amor*) of the ultimate end which loves (*diligo*) itself and all things because of itself; and thus it is everlasting: in everlasting love (*caritas*)" [Jer 31.3].[49]

And therefore three things are attributed to him:[50] (ad a) Union,[51] so that it may be clear that he is not lacking anything, for deprived love (*amor*) causes discord.[52] But the Holy Spirit is proper to the highest good, and therefore it is the One who binds together (*nexus*). (ad b) Goodness, so that it may be clear

---

46. For Thomas's terminology, see Sermon 01 *Veniet desideratus*, note 39.

47. Sharing and giving away what you have are good acts (ST I 5,4,2, 106,4; III 1,1), acts of love: ST II–II 32,1 and 10.

48. Cf. Ps 42.6 (*perturbatus*); Mt 2.3, 16 (Herod, *turbatus*, and so much that he had all boys killed who could have been the rival king). On the other hand, Mary, *turbata* (Lk 1.29), found peace again as soon as she heard of the final end (Lk 1.32–33, 37 and 38).

49. The love of the Eternal One is not selfish love, as also the second part of this verse shows: "I have loved you and therefore I drew you towards me in my mercy"; cf. ST I 20,1,3: "Love is a unifying force."

50. I.e., the Holy Spirit.

51. *Connexio*. ST I 39,8,2 (with reference to Augustine): unanimity (*concordia*) or the connection/bond between the equal Father and the equal Son; cf. also I 37,2. The name *Unio* signifies God as for his unity. See note 44.

52. ST II–II 37,1.

that [the Holy Spirit] is not closed, "for a good spreads itself";[53] Wis 12.1 (Vg) says: "O, how good is the Spirit." (ad c) Use, so that it may be clear that he is peaceful and that he concerns the end.[54] Also, Augustine points out that he is use, that is, enjoyment, since God enjoys himself with divine love (*amor divinus*) and loves (*diligo*) the Son with the love (*amor*) of enjoyment.[55]

❖

But are these three holinesses? No. For in us, being, willing, and understanding are three different things; thus the holiness of being is different from the holiness of will and of understanding. But in God, being, understanding, and willing are the same;[56] and so the holiness of these three is the same.[57] But it is repeated thrice [in Is 6.3], not in order to show a triple holiness, but the holiness of three.

❖

(2.2) He shows that the image of the Holy Trinity is impressed upon rational creatures, when he says: "Lord, God of the hosts." Regarding this we must know that the resemblance to him is the more explicit in things the nearer they are to God and the closer they are to him.[58] Well, such are the rational creatures, and hence the resemblance to the Trinity is reflected more in them. This resemblance is shown in three respects:

(2.2.1) First, in respect of a special providence that God has for the rational creature, by punishing, by instructing, and by rewarding him.[59] And therefore it says: "Lord."

(2.2.2) Second, because in a special way he is the end and the reward of a rational creature, while, in general, he is the

---

53. ST I 5,4, 39,8,3 (with reference to Augustine). This name signifies God as cause (*causa finalis*).

54. ST I 39,8,1 (with reference to Hilary). This name signifies God as such.

55. Cf. ST I 37,2. Thus Thomas explains the paradox of Hilary's *Usus* as a name of God and Augustine's distinction between *uti* (towards things) and *frui* (towards God only); cf. ST I–II 11, 12,2,3 and 34,4.

56. But we must distinguish them according to our understanding: ST I 13,4.

57. ST I 42,2–6.

58. Cf. ST I 4,3.

59. Respectively, Prv 3.11–12 (cf. ST III 59,1); Heb 12.5–7; Gn 1.28–30 (cf. ST I 96,2); Ps 8.6 (cf. ST I 20,4,2); Lk 6.35; Heb 10.35–38, 11.6, 26.

end of the whole of creation.[60] Therefore, it says: "God." In Heb 11.16 it says: "He is not ashamed to be called their God, (for he has built a city for them)"; and in Gn 15.1: "I am (your protector, and) your reward (will be very big)."

(2.2.3) Third, in respect of freedom. For the other creatures lead their lives, yet they do not lead themselves to their actions and thus they are like slaves, in particular because they exist for the sake of other things. A rational creature, however, leads himself, because he is free and lord over his own actions.[61] And therefore they are soldiers, whence it says: "of the hosts," meaning: of the angels—about which Jb 25.3 says: "Is there a number of his soldiers?"—and of the people, as Jb 14.14 reads: "All the days that I have served now as a soldier."[62] In this host the image of the Trinity is reflected: in the angel, namely, because he is "the seal of resemblance" [Ezek 28.12];[63] in humankind through memory, intellect, and will.[64]

(2.3) Furthermore, he makes known a trace that is reflected[65] within other creatures, when he says: "Full is the[66] earth," et cetera. And this is clear in the first establishment of the things.

For, there [that is, in the first establishment of things] we find the power of the God who creates, so that the Father would be recognized: "In the beginning God has created heaven and earth" [Gn 1.1], et cetera. And when we read that "the earth was waste and empty" [Gn 1.2], we understand this [as waste

---

60. Cf. also Rom 11.36, 1 Cor 8.6, and Heb 2.10. Theses texts underlie the *exitus-reditus* scheme of the ST, although Thomas never refers to these texts explicitly.

61. Cf. ST I 83 (free will); I–II 6,8 and 76 (ignorance) and 80 (the devil).

62. Only, however, if he is obedient will he win the battle; cf. ST III 47,2 (citing Prv 21.28), aiming at Christ, esp. in the Passion.

63. Curiously enough, these words in Ezek 28.12 refer to a human being (*filius hominis*, namely, the prophet Ezekiel), not to angels.

64. As Augustine says. *Memoria* refers to the Father, since it retains what it knows (the Word, the Son) as well as love (the Holy Spirit); cf. ST I 93,7,3. Intellect and will obviously refer respectively to the Son and the Spirit.

65. ST I 45,7, 93,2.

66. The text leaves out *omnis*, "the whole," from Is 6.3, which would strengthen Thomas's interpretation.

and empty] if it is considered in itself, because its fulfillment comes from the glory of God.[67]

There we find the art of the God who forms all the things,[68] so that the Son would be recognized. For just as an artist by means of his art renders form to the matter, so God has given to all things their proper form by means of his Word, who is "the full art of living rational beings."[69] Hence it is said: "And God said: 'Let there be light'" [Gn 1.3], meaning: he brought forth the Word, in whom was [the power] to bring them into being.

There we find the pleasure of the God who approves, so that the Holy Spirit would be recognized. Thus it is said: "God saw all the things that he had made (and that they were very good)" [Gn 1.31], meaning: he approved of them.[70]

There we also find a trace insofar as the property [of each of the three Persons] is concerned. For every creature whatsoever remains through the power of the Father, has an appearance because it is formed by the Word of God, and is ordered through the love (*amor*) of the Holy Spirit towards [its] end.

---

67. ST I 65,2; I–II 114,1,2: God's glory is the manifestation of his goodness, as in Ps 19.2; cf. ST I 44,1–2, 45,1: "and God saw it was good."

68. ST I 44,3.

69. A quotation from Augustine, also used in his *Commentary on the Gospel according to John*, c.1 (*lectiones* 2 and 4) and SN II 11,2,2,3.

70. ST I 47,2, 65,1,2, 74,3,3.

SERMON 13

HOMO QUIDAM FECIT CENAM MAGNAM

Sermon on the Second Sunday after the Feast of the Trinity[1]

Luke 14.16: *Someone made a great dinner and invited many.*

PART 1: *Prothema*

IT SEEMS THAT there is a difference between physical and spiritual pleasures, for physical pleasures are manifest to people who have surrendered to the senses, and the spiritual pleasures are hidden to them, whereas the latter are manifest to spiritual men. Hence it says in Rv 2.17: "To the one who gains the victory I shall give the hidden manna."[2] And since this homily is about our spiritual refreshment, let us ask the generous distributor of this delight that he may give me something to say in praise, et cetera.

PART 2: *Sermo*

"Someone made a (great) dinner" [Lk 14.16], et cetera. Just as the body cannot be maintained without physical refreshment, so also the soul is in need of spiritual refreshment for its maintenance. About this spiritual refreshment Ps 23.2–3 says: "He has led me out unto the water of refreshment. (He refreshes my soul.)" Conspicuously it says "unto the water of refresh-

---

1. This sermon dates from the second Parisian period: 1268–1272.
2. In ST I–II 112,5, Thomas uses this text to explain that through signs or experiences someone can know whether he/she has grace, although this knowledge is not as certain as knowledge through revelation.

ment," for just as physical refreshment is necessary against a total destruction brought about by taking in natural heat, so the soul is in need of spiritual refreshment because of the heat of concupiscence, which harms us and which hinders the salvation of our souls. Thus spiritual water is necessary because it extinguishes this heat. Physical water cools, but does not nourish [cf. Jn 4.13]; spiritual water, however, cools and nourishes. About this water it is said in Jn 4.14: "In someone who drinks from this water, a fountain shall well up of water that is salutary unto eternal life."[3]

Concerning this spiritual refreshment the Lord makes a comparison in today's Gospel. We can see two things: first [in the *Sermo*], the preparation of this refreshment, where he says, "Someone made a great dinner"; second [in the *Collatio in sero*], the announcement of the feast when it was prepared, where it says, "and he invited many."

Regarding the preparation there are three aspects that must be considered: (1) first, who this man is who made the dinner; (2) second, what kind of dinner it is; and (3) third, how big it is.

(1) As for the first aspect, I say: we must take a look at who that man is. I say that this man is the Son of God, who is truly a man in view of the truth of the assumed human nature.[4] Thus the Apostle says in Phil 2.6–7: "Who, although he was in the form of God, emptied himself, taking the form of a slave, became like the people, and through his way of life was found a man." Jer 17.9 reads: He is a man and "who will know him?"

Jesus says in Lk 14.16: "Someone" or "a certain man," as if he says: Some particular things are in him that are not in others. For he is a distinct man, since he has (1.1) the fullness of divin-

---

3. In ST II–II 25,5 Thomas advocates that we must take good care of our body, but that the care for the soul is more important, since the soul does not die.

4. Thomas identifies the inviting man with Jesus Christ on account of his humanity; the Latin text reads *Homo quidam*, that is, "someone," "a certain human being" or "man."

ity, (1.2) the fullness of truth, and (1.3) the fullness of grace.[5]

(1.1) First, I say: [the man] Christ had the fullness of divinity.[6] Other people are called gods, but only in the sense that they take part;[7] this man, however, is the true God.[8]

(1.2) Furthermore, other people know a little about the truth, but this man had the fullest knowledge, not only according to his divinity, but according to his humanity [as well].[9] "For in him are all hidden treasures of wisdom and knowledge" [Col 2.3].

(1.3) Moreover, others had some grace—some the grace of eloquence, others the grace of wisdom, because "there are varieties of graces" [1 Cor 12.4]—but Christ had the fullness of grace. Therefore, the Apostle says in Col 1.19: "It was pleasing that in him all fullness dwelt." Jn 1.14 speaks about the fullness of divinity, of truth, and of grace that was in Christ: "We have seen his glory, a glory as of the Father's only Son" in view of the fullness of divinity; it says "full of grace"[10] in view of the fullness of grace; "and of truth" is added, referring to the fullness of truth that was in Christ.[11]

Now it is clear who that man is.

❖

(2) As for the second aspect, we must look at what kind of dinner it is that this man has prepared. I say that he has made a triple spiritual refreshment: (2.1) one has to do with the sac-

---

5. Christ was a true man, but because of the hypostatic union he had certain qualities which other people do not have; cf. ST III 7.
6. Jn 1.14; cf. ST III 7,9–10; from the very beginning of his conception: ST III 7,12, 34,1.
7. In Ps 82.6; cf. ST II–II 85,2,1; III 16,1, as it is said in Jn 1.16.
8. ST III 16,2.
9. ST III 9–12, esp. 9,1–4.
10. Scripture also speaks of John the Baptist (Lk 1.15), Mary (Lk 1.28), Stephen (Acts 6.8), and the addressees in Eph 3.19 as being full of grace. But they have it because they have received it at a certain point in their lives, *from the fullness of Christ* (Jn 1.16, Eph 4.7; cf. ST III 7,10); *participatiue*, as Thomas says in 1.1. Thus only Jesus Christ has the fullness of grace for as full as grace is: his grace has no end (ST III 7,11), whereas others are full of grace, or rather, filled with grace insofar as a limited human being can contain it.
11. For all truth is from God: ST I 16,5; cf. Jn 14.6.

rament, (2.2) another with the intellect, and (2.3) a third with our affection.

(2.1) First, I say: that a man "made a dinner" refers to the sacrament.[12] We understand what is said in Sir 29.26 as concerning this sacramental refreshment: "Come over, stranger, and set the table and give what you have in your hand to the others to eat." Christ is a stranger in the world: "though the world was made through him" [Jn 1.3], "still it has not known him" [Jn 1.10]. He came into the world as if he were a foreigner [cf. Jn 1.26, 9.29]. He has set the sacramental table, and what he had in his hand, that is, in accordance with the power that was given to him by the Father [cf. Mt 28.18], he has given to the others to eat [cf. Is 58.7], namely, to the believers. Christ has established this refreshment insofar as he had the fullness of grace.

This refreshment contains the early meal as well as the dinner; the early meal is the sacramental refreshment in the Old Testament;[13] dinner, the one in the New Testament.

We understand that the Gospel speaks about the sacramental refreshment of the early meal as referring to the Old Testament: "Behold, my early meal is ready; bulls and the fattened animals are slaughtered" [Mt 22.4]. After all, in the Old Testament slaughtered bulls were offered, according to the letter. The early meal takes place in the first part of the day; likewise, in the Old Testament the feast of the sacramental refreshment took place under the First Law, as bulls and fattened animals were killed and offered to the Lord.[14]

Since an early meal was made, it was becoming[15] that also a dinner would be made. We read about this meal in Mt 26.26: "While the disciples were eating,[16] the Lord took bread and broke it and gave it to his disciples and said: 'Eat and drink;

---

12. For the Eucharist as a spiritual refreshment: ST III 84,6.
13. ST I–II 102,5.
14. The Old Testament sacrifices are prefigurations of the sacrifice of Jesus Christ: ST III 75,1. For the four senses of Scripture texts (literal, spiritual, allegorical, anagogical), see ST I 1,10.
15. *Decens* indicates beauty, harmony, and order. See n. 14 on Sermon 18 *Germinet terra.*
16. In the evening; cf. Mt 26.20; so the Eucharist is the dinner, the evening meal.

this is my body.'" To an early meal people from outside are very welcome, but only relatives and close friends and the people with whom one lives [cf. Eph 2.19] come to a dinner. Jb 31.31 reads: "If the men of my tent never said: 'Who shall give us of his meats, that we may be sated?'" as if he says: only relatives and close friends are admitted.

(2.1: 3) See that this dinner was great and in what way it was great.[17] I say that the dinner is called "great" because of (3.1) the magnificent provision, because of (3.2) the greatness of the delight in taste, and (3.3) because it results in a great virtue. These characteristics were in that refreshment. Hence it was great.

(2.1: 3.1) If you seek what the provision of this dinner was, you would find out that it was a magnificent provision. Ps 78.24: "He has given them bread prepared from heaven; a man has eaten angels' bread." If someone wants to praise a meal well, he praises it in two ways: by reason of the place where it comes from, and by reason of the dignity of the ones who eat it. By reason of the place when it is said: "This wine comes from such-and-such a place," namely, where usually precious grapes grow. In the same way a wine is praised for the dignity of the consumers when it is said: "This is the wine of which a king drinks." Because of this the Psalmist, intending to describe the great provision of the dinner, first describes it in view of its place [of origin] when he says: "He has given them bread from heaven" [Ps 78.24]. Where did it come from? From heaven. Believe the Bread, who says: "I am the living bread that came down from heaven," [Jn 6.41],[18] that is: by taking on our weakness according to his divinity, not by abandoning the height of heaven.[19]

---

17. Thomas announced the greatness (*magnitudo*) of the meal as a separate point, but he discusses it as an aspect of 2.1, 2.2, and 2.3: the sacramental, intellectual, and affectionate meal are all great in their own way.

18. Thus Thomas follows a sacramental rather than a Christological interpretation here. He does so throughout this homily. This is also how John 6 functions in ST III on the Eucharist (especially in 79–80).

19. Coming down from heaven means neither that he is not in heaven any more nor that he was not on earth before; cf. ST I 43,1.

Likewise, that food is described as being precious by reason of the dignity of the consumers, because the greatest are refreshed by it, namely, the angels who are refreshed by the Word of God. This food is set out before you in the dinner.

So the dinner is great because of the magnificent provision.

(2.1: 3.2) But if expensive foods are placed in front of you that are not pleasant to eat, they are not considered great. Because of this, the dinner is described subsequently as great because of its greatly delightful taste. As it says in the Book of Wisdom 16.20: "You have bestowed on them bread prepared from heaven; it contains every delight and sweetness of taste." Delight is caused by three things: (3.2.1) by the memory of things past, (3.2.2) by the hope of future things, and (3.2.3) by the experience of things present. Well, all three delights are in this dinner.

(2.1: 3.2.1) If you consider things past, the memory of them is delightful. What is more delightful than to call to mind that man is redeemed by the blood of Christ?[20] In Leviticus we read: "Remember my poverty," et cetera [Lam 3.19]. And in the Gospel: "Do this in memory of me" [Lk 22.19]. And the Apostle calls to mind: "Whenever you do this, you proclaim[21] the death of the Lord" [1 Cor 11.25].

(2.1: 3.2.2) Moreover, in this dinner is a great delight because of the hope of things to come.[22] For this sacramental refreshment is a sign that announces things to come,[23] and it gives us hope of future happiness.[24] Therefore, we read in the Gospel: "Unless you eat the flesh of the Son of man (and drink his blood, there is no life in you)" [Jn 6.54].

(2.1: 3.2.3) Even more, this refreshment is the greatest de-

20. Cf. 1 Pt 1.19. The memory of a fact or event in the past can as such already be consoling. But here Thomas points to an event in the past that is prolific for us for the present and the future: thus we can live as free human beings now and we will enjoy eternal happiness in the hereafter; cf. ST I–II 32,3.

21. That is: call to mind, remember (*recordor, memoror*), for yourself and for others.

22. Hope, like memory, generates delight; cf. ST I–II 32,3.

23. It is a sign and more than a sign; cf. ST III 75,1.

24. Hope can be one of the principal passions of the soul (ST I–II 25,3–4, 40) and a theological virtue (ST I–II 62; II–II 17–22).

light if you focus your attention on what is present: the thing signified that is contained [in it] and the thing signified that is not contained [in it]. The thing signified that is contained [in it] is the body of Christ.[25] Man truly ought to boast of having the body of Christ in him, for "there is no other nation so great that has gods who are so close as our God is close to us" [Dt 4.7].[26] Just as delightful is the thing signified that is present and is not contained [in it]: the unity of the Church. What is more joyful than this unity? Ps 133.1: "Behold how good and how joyful (it is for brothers to dwell together in unity)."[27]

Thus this dinner has the greatest delight whether you focus on the past or the present or the future.

(2.1: 3.3) Third, this dinner is great because it results in a great virtue [or strength], for it unites us with God and makes us live in God. Thus it says in Jn 6.55: "Someone who eats my flesh and drinks my blood," et cetera [6.57], "remains in me," that is, through faith and love (*caritas*),[28] "and I in him," namely, through grace and the sacrament.[29]

But if God is in us and we are in him, we ought not fear anything.[30] As we read in Jb 17.3: "Place me next to you, and let anyone's hand fight against me." And in Ps 23.5: "You have prepared a table for me (in the sight of my enemies)." Now something is made one out of two: a less noble thing follows the movement of a predominant thing. So it is necessary that the soul that is united with God follow God [cf. Eph 5.1]. Therefore, it must not fear anything, since God is in us through the

---

25. Thomas speaks of the *praesentia realis* in the sacrament of the Eucharist; cf. ST III 75–76. Since this bread and wine contain Christ *realiter*, we should eat and drink them with joy: Eccl 9.7.

26. Also through baptism: Gal 2.20; cf. ST III 69,5.

27. An implicit reference to the *corpus mysticum Christi*. 1 Cor 12.27: "You are the body of Christ and each one of you is a member of it" (cf. ST III 8,1, 49,1). This body is one: *unitas*, which is stronger than *unio* (ST II–II 25,4): 1 Cor 10.17 (cf. ST III 67,2, 73,2).

28. Cf. ST III 75,1.

29. As in 1 Jn 2.14; cf. ST III 62 and 79,1.

30. Here is meant fear (*timor*) as one of the principal passions of the soul (ST I–II 25,4: 41–45), which is a sign of a lack of faith and trust. For fear as a virtue, fear of the Lord, see: ST II–II 7,1 and 19.

sacrament.[31] In the strength of this food Elijah walked to the mountain of the Lord, Horeb [1 Kgs 19.8].

If we are worthy of this food, it will lead us to eternal life. Happy, therefore, those who are worthy to taste this food, but unhappy those who taste of it although they are not worthy of it, for "they eat judgment on themselves" [1 Cor 11.29].

This, then, is the sacramental refreshment.

❖

(2.2) Another refreshment is the intellectual one, which pertains to the intellect. This refreshment is prepared for us by Christ insofar as it is full of truth.[32] Hence the uncreated Wisdom says in Prv 9.2: "Wisdom has mixed the wine and prepared a table," and has sent out an invitation saying: 'Come and eat my bread and drink the wine that I have mixed for you; (leave your foolishness and live, and walk in the ways of prudence)'" [Prv 9.5–6]. The Wisdom of God is Christ [cf. 1 Cor 1.24]. He has "mixed" the "wine," that is, the dogma[33] of the spiritual wisdom: that wine was so strong that man could not tolerate it unless it were mixed, and so he has mitigated it when he put out the spiritual dogmas.[34] "He has placed a table," meaning: the whole creation. The dogma of wisdom is called bread and wine: bread so that we may keep our footing, and wine which makes joyful [Ps 104.15] and sets ablaze [cf. Acts 2.13].[35]

In this refreshment we find the early meal and the dinner. The early meal consists of the teaching of the philosophers.

---

31. In ST III 63,1–3 Thomas speaks of a sacramental *character* which provides the recipient with spiritual power. It brings the recipient to a virtuous way of life through which he/she honors God.

32. Cf. ST III 78,5.

33. Thomas uses the term *dogma* here (*dogma sapientiae spiritualis, spiritualia dogmata, dogma sapientiae*) in contrast with the term *doctrina*, used in the next paragraph for the teachings of the philosophers (*doctrina philosophorum*). A dogma is in the usual sense of the word an infallible teaching of the Church as the formulation of revealed truth.

34. In ST III 42,3 Thomas expounds that Christ used parables for those who could not understand his spiritual teachings (cf. Mt 13.10–11). Thomas refers in this context to Nm 4.5, where the Levites cover the Ark when the Israelites break the camp.

35. Bread belongs to our daily food, that we may live (cf. ST III 74,1 *Primo*); joy belongs to a Christian life (ST II–II 28) and is one of the effects of devotion (II–II 82,4).

This is pointed out in the prophet Habakkuk where we read that he made a meal for the reapers in the field [Dn 14.33]. The reapers are the philosophers who gather the crops from the field, that is: the truths from creation. Hence we read in Rom 1.20: "God's invisible (eternal power and divinity have been understood through the things that were made)."

The dinner is the refreshment of Sacred Scripture. Thus it says in Rv 3.20: "If someone opens for me, I will enter his house and have dinner with him." This is the difference between the teaching of Sacred Scripture and that of philosophy: the teaching of philosophy is from creation, but the teaching of Sacred Scripture is from inspiration.[36] Therefore, he says: "If someone opens for me, I will enter his house," namely, through the inspiration of the Holy Spirit. Thus we read in Jn 16.12: "When he comes, that Spirit of truth, he will teach you every truth." Sacred Scripture is called a "dinner," because it is given for relatives [cf. 1 Jn 3.1] and close friends [cf. Jn 15.15]. Hence it says in Prv 31.15, concerning the wife: "She gives game to the ones who live in the house and ordinary food to her servants."

❖

(2.2: 3) This dinner is great since it has three characteristics, mentioned above.

(2.2: 3.1) First, it is great because of the greatness of the splendor of the provision, for it is taken from the best things [cf. Is 25.6]. Hence Wisdom says: "Hear me, for I will speak about great things" [Prv 8.6]. They are great, because they exceed every sense. As we read in Sir 3.25: "Many things that are above the senses of people have been shown to you."[37] These are

---

36. So both are about the truth, but philosophy is about a lower truth, and thus it is a lower science. In his days there was a fierce debate between theologians and some philosophers who were influenced by the thoughts of Averroes (1126–1198). The latter came to the conclusion that faith and reason were incompatible. These philosophers taught things that were incompatible with aspects of the Catholic faith (e.g., creation as an event "in the beginning" [*in principio*] and "from nothing" [*ex nihilo*] [ST I 44 and 46], and the resurrection of the body [ST III 53–54; SCG IV 79–89]). We see this discussion reflected, for instance, in ST I 1,1, and II–II 1,1: The first truth from which all other truths are derived can only be known in faith through revelation.

37. This text is cited in the opening question of the first part of the ST:

useful things, as the Lord says in Exodus: "I am the Lord, who teaches you useful things, leading you in the way in which you walk" [Is 48.17]. Other sciences do not lead you on the way.[38]

(2.2: 3.2) Likewise, this dinner is great because of the greatness of the delight in taste. After all, there is sweetness to the highest extent in the words of Sacred Scripture, as Ps 119.103 says: "How sweet to my throat is what you say, (sweeter than honey in my mouth)." Its sweetness is above the sweetness of every other science. For a consideration is called delightful in two ways: either because of the thing considered or because of the consideration itself. A demonstration concerning a triangle[39] is not delightful because of the thing demonstrated—since no one really cares about a triangle—but it is delightful because of the consideration itself, which befits the intellect. But when the consideration is about a thing that is loved (*amatus*), and with this also the consideration itself is delightful, then it is perfectly delightful. This is the case in Sacred Scripture, since in it there is not only delight about getting to know the truth, but it even concerns beloved (*amatus*) things.[40] Thus Augustine says in *Confessions*: "Other writings do not have the features of this devotion, the tears of confession, the pledge[41] of the Holy Spirit,"

"Whether it is necessary to have another doctrine than the philosophical disciplines" (ST I 1,1,1); likewise in the context of our salvation: "Whether believing something beyond natural reason is necessary for salvation" (ST II–II 2,3,3).

38. Other sciences, practical as well as speculative, are by no means useless according to Thomas, but in view of the ultimate end of our life they cannot compete with the science which we receive from God through revelation: Scripture and tradition, which contain the *Sacra Doctrina* (cf. ST I 1,1–3 and 5). Therefore, these other sciences must be seen and practiced in the light of the highest science.

39. It seems that Thomas refers to Euclid's *Elements* (around 300 BCE), in which Euclid formulates a comprehensive mathematical theory (which never lost its significance until today).

40. Thus Sacred Doctrine must not only be a matter of the intellect; a theologian must be involved, heart and soul; a theologian must be someone of faith, for theology is not without engagement; cf. ST I 1,4,1 where Thomas cites James 1.22 ("Be doers of the word, not only listeners"). See also paragraph 2.3.

41. There are two words for "pledge" in Latin: one is *pignus*, which is given for an entrusted thing; when it is returned, the state of pledge is abolished. The other term, *arra*, which Augustine uses here, is something given in confidence,

and other things that he mentions there. So the refreshment of Sacred Scripture is great because of the greatness of the abundance in provision and because of the greatness of the delight in taste.

(2.2: 3.3) Third, because of the greatness in effect. What is the effect of it? I say that it gives life, as Saint Peter says: "Lord, to whom shall we go? You have the words of everlasting life" [Jn 6.68]. By means of words people are brought to the faith, through which they live and are incited to love (*caritas*) [cf. Lk 10.28]. Hence it says in Sir 15.3: "She [Wisdom] fed him with the bread of life and of understanding (and made him drink the water of the wisdom of salvation and took him up to her close relatives)."

(2.3) Third, Christ prepared for us a refreshment that pertains to our affection. Thus we read in Song 5.1: "Eat, my friends!" that is, here and now, through grace, "and get drunk, my dear!" that is, in the future, through glory.[42] Christ makes this refreshment for us insofar as he has the fullness of divinity, as Ps 84.12 reads: "The Lord will give grace and glory."[43]

In this refreshment is the early meal of grace, namely, in the present. The Lord calls us to this early meal in Jn 21.12, where he says: "Come and take breakfast."[44]

We expect the dinner of this refreshment in the future, which will be in glory. Therefore, it says in Rv 19.9: "Happy those who are called to the wedding feast of the Lamb." This is the dinner to which no one is called unless he is a worthy member of the household. Thus we read in Is 65.13: "My servants will eat, but you will be hungry."[45]

---

first in part, so that may be made full or given to the full in the future (although in Eph 1.14 *pignus* is used in the meaning of *arra*).

42. In ST III 79,1,2 Thomas uses this verse to speak about the Eucharist as a spiritual refreshment for the soul.

43. Cited in this context in ST I–II 7,1 and 62,1,3 (necessity of the sacraments); cf. ST I–II 108,1; II–II 183,2; III 19,4,2 and 26,2,1. This leads to happiness, according to Ps 84.13.

44. *Prandeo:* this meal takes place in the morning; cf. Jn 21.4.

45. It may seem that Thomas is excluding people here. But in the *Collatio in*

(2.3: 3) This dinner is greater than other ones because of the three characteristics already mentioned.

(2.3: 3.1) First, because of the great splendor of the provision. The greatness of the provision is found in the fact that man would sit at the table of God. Someone who sits at the king's table has a splendid provision. In Lk 22.29–30 it is said: "I have given you a place," et cetera, "so that you may eat and drink at my table," et cetera. Does he have a tangible table then? Certainly not! God's refreshment is joy [cf. Ps 43.4]. But about what does Christ rejoice? Surely about himself, for he would not be happy unless he would rejoice about himself.[46] Then he will bring to pass that they see him by essence [1 Jn 3.2] and thus they will rejoice in him. Jb 22.26 reads: "Then you will be full of delights because of the Almighty."[47] Which food is more precious than God? Surely none.[48]

(2.3: 3.2) If someone tries to find out how great the delight in taste is, his seeking is redundant. For everything (of this meal) is delightful. Something is delightful insofar as it is good or insofar as it appears to be good.[49] But if minor good things or things that participate in the good are already delightful, then how great a delight is caused by that thing whose goodness is infinite.[50] As we read in Ps 16.11: "The delights in your right

---

sero he will point out how everybody ought to be made worthy, in accordance with Lk 14.21–23.

46. Our ultimate happiness is found in God (cf. ST I–II 2,8, 3,1). Since Christ as a human being is full of God, and as God is the fullness of God, he therefore rejoices in himself. The image of indulgence in navel-gazing is not what is meant; Thomas tries to formulate the mystery of the fullness of Christ's happiness and joy.

47. In ST I 42,6 Thomas speaks of the almightiness of the divine Son (here he shows the consequences of the steps taken in the preceding *articuli*); in ST III 13 he contemplates the almightiness of the Son's human soul (where he shows the consequences in regard to this subject of the faith in the true humanity of Christ).

48. Cf. Jn 4.34 (in ST I–II 69,2,3). Also: Wis 7.9 (in ST I–II 2,6); Prv 3.15 (in ST II–II 100,1).

49. Cf. ST I 5,6.

50. Which is God; cf. ST I 6,2–3 and 7,1, from whom all good things come. Everything that is, participates insofar as it is good in God's infinite goodness; cf. ST I 6,4 and 7,1.

hand are till the end," and Ps 31.20: "How great the multitude of your sweetness, Lord."

(2.3: 3.3) Third, this dinner is great because of the greatness of the virtue [or strength] in its effect,[51] for it contains the eternity of life [cf. Jn 6.50–51]; the rejoicing saints will never be deficient in it. Ps 22.27a reads: "The poor will eat and be satisfied," et cetera. "The poor will eat"—and who are the poor? Surely the poor in spirit, since we read in Mt 5.3: "Happy are the poor in spirit (for the Kingdom of heaven is theirs)." Or the poor are the humble, or the poor in will [cf. Ps 40.9], namely, those who have riches but despise them. These come to the dinner, whereas the ones whose mind is set on temporal things do not come [cf. Lk 14.18–20]. Thus we read in the Gospel: "Happy those who hunger and thirst for justice, for they will be satisfied" [Mt 5.6].

And [the Psalm continues]: "They who seek him will praise the Lord" [Ps 22.27b]. Augustine says: "We will see, we will love (*amo*), and we will praise. Their hearts will live forever and ever"—not just a physical life, but a life of the soul, a life that is united with God.[52]

May we be found worthy of this by him who with the Father, et cetera.

PART 3: *Collatio in sero*

"Someone" [Lk 14.16], et cetera. Today we have spoken about the preparation of this dinner; now we must speak about its announcement. For the "someone" [in this biblical story] certainly has not prepared the dinner for no one to sit at the table, but in order to make it known to others. See that this dinner is not made known to anyone but to one who is called to it. One

---

51. The Latin text used reads *affectu;* but in the context of the sermon (see the parallel paragraphs 3.3 above, in 2.1 and 2.2) it is obvious it should be *effectu.*

52. *Vita anime Deo coniuncta.* Cf. ST I 12,4sc and 6sc on eternal life (which consists in the vision of the divine essence); cf. ST I–II 11 and 104,4, on the enjoyment of God; and ST I–II 5,4 on the difference between imperfect happiness in this life and perfect, eternal happiness after life on earth.

who is not called can approach the things that he knows and desires, but he cannot approach what exceeds our desire unless he is called.[53] Such is this dinner. Hence the Apostle says in 1 Cor 2.9–10 and in Is 64.3: "Eye has not seen, ear has not heard, and in the heart of a man it did not (come up: the things that God has prepared for them who love [*diligo*] him. Yet he has revealed it to us through the Holy Spirit)." And therefore someone does not come to this dinner unless he is called, whence Rom 8.30 reads: "the ones he has called he has also justified, (and the ones he justified he has also glorified)."

We must note that there are two kinds of vocation [or calling]: (1) one interior, (2) the other from outside.

❖

(I) The interior vocation, through which the Lord addresses man internally, is never in vain, since a human being does not reject it. Jb 14.15: "You will call me and I will respond to you." Augustine says in his book *On Predestination:* "The grace which is infused in human hearts by the divine abundance is not repelled by any hard heart; therefore, we say in this case that rather the hardness of the heart is repelled." Hence the Lord's interior calling is not in vain.[54] Thus we read in Jn 6.45: "Everyone who hears and learns from my Father comes to me."[55]

❖

(II) The other vocation, which occurs through an angel or a human being,

---

53. In general in ST I 12,13,4, in respect of our happiness in I–II 5,5, and in respect of the resurrection in III 55,1.

54. Thomas uses the term *vocatio* (vocation, calling) for God's calling as an execution of what he has predestined; cf. ST I 23,2.

God's calling from within is never in vain, Thomas says: all people are naturally created towards God; God made us as beings who naturally will what is good. Through sin, however, this will is disordered; sinning goes against our will. So if we are inspired by God himself to do what we are naturally inclined to do, we would not refuse but would do it, happily and voluntarily. The working of inspiration is in our soul from the inside out, instead of the less effective, indirect calling of God, which comes from outside us, through angels or fellow-human beings. Cf. ST I 105,4 and 5; I–II 6,4, 9,6 (where he cites Phil 2.13: "It is God who works in you both to will and to do in order to realize what is good in his eyes") and 113,1,3.

55. ST I 43,5,2; cf. III 69,5,2.

(1)[56] is not as effective as the one that is directly from God; indeed, often it is in vain, and many reject it. Hence[57] we read in Prv 1.24: "I have called and you have rejected." And Mt 20.16: "For many are called, but few elected." Concerning this vocation the Lord speaks here, as he says, "he called many" [Lk 14.16]. And it shows that he speaks of this vocation, because this is done by a servant [Lk 14.17]. Therefore: "At the time of the dinner he sent his servant to say to the ones who were invited: 'Come!'"

(2) But who is the servant? The Apostle Paul and the other preachers, prelates, and teachers; all such people who remind us of the good [that God has done for us] are called servants of God.

Here two things that must be considered come up, namely, (3) who are called and (4) how they are called.[58]

(3) In this multitude of people called we find a threefold distinction, as the Gospel clearly shows: (3.1) some of the ones called are those who were invited to the dinner, (3.2) others were the downtrodden citizens, and (3.3) yet others were strangers.

(3.1) Now who were the ones who were invited? I say that those properly invited were those who received the privilege of a divine office, for the invitation is sent out to relatives and close friends. If someone is a religious, a cleric, or if someone happens to have the gift of wisdom or something the like, that is the invitation.[59] In Est 1.7 it is said that "the ones who were

---

56. The structure of section II on the calling from outside is: (1) its effectiveness, (2) its subject (who are calling), (3) its object (who are called), and (4) the way in which the dinner is announced.

57. The Latin text used reads *undo*, but obviously it should be *unde*.

58. Thus the emphasis of this part of the sermon is on the practical.

59. So Thomas makes the preachers-to-be and the teachers-to-be aware that they themselves are called and need to respond. The invitation is a gift: becoming a religious, a priest, et cetera, is not something you do, but something God is doing to you (cf. Heb 5.4), and you are the one to respond to it by realizing what you are called to do or to become. Likewise, talents are gifts, and someone

invited to the feast drank from golden cups." The golden cups are God's precious gifts.

The ones invited were to come to the wedding, but did not come because of a triple hindrance, which is mentioned in 1 Jn 2.15: "Do not love (*diligo*) the world nor the things that are in the world. If someone loves (*diligo*) the world, the love (*caritas*) of God is not in him." What is it that hinders the ones who were invited from coming to the wedding? Certainly, that a human being clings to the world. And how does someone cling to the world? Certainly, by pursuing things that are in the world. And which are the things that are in the world? The concupiscence of the flesh or the concupiscence of the eye or the pride of life, as it is said in 1 Jn 2.16.[60] Thus in three ways people are hindered from coming to the dinner, even though they are invited, namely, (3.1.1) because of pride, (3.1.2) because of the concupiscence of the eye or (3.1.3) that of the flesh.[61]

(3.1.1) First, I say, someone is hindered from coming to the dinner because of pride.[62] It happens that some people have received many good spiritual and temporal things from God, and although they ought to subject themselves to God because of those things, they become proud because of these things. Hence we read in Ezek 28.17: "Exalted is your heart because of your ornament." And in Jer 5.5: "You will speak to their aristocrats, and, behold, they have broken the yoke of the counsels and have torn the bonds," that is, the bonds of the Commandments. And these are signified by him who has said: "I have bought a house, and I am going to see it" [cf. Lk 14.18]. Augustine says that "house" is understood as absolute dominion, that with the word "absolute dominion" pride is expressed,[63] where-

---

who receives such a gift is therefore called to live according to it; cf. Mt 25.14–30. See also ST II–II 24,3, 62,4,3.

60. The formation of our judgment is hindered because it is connected with our senses: ST I 84,8; I–II 33,3.

61. Cf. ST I–II 77,5.

62. ST II–II 162–165: it is willed and contrary to good reason. Cf. Sermon 08 *Puer Jesus, Collatio in sero,* paragraph 4.3.

63. The Latin word for house is *domus*. Because *dominatio* (absolute dominion) belongs to the *Dominus* (the Lord) alone, therefore not acknowledging God as the Lord, turning away from God, and taking the Lord's place are characteristic of

as the dinner is proper to the humble. Note also that he says: "I have bought a house and I need to see it" [Lk 14.18]. Often those who are proud of the gifts given to them by God think of the gifts, not of the One from whom the gifts came. Against such a man it is said in 1 Cor 4.7: "What do you have that you have not received?"

Imagine, you are a highly placed man (*prelatus*) or a scholar. You ought to ponder from where you have it: you do not have it from yourself, but from God, so that you may subject yourself to him. And this realization not only takes away pride, but even brings on humility.[64] For as the gifts increase, the reasons for giving honor increase;[65] the more goods you have, the more obliged you are to God. But someone who does not know[66] that the goods he has come from God, cannot thank God. Because of this [I say]: think this over, that whatever you have, you have from God [cf. also Jn 3.27], and that you are bound to give him thanks [cf. Eph 5.20, Col 3.15, *et alibi*] or, better, give to him thanks in return.[67] Then those gifts will not lead to pride.

(3.1.2) Others look down on going to the dinner, even though they have been invited, and this because of the concupiscence of the eyes. It is understood that Hos 2.8 says about them: "I have multiplied for them silver and gold which they have made into a Baal." By "gold" wisdom is meant;[68] by "silver" eloquence;[69] some have obtained the grace of eloquence or the gift of wisdom, and hence they ought to serve God. Those who turn these gifts around and use them for concupiscence and the acquisition of earthly things serve the devil. He says that

---

pride. In this respect pride is the beginning of every sin; cf. ST I–II 84,2; II–II 162,6–7.

64. Humility is the opposite of pride: ST II–II 161.

65. Cf. ST II–II 106,1 and 3.

66. *Ignoro*: Thomas distinguishes between *ignoro* (*ignorantia* as a result of neglect; people who do not make an effort to find the truth) and *nescio* (*nescientia*, not knowing as such), ST I–II 76,2.

67. *Gratias agere, gratias reddere*: ST II–II 58,11. Therefore, gratitude is a virtue of justice: ST II–II 80, 81–91.

68. Sir 6.18–37 (especially verse 30); cf. Jb 23.10, Ps 18.31, Wis 3.6–9.

69. Prv 10.20; cf. Sir 28.24b–25a. Thus we still say that an eloquent person has "a silver tongue."

"they have made a Baal," because avarice is slavery of idols.[70] These are signified by the one who was invited and said, "I have bought five yoke of oxen, and I am going to try them out" [Lk 14.19]. By the five yoke the five senses are signified, which completely enslave someone to sensory things. He says: "I have bought five yoke of oxen, (and I am going to try them out)." Here not only cupidity but also curiosity[71] is repudiated. Some are very curious about external things and about what others do, so that they try to find out what others do and neglect their own deeds. Such people are like an eye which sees another eye, but it does not see itself. For some do not want to believe anything except what they see.[72]

(3.1.3) Third, the ones invited are hindered from coming to the dinner because of the concupiscence of the flesh. For some turn themselves to pleasures when they have been exalted through the gifts of God. Hence we read in Ezek 16.15: "You trust in your ornament; you have committed fornication."[73] Is 22.12: "On that day the Lord will call you to weeping and mourning," namely, when he has said in the Gospel, "Happy those who lament (for they will be comforted)" [Mt 5.4]. And [Isaiah continues]: "Behold, their joy, their killing of the calves." The condemned say: "Let us eat and drink, for tomorrow we will die" [Is 22.13]. They are referred to by the one who married a wife and therefore could not come to the dinner [Lk 14.20]. By the wife the concupiscence of the flesh is signified. Only this one and not anyone else said: "*I cannot* come."

---

70. Desire (*cupiditas*) is the root of every sin in respect of our turning towards a created good (instead of towards God); cf. ST I–II 84,1–2. Contrary to slavery in the general sense of the word, this slavery not only concerns the body, the exterior life (ST II–II 104,6,1), but even the soul, the interior life: ST II–II 122,4,3.

71. ST II–II 167.

72. Cf. Jn 4.48, 20.29. Faith is about things that we cannot see: Heb 11.1; cf. ST II–II 1,4. Since Jn 20.29 ("Happy those who have not seen and yet believe") is said in the context of the Resurrection, it seems that Thomas echoes the critique that he had voiced earlier, in the *Sermo*, against the philosophers who deny the resurrection of the body.

73. This can even be because of a spiritual beauty, if someone is proud of it: ST II–II 145,2,3.

For because of the enticement of the flesh he could not come.

There is a difference between the sin of pride and of cupidity,[74] on the one hand, and lustfulness,[75] on the other. For the proud and the ones who desire (*cupidus*) commit a sin intentionally and do not want to come to the dinner.[76] But those who sin through the sin of the flesh, sin because of weakness and incapability. These have the intention of going to the dinner but are hindered by the concupiscence of the flesh.[77] Hence the Apostle says: "The flesh desires (*concupisco*) against the spirit, the spirit against the flesh, so that you do not do everything you want" [Gal 5.17].

These, although they were invited, have not come to the dinner either because of pride or because of cupidity or because of the concupiscence of the flesh. But it is written that "a servant who knows the will of his lord and does not do it, will be flogged with many lashes" [Lk 12.47]. So, the more important you are, if you act against the will (of the Lord), you are worthy of a heavier punishment.[78]

And the *paterfamilias* was furious when he heard that the ones invited did not want to come [Lk 14.21]. By the anger God's wrath[79] is signified.[80] So the first that are called to the meal are the ones who are invited.

(3.2) Another category of those who were called to the din-

74. For the difference between these two, see ST I–II 84,2.

75. *Luxuria* is a collective term for all kinds of sexual activity which are against the virtue of temperance: ST II–II 153–154.

76. On intention: ST I 79,10,3; I–II 12; cf. 19,7–8.

77. Thus the first two were hypocrites because they said, "Please, accept my regrets," while they did not regret it at all (ST II–II 111,1–3), whereas the third man spoke the truth; he *could* not come. Furthermore, the first two did not even have the *intention* of coming, Thomas says; they sinned consciously, whereas the third man sinned because of weakness, namely, passion: ST I–II 77,2–3 and 6–8.

78. Cf. ST I–II 73,9.

79. Since God is not composite, his wrath and anger must be understood as metaphors; cf. ST I 3,2,2.

80. Thomas has identified the one who made the dinner as Jesus Christ because of the word *homo*—a man, a human being—in the text. Here Thomas reads the parallel text of Mt 22.2–10 into Luke's version; in Matthew it is a king who invites people to the wedding feast of his son.

ner are the downtrodden citizens, as it says in the Gospel: "Go to the streets and the broad ways of the city, and call the weak, the blind, and the lame" [Lk 14.21], et cetera. And see: the last are made the first [cf. Mt 19.30, 20.16]. For the great do not arrive at that dinner, neither do the mighty, but the weak and the poor do. We have the example in Lazarus and the rich man [Lk 16.19–26]. The ill are often converted, whence Ambrose says: "Weakness of the body excludes no one from the Kingdom, and sometimes [this weakness] is even absent from someone who is not allured by sin." The Apostle explains why: "God has chosen those who are the weak of the world to shame whatever is strong" [1 Cor 1.28]. You must understand this in a spiritual way, that the poor in temporal things who are, however, rich in spiritual things are chosen; these are in the streets and the broad ways; whence the Prophet says: "Scattered are the stones of the sanctuary on the corner of all the broad ways" [Lam 4.1].[81]

But concerning the man who is rich in temporal things but poor in spiritual things, Rv 3.17 says: "You say that I am rich and do not need anything, whilst you do not know that you are wretched, (miserable, poor, blind, and naked)," for "sin makes peoples wretched" [Prv 14.34].

But from which defect of riches do sinners suffer? I say that they fail (3.2.1) in knowledge, (3.2.2) in strength, and (3.2.3) in rectitude.[82]

(3.2.1) First, I say that those blinded through sin suffer from a defect in knowledge, namely, because they disdain what is good and choose what is evil.[83] Thus the Apostle says in 2 Tm 3.4: "The ones who love (*amator*) pleasures more than God are swollen (with passionate excitement) and blind." It is on the ground of this blindness that rich people despise divine things and would rather have temporal things.

(3.2.2) Others fail in strength of the mind and virtue[84]

---

81. Citing this verse here seems to be an implicit reference to 1 Pt 2.5: "Let yourselves, like living stones, be built into a spiritual house," et cetera.
82. Cf. ST II–II 15,1.
83. ST I–II 76,1; cf. I–II 100,1 and II–II 173,2.
84. ST I–II 85,1–4. Thomas's formulation is: *in fortitudine animi et virtute;* the

through sin. Hence it says in Neh 4.10: "Weak is the virtue[85] of the one who carries (heavy loads)," of whom it is said: "My virtue[86] was for nothing" [Jb 30.2], and these are the weak.

(3.2.3) Others who are blinded through sin fail in rectitude,[87] that is, in their intention. Hence it says in Mi 7.2: "The saint has disappeared from the earth, and a righteous man is not found among the people." These are the lame; from the outside they seem to follow the Lord, but if anyone sees their intention, it becomes clear they are lame. About this lameness Elijah says: "How long will you be lame, in two minds?" [1 Kgs 18.21] Whenever the poor are enriched, the blind illuminated, the weak strengthened, and the lame cured,[88] "then," says Is 35.6, "the lame will leap like a deer."

(3.3) See that when the servant had led those people in, he said to his lord: "There is still room" [Lk 14.22], by which predestination[89] is indicated: for not only the great and the faithful are called. Therefore, the Lord says: "I have other sheep, which are not from this flock (and I must lead those to me, and it will be one flock, one shepherd)" [Jn 10.16]. Because the Lord has other sheep, he calls people who are outside the flock. Therefore, it says in the Gospel: "Go out into the roads and hedges, and compel (them to come in, that my house may be filled)" [Lk 14.23 (Vg)]. By the people who are outside, the unbelievers are signified. Now, we find a triple distinction within the unbelievers:[90]

(3.3.1) The first are the Gentiles and the pagans who do not at all share in the faith; the light of faith does not shine for

---

word *virtus* means "virtue" as well as "effort" and "strength"; *fortitudo* also means "strength," but not "virtue." In the verses quoted from Nehemiah and Job the term *virtus* is used.

85. Or "strength."
86. Or "effort."
87. ST I–II 75,4; II–II 15,3; sin makes the will turn to what is evil (contrary to rectitude) and causes (a greater) blindness of the intellect, and such blindness leads to (more) sinning.
88. In the prayer before receiving holy Communion attributed to Thomas, *Omnipotens sempiterne Deus ecce accedo ad sacramentum unigeniti Filii tui,* we find a remarkable parallel with these pairs of words.
89. ST I 23–24; also SCG III 163.
90. Cf. ST II–II 10–11, esp. 10,5 and 6.

them. These are in dark roads. Hence it says: "The roads of the godless are dark roads" [Prv 4.19].

(3.3.2) Other unbelievers are the Jews, who share something with us, namely, the sacred doctrine of the Old Testament. Of them it is said: "There is still a little light in you" [Jn 12.35]. These are signified by the scattered roads, in Is 33.8: "Scattered are the roads." The figurative observances have passed away; they have become scattered roads, because since the truth has come, the prefiguration has passed. Thus someone who preserved the figurative observances would sin. Hence the Apostle says: "If you let yourselves be circumcised, Christ will bring you nothing" [Gal 5.2].[91]

(3.3.3) The third group of unbelievers are the heretics in the hedges [Lk 14.23 (Vg)]. Hedges are conceived as making divisions. Heretics do not serve for anything; the only thing they do is making a division. Heretics are thorns because they sting, and hedges because they divide.[92]

These three categories of people are pointed out to us, in order to show that the Gospel was preached first to princes and priests who refused to come [Mt 2.1-8, 16]; then Peter preached to the lower people of the Jews and converted 3,000 of them [Acts 2.41]; subsequently preachers went into the hedges and the broad ways in order to proclaim the Gospel,[93] and all were brought to the faith. Hence the Church prays not only for highly placed people (*prelatus*), but also for the weakened and the unbelievers.[94] So these are the ones who are called.

---

91. So as for the Jews, *infideles*, "unbelievers," is said in view of the faith in Christ and so in the Trinity, not in the sense that they do not believe at all; cf. ST 104,2.

92. Schismatic groups like the Cathari were a serious threat to the unity of the Church (and of the secular society) and could, therefore, eventually not be tolerated: ST II–II 11,3, 39.

93. In the first two instances Thomas uses the verb *praedico* + the dative case: the Gospel was preached for the benefit of the addressees. When he speaks of the heretics, he says that the Gospel "was preached into the hedges and the broad ways," *praedico in* + the accusative case. Thus he points out to his audience, preachers-to-be, that they should (not preach from afar, but) actually go into the places where these heretics live and preach, and proclaim the Gospel from within these communities.

94. ST II–II 83,7–8.

(4) But how are they called? A triple way of vocation is presented.

(4.1) The ones who are invited must be called by a simple summons, as it happens in the Gospel: "He sent his servant at the time of the dinner to say to the ones invited that they come" [Lk 14.18]. Neither being loud nor being rough is better. Thus we read: "Do not chide an old man, but honor him as your father" [1 Tm 5.1] and elsewhere: "Give honor to the wise man" [Sir 10.31 (Vg)].[95]

(4.2) Furthermore, the poor and the downtrodden must be led inside. Some have taken up the plan to come to God in baptism; they have renounced the devil and his whole train. Now they need someone who instructs them and leads them in and makes them acquainted with the King. Hence it says in Ex 23.20: "Behold, I will send my angel to go before your face so as to protect you as well as to lead you into the place."

(4.3) Third, the unbelievers and the heretics must be compelled to come to the dinner, as we read in the Gospel: "Go out in the streets and hedges, and compel them to enter" [Lk 14.23 (Vg)]. Those who are in the hedges must be compelled in two ways. "Signs are not given to believers, but to unbelievers" [cf. Mt 12.39, 16.4]. Hence heretics are compelled to enter on the ground of the evidence of miracles.[96] Likewise, to the letter, they must be compelled by giving them a hard time (*per vexacionem*). Thus we read in Ps 32.9: "(Be not senseless like horses or mules:) jaws in bridle and bit, (that is how their temper must be curbed.)" Heretics say that no one must be urged to come to faith by means of punishment. On the contrary rather, whence it says in Is 28.19: "Only distress (*vexacio*) will give understanding to the hearing."[97]

We do not read that they who were on the roads and in the

---

95. Neither force nor threats must be used, Thomas impresses upon his audience: converting someone must be done with respect; cf. ST II–II 10,11–12.

96. As in Mt 2.1–11 and 27.45, 54 (the star and the darkness and the confession of the centurion; cf. ST III 44,2) and as Christ did during his life on earth (cf. ST III 44,3–4).

97. Cf. ST II–II 11,3co, ad 3: excommunication and the death penalty are the ultimate measures.

hedges have excused themselves; only those who were invited did. In this it is pointed out that cold sinners are converted more quickly than the ones who stray from the way on which they were going.[98] Hence we read in Hos 8.5–6: "He cannot thoroughly be cleansed, because he is from Israel."

We will ask, et cetera.

---

98. *Decidere a statu viae*, which is *apostasia*: once they were *viatores*, pilgrims on the way to the *patria*. Cf. ST I–II 84,2,2; II–II 12,1.

SERMON 14
ATTENDITE A FALSIS

Sermon on the Third Sunday after the Feast of the Apostles Peter and Paul[1]

Matthew 7.15–16: *Beware of the false prophets who come to you in clothes of sheep; inside they are grasping wolves. You will know them by their fruits.*

PART 1: *Prothema*

HE APOSTLE demonstrates in the following words that there are two things that are contrary to one another. "The spirit," he says, "desires (*concupisco*) against the flesh and the flesh against the spirit" [Gal 5.17]. And yet it happens that sin comes forth from both; sometimes sin comes forth from the weakness of the flesh, sometimes from the ignorance of the spirit.[2] Thus the Apostle says in 2 Cor 7.1: "Let us cleanse ourselves from every impurity of the flesh and of the spirit." And just as the sin of the flesh comes forth from the weakness of the flesh—as it is said in Mt 26.41: "the spirit is willing indeed, yet the flesh is weak"—so the sin of the spirit comes forth from ignorance of the spirit, namely, when the spirit is deceived.[3] And therefore we are strengthened in this Sunday reading against both sins. We are strengthened against the sin that

---

1. Or the 7th Sunday after the Feast of the Trinity, as the Nürnberg text says. This sermon was given on the 14th of July 1269.

2. ST I–II 77,1–3, and I–II 76,1, respectively. In this sermon the focus is on the latter, as Thomas indicates in this *Prothema*.

3. Other internal causes are our passions and our misery (ST I–II 77–78). In I–II 79–81 Thomas examines the external causes: the roles of God, of the devil, and of human beings themselves.

195

occurs by reason of the weakness of the flesh by the Apostle in the Epistle reading that says: "We are indebted to the flesh not to live according to the flesh" [Rom 8.12]. We are strengthened against the sin that occurs by reason of the deception of the spirit, where it says in the Gospel reading: "Beware of the false prophets, (who come to you in clothes of sheep; inside they are grasping wolves. You will know them by their fruits)."

Let us ask the Savior, who wanted us to be careful of both sins, that he may grant that I say something that is to his praise, et cetera.

PART 2: *Sermo*

"Beware" [Mt 7.15], et cetera. It belongs to the task of a good commander that he advises his soldiers to be careful of ambushes [cf. 2 Kgs 6.8–10]. It is true that we have a cunning and wily enemy. Hence we read in Sir 11.29: "Many are the ambushes of a wily man." The Psalmist says: "He sits in ambushes with the rich" [Ps 10.8], that is: with the proud. The Apostle explains what these ambushes are, when he says that "Satan transfigures himself into the Angel of light, and his servants (transfigure themselves) into the servants of righteousness" [cf. 2 Cor 11.14–15].

Against Satan's servants the Lord advises us in the words mentioned above to be careful. In these words he teaches us four things: [*Sermo*] (1) First, he teaches of what kind the enemies are, where he says: "Beware of the false prophets." [*Collatio in sero*] (2) Second, he teaches what ambushes they make, where he says: "They come to you in clothes of sheep. (3) The third thing is that it threatens to damage us, where he says: "Inside they are grasping wolves." (4) Fourth, he teaches how to recognize them, where he says: "You will know them by their fruits."

These enemies are false prophets, and they are very dangerous, and therefore we must watch out for them, for they are as dangerous for us as good angels are necessary and useful for us. Hence we read in Prv 29.18: "When prophecy ceases, the population will be scattered."[4] About the false prophets it says

---

4. They can enlighten, guide, and protect us; cf. ST I 111 and 113. In ST II-II 172,1,4 Thomas argues, referring to this verse, that prophecy is necessary for

SERMON 14

in Jer 23.15: "From the prophets of Jerusalem defilement has spread over the land."

※

(1) And in order to see who the false prophets are, (1.1) let us first see what the definition is of a prophet and then (1.2) why someone happens to be a false prophet.

(1.1) I say that four things belong to the definition of a prophet.

(1.1.1) The first is divine revelation.[5] Hence it says in Am 3.7: "The Lord God will not speak a word without revealing his secret to his servants, the prophets."[6]

(1.1.2) At times some things are divinely revealed to a person, but he does not understand it, as when Nebuchadnezzar saw a statue [cf. Dn 2.31]; and when something was announced to the Pharaoh—he saw spikes of grain and cattle—but he did not understand it [cf. Gn 41.2–7].[7] For this, understanding is required[8]—a second characteristic of a prophet. Thus we read in Dn 10.1: "A word was revealed to Daniel and he understood the message." So, "understanding is needed with visions" [ibid.].

(1.1.3) If a person had a revelation from God and, although he understood it, kept it to himself, it would be of no avail. Because of this it is required in the third place that the things that are revealed to a man and that he understands, are made known by him to others. Is 21.10 reads: "I have made known to you the things which I have heard from the Lord of hosts, the God of Israel."

(1.1.4) Some things that are revealed and made known from God are above human perception. But people do not believe

---

the guidance of people, in particular in view of the way in which we ought to serve God. What has been revealed to the prophets has been revealed to angels in a more excellent way: ST I 57,5,3.

5. ST II–II 172,1: prophecy is something supernatural. For the other three characteristics mentioned in 1.1.2 – 1.1.4 see also ST II–II 171,1.

6. I.e., insofar as they are necessary for the instruction of a faithful people; cf. ST II–II 171,4,1.

7. Therefore, it is clear that prophecies can be given to people who do not believe or do not live an exemplary life; cf. ST II–II 172,4.

8. I.e., understanding of the prophecy itself, not necessarily of the ultimate end and how we attain it; cf. ST II–II 8,5,2, 173,2,2.

unless things are proven, and this proof is the working of miracles.[9] And this is signified in 2 Kgs 5.8, where we read that when Naaman the Syrian had come to the king of Israel to be cured of leprosy, Elisha said: "Send him to me, so that he knows that there is a prophet in Israel."

So, along the line of what has been said above, I come to the conclusion that the name "prophet" can be interpreted in four ways.

(ad 1.1.1) At times someone who receives a divine revelation is called a prophet, as we read in Nm 12.6: "If someone among you were a prophet of the Lord, I could speak to him in a dream."[10]

(ad 1.1.2) Yet sometimes we call someone a prophet although he has not received a divine revelation, but because it is given to him to understand the things revealed. Thus we read in 1 Cor 14.29: "Let two or three prophets speak, and let others determine." In the same letter [the Apostle] calls teachers and preachers prophets [cf. 1 Cor 12.8–10], in accordance with Sir 24.33: "Still" all teachers "will pour out the teaching as a prophecy."

(ad 1.1.3) Sometimes we call people prophets who recite the revealed things, as it is said in 2 Chr 35.15: "The sons of Asaph and of Idithun" prophesied.

(ad 1.1.4) Sometimes those who work miracles are called prophets. Hence it is said in Sir 48.14 that "the dead body" of Elisha "prophesied," meaning: he has worked a prophetic miracle.[11] In 2 Kgs 13.21 it is told that some robbers were terrified: they threw the dead body of someone who was killed into the grave of Elisha, and that that man lived again. And likewise it is

---

9. ST I 105,7: Things done by God which are beyond our knowledge of the natural causes are called miracles. To some people the grace of working miracles is given in order to confirm what is being preached or to underline someone's holiness; cf. ST II–II 178. At the very end of Sermon 13 *Homo quidam* (in 4.3) Thomas points out that signs and miracles are for unbelievers.

10. Dreams, however, can also be deceptive; cf. ST II–II 95,6. Like visions, they are enigmatic: ST III 7,8,1.

11. It is a prophetic miracle because it is a prefiguration of what Christ did to Lazarus (Jn 11.34–44) and does to all who believe in him (Jn 11.25–26): ST II–II 1,6,1; cf. also I–II 111,4; II–II 95,2,3.

said in the Gospel that, when Christ worked miracles, the Jews said: "A great prophet has arisen among us" [Lk 7.16].[12]

Therefore, he says: "Beware," et cetera.

But how is "prophet" conceived here and now? Chrysostom says that those who prophesy about Christ are not called prophets nowadays, but those who interpret a prophecy about Christ, since no one can interpret the prophetic meanings unless through the Holy Spirit [cf. 1 Cor 12.3].[13]

(1.2) Let us see who are called false prophets. In four ways a prophet can be false: (1.2.1) first, because of the falseness of the teaching; (1.2.2) second, because of the falseness of the inspiration; (1.2.3) third, because of the falseness of the intention; and (1.2.4) fourth, because of the falseness of life.

(1.2.1) First, some are called false prophets on the basis of the falseness of the teaching, as when they preach and teach false things. It belongs to the task of a prophet that he preaches and teaches true things.[14] Hence we read in Dn 10.1: "a word is revealed to Daniel and the word is true"; and the Lord says: If anyone makes my words known, "let him speak in truth" [Jer 23.28]. But many preach in a false way. Thus it says in a Letter [of the New Testament]: "There will be pseudo-prophets among the people; yes, also among you there will be deceitful *magistri*" [1 Jn 4.1] who do not hesitate to induce a direction that leads to doom. Arius[15] was a liar—was he not?—as well as the ones like

---

12. Still, the working of miracles can also deceive us; demons are capable of performing works that look very much like true miracles; cf. ST 114,4.

13. Cf. ST I 43,3,4. Thus Thomas has formulated a definition distilled from Scripture; he surveyed those whom we in our faithful speech in fact call prophets. For the role of the Holy Spirit and of the angels, see: II–II 172,1–2.

14. A prophet worships God by preaching what is true. False teachings may contain some truth. Because of this they are more plausible and acceptable for the listeners and so more dangerous too; cf. ST II–II 172,6.

15. Arianism, based on the teachings of the Libyan priest Arius (256–336), was a popular heresy in the early Church. Arius denied the eternity of the Son: Christ is not God. The Ecumenical Council of Nicea was called together in 325 by the emperor, upon whom Arius had called as he was condemned by his own bishop, Alexander of Alexandria, in 311. The *homoousion* ("one in being with the Father") was formulated by this council as an answer to Arian teaching. The con-

him, who wanted to "correct" the doctrine of Christ. Hence we read in Lam 2.14: "Your prophets have seen false and stupid things."

But which things are stupid? Someone who freely says things to please the people is someone who speaks false things.[16] Is 30.10: "Speak things that are pleasing to us, see errors for us." Jeremiah, being asked what false prophets see, says: "They did not reveal your iniquity, in order to call you to repent" [Lam 2.14].

If some call "good" what is evil, and "evil" what is good, they are false prophets. Jer says [in Lam 2.14]: "They have false assumptions and make false statements." What is accepted is elevated, and what is dismissed is condemned. So when the things that must be lifted up are pressed down, and the things that must be pressed down are lifted up, you have false assumptions. Through the teaching of the Lord it is clear what must be lifted up and what must be pressed down. Profane language and a worldly life must be pressed down. If someone says that it is better to fast without a vow than with a vow, and pulls others back from the religious life where people fast with a vow, and persuades [them] to fast in the world without a vow, he teaches falsely. The Prophet says: "Make vows and render (to him)" [Ps 76.12]. He says this because it is better to fast with a vow than without a vow; otherwise he would just have said: "Do it."[17]

In his book *On the Parables* Anselm gives an example, saying that someone who gives a tree with fruits gives more than

---

troversy even led to a schism: the schism of Alexandria, in 330. After the death of Emperor Constantine, Arianism grew in popularity again and remained very much alive, especially outside the Roman Empire, until the 7th century. The discussion on who Christ is and how we are to formulate this has never disappeared from the theological agenda. Arius's heresy is very much present in ST III where Thomas discusses the mystery of the Incarnation.

16. This was part of the popularity of Arianism: a mystery (e.g., that Christ is a human being as well as God) is more difficult to accept than something that can be fully understood (e.g., that Christ is a human being and not God). Pleasing others is in itself not bad; it can even be virtuous, but it is bad when the truth is neglected; cf. ST II–II 115,1,1.

17. Cf. ST II–II 88,4. This example reflects a discussion between the regular and the secular in Paris in Thomas's days; cf. ST II–II 88,6 and 186,6.

someone who only gives the fruit. Likewise, someone who takes a vow and renders it does better than someone who does good without a vow.[18] "Still it is better not to vow than not to render what is promised" [Eccl 5.4].[19]

(1.2.2) Furthermore, prophets are called "false" because of the falseness of inspiration. So whence are true prophets inspired? Certainly from God and the Holy Spirit, as it is said in the Letter of Peter: "A prophecy was never proclaimed to the people through the human will, but holy people of God spoke, inspired by the Holy Spirit" [2 Pt 1.21]. Someone can be falsely inspired by the devil, and even by his own spirit;[20] we find both cases in Holy Scripture.

First, I say, someone can be inspired falsely by the devil. As we read in Jer 2.8: "His prophets prophesied in Baal." "To prophesy in Baal," which means "in the devil," is to say occult things. Those who practice black magic, who seek truth about secret matters through inspiration by the devil, prophesy "in Baal." And this is the worst among the sins as well as the worst type of idolatry.[21] And it is not excused on the ground of what they say, that they do it for a good purpose, because evil should not be done for good.[22] Thus the Apostle says of those who say: "Let us do evil things, so that good things may come about," that "the condemnation of them [that reason like this] is just" [Rom 3.8].

Others are inspired in a false way by their own spirit. Thus we read in Ezek 13.3: "Thus says the Lord: 'Woe to the unwise prophets, who follow their own spirit and do not see anything.'" Jer 23.16: "They speak of the vision of their own heart; they do not speak from the Lord's mouth." They who follow human reasoning speak from their own spirit.[23] Such are they who speak

---

18. The same example is given in ST II–II 88,6.
19. Because a vow obliges to the highest extent: ST II–II 88,3.
20. Cf. ST II–II 94,4 vs. 172,1.
21. Cf. ST II–II 95 esp. 95,4. Idolatry is considered a very grave sin, in particular for those who have taken on the faith: ST II–II 94,3.
22. Cf. Rom 12.21; cf. ST I–II 79,4sc; II–II 98,4,4 (which is Thomas's answer to the *sed contra*); III 68,11,3. That God can bring something good out of evil (I 2,3,1) does not make evil itself good.
23. Is 55.8; cf. ST II–II 171,1,3.

according to Platonic ways of thinking, which cannot arrive at truth. For instance, those who say that the world is eternal.[24]

We find some people who study philosophy and say some things that are not true according to the faith. And when someone tells them that this is opposed to the faith, they answer that the Philosopher [namely, Aristotle] says this, but that they themselves do not maintain this; yes, that they only repeat the words of the Philosopher. Such is a false prophet, or a false teacher, because causing doubt and not solving it is the same as giving way to it. This is signified in Ex 21.33–34, where it says that "if someone digs a pit and opens the cistern without covering it over," and a cow belonging to his neighbor comes and falls into the cistern, he who left the cistern open is bound to pay him restitution. Someone who causes doubt about these things that regard the faith, opens the cistern. Someone who does not solve the doubt, although he has a sound and bright intellect and is not deceived, is the one who does not cover over the cistern. Still, someone else, who does not have such a bright intellect, may well be deceived, and then the one who caused the doubt is bound to restitution, since because of him that person fell into the pit.[25]

See, my dearest brethren,[26] there have been many philosophers and they have said many things that pertain to the faith, and yet you will scarcely find two of them who harmonize in one conclusion. And any philosopher who has said something that belongs to the truth has not said it without a mixture of falseness.[27] Just one old woman knows more about these things that pertain to the faith than heretofore all philosophers.[28] We

---

24. See Sermon 06 *Celum et terra transibunt*, note 7.

25. Because the person falling falls because of ignorance: ST I–II 76,2–4. Here Thomas speaks of a sin against the neighbor; cf. ST I–II 72,4 (*peccare in proximum*).

26. *Karissimi*. This little interjection reflects Thomas's zeal and his passionate concern with the well-being of his audience.

27. ST II–II 2,4: because the fullness of truth is God (ST I 16,5) and we know it through faith insofar as he has revealed it (ST I 1,1 and II–II 1,1), whereas for philosophers revelation is not a source of knowledge, and faith is not the gate to it; cf. SCG III 154.

28. *Vetula*: see how Jesus, too, presents an old woman (*vidua*) as a great example, in Lk 18.3–8 and 21.2–3 (cf. ST II–II 32,4,3; III 79,5).

read that Pythagoras first was a boxer. He heard a *magister* disputing on the immortality of the soul, arguing that the soul would be immortal. And he was enticed so much that he left everything and gave himself over to the study of philosophy. But which old woman nowadays would not know that the soul is immortal?[29] Faith is capable of much more than philosophy is. Hence, if philosophy is contrary to faith, it must not be accepted.[30] Thus the Apostle says in Col 2.8, 18–19: "See that no one deceive you by a false philosophy or seduce you, in his desire for empty glory," "someone who walks by things he does not see, in vain with his spirit full of his flesh, and not holding on to the head," which is Christ.[31]

(1.2.3) Others are false prophets because of a false intention. But what is the true intention of a prophet?[32] Surely, the benefit of the people. Hence the Apostle says in 1 Cor 14.13: "Someone who prophesies speaks to the people for the sake of their advancement, exhortation, and consolation." He speaks for the sake of their advancement, so that he renders them devout [cf. Ps 76.12]; for the sake of their exhortation, so that he renders them ready and willing in good works; and for the sake of their consolation, so that he renders them patient in adversities. If anyone seeks from his teaching something else than the benefit of the people, he is a false prophet.

Someone who is a bishop takes up the task of governing and preaching and ought to seek the benefit of the people. If he actually seeks something else, like temporal gain or empty glory,[33]

---

29. In other words: with faith, even if it is a little (or as little as a mustard seed), you know more than the great pagan philosophers; cf. ST I 44,2; II–II 1,8,1.

30. This is how Thomas uses Aristotle's philosophical insights in his theology: if Aristotle says something which is incompatible with the Christian faith, Thomas does not hesitate either to change (slightly) what Aristotle said in order to make his point or to show his readers that Aristotle cannot be used for a better understanding of a particular aspect of the Christian faith. E.g., in ST I 25 we see two examples of this: in 25,2,1 on a Christian understanding of infinity and in 25,3,2 concerning the way Christians ascribe characteristics to creatures and God.

31. Col 1.18. Cf. ST III 8,6sc. Otherwise, schisms occur: ST II–II 39,1.

32. Cf. ST I–II 19,7–10.

33. Cf. II–II 132.

he is a false prophet, because he does not hold on to the right intention. Therefore, Chrysostom says that many priests do not care how the people live, but how much they give to the Church. For this reason the Lord complains in Ezek 13.19: "They profane me with my people for a little bit of barley and a piece of bread." Against them the Apostle says: "We are not like the very many who commit adultery with God's word" [2 Cor 2.17]. Also, Gregory says that someone is a prisoner of the thought of adultery if he seeks to please the eyes of his wife by means of the thing with which a husband conveys gifts to his wife.[34] An adulterer does not seek in a woman to generate offspring, but seeks only temporal delight. In the same way does the one who does not seek spiritual offspring, but only temporal gain or empty glory, commit adultery against the word of the Lord.

(1.2.4) Furthermore, some are false prophets through a bad life, such as when someone teaches one thing and lives another [cf. Lk 11.46, versus 1 Tm 4.12, Ti 2.7–8]. Then his teaching is not accepted. And because of this, Christ "began to do and teach" [Acts 1.1]. And in Lk 1.70 it says: "As was said through the mouth of the holy ones, who from centuries are his prophets"; as if it says: the prophets through whom the Lord speaks ought to be holy.[35] But about them the Lord complains through Jer 23.11: "The priests and prophets have become filthy; in my house I have seen their evil."[36]

We will ask the Lord, et cetera.

PART 3: *Collatio in sero*

"Beware of the false prophets" [Lk 7.15–16], et cetera. Today we have spoken about the enemies of the Christian people, namely, the false prophets.

---

34. "the thing with . . . his wife": a rather cryptic description in order to avoid the word "penis." Adultery in the strict sense of the word: ST II–II 154,8; the spirit of adultery is found in *luxuria* (lustfulness) in general: ST II–II 154,1.

35. Wis 11.1, Sir 48.23 (Vg; cf. Sir 48.22); cf. also Jn 13.15, in ST III 37,1,2.

36. Cf. ST II–II 186,10: the sins of the ones who are addressed are worse since they are supposed to live an exemplary life.

SERMON 14

(2) Now we must see how they have made ambushes for us. Well, the Apostle lays bare their ambushes in the Letter to the Corinthians,[37] and likewise does the Lord in the Gospel when he says: "Beware of the false prophets who come to you in clothes of sheep," et cetera. This is what we understand by hypocrisy,[38] because the hiding place of false prophets is hypocrisy. Hence the Apostle says in 1 Tm 4.1–2: "The Spirit explicitly says: 'In the last days deceivers will come who abandon the faith because they listen to spirits of error and to teachings of demons who speak lies in hypocrisy.'" If someone considers the life and manners, they who lead an austere life and abstain from marriage and delicate foods[39] will seem good to him, but they listen to the spirits of error and the teachings of demons.[40] Take heed to what it is that he says: "who come to you in clothes of sheep." "Sheep" are the Christians who obey Christ, as we read in Jn 10.27: "My sheep listen to my voice." The sheep's pelts are the imitations of Christ. In this way the Apostle says: "Be renewed in the spirit of your mind, and put on the new man, who is created after God in righteousness and holiness of truth" [Eph 4.23–24].

Here he touches upon two things, for righteousness seems to pertain to neighbors, outside ourselves,[41] and holiness of truth to the interior disposition of the soul.[42] Thus that word in Prv 31.21 is fulfilled which says: "All the members of her household are clothed with double (garments)," meaning: inside with the virtues of the soul and outside with good works.

It is true that if the false prophets had both garments, they

---

37. It is in fact Eph 6.11.

38. Which is simulating, incompatible with truth: ST II–II 111,2–3.

39. Thomas is preaching for religious and students preparing for religious life; religious do not marry (cf. ST II–II 152,4; 186,4), as a part of the vow of chastity, and live a simple life (as part of the vow of poverty): ST II–II 186,3. There were, however, in his days many sects and false prophets (heretics) who went to extremes. Thomas warns his listeners not to judge by appearance alone.

40. Cf. the vow of obedience: ST II–II 186,5.

41. ST II–II 58,2; 80,1.

42. ST I–II 81,8; II–II 23,7; cf. Thomas's explanation of Eph 4.23 in ST I–II 72,2,3.

would have been sheep of Christ. By means of exterior clothes a man approaches men: and thus we understand what the Lord says, "they come to you in clothes of sheep," as that they take up exterior works through which "they come to you"—since through interior works [people] approach the Lord.

We must notice that the clothing of Christ's sheep is fourfold: namely, (2.1) worship, (2.2) righteousness, (2.3) penance, and (2.4) innocence.

(2.1) The garment of worship is the garment of the worship of God. The sheep of Christ wear it in the sense that they are intent upon the worship of God.[43] The sheep of Christ receive this garment in baptism, as the Apostle says in Gal 3.17: "All you who are baptized in Christ have put on Christ." The sheep of Christ put on this garment when they are going to pray. Thus we read in Sir 50.11: "By going up to the altar" of incense "he gave glory to God."[44]

Hypocrites put on this garment [cf. Mt 15.7–9] for two reasons: (2.1.1) for empty glory[45] and (2.1.2) for gain.[46]

(2.1.1) They put it on for empty glory by praying in public and out in the open. Thus we read in the Gospel: "who love (*amo*) to pray in the synagogues and on the corners of the broad ways, so that they may be seen by the people" [Mt 6.4]; "in the synagogues," that is: in public.[47]

But is it bad, then, what is written: "Bless the Lord, all his angels" [Ps 103.20–21]? Chrysostom says that this[48] does not so much refer to a place as to the soul. The one who has his soul not with the people, but with God, prays in a hidden place. If someone prays alone in his room, but wants to be seen by the people, he prays in public.[49] What, then, is forbidden? That people have their soul aimed at being seen by the people as

---

43. Garments are external; Thomas counts worship among the exterior acts of religion, like adoration, sacrifices, and tithing (ST II–II 84–91); interior acts are devotion and prayer (ST II–II 82–83).

44. In Sir 50.5–11 the splendor of the vestments of the high priest Simon are described.

45. Hypocrisy is one of the daughters of empty glory: ST II–II 132,5.

46. ST II–II 58,11,3.

47. A synagogue, like a church building, is a public space.

48. What is said in Mt 6.4.

49. Cf. Christ's way of reasoning in Mt 5.21–48.

they pray; this must be avoided by Christians. Hence Chrysostom says: "Let the one who prays not do anything new, so that he could not be seen by the people because of any shouting, breast-beating, or raising hands." But when you pray with others, pray as the others, in secret. Seeking new gestures and ways pertains to what [Christ] calls praying in the synagogues. A man in his praying ought to be in conformity with others;[50] he should not seek new ways as the hypocrites do, who pray in public for empty glory.

(2.1.2) And the same applies to those who pray abundantly for gain. Thus we read in the Gospel: "Woe to you, scribes and Pharisees, hypocrites, who devour houses of widows, while you say long prayers" [Mt 23.14], because they pray in order to acquire gain. Some seek in a most scandalous way gain from little women: they say "long prayers," in order to make them devout and receive gifts from them.

But is it bad, then, to pray abundantly? Augustine answers, saying: "Let much speech be absent from prayer, but let praying much not be missing, if someone wishes to persevere in his intention. For this labor is done much more by sighs than by spoken words,[51] more by tears than by addressing."[52]

(2.2) Another garment of Christ's sheep is that of righteousness and mercy,[53] about which we read in Jb 29.14–16: "I am clothed with righteousness as with a garment. I have been an eye for the blind and a foot for the lame; I have been the father of the poor." Hypocrites always pretend to wear this garment. Therefore, it says in the Gospel: "Watch out that you do not do your justice before the people, in order to be seen by them; when you give alms, do not blow the trumpet, as the hyp-

50. Thomas says something similar in regard to fasting practices in Sermon 08 *Puer Iesus*, in 2.2 of the *Sermo*.

51. Cf. ST II–II 83,12.

52. With Augustine, Thomas advocates for praying from the heart, as an attitude; cf. ST II–II 83,14.

53. *Iustitia et misericordia*: cf. Mt 23.23. Righteousness, or justice, and mercy are named in one and the same breath, as in ST I 21; one should not be without the other. Righteousness is one of the cardinal virtues (ST II–II 57–122; ST I–II 61); mercy is the greatest of the virtues that are directed towards the neighbor (ST II–II 30,4) and pertains to the theological virtue of love (*caritas*: ST II–II 23–46; ST I–II 62).

ocrites do" [Mt 6.1]. Chrysostom says that the trumpet is every act or spoken word through which one boasts of himself. For instance, you give alms, but you would only give it to a more honorable person, who can give you something in return: that is a trumpet. Likewise, if you want to give alms in secret in order to look more praiseworthy: that is a trumpet.[54]

(2.3) The third garment of Christ's sheep is penance,[55] about which the Psalmist says: "I have made a sackcloth my clothing" [Ps 69.11]. These garments—that is to say, things that simulate [penance and] an austere life—are employed by hypocrites. Hence it says in the Gospel: "When you fast, do not become as the hypocrites: sad. They neglect their face, so that it is seen by the people that they fast" [Mt 6.16]. This is what they seek, and this is what they long for: that it is seen by the people that they fast.

Augustine says: "In this chapter we must notice that there can be ostentation not only in the splendor of physical things but even in vulgar things of filth, and that this is the more dangerous because he [the hypocrite] deceives with an appeal to the name of the Lord." The Philosopher says that it can pertain to [ostentation or] being boastful of oneself, if a person has a poorer way of life than his position requires. These exterior things are certain distinguished signs: in any army a battle-array carries its sign; that is not presumptuous. In any state whatsoever a man ought to be content with moderate things and not seek the low things too much. Hence Augustine says: "We should neither use precious things too much nor poor things too much." And why? Because we can seek glory in these two. About that poor garment we read in Zec 13.4: "They [that is, the prophets] will not be covered with a sackcloth over their upper garment," namely, in order to pretend.[56]

---

54. The will to give alms with the intention to be praised for it by others cannot be called a good will, although the act is good in itself; cf. ST I–II 19,7,2.

55. Both penance and innocence (in 2.4) are great gifts from God that excite us to being grateful to God while God loves those who are innocent and penitent; cf. ST I 20,4,4 and II–II 106,2.

56. Thomas argues in favor of temperance (ST II–II 141–170), the fourth cardinal virtue, as he does in II–II 141,6.

(2.4) The fourth garment of the sheep of Christ is innocence,[57] which is a bright and beautiful garment, as we read in Prv 31.25: "Strength and elegance are her clothing."[58] Hypocrites have put on this clothing, that is: the garment of simulated piety and cleanness. Therefore, it says in the Gospel: "Woe to you hypocrites, who are like whitened graves" [Mt 23.27], the things that seem whitened to the people, but "on the inside they are full of bones of the dead and every foulness," meaning: plundering and uncleanness. And Chrysostom says: "Appearing [to be a hypocrite] is shameful, but being [a hypocrite] is more shameful; and what is beautiful in appearing is more beautiful in being." These are the ones who come in the clothes of sheep.

But we must notice that some come in clothes of sheep who are not sheep, like those who seek temporal gain and their own honors. Hence Augustine makes a distinction saying that there is the figure of the thief, of the wolf, of the shepherd, and of the hireling. For the shepherd intends the benefit of the sheep; the wolf and the thief destroy the sheep; and the hireling seeks his own gain from the sheep. Augustine continues: "The hireling must be endured; the shepherd must be loved (*amo*); and from the wolf one must flee." And this is what is meant when it says: "They come to you in the clothes of sheep, yet inside they are grasping wolves."

❖

(3) We must also note that hypocrites are compared to wolves because of four things: (3.1) because wolves grasp sheep, (3.3) they do not spare them, (3.2) they disperse them, and (3.4) they persevere in their malice.

(3.1) First, I say that hypocrites are compared to wolves because wolves grasp sheep, and hypocrites grasp the goods of soul and body [cf. Mt 23.13–14]; they lead people to err [cf. Eph 4.14], and persecute them physically and rob them of things [Mt 23.25].[59] Thus we read in Ezek 22.27: "Her princes in her

---

57. See note 55.
58. The word *innocentia* does not occur in Prv 31.10–31. Thomas has distilled this word from the description of the virtuous woman in this pericope.
59. Avarice: ST II–II 118.

midst are like wolves that take prey in order to pour blood, to destroy souls, and to pursue gain greedily."

(3.2) Second, hypocrites are compared to wolves because wolves disperse sheep, as we read in the Gospel: "A wolf grasps and disperses sheep" [Jn 10.12]. The Lord says: "Someone who is not with me is against me," so: "And someone who does not gather with me" disperses [Mt 12.30]. But what is dispersing? Certainly, someone is dispersed when he deviates from what the Church teaches.

(3.3) Third, hypocrites are compared to wolves because they do not spare in any way. Hence the Apostle says in Acts 20.29: "I know that after my departure grasping wolves will enter among you, which do not spare the flock." A person who would kill someone and would not spare him unless one silver coin could be gained, is called very cruel. Hypocrites act in such a way. The life of the soul is better than that of the body [cf. Mt 20.28], and hypocrites seduce souls in order to have followers and honors [cf. Mt 23.14].

(3.4) Fourth, hypocrites are compared to wolves because, like wolves, they persevere in their malice.[60] Hence we read in Zep 3.3: "His judges are wolves until the evening," that is: until the end.

So, because of the four reasons mentioned, false prophets are like wolves of which we must beware.

❖

(4) But how are wolves detected?[61] It is shown when it is said: "You will know them by their fruits" [Mt 7.16].[62] Augustine says that many are deceived because they mistake the clothes of a sheep for the fruits. Some simple people see others doing good exterior works: fasting as well as praying and the like, which are the clothes of the sheep, but these are not their own clothes. Yet

---

60. Malice, which causes a person to sin: ST I–II 78.

61. It is not a sin to believe that a wicked messenger is a good one (because this is a deception of the bodily senses and not of the mind); the danger is, however, to adhere subsequently to the evil one when he tries to allure you, which is sinful: ST II–II 10,2,3.

62. Just as God can be known by his gifts; cf. Rom 1.20, in ST I 65,1,3; I–II 111,4; and II–II 9,2,3 among others.

SERMON 14   211

the sheep of Christ should not hate their own clothes if wolves disguise themselves with these [cf. Eph 4.26–27].

What, then, are the fruits that sheep produce? We can properly say that there are four fruits that sheep produce, on the basis of which wolves or hypocrites can be detected. (4.1) The first occurs in the affection, (4.2) the second in the speech, (4.3) the third in the operation, and (4.4) the fourth occurs in times of trouble. The first concerns the heart; the second, the mouth; the third, the work; and the fourth, patience and strength.[63]

(4.1) First, I say that the sheep of Christ, or the saints, have their proper fruit of the heart, which is the love (*amor*) of God and the neighbor. Thus the Apostle says in Gal 5.22: "The fruits of the Spirit are joy, love (*caritas*), and peace." But hypocrites have another fruit, namely, ambition,[64] because they love honors, as we read in Is 10.12: "I will visit upon the fruit of the magnificent heart of the king of Assyria."[65] Hypocrites "love (*amo*) the first places at the dinners and the first seats in the synagogues" [Mt 23.6]. If someone wants to be received with full honors while he shows humility on the outside, the garment does not correspond with the fruit.

(4.2) Another fruit that Christ's sheep have is in speech, since good people say good things and speak about good things always. Hence the Apostle says in Heb 13.15: "Let us offer sacrifices through him, the fruit of the lips that" suit "his name." If someone says something that is not in tune with his works, he does not have clothes that are like his fruit. Thus we read in Prv 18.20: "A man's stomach will be filled by the fruit of his mouth." It is difficult for a heart full of jealousy not to utter something of that once in a while, since "out of the abundance of the heart the mouth speaks" [Mt 12.34].[66] Therefore, Gregory says: "It is

---

63. These four themes (cf. Bach's cantata 147, "Herz und Mund und Tat und Leben") are derived from the Magnificat (Lk 1.46–55), sung during Vespers; the third part of the sermon is given during Vespers. Implicitly Mary is presented here as the example for all Christians.

64. Which is always (*semper*) a sin: ST II–II 131,1; it is opposite to humility (ST II–II 162).

65. I.e., the fruit of his pride; cf. the themes in Is 10.1–13.

66. Cf. ST II–II 153,5,4.

very difficult for the vicious whenever they preach right things, not to utter things from time to time that silently go round in them."

(4.3) The third fruit of Christ's sheep on the basis of which hypocrites can be detected, is the fruit of good operation, for in good people there is good fruit. The Apostle says in Rom 6.22: "You have your fruit in sanctification." Yet in evil people the fruit is evil. Hence it says in Prv 10.16: "The fruit of a godless person leads to sin," that is: to a sinful work. Augustine says in one of his sermons: "When a professing Christian draws the people's attention to himself through an unusual foulness or uncleanness, we can know when he does this voluntarily and not because he has no choice; we can know from his other works whether he does so out of contempt for a finer habit, or whether he does so out of ambition."

It can happen that at one time a person acquires a great habit out of humility, yet at some other time out of ambition.[67] Take a look at his other works: if you see in those a contempt of ambition, he is acting out of humility; if not, he says, you can know a person by his works. Because those who, on the one hand, convey a worthless habit, but, on the other hand, show signs of penitence and gentleness, are his sheep. If not, they are pretenders. "Therefore, hypocrites can be detected easily," [Augustine] says. "The road on which we are ordered to walk is laborious; hypocrites do not choose to work hard."[68]

Furthermore, hypocrites show themselves moderate, but when they have a chance to pursue their desires, they pursue them to the highest extent. Hence Gregory says: "If any temptation of faith comes up, the savage mind of the wolf would immediately lay aside the habit of the sheepskin; then he shows how much he would rage against the good ones."

(4.4) The fourth sign by which hypocrites can be detected is found in time of trouble. Thus we read in Prv 15.6 (Vg): "There will be disquiet for the fruits of the godless; the teaching of a man is known through patience." Augustine, comment-

---

67. E.g., when someone boasts of his humility; cf. ST II–II 38,2,3.
68. "Because those who on the one hand.... choose to work hard": these words echo Sir 7.15–17.

ing on the Lord's Sermon on the Mount, says about hypocrites: "As soon as through some temptations they begin to withdraw or negate the things that follow from that clothing or pursue what they desire, it becomes necessarily clear whether it is a wolf in a sheep skin or a sheep in its own skin." Because of this, James says in his letter: "If someone cleanses himself from these things," from sins, that is, "he will be a vessel prepared for honor to the Lord."[69]

May he make us worthy to perform this, he who with the Father, et cetera.

69. It is, in fact, 2 Tm 2.21.

SERMON 15

HOMO QUIDAM ERAT DIVES

Sermon on the Ninth Sunday after the Feast of the Trinity

Luke 16.1: *There was a rich man who had a steward; and he was discredited with him because he had squandered his goods.*

PART 1: *Prothema*

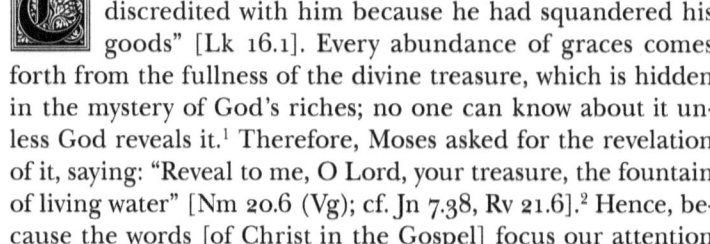HERE WAS a rich man who had a steward; and he was discredited with him because he had squandered his goods" [Lk 16.1]. Every abundance of graces comes forth from the fullness of the divine treasure, which is hidden in the mystery of God's riches; no one can know about it unless God reveals it.[1] Therefore, Moses asked for the revelation of it, saying: "Reveal to me, O Lord, your treasure, the fountain of living water" [Nm 20.6 (Vg); cf. Jn 7.38, Rv 21.6].[2] Hence, because the words [of Christ in the Gospel] focus our attention on the divine riches, let us take refuge with him in whom "all hidden treasures of wisdom and knowledge are" [Col 2.3] and let us ask, et cetera.

---

1. Hence St. Paul's warning in Col 2.4 not to be deceived by specious arguments. So we can only know about it through faith, not through philosophy: ST I 1,1,1; II–II 2,3,3. See also Sermon 13 *Homo quidam fecit*, section 2.2.

2. We do not find this text in the standard version of the Vulgate. But Thomas's version of the Vulgate reads: "clamaveruntque ad Dominum, atque dixerunt: Domine Deus, audi clamorem hujus populi, et aperi eis thesaurum tuum fontem aquae vitae, ut satiati, cesset murmuratio eorum."

PART 2: *Sermo*

"There was a (rich) man" [Lk 16.1], et cetera. It is most dangerous for someone not to pay attention to his manner and his measure, for this negligence is the reason why manner and measure grow beyond themselves into pride;[3] they consider themselves lords instead of the keepers of the things.[4] They say what we read in Jb 21.15: "Who is the Almighty, that we would serve him?" And likewise it is said in Jb 11.12: "An idle man grows into pride, and like a young wild ass he thinks he is born free." A wild ass is a forest donkey that is not owned by anyone. Some believe that they are without a yoke, and to them it seems that whatever they like is allowed to them.[5] And in order to take away this haughtiness from our heart, the parable about the steward is presented to us.

Now two persons[6] are presented here: (1) the person of the lord, where it says: "There was a rich man"; and next (2) the person of the steward, where it says: "who had a steward."

(1) So, first the person of the lord is presented to us, where it says: "There was a man," et cetera. Three things are mentioned concerning the person of the lord: (1.1) what he is, where it says: "a man," (1.2) his wealth, where it says that "he was rich," and (1.3) how he takes care of his wealth, where it says: "who had a steward."

(1.1) First, I say, the person of the lord is touched upon, where it says "a man." This man is God. Although God, insofar as the [assumed] human nature is concerned, truly is a man, he

---

3. Modesty and humility (ST II–II 160–161, 166,2, 168–170), fruits of the Holy Spirit (ST I–II 70,3), are opposite to pride (ST I–II 84,2; II–II 162).

4. See also how careful Thomas's formulation of the right to possess things is, in ST II–II 66,1–2. Also the introduction to the *Secunda Pars* of the ST: "*quasi* *liberum arbitrium habens et suorum operum potestatem.*

5. In Jb 39.5 the wild ass (*onager*) is mentioned as one of the wild animals. In Jb 24.5 it is the symbol of the godless who violate the Law and rob the poor, but harvest from empty acres; cf. Is 32.14, Jer 2.24, 14.6, Dn 5.21.

6. Here Thomas uses *persona* in the non-theological sense, as in Sermon 05 *Ecce rex tuus*, note 24.

cannot be defined or understood with respect to his divine nature.⁷ And yet he is called a man here insofar as his divine nature is concerned⁸ because of three things: (1.1.1) the similarity,⁹ (1.1.2) the intimacy, and (1.1.3) what is proper [to man].

(1.1.1) First, I say that God insofar as the divine nature is concerned is called a man by reason of the similarity [between the two]. According to our ordinary way of speaking, things are named by the names of their images, and images by the names of things.¹⁰ We read about this similarity of God with man in Gn 1.26: "Let us make man to our likeness and image."¹¹ Amidst the other lower creatures,¹² man has this privilege that he is created to God's image: not of the body, but of the mind.¹³ And because of this he is chosen above other creatures [cf. Gn 1.26, 28; Ps 8.6–9]. The image of Hercules is called Hercules; he is called Hercules through the name of his image—[in the same way] God is called a man.¹⁴ If man is created in the image of God, he ought to be careful to keep himself uncorrupted and pure.¹⁵

Behold, we have the image of God carved in wood. If someone threw mud at it or spat on it, would he not be called blasphemous? Much more so the one who corrupts the image that is created in God's likeness, because much more excellent is the image of God in the soul than the image of Christ in wood. Augustine says: "You are the image of God, which you corrupt through fornication and revelling in lust, while you do not pay

---

7. Therefore, Thomas employs a negative theology, the basis of which is found in ST I 1–13.

8. Hence it is a metaphor: ST I 1,9.

9. Which must be distinguished from the image: ST I 93,9.

10. Thomas refers to Aristotle: when we perceive a thing through our senses, we form an image of it in our intellect. Subsequently we give the image a name as we understand it: we call a table "a table," because the thing we want to name matches the image in our mind of what a table is. Cf. ST I 13,1.

11. ST I 4,3.

12. Lower creatures are the creatures on earth; higher creatures are the angels and the heavenly bodies (stars, planets).

13. Cf. ST I 93,6. For God does not have a body (Jn 4.24; cf. ST I 3,1), but God has an intellect (ST I 14). Cf. note 7.

14. ST III 16,1.

15. Purity (*mundicia*) is necessary for being focused on God: ST 81,8. The pure of heart will see God: Mt 5.8; cf. ST II–II 8,7.

attention to whose image you violate."[16] If this image is corrupted through sin, man ought to take off all foulness and be renewed. Hence it says in Col 3.9–10: "As you take off the old man with his actions, clothe yourself with the new man, who is renewed in the recognition of God, in accordance with the image of him who created him." We ought to take off everything that has to do with sin and foulness in us, and we ought to clothe ourselves with the new man, so that we may get to know him in our mind and through our work.[17]

(1.1.2) Second, God is called a man by reason of the intimacy. If someone lived with the French, we could say: by contact with the French he has become a Frenchman." By a certain intimacy and contact [with us] God can be called a man,[18] because it is delightful for him to be with people, as we read in Prv 8.31: "It is my delight to be with the people's children."[19] Yes, so great was his delight to live with people, that it was not enough for him to live with them in a spiritual way, but that he wanted to take on our flesh, so that he could live with people in a physical way. Thus we read in Bar 3.38: "After this he has been seen on earth, and he has lived with the people." "He has been seen on earth": in what way? Jn 1.14 says: "The Word has become flesh and dwelt among us." If God has proved himself so intimate with us, then we also ought to prove to him that we are intimate with him.[20]

Hence, someone who does not care about living with God is ungrateful.[21] It would be very presumptuous if a king sought friendship[22] with a poor man and the latter refused the king's

---

16. Cf. spiritual fornication: ST II–II 151,2.

17. Thus getting to know God is not only a matter of meditation and thinking things through (cf. ST I 62,9,1, 88,2–3; II–II 5,1,1, 188,8,2), but also of actively following in the footsteps of Jesus Christ (cf. ST I–II 52,2, 76,2,2; III 69,5).

18. See note 13, above.

19. In order to be friends there must be a similarity, a connection (cf. ST II–II 26,8); since human beings are created in his image, there was similarity (cf. ST III 4,1) and even more so after the Incarnation.

20. By becoming like him: Eph 5.1; cf. ST I–II 24,3,2; II–II 132,1,1.

21. Cf. ST I–II 76,4,3; II–II 35,1,3; ingratitude in general: II–II 107.

22. For Thomas's view of love and friendship, see: Sermon 01 *Veniet desideratus*, note 39.

friendship. The almighty King seeks your friendship [cf. 2 Sm 3.12–13]. In what way? The Lord says in Rv 3.20: "I stand at the door,"—that is: at [the door of] our affection, approaching the heart through the will—"and I knock," by making a good proposal; "if someone opens for me, I will come in and share a meal with him."[23] When someone opens the affection of his heart for Christ, God comes in [cf. Jn 14.23] and refreshes and is refreshed; he rejoices in you, and he makes you rejoice [cf. Ps 16.11]. If God is so intimate with us, we ought to apply ourselves to being intimate with him, in accordance with the Psalmist who says: "One thing I have asked of the Lord, for this I long: (to live in the house of the Lord all the days of my life)" [Ps 27.4]. "Living with him[24] has no bitterness, and his[25] companionship no weariness" [Wis 8.16]. There are some people whose social life is bitter; they fight with others and make them sad. The social life of others is weary because they say empty things or unpleasant things. In God you will find nothing that is displeasing and in all things you will not find anything but what delights [cf. Wis 8.18]. Every delight is nothing compared to a delight of God [cf. Wis 7.14].

(1.1.3) Third, God is called a man because of what is properly human. What is proper to man? Being mild in nature, since by nature man is a social being [cf. Gn 2.18]. Some living creatures live separately: wild animals, lions and bears. Yet this property is only natural to man, because kindness (*benignitas*) is called humanity.[26] If someone happens to be destructive and harmful, he is called inhumane,[27] as if he has taken on the nature of a wild animal, like a lion or a bear. Hence we read

---

23. But people may refuse: Prv 1.24, Zec 7.11–12, Heb 12.25. Friendship with the world, however, implies enmity with God: Jas 4.4.
24. Or "her": that is, wisdom. Latin: *(conversatio) eius*.
25. Or "her": that is, wisdom's. Latin: *illius*.
26. For living together people must also trust one another: ST II–II 109,3,1; cf. II–II 114,2. In Ti 3.2 Paul explains what *benignitas* is: slandering no one, being peaceable, considerate, exercising all graciousness towards everyone; cf. ST I–II 70,3. Note how positive Thomas's view of the human nature is (cf. also, e.g., ST I 75,6, 77,4 and 79,9).
27. Inhumanity is continually being and acting contrary to mercy and compassion: ST II–II 118,8,3.

in Prv 28.15: "A roaring lion, a hungry bear, is a godless prince over a poor people." This property [of *benignitas*] befits God to the highest extent, because "his merciful deeds are over all his works" [Ps 145.9]. Indeed, he is goodness and leniency itself. Thus the Apostle says in Ti 3.4: "The kindness (*benignitas*) and the humanity of our Savior have appeared; (he saved us not on the basis of works of justice that we have done, but according to his mercy)."

So, because of our similarity and intimacy with God and his property, anyone ought to be uncorrupted, devoted to God, and kind to his neighbor. It is clear now what kind of man the man in this story is when Christ calls him "a man."

(1.2) Next we look at his wealth, which is mentioned when he says "rich." But of what kind was his wealth? I say that he was rich in three respects: (1.2.1) first, in the sense of a perfect nature; (1.2.2) second, in the sense of an affluence of gifts; and (1.2.3) third, in the sense of the multitude of things that he possessed.

(1.2.1) First, I say, God is rich in the sense of a perfect nature.[28] It happens that some are rich in things owned, but are poor inside, like the stupid, who do not have wisdom. Someone was to give his daughter in marriage. There were two men who courted her: one was rich in possessions but poor in wisdom; the other one was wise, but not rich. He went to a wise man and asked him to whom he was to give his daughter. He answered: "I prefer a man lacking riches over riches that lack a man." But God is rich in himself, for every good whatsoever that is found in a creature comes from him.[29] If you seek knowledge or goodness, all of it is in the most excellent and original way in God.[30] These are the riches of which the Apostle says: "O the depth of the riches of God's knowledge and wisdom" [Rom 11.33].[31] By reason of this, that the endless highest riches are in him, we ought to exert ourselves with the highest desire to hold on to

28. ST I 3,4, 4,1.
29. ST I 4,2, 47,1; on evil and its cause, resp. I 48 and 49.
30. Sir 1.5, Mt 19.17; cf. ST I 6,4, 15,1 and 3; cf. (on evil) I 48,1–3, 49,2.
31. Cf. ST I 14.

God [cf. Ps 63.9]. Someone who knows the location of a treasure full of riches that he can obtain is stupid if he does not apply himself totally to acquiring that treasure. The treasure of riches is in God, and you can obtain it.[32] Hence it says in the Gospel: "The Kingdom of heaven is like a treasure hidden in a field; when a man finds it, he goes and sells everything he has and buys that field" [Mt 13.44]. If you have these riches that are in God, you will not lack anything [cf. Prv 8.21, Wis 7.14]. Thus we read in Wis 7.11: "With her all goods together came to me." And the Lord said to Abraham: "I will show you every good."[33] God alone can fulfill our desire.[34]

(1.2.2) Second, God is called "rich" according to an affluence and abundance of gifts. We are right in calling someone rich who does not have many riches, but has much to give. God "gives affluently" [Jas 1.5], and still his treasure is not diminished.[35] The Apostle says: "God who is rich in mercy," that is, who grants mercy abundantly; "for he is rich for all who call upon him" [Eph 2.4].

If someone gives abundantly, many would thrust themselves forward in order to receive [cf. Mk 1.33, 2.2]. But, if you want to receive [from him], God is ready to give to you. So you ought to thrust yourself forward in order to receive. The Psalmist says: "Approach him and you will be illuminated" [Ps 34.6]. And in Rv 22.11 we read: "Let the holy one become even holier."

Man always ought to long more and more for the possession of spiritual things. The appetite for an end has neither manner nor measure,[36] whereas the appetite for the things that are for an end is regulated according to the measure of the end. For instance, the end for which a doctor reaches is health; the means to this end are the medicines. A doctor does not say: "I want to cure this man but not completely," but rather: "as well as I can." So, in respect of the end, he does not set a measure.

---

32. Namely, by contempt of worldly riches; cf. ST II–II 161,5,3, citing Mt 6.19–20.
33. It is in fact Moses who is addressed, in Ex 33.19.
34. Ps 63.6, 103.5; cf. ST I–II 2,8 and II–II 28,3.
35. God's goodness is without end: Psalm 136; cf. ST I 7.
36. Especially not if the ultimate end itself is concerned; cf. ST I–II 30,4.

But if he said: "I will give him the strongest medicine I can get," he would make a mistake, because medicines are [not the end, but only] for reaching the end. So for these there ought to be a measure. The goods of the soul are an end; the goods of the body are *for* an end. Hence concerning temporal goods we ought to seek according to a measure, but concerning the goods of the soul we ought to seek as much as we can.[37] Now, some want to limit their virtue.[38] They say: "It is enough for me to do this," and do not want to limit their riches. Therefore, it is not enough for them to give up one thing: they are to give up all the many things they have as well as the many things for which they strive.[39]

Well, God is rich in mercy and in an affluence of gifts. Thus we always ought to approach him for spiritual goods [cf. Heb 4.16]; and as for temporal goods, we ought to leave it up to him, that he may give us from these in accordance with what seems best to him. Thus we read in Mt 6.33: "First seek the Kingdom of God, and all these things will be given to you with it."[40]

(1.2.3) Third, God is rich in possessions, because all things are his. The Psalmist says: "The earth is the Lord's, and its fullness, (the world and those who dwell in it)" [Ps 24.1].[41] Furthermore: "Glory and riches are in his house" [Ps 112.3], et cetera. Moreover: "Although he was rich, he became indigent for our sake" [2 Cor 8.9].[42] And in view of this we should realize that we should not put our trust in temporal [Ps 49.7, 146.3–4], but in spiritual things [Ps 118.8–9]. If a man sees someone else's servant, and if that servant promises to serve him, he must not trust in that servant's promise, because his lord could stop him. But

37. ST II–II 184,3.

38. Cf. ST I–II 64: the middle in virtue is not about a mediocrity but about a balance. As Thomas shows in ST I 21: God is rich in mercy, but in such a way that justice is not violated.

39. Cf. Mt 19.21: ST I–II 108,4,1; II–II 32,6 (that it is "necessary" to give alms).

40. Cf. ST II–II 83,6: we should also ask for temporal things, at least insofar as they help us to focus on eternal happiness.

41. Cf. ST II–II 66,1. See also how this verse functions in III 48,4 (on redemption). Possession of something implies dominion over it: II–II 136,2,2.

42. ST III 40,3.

if the lord of the servant promises that this servant will serve this man, then he can trust him. Therefore, we ought to trust in God, because he can give all things.[43] Hence the Apostle says in 1 Tm 6.17: "Tell the rich of this age not to be wise in a lofty way,"—that is: not to be proud of the things that belong to God—"and not set their hope on the uncertain riches," but to hope in the living God, "who gives all things affluently" [Jas 1.5]. In him is the foundation of hope.[44]

Thus God is rich in a threefold way. Now it is clear what this man and his wealth are.

❖

(1.3) Let us look at how he takes care of his wealth, which is mentioned where it says: "who had a steward." But who is this steward? I say that the steward is the manager of the house. So by means of his power God could do all things by himself, but he did not want it:

(1.3.1) Indeed, he has commissioned some to be keepers, whereas he reserved the governance for himself,[45] and he willed that the beauty of the order and the perfection of the universe be preserved. Imagine that we would not need one another; this would not be the beauty of the universe;[46] as the Psalmist says: "How magnified are your works, O Lord: you have made all things in wisdom; the earth is filled with your possession" [Ps 104.24].

(1.3.2) Furthermore, he wanted to govern all things by himself because of the usefulness, because he did not want anything to be superfluous.[47] Hence, "although you are able to heal all things," in Wis 14.4, is followed by: "so that none of your

---

43. For he has the riches, the power, and the freedom to do so.

44. Because of God's mercy and almightiness we should never despair; cf. ST I–II 62,3,2, 64,4; II–II 14,2 and 14,3,1.

45. Cf. Wis 14.3; cf. ST I 22,1,2: God created good things and placed them in a good order. The eternal idea of this order in God is called "providence" (*providentia*); its execution in time is called "governance" (*gubernatio*): I 103–119.

46. ST I 5,5, 47,3, 61,3 (*ordo rerum ad invicem est bonum universi*); I–II 111,1 and II–II 81,2.

47. Everything has its place and function in the order of creation; that is what makes it "very good" (Gn 1.31); cf. ST I 47,2.

works would be superfluous, people entrust their lives to a little piece of wood." Why has God made the sun? So that we would not lack its warmth and light. If it had no use, it would have been superfluous. Also you are superfluous in the world if you do not do something useful. Job reads: "Have you created the children of the people in vain?" [Ps 89.48]. As if it says: "No." Well, the Lord judges that a "useless servant" is thrown out into the "outer darkness" [Mt 25.30]. So what is there to say about the servant who causes damage [in Lk 16.1]?

(1.3.3) Moreover, God willed to commission some to be managers out of liberality.[48] God willed that the goodness of a thing would go over onto other things. Dionysius says that nothing is more divine than becoming a co-operator of God[49]—and when you preach for the salvation of the soul or do other good things, you co-operate with God. Thus God says to Moses: "I have made you god for Pharaoh" [Ex 7.1].

(2) He says: "who had a steward." Who are stewards? I say that God has appointed stewards on different levels in an order:

(2.1) First, he appointed the angels who manage the things that are above all creation. Hence Augustine says in his commentary on Genesis: "All bodies are governed by a spiritual creature."[50] The Apostle says: "All of them are the Spirit's managers (sent for the benefit of those who receive the inheritance of salvation)" [Heb 1.14]. These are great instruments.

(2.2) There are other great instruments, but they are smaller than these, who are set over earthly things [only]. Thus we read in Gn 1.26: "Let us make man to our likeness and image, that he may be over the fish and the animals and the birds": in brief, over all things. Ps 8.8: "You have subdued all things under his feet," but: "Know that the Lord himself is God" [Ps 100.3]. Hence Chrysostom says: "You are a stranger, and the things commissioned to you are only of a transitory and short

---

48. Cf. ST I–II 32,6; III 7,2,3.
49. Cf. 1 Cor 3.9 (in ST I 23,8,2), 4.1 (in ST II–II 63,2,1, 100,1), and Col 1.25–29.
50. Cf. ST I 110,1–3.

use" [cf. Ps 49.11]. And he gives two examples, saying: "You have a field or landed estate now; just imagine how many owners it has had before you: an infinite number; it barely contains so many clods of earth. Likewise, it is with you as with someone who rests in the shade: you pass away and someone else comes who rests there as you did. In this way things come and go for you in the world according to the divine providence, not according to yours." Thus you are a steward, not a lord.

(2.3) Furthermore, there are mediating instruments between people and angels, who are above the people and are appointed to lead the people.[51] The Apostle says: "Thus let a man regard us as" leaders and managers [1 Cor 4.1].

(2.4) Furthermore, the Lord has raised up glorious servants, like St. Dominic and St. Francis, who work with care for the salvation of the people;[52] their special concentration has been focused on leading the people to salvation [cf. Acts 13.26, 47]. Yes, all saints have sought to work with care for the salvation of the people. Glorious is the fruit of their good efforts [1 Pt 5.4; cf. 1 Cor 9.23–25]. Hence they are glorious now in the heavenly homeland, to which may we be led by the Son of God. Amen.

PART 3: *Collatio in sero*

"There was a rich man" [Lk 16.1], et cetera. As it was said today, in these words two persons are introduced: the person of the lord and the person of the steward. Some things have been said about the lord; now we will speak about the steward. And concerning the steward we can consider three things: (1) his task, (2) his abuse, and (3) the danger threatening him. We can consider his task because he was a steward, his abuse because he squandered the goods of his lord, and his peril because he was discredited.

---

51. Cf. Mt 24.45 (also 2 Tm 1.8). In this sermon Thomas refers to the apostles and their successors; in ST I 22,1, to leading figures in a family, a city, and a state.

52. The saints in heaven pray for us: ST II–II 83,11. *Amministro* (from *minister*: servant, helper) is here translated as "to work with care" rather than "to manage."

(1) I have said that stewards are managers, like angels[53] and people.[54] And since we are people, let us say that the care for the regulation of the goods is commissioned to man. The Lord entrusts three things to man: (1.1) himself, (1.2) spiritual goods, and (1.3) exterior things.

(1.1) First, I say, the Lord entrusts man to himself. A difference between humankind and all other [living creatures] is that God has given to man power over himself: a man can do of his own accord what he wants to, whereas other living creatures are moved by their natural instinct. Thus it says in Sir 15.14: "From the beginning God established man and he gave him up in the hand of his own plan."[55] If you have entrusted something to someone, you demand an account of him; if not, you don't. If a lion kills a man, God does not punish the lion, because he has not entrusted responsibility for itself to a lion. The Apostle asks: "Does God care about cattle?" [1 Cor 9.9] But God has entrusted man to himself. Therefore, he ought to render account to him. Thus we read in Sirach: "Walk in the way of your heart" [Eccl 11.9], that is, according to the desires of your will, "according to what you observe with your eyes," that is, according to your intellect, "and know that for all these things" the Lord "will bring you to judgment."

(1.2) Second, God has entrusted the spiritual goods to man, since man is able to use spiritual goods:[56] he can use them in a good or in an evil way. Thus it says in the Gospel: "Someone who was setting out on a journey to a foreign land called his servants and gave them his goods" [Mt 25.14], that is, the spiritual goods. And he said to them: "Trade with it until I come" [Lk 19.13]. If you have love (*caritas*), you can use it in a good or evil way,[57] but [eventually] you will have to render account

---

53. The higher angels help (*illuminare*) the lower (ST I 106,4), and angels help, serve, and guide (*amministrare*) corporeal creatures (ST I 110,1).

54. Gn 1.28; cf. ST I–II 106,3,3 (*deservire*).

55. The human being has a free will: ST I 83,1; I–II 10,4, which does not mean he/she should just do as he/she desires: Sir 15.15–20; cf. ST I 91,4,2 (God's laws); I–II 104,1 (obedience to those who are higher).

56. The virtues (ST I–II 55–67), the gifts (ST I–II 68), the beatitudes (ST I–II 69), and the gifts of the Holy Spirit (ST I–II 70).

57. See also note 40. Someone can love what is good, but also what is evil, or

of this. Hence the Apostle says in 1 Cor 14.32: "The spirits of the prophets are subject to the prophets" and so eventually they must give account of it. Gregory states that "when the gifts grow, the responsibilities for the gifts grow."

(1.3) Third, God has entrusted exterior goods to man, that we may use them, as the Psalmist says: "You have subdued all things under his feet" [Ps 8.7], et cetera. Therefore, you ought to render account. If a certain lord has entrusted his goods to you, you ought to render account of those by the end of the year [cf. Lk 16.2]. In the same way God demands at the end of your life an account of the things granted to you (*prebenda*). Hence it is said against the evil ones in Jas 5.1: "Come now, you rich men, weep and cry out over the miseries that will come to you." And it continues. "Behold, the judge is standing at the door already" [Jas 5.9].

Now it is clear what is said about the steward.

❖

(2) Let us look at the abuse of the steward, which is mentioned where he says: "he squandered his goods." So, in what way does the steward squander the goods of his lord? In three ways: (2.1) first, by using them for himself; (2.2) second, by keeping back things that did not belong to him; (2.3) third, by a superfluous and prodigal diversion.

(2.1) First, the steward squanders the goods of his lord by using them for himself. For instance, a steward to whom his lord has entrusted the house or other goods, would not want to hand the proceeds over to his lord, but would keep them for himself [cf. Mt 21.33–36]; he would be called a thief.[58]

God has entrusted you to yourself not in order to be your own, but that you may be his [cf. Rom 14.8] and that you seek God's glory, not your own [cf. Prv 25.27 (Vg)]. The Apostle says: "I urge you: be eager to present yourself to God as an irreproachable worker who cannot be confounded" [2 Tm

---

can love what is good in an evil way. In the latter two cases the love is called "unordered" or "disordered"; cf. ST I 60,5; I–II 100,5,1; and II–II 26,1–12.

58. Cf. ST II–II 66,2–3. Therefore, Thomas discusses theft as a sin against the virtue of justice, which is defined as giving to another what is due (ST II–II 58,1–3), and the virtue of liberality (ST II–II 58,9,2).

2.15].⁵⁹ But some do not consider themselves servants of God, but free men. They say with Jb 21.15: "Who is the Almighty, that we would serve him?"

Likewise, if God has given you knowledge or virtue, to what purpose has he given it to you except that you may serve him and give him glory? Hence we read in Sir 51.17: "To the One who gives me wisdom I will give glory." Hilary says: "Almighty Father, I am aware that I owe this privileged task for my life to you, so that every word and thought of mine may speak of you." But others, of a different mindset, have said: "Our lips are ours; who is our lord?" [Ps 12.5] From this way of thinking they want to oppose God and the faith when they know how to discuss and to read well, as we read in Is 3.8: "Their speech and their ideas are against the Lord."

Likewise, God has given you riches, so that you may turn them into the honor of God [cf. Psalms 145, 147]. Thus David has said to him: "Everything is yours, and we have given to you the things we have received from your hand" [1 Chr 29.14]. Contrary to this, some hold that all things are theirs, not God's. Jb 22.18 reads: "They have thought of the Almighty as someone who could not do anything, although he had filled their houses with good things."⁶⁰ Is 24.5: "They have squandered the everlasting Covenant," which contains that all creatures ought to exist for the glory of God.⁶¹

So the steward squanders the goods of his lord by using them for himself.

(2.2) It also happens that a steward or regulator squanders the goods of his lord by keeping back things that did not belong to him. Someone who ought to sell wine but would keep something back, so that he is corrupted [cf. Prv 11.26, Am 8.5–6], squanders the goods of his lord by keeping back what is not due to him [the steward]. Taking care of yourself does not mean that you only think about yourself and only care about your-

---

59. Cf. ST II–II 129,7.
60. N.B.: Even the powers in the created world are from God: SCG II 3.
61. Cf. Jer 31.33, 1 Cor 10.31 (concretely: ST I–II 88,1,2, 100,10,2; II–II 83,14).

self.⁶² Just as the eye is not made for itself alone, but so that it is of service to the whole body [cf. 1 Cor 12.21–26]. A certain old man has said: "Because I am a human being, I consider nothing human alien to me."⁶³

Likewise, you have received grace from God. Do you believe, therefore, that you have it in order to have it for yourself alone? Certainly not. Just as the sun does not have brightness for itself alone, but in order to pour it out for others, so God has given you grace, so that you may distribute it to others [cf. Mt 5.15–16, Rom 12.8]. Hence St. Peter says: "As each one has received grace, use it for one another as managers, as Christ's good distributors" [1 Pt 4.10]. And the wise one says: "I have learned (wisdom) without delusion, and I share it without envy" [Wis 7.13].⁶⁴

Likewise, you ought to distribute temporal things to others; you should not have them for your own use. The Apostle says: "Tell the rich of this age not to be wise in a lofty way (and to give easily)" [1 Tm 6.17]. The Philosopher has said that those cities are the best in which things are privately owned, while the use of them is communal.⁶⁵ In Jl 1.17 it is said: "The storehouses are squandered, because the wheat is mingled," meaning, to the letter:⁶⁶ "is corrupted." And because of this it is said in the Letter of James 5.2–3: "Your riches have become wholly putrid; your garments are eaten by the moths; (your gold and silver have rusted, and the rust of it will be a testimony against you)." Basil says: "People usually say: 'God is not just.' Is God unjust because he is distributing things to us and does not give the same to everyone?⁶⁷ Is God unjust? It is not unjust that a thing is unequally portioned out to us. Why, then,⁶⁸ do you have abundance and does someone else beg, but that by distributing well you may obtain the reward of life, and that he may be crowned

---

62. Loving yourself, loving your neighbor: ST II–II 25,4–5 and 26,3–5.

63. In a play called *Autotimus* (act 1 scene 1) by Publius Terentius, a playwright from Carthage who lived from 190 to 158 BCE.

64. See also Sermon 08 *Puer Iesus*, section 3.2.3.

65. ST II–II 66,2.

66. Thomas distinguishes four senses, four layers in Scriptural texts: the historical or literal, the spiritual, the allegorical, and the moral or anagogical: ST I 1,10.

67. ST I 65,2,3; also 47,2,3.   68. In the text *ego* should be *ergo*.

with the trophies of patience? But are you not a looter by keeping for yourself the things entrusted to you to be distributed? It is the bread of the poor that you hold in your hand, the tunic of the nude which you keep in your room, the shoe of the unshod that decays in your possession; you have the silver of the needy that you have hidden underground. Regarding these things you could have given as much as your injustices are many."[69]

(2.3) Other stewards, or distributors, are distributors by being prodigal all around. First they give themselves up to the devil for a mediocre delight. Against them we read in Prv 5.9: "Do not give your honors to a stranger and your years to someone cruel."[70]

Others sell their grace if they have it[71] for a favor of the public. Against them it is said: "Do not give what is sacred to the dogs" [Mt 7.6]. They give temporal things to stage-players, but they would not give anything to a good man.[72] It is said against them: "Give to the just man and do not receive the sinner" [Sir 12.4], that is, insofar as he is a sinner, in order not to favor him in his sin. We read that a prodigal son spent a part of his wealth by living "a life of lustfulness" [Lk 15.3].[73] O, I wish that not so many would waste their soul!

It is clear now what was said about the steward's task and his abuse.[74]

(3) Let us look at the danger that threatens the steward. We see a danger for this steward on three grounds: (3.1) first, by reason of scandal; hence it is said that he was discredited [Lk 16.1]; (3.2) second, by reason of the loss of his function; hence it

69. This view has consequences for how we assess stealing out of necessity: ST II–II 66,7.

70. Cruelty is opposed to clemency: ST II–II 159,1. The devil is called cruel because, although it is in accordance with justice that humankind is enslaved by him, he is without devotion, compassion, etc.; cf. ST II–II 157,1,3, 159,2,2; III 46,3,3.

71. Cf. Prv 23.23. Cf. ST II–II 100,3–4.

72. On the question to whom we should give alms: ST II–II 32,5 and 9.

73. On *luxuria*: ST II–II 153.

74. The whole text of section 2 echoes 2 Cor 6.1 (and Heb 12.15): "As his [God's] co-operators we beseech you that you do not receive the grace of God in vain."

says: "You cannot be a steward any more" [Lk 16.2]; (3.3) third, we see the danger for the steward that he can not help himself any more; hence he said: "I do not have the strength to dig, and I am ashamed to beg" [Lk 16.3].

(3.1) First, I say, we see the danger that threatens the steward or distributor, by reason of scandalization. Someone has possessed many goods. He dies. His sins do not remain hidden [cf. Mt 10.26]. Who has discredited him? His conscience[75] and the saints, as well as God himself, "for whom all things are bare (*nuda*) and open" [Heb 4.13].[76]

(3.2) Likewise, we see the danger of the steward by reason of the loss of his function, because it is said to him: "You cannot be a steward any more." You have had knowledge and money. You die. You cannot have them any more, as the Psalmist says: "When a rich man dies, he will not take all things with him" [Ps 49.18], meaning: nothing. Jb 1.21: "I have come from my mother's womb naked (*nudus*); I will return to it naked."

(3.3) Maybe you will say: "I will be able to acquire something for myself." Surely not, for you will not be able to help yourself. Hence he says: "I do not have the strength to dig, and I am ashamed to beg." Because of this, it is said in Sirach: "Whatever your hand can do, do it immediately, because there is no work, no thought, no knowledge, no wisdom with the inhabitants of the netherworld, whither you will hastily go" [Eccl 9.10]. Maybe you will say: "I will ask the Blessed Virgin and the saints to help me." Certainly, that will not be the place and time for begging.[77] Hence it says: "I am ashamed to beg." The foolish virgins wanted to beg, but nothing was given to them; "but those who were ready entered with the groom into the wedding" [Mt 25.10].

So the steward is in danger.

❖

(4) But what is the remedy?[78] Who would have a case before a judge when he is accused and his offense is known? What

---

75. Cf. ST II–II 33,7.
76. Cf. ST I 14,5–6.
77. Cf. Mt 7.21. Asking in prayer requires that your heart be with it: ST II–II 83,4,2.
78. Thomas did not announce this fourth point. To conclude his homily he gives practical advice.

would be the salutary counsel? I say that the salutary counsel would be the one that the king would give him, namely, if the king told him: "Do this, and you will be free" [cf. 2 Kgs 5.10, Lk 10.28]. This would be the salutary counsel. Christ gives you the counsel. When people are discredited and can no longer be stewards, and they can neither dig nor beg, they ought to do what Christ recommends, who says: "Make friends for yourselves with the mammon of iniquity, so that, when you are wanting, they may receive you in eternal tents" [Lk 16.9]. But what is this counsel about the mammon? This is the same counsel that Daniel gave to Nebuchadnezzar, saying: "May my counsel be pleasing to you, O King: buy off your sins through almsgiving" [Dn 4.24].

He says: "with the mammon of iniquity." Should we then give to the poor from unjust riches, as from theft?[79] Certainly not, because Augustine says in *On The Word of the Lord:* "Do not conceive of such a Lord as a man whom you would despise." And the Lord says: "I hate robbery in the camp" [Is 61.8]. We usually explain or understand the expression "with the mammon of iniquity" in four ways.

(4.1) Basil explains it in one way, saying that the Lord says "mammon of iniquity" because riches are iniquities. For it rarely occurs that someone has riches which one of his ancestors has not acquired unjustly.

(4.2) Augustine says that riches are called the "mammon of iniquity" because an unjust man values these riches highly.

(4.3) Or riches are called "mammon of iniquity" because they lead to iniquity.[80]

(4.4) Chrysostom says that riches are called "mammon of iniquity" because you have kept them for yourself unjustly.[81]

Do you have 20 or 40 pounds[82] of income in storage now? At least when you die you would distribute it. And to whom should [these riches] be given, then?

---

79. Cf. ST II–II 32,7, 66,8.
80. Therefore, it was becoming that Christ, who goes before us leading a virtuous life, lived in poverty (although he himself could not have sinned; cf. ST III 15,5,1, 22,4,1): ST III 40,3,1.
81. Cf. ST II–II 66,2.
82. The *libra aurea:* the Roman pound.

Some are worried about themselves with regard to their reputation. Christ says: "so that, when you are wanting, they may receive you in eternal tents." Augustine connects the two words of Christ and of the steward: the steward says: "so that when I am removed, they may receive me in their homes" [Lk 16.4], whereas the Lord says: "in eternal tents" [Lk 16.9]. Therefore, we ought to distribute [our riches] to the ones of whom the eternal tents are. Augustine says: "Who else are those of whom the eternal tents are than the saints of God? And who else are the ones that are received by them in the eternal tents than they who serve their needs and give to them with gladness what they lack? These are Christ's little ones, who, after leaving "everything" behind, "have followed him" [Lk 5.11].

Must, then, alms be given to sinners?[83] I say that, all other things being equal, it is better to give to a just man than to a sinner, because by giving to a just man you do a work that is meritorious and in a similar way the work of the one who receives is. But this is not so in the case of a sinner; indeed, only the work you do is meritorious, but not what he does. Chrysostom says: "Almsgiving is the most powerful art of the arts, because it does not build houses for us made of mud [cf. Jb 4.19]; for us it is a spending for everlasting life."[84]

And that this may be fulfilled for us by him who, et cetera.

83. Cf. ST II–II 32,9,2.
84. Cf. ST II–II 32,4.

SERMON 16
INVENI DAVID

Sermon on the Feast of St. Nicholas, the Sixth of December

Psalm 89.21-22: *I have found David, my servant.*
I have anointed him with my sacred oil;
my hand will help him and my arm will make him firm.

PART 1: *Prothema*

THE MIRACLES of God cannot be scrutinized by man, as we read in Jb 37.5: "Who works great wonders and things that cannot be scrutinized." Some of the miracles God performs in his saints. Augustine teaches this, saying that justifying man is more than creating,[1] because creation passes whereas justification remains [cf. Mt 24.35]. Thus "God is wondrous in his saints" [Ps 68.36]. We cannot scrutinize these wonders of God in his saints, unless he who is the scrutinizer of hearts and reins [cf. Ps 7.10] teaches us.[2] Therefore, let us take refuge with him in prayer and ask him at the beginning that he may give me something to say, et cetera.

PART 2: *Sermo*

"I have found David, my servant," et cetera. From these words we can learn four praiseworthy things of this holy bishop: (1) first, his wondrous election; (2) second, his unique consecration; (3) third, the effective execution of his task; (4) fourth, his

---

1. ST I–II 113,9; III 43,4,2. It is even more than creating another world: I 25,3,3.
2. Because it is through grace; cf. ST III 2,10.

immovable and firm stability. His wondrous election is shown in the words: "I have found David, my servant." His special consecration is shown where it says: "I have anointed him with my sacred oil." The effective execution of his task is shown in the words: "My hand will help him." His stable firmness is shown where it says: "and my arm will make him firm."

❖

(1) So let us take a look at what he says: "I have found David, my servant." Here we can consider four things concerning the meaning of "finding": it implies (1.1) rarity, (1.2) inquiry, (1.3) appearance, and (1.4) experimental proof.

(1.1) First, I say that finding implies rarity, for we say of rare things that they are found; it would be ridiculous to say: "Finding people on the Petit Pont."[3] Now, what is rare is said to be found, as in the question in Prv 31.10: "A strong woman, who will find her?" As if it says: "She is difficult to find," for a woman is by nature soft and weak.[4]

(1.2) Second, we speak of being found when things are sought after. Hence it is said in Prv 2.4: "If you seek her as if she were money, you will find her," namely, divine knowledge. And the Gospel speaks of a woman who seeks a lost drachma, "until she finds it" [Lk 15.8–9].

(1.3) Third, finding implies that it appears clearly to you.

---

3. The *Parvus Pons* was one of the two bridges over the Seine in 13th-century Paris; it connected the banks with the Ile de la Cité (on which Notre Dame is situated), the very center of the city and thus very busy.

This example is a clear sign that this sermon was delivered in Paris. It might have been on a Sunday or—since St. Nicholas was a very popular saint—on a weekday, probably when Thomas was Regent Master. Also the exact location is uncertain; Kwasniewski (29, note 40) suggests it might have been delivered to the Franciscans, in view of the reference to the stigmata of St. Francis (in 2.4).

4. Thomas shows himself a child of his time when he bluntly speaks of women as the weaker and softer sex. His view originates from the Genesis story—the woman is the one seduced by the serpent (ST I 94,4,1; I–II 89,3,2)—as well as Aristotle's ideas (e.g., in ST II–II 156,1,1). This view was confirmed by his experience, namely, the reality in the society of his time that women did not have responsible positions and were treated as second-class citizens; cf. ST I 98,2sc; I–II 105,3,1. Thomas, however, also says, not quite in tune with the reality in the society, that in Christ women should not be treated as secondary people: ST III 72,10,3, in the light of Col 3.11 ("in Christ there is neither male nor female").

Thus we read in the Gospel: "The Kingdom of God is like" a *paterfamilias* seeking "a hidden treasure in a field, who, when he finds it, goes and sells all he has (and buys that field)" [Mt 13.44]. When a treasure is dug up from the earth and shown, then we call it found.

(1.4) Fourth, finding implies experimental proof. When someone doubts about something and later on he knows it for sure, he says: "I have found[5] that this is how it is." And in this way Solomon says: "I have found a woman more bitter than death" [Eccl 7.26].[6]

In these ways the Lord has found St. Nicholas.

(ad 1.1) First, he found in him something very rare, namely, a matured[7] virtue that is rare in young men.[8] Thus it says in Proverbs: "Adolescence and pleasure are vain" [Eccl 11.10 (Vg)]. It is a rare characteristic that a young man is not enslaved to vanity, and because St. Nicholas was preserving his sanctity in his youth, we say that he was found. For "even as a little boy he tormented the body by fasting a lot."[9] In Hos 9.10 we read: "Like unripe grapes in the desert I found the sons of Israel, as the first fruits of the fig tree."[10] Figs ripen later than other fruits, and if they ripen at the right time, they are called found. In this sense, boys who preserve their sanctity in their boyhood are called the first fruits of the fig tree and are called found— and that is pleasing to God. Hence we read in Mi 7.1: "My soul has desired early-ripening figs." Fish of the season and fruits of the season are in great demand; so great is God's demand that man carries the yoke of the Lord in his youth. Hence it says in Lam 3.27: "It is good for a man to carry the yoke of the Lord

---

5. Or: "I have found out": *inueni*.

6. Note that Thomas's audience consists of religious and religious-to-be; the attractiveness of women may be a threat to their life as religious.

7. *Tempestiuam*: translated here as "matured" in view of the comparison made later with ripe fruits.

8. So Thomas is also critical towards the young men in his audience; in view of virtue and temptations they are certainly not presented as superior to women.

9. An antiphon from the office of the Feast of St. Nicholas.

10. The Hebrew text seems to make more sense: the grapes are ripe there.

from his adolescence," for [Prv 22.6] "the adolescent will walk along his path; even when he is old he will not recede from it." And even if such people leave the path of sanctity, they return more easily.[11]

(ad 1.2) Second, the Lord found in St. Nicholas what he is looking for. And what does the Lord seek? Certainly a devout mind. Thus it says in Jn 4.24: "God is Spirit" and he seeks "those who worship him in spirit and truth." And why does the Lord seek a man with a devout mind? I say: Someone who delights in living with someone else, seeks someone who is the same.[12] This also applies to God; since it is delightful to him to live [with someone] with a devout mind, he seeks [someone with] a devout mind. Hence it says: "My delights are living with the sons and daughters of people" [Prv 8.31]. And in St. Nicholas God found a devout mind, since he was constantly in the church and in devout prayer. Therefore, it befits him what is said in Hos 12.5: "He implored him in Bethel in tears and he found him." Bethel is, in translation, "house of God."[13]

See also that it is rightly said, "He found David," for David was in his boyhood great in power and virtue;[14] he killed a bear and a lion, and he was chosen in preference to his brothers, and he was also most devout.[15] The Psalmist says: "As with fat[16] and wealth"—meaning: with devotion—"my soul is filled" [Ps 63.6]. And in Sir 47.2 we read: "Like the fat separated from the meat, so David" was set apart from "the sons and daughters of Israel." Also St. Nicholas was holy[17] in an eminent way.

11. Cf. ST I–II 52,1, 53,2; with God's help, ST I–II 114,7.
12. ST II–II 25,6,5.
13. Cf. Thomas's explanation of Jn 2.16 on the question whether it is necessary to worship in a church: ST II–II 84,3.
Obviously "house of God" is interpreted by Thomas in this instance as the church building; cf. Jn 2.16.
14. In view of Thomas's following exposition, *virtus* is translated as "power and virtue."
15. Cf. 1 Sm 17.34–36 (killing bear and lion), 16.12 (being chosen), and the Psalms (devotion).
16. I.e., the part of the animal offered to God; cf. Lv 3.3–4; devotion is towards God: ST II–II 82,1.
17. Connotations of "holy" are, among others, "separated/set apart" (ST III 4,6) and "purely good" (ST I 36,1,1): Heb 7.26.

SERMON 16

(ad 1.3) Third, the Lord found in St. Nicholas something that shone clearly, namely, dedicated affection. What makes a man shine? I say that nothing makes a man so radiant as dedication and kindness (*benignitas*) to others [cf. Mt 5.16]. God is hidden in himself. Still he is revealed to us through his works of kindness (*opera beneficientie*) [cf. Rom 1.20]. Hence it says in Sir 44.10 about those who act with piety towards others: "These are men of mercy, whose dedicated works have not been wanting," and the Church proclaims "their praises" [Sir 44.8]. And elsewhere we read: "May the lips of many praise the man illustrious in handing out bread" [Sir 31.28 (Vg)]. St. Nicholas was to the highest extent "compassionate and he felt deeply for the afflicted."[18] And by a gift of gold he relieved the poverty of virgins.[19] Thus we read in Hos 14.9 what applies to him as well: "From me his fruit is found."[20]

And because of this the Lord rightly says: "I have found David, my servant." A servant is someone who carries out the operation of the Lord.[21] The pre-eminent operation of the Lord is mercy, as the Psalmist says: "And his acts of mercy are over all his works" [Ps 145.9]. So a servant of the Lord is someone who tries to carry out his mercy towards the poor. The Apostle says: "We are servants because of Jesus."[22]

(ad 1.4) Fourth, the Lord found in St. Nicholas something proven by experience: faithfulness that is much sought-after.[23] Thus the Apostle says: "Still it is sought-after among the managers," only "that someone may be found faithful" [1 Cor 4.2]. And

18. A responsory from the night office of the Feast of St. Nicholas.

19. A reference (which Thomas also makes in ST II–II 107,3,4) to the story that by a generous gift of gold that Nicholas made to an impoverished family, three young girls were rescued from a life in the prostitution that was hanging over their heads.

20. *Ex me*: the fruits of the Holy Spirit: ST I–II 70,3.

21. Cf. the angels as servants of God in ST I 111–113.

22. The expression *propter Iesum*, "because of Jesus," is in Paul's letters found only in 2 Cor 4.11 ("constantly we are handed over to death because of Jesus" or "for the sake of Jesus"). We find the expression *servi Iesu* ("servants of Jesus") in Phil 1.1, where St. Paul refers to himself and Timothy; cf. Phil 2.5–8.

23. *Fidelitas*, in terms of keeping the Lord's word, being trustworthy, is first of all towards God, but also towards fellow human beings (ST I–II 100,5; II–II 88,3).

in Wis 3.6 we read: "He has tested them and found them worthy of him."[24] A servant ought to be faithful, so that he refers everything he has and does to God. Whether you pray, or do works of mercy, every good thing you do, you must refer to God. Hence it is said: "He who is tested in it,[25] is found perfect" [Sir 31.10]. This is St. Nicholas and because of this it says: "my servant."

Yet, contrary to this, many do not serve the Lord but themselves. Thus the Apostle says: "Such people do not serve Christ, but their belly" [Rom 16.18]. If you do good in order to have allowances (*prebenda*), you serve yourself, not God [cf. Mt 6.1]. A good bishop should not be like this, but he ought to be innocent as for himself [cf. Heb 7.26], devout in his relation to God, and merciful in his relation to his neighbors[26] as well as faithful in everything and in respect of everything [Lk 16.10, 1 Tm 3.2–13].

(2) Next is his consecration, which is mentioned where it says: "I have anointed him with my sacred oil." We are to observe that the sanctification of bishops and some others is done with oil; there is hardly any sanctification in which oil is not used [cf. Ex 30.31–32, 40.9]. In order to signify the power of oil, we must notice that we use oil for four purposes: (2.1) for the healing of a wound, (2.2) as the fuel of a light, (2.3) to season the taste, and (2.4) to soften.

First, I say, we use oil for healing. Is 1.6 reads: "Injury, bruise, and swollen wound are neither bound up, nor healed by medicine, nor bathed with oil." Second, we use oil as the fuel of a light. Hence we find a precept in Ex 25.6 [and 35.9, 28] for the children of Israel to offer "oil for the light to be made." Third, we use oil to season food. Thus we read that King Solomon sent Hiram oil for meals [cf. 1 Kgs 5.25; cf. 2 Chr 2.9]. Fourth, I say that we use oil to soften. Thus it says: "His words are smooth, more than oil" [Ps 55.22].

---

24. Thomas distinguishes between temptations from the devil (which are aimed at leading us astray) and being put to the test by God (to make sure that we love him: Dt 13.4; cf. Mt 25.21, 23): ST I 114,2.

25. I.e., in gold.

26. Devotion to God and mercy towards neighbors: ST II–II 30,4,2, where Thomas cites 1 Tm 4.8.

(2.1) First, I say that oil is used for the healing of a wound. By this we understand healing grace, as in Lk 10.34: the Samaritan who wanted to take care of the injured man "poured on wine and oil."[27] The sick are anointed with oil, as James [instructs]: "If someone among you gets sick, call for the presbyters of the Church, that they pray over him and anoint him with oil" [Jas 5.14].

And when St. Nicholas was anointed with the oil of healing grace—we say this because he was full of health[28] and thus equipped to anoint others—it says that he poured out "wine and oil," the wine of severe correction and the oil of mercy and comfort.[29]

(2.2) Second, we use oil for light to be made, by which the study of wisdom is signified [cf. Ps 119.130, Prv 6.23]. Concerning this oil it is said: "May oil not be absent from your head" [Eccl 9.8], and in Zec 4.14: "These are the two sons of gleaming oil." Since oil is used as fuel of a light, prophets are anointed with oil [cf. Is 61.1].

(2.3) Third, we use oil to season food, by which spiritual joy is signified. For tasteful ingredients make the seasoning; in the same way, spiritual joy makes it easier to do good works. For with sadness even ordinary work is difficult; with joy even hard work is easy [cf. Is 12.3]. The Psalmist says: "So that he makes his face cheerful with oil" [Ps 104.15], and: "God, your God, has anointed you with the oil of joy before your companions" [Ps 45.8]. And Is 61.3 reads: "Oil of mirth instead of mourning."

Hence priests are anointed with oil [cf. Ex 28.41], namely, with the oil of joy. Thus it seems that spiritual joy belongs to those who are dedicated to the divine cult, as the Psalm reads: "May your priests be clothed with gladness,"[30] et cetera.

---

27. Thus the good Samaritan is an image of Christ.

28. He was full (*plenus*) of it, so that he could pour it out for others; cf. ST III 7,10, referring to Eph 3.8–9.

29. Wine of correction, e.g., in Ps 60.5 and Jer 25.15–38. Oil of mercy because oil softens (see section 2.4); oil of comfort or strengthening; cf. Is 61.1 and Lk 4.18.

30. This is a quotation from Ps 132.9: "Your priests will be clothed with jus-

(2.4) Fourth, we use oil to soften, by which mercy and kindness (*benignitas*) of heart are signified—and these were in St. Nicholas, for he was completely filled with mercy and devotion. In Dt 33.24 it says: "May he be pleasing to his brothers; let him dip his foot in the oil." Oil spreads itself; mercy in a similar way. Oil flows; in a similar way mercy flows over all good works. So, unless you have mercy, your works are nothing [cf. 1 Cor 13.1–3]. Hence the Apostle says: "Devotion avails for all things" [1 Tm 4.8b].[31]

You ought to consider that in the future the marks of rewards will reflect in the bodies of the saints [cf. 1 Tm 4.8c] in accordance with the merits of the graces. Also, in our days the marks of the affection show, as we clearly see in St. Francis: the marks of Christ's Passion were in [his body], because he was intensely affected by the Passion of Christ. Likewise, the marks of mercy reflect in St. Nicholas, for "oil dripped from his tomb,"[32] as a sign that he was a man of great mercy. Dt 32.13: "So that he may cause honey to flow from the rock, and oil from the hardest stone." That belongs to a king.[33]

(3) Then the execution of his task follows, when he says: "My hands will help him," et cetera. God does not have a physical hand, but his power is called his hand.[34] See that God's hand has helped him in four ways: (3.1) by drawing him to himself and tearing him away from evil things, (3.2) by leading him, (3.3) by comforting or strengthening him, and (3.4) by performing miracles.

(3.1) First, I say: the hand of the Lord, that is, his power, has helped him, St. Nicholas, by drawing him to himself and tear-

---

tice and your holy ones will exult," and/or from 2 Chr 6.41: "May your priests, Lord God, be clothed with salvation, and your holy ones will be glad over good things."

31. In ST I–II 68,7,2 Thomas explains this verse as referring to good exterior works.

32. A responsory from the night office of the Feast of St. Nicholas. This legendary oil is called the "manna of St. Nicholas."

33. See Sermon 05 *Ecce rex tuus* under 2.2.2–2.2.4.

34. Hence, "the hand" of God is a metaphor: ST I 1,9 and 3,1,3. See also note 14.

ing him away from evil things. The Psalmist says: "Stretch out your hand from on high, and tear me away and rescue me from the many waters and from the hand of the sons of strangers" [Ps 144.7].

(3.2) Second, the hand of God has helped St. Nicholas by leading him. People who lead others usually take them by the hand. Thus the Lord leads the just ones by means of his power, as the Psalmist says: "Let the wickedness of sinners be brought to nothing"; yet the Lord "leads the just one" [Ps 7.10]. Likewise, Is 8.11 reads: "He has instructed me by his strong hand, that I may not proceed on the path of this people."

(3.3) Third, the hand of the Lord, that is, his power, has helped St. Nicholas by [comforting or] strengthening him. Thus it is said in Ezek 3.14: "And the hand of the Lord was with me to strengthen me." He was greatly strengthened.

(3.4) Fourth, the Lord's hand, that is, his power, has helped St. Nicholas by working miracles.[35] Thus we read in Acts 4.30: You will stretch out "your hand, and signs and wonders occur in the name of your Son." St. Nicholas was filled with [the power to work] miracles. Who has ever sought the glory of the world and has received it like St. Nicholas, who was a poor bishop in Greece?[36] The Lord has adorned him with miracles, because he was most merciful. Ps 4.4 says: "Know that the Lord has made his saint work wonders." Mercy has made St. Nicholas wondrous, and the Lord has strengthened him until the achievement of the goal of eternal life.[37]

May he lead us to this, who with the Father and the Holy Spirit lives, et cetera.

---

35. For only the Lord works miracles; people who work his miracles are instruments of him: cf. ST I 105,7, 110,4, 114,4; II–II 178; and as for Christ, cf. ST III 43.

36. Myra, where St. Nicholas was bishop, is in southern Turkey; in St. Nicholas's days the language of the people living there was Greek.

37. The fourth point, Nicholas's stable firmness, announced at the beginning of the *Sermo*, is missing in the manuscripts. Bataillon gives three possible reasons: (1) the copyist did not write it down or copy it, e.g., because he became tired; or (2) Thomas never came to the fourth point (cf. Sermon 20 *Beata gens*); or (3) the fourth point was discussed in the *Collatio in sero*, which did not come down to us.

SERMON 17
LUX ORTA

Sermon on the Feast of the Birth of the Blessed Virgin Mary, the Eighth of September

Psalm 97.11: *A light has gone up for the just, and joy for the upright of heart.*

PART 1: *Prothema*

"LIGHT has gone up for the just, and joy for the upright of heart" [Ps 97.11]. "Every very good endowment and every perfect gift from above is coming down from the Father of lights."[1] This second quotation is from the Letter of James 1.17. Temporal things are a good (*bonus*) endowment. The things that belong to us naturally, like the body and the soul, are a better (*melior*) endowment. Eternal glory and the goods bestowed by grace are the best (*optimus*) endowment. Every very good (*optimus*) endowment—we understand this as grace—comes from the Father of lights. Grace is called the best (*optimus*) gift, given to us so that we may perform meritorious works.[2] Hence it says in Jn 15.5: "Without me you cannot do anything." Likewise, we call grace the perfect gift, given to us so that we may receive the good of glory. And this grace comes from the Father of lights, as we read in Ps 84.12: "The

---

1. Since *donum* is usually translated as "gift," *datum* is translated as "endowment." In ST I 49,1–2 Thomas discusses how it can be that the Creator is perfectly good whereas evil is a reality in his creation, in view of Mt 7.18, where Christ says that a good tree bears good fruit.

2. Grace (*gratia cooperantis*) is the origin of our merit, in the first place through love (*caritas*): ST I–II 114,4.

Lord will give grace" in the present, "and glory" in the future.

So, because the grace of God is so effective a gift for working the good in the present and for arriving at eternal glory in the future, let us ask at the beginning that the Lord may give us grace, et cetera.

PART 2: *Sermo*

"A light has gone up for the just." This is a short saying, but it holds a manifold meaning. We find it in Ps 97.11.

(1) We read that the birth of the Blessed Virgin is shown beforehand by many figures in the Old Testament.[3] Among other figures it is pointed to by three figures in particular, namely, (1.1) in the ascent of dawn, (1.2) in the rising of the morning star, and (1.3) in the sprouting of a twig from the root. In the dawn her birth is designated insofar as her sanctification is concerned. In the rising of the star we find a prefiguration insofar as it concerns the integrity of her virginity. In the sprouting of a twig her elevation and great contemplation are prefigured.

(1.1) Concerning the ascent of the dawn,[4] through which the birth of the Blessed Virgin is prefigured insofar as it concerns the sanctification she brought,[5] we read in Gn 32.27 that the angel has said to Jacob: "Let me go; the dawn is already ascending." The struggling of Jacob is a sign of the company of the Old Fathers [Patriarchs], who struggled with the angel with two arms, namely, tears and prayer. Thus we read in Hos 12.5: "He fought with an angel and was strengthened; he asked him in tears." But after the angel got to know about the dawn in the

---

3. In the figurative reading of the Old Testament, things and events are seen as referring to the Christ event to come; cf. also the Law (ST 101,2, 102,2, 103,3 and 104,2) and the Eucharist (ST III 73,6).

4. Dawn or daybreak (*aurora*) announces the coming of the sun. In Scripture the sun is identified with Christ, e.g., Mt 4.16 (citing Is 9.1), Lk 1.78–79 (ST III 35,8,3), Jn 8.12. Traditionally also the "sun of justice" in Mal 3.20 (4.2) is identified with him.

5. Not only by giving birth to Christ, but also as a great example of a virtuous life, as Thomas expounds in the following in the *Sermo;* cf. ST III 27,4 and 27,5,2.

birth of the glorious Blessed Virgin, he said: "Let me go," as if he was saying: "Ask me no more, but take refuge with the Blessed Virgin." Dawn is the end of the foregoing night and is the beginning of the day that follows. Likewise, in the rising of the Blessed Virgin Mary the night of guilt has ended, and the day of grace[6] has begun. Hence Sedulius[7] says: "She has put an end to vices and taught the way of life."

(1.2) Second, the birth of the glorious Virgin is prefigured in the rising of a star insofar as it concerns the integrity of virginity.[8] Thus Balaam prophesied in Nm 24.17: "A star will rise from Jacob, and a twig will rise up from Israel." Now, the rising of her star is compared to the integrity of her virginity, because, just as a star shines without being corrupted and without diminution or loss of light, thus the Blessed Virgin brought forth her Son, without a violent opening of the flesh and without the loss of her virginity. Thus Bernard of Clairvaux has said: "The Blessed Virgin is justly compared to a heavenly body, because, just as a heavenly body shines without being corrupted, and just as the shining does not diminish the clarity of the heavenly body, so does the Son not affect the virginity of his mother.[9]

(1.3) Third, the birth of the glorious Virgin was shown beforehand in the sprouting from a twig insofar as it concerns her contemplation. Is 11.1 reads: "A twig will sprout from the root of Jesse, and a flower will come up from his root," et cetera. The twig[10] is raised up towards heaven. In this the contem-

---

6. Cf. ST III 36,7sc: the star is not one of the ordinary stars in the sky.

7. Sedulius: an Italian poet and priest who worked in Greece in the 5th century. These words occur also in a homily by Jerome on the Assumption. It is not really clear which text is older. Apparently Thomas knew the text through Sedulius, who wrote a poem in five books, the "Paschal Song (*Carmen Paschale*)," on the life of Christ. Some of the verses of this poem became part of the liturgy of the Church. Later on in this homily Thomas quotes from this work without explicitly referring to it.

8. ST III 28 and 29,2.

9. Although we know that stars actually burn up and that planets only reflect the light of a star, the point Thomas makes remains clear. Also, by this figurative interpretation Thomas enforces the argument against astrology, as in ST II–II 95,5.

10. Thomas is playing on the words *virgo* (virgin) and *virga* (twig).

plation of the Blessed Virgin is signified, who overcame these earthly things and who lifted up her heart to the things that are above.[11] Thus Bernard says: "O sublime Virgin, in which sublime [realm are you]? You raise up your mind to the One who sits on the throne, to the Lord of majesty."

Therefore, in this way, with a triple figure, the birth of the Blessed Virgin Mary was prefigured for us: it was as the dawn in birth, as a rising star in bringing forth God's Son, and as a twig sprouting in a commendable life. David comprehends these figures in one verse when he says: "A light has gone up for the just," et cetera. The light puts an end to night and starts the day, shines and does not fall into corruption; and after the lower things of nature have been bypassed, it aims at higher things.

(1.4) Also, however, the company of the apostles is called "light" in the Gospel. In Mt 5.14 we read: "You are the light of the world." Likewise, the angels are called "light." Gn 1.3 reads: "God said: 'Let there be light,' and light was made"; a gloss says that this is understood as concerning the blessed spirits, that is, the angels.[12] And since the Blessed Virgin transcends the companies of the apostles and angels because of her excellence, she is suitably called "light."

(1.5) Moreover, with another reasoning she can be called "light." In Jn 8.12 we see God,[13] who says, "I am the light of the world." Well, the Blessed Virgin has given birth to that light, and it is impossible that light be brought forth unless from light, at least in a univocal generation. Hence, she is suitably called "light."[14]

---

11. SCG III 37: the way to ultimate happiness is found in contemplation of God (cf. also ST I–II 38,4), who is "above," "in heaven."

12. Cf. ST I 61,4sc, 63,5,2. And yet another interpretation of Gn 1.3 is found in ST I 32,1,3.

13. That is, Christ insofar as he is God; cf. the linguistic rules in ST III 16,1–2.

14. In a univocal generation the one bringing forth and the one brought forth are of the same nature: a man brings forth a man (in time), and the divine Father brings forth the divine Son (eternal generation), as in "God from God, Light from Light, True God from True God" (cf. ST I 27,1–2). Since Thomas interprets Jn 8.12 as concerning the divine Son, the speech of generation of the

Thus those words befit her well: "A light has gone up for the just," et cetera.

❖

Now, two things in particular are brought to our attention in this verse: (1) first, the rising of the Virgin's glory, when it says, "A light has gone up"; and (2) second, the fruits of the birth: "for the just, and joy for the upright of heart."

❖

(2) "A light has gone up for the just."[15]

(2.1) This just one is her father Joachim, as she is his daughter.[16]

(2.2) But "for the just" also refers to the fact that for Christ a light has gone up, meaning that the Blessed Virgin is, so to speak, a special mother-to-be.

(2.3) "A light has gone up for the just" is also interpreted as "for the penitent," for whom she is, so to speak, an advocate. Hence we sing: "O Virgin, our advocate."[17]

(2.4) Furthermore, "a light has gone up for the just" means "for those exercising justice," the active ones; "and joy for the upright of heart" refers to the contemplative ones. Those who work for justice are called the actives; those who are lifted up towards the things above through contemplation are called the contemplatives.[18] These long for doing well through the guidance of the light as well as for the contemplation of God.

---

light from Mary must be understood in the same way as that we call Mary the Mother of God; Mary is not God. But since the one Christ has the divine and the human nature, we can and do in fact use words that signify the divine nature (e.g., "Son of God"), and words that signify the human nature ("he died") for him who is born of Mary, whether we mean Christ insofar as he is God or Christ insofar as he is a man; cf. ST III 16,1–5. Consequently, on the veneration (rather than adoration) of the Mother of God: III 25,5.

15. The part "and joy for the upright of heart" is the subject of the *Collatio in sero* and is briefly touched upon in 2.4.

16. Since *justo* in Ps 96.11 (Vg) is masculine and singular, Mary's mother, St. Ann according to the same tradition, is out of Thomas's sight.

17. Thomas quotes the *Salve Regina,* but in a slightly different wording: *"eja virgo,* advocata nostra," instead of *"eja ergo,* advocata nostra." Quite a few names that were originally given to the Holy Spirit were in the course of time also attributed to Mary, e.g., advocate, comforter, and counselor.

18. On the distinction and the nature of these two: ST II–II 179–182, where

In this way it is obvious why the Blessed Virgin is called "light" and through which figures she is prefigured. The *Sermo* will be on this part: "A light has gone up for the just"; the *Collatio* will be about what is left.

We have seen the reasons why the Blessed Virgin is called "light." Let us add some more.[19] We see that physical light is (1.6) a source of joys, (1.7) the leader of travelers and of those who are on the way, (1.8) the expeller of darkness, (1.9) the spreader of its likeness, (1.10) the mother of the heavens' graces, (1.11) the most splendid of creatures, and (1.12) a delight as well as a consolation to the eyes. These are found in the Blessed Virgin; because of these, the sight [of her] is called good.

(1.6) First, I say that light is the source of joys, because someone who lives on the sea longs for the light[20] and rejoices in it [cf. Ps 21.7]. Hence it befits the Virgin well, who is prefigured in Est 8.16. For there it is said that "for the Jews," that is, the ones who believe, and thus for the Christians who confess Christ as God and man, "there is a new light," that is, the Blessed Virgin. She is called "new light" because "neither was she seen to have a woman [as an equal] before her nor after her" [Sedulius]. And she is called "light" because she is without darkness of sin and ignorance.[21]

Her rising is seen with the eyes of the heart, and how it takes shape is now seen with the eyes of the body and [results in] interior joy, honoring your neighbor and dancing for God [cf.

Thomas refers several times to Lk 10.38–42, on Martha and Mary (II–II 180,8, 182,1–3).

19. Thomas mentioned three *figurae*, prefigurations (1.1–1.3), which may be an allusion to the Trinity, then two arguments based on sayings of Christ (1.4–1.5), which may refer to his divinity and humanity, and now he adds seven reasons connected with life on earth (1.6–1.12), which may be a hint at the fullness of life on earth (seven days, virtues, etc.). Together this makes twelve, which seems to be by reason of the twelve lights, stars, in Mary's crown in Rv 12.1.

20. An implicit reference to *Ave Maris Stella* (also explicitly mentioned later on, in 1.8) and to Ps 130.6.

21. She was conceived like any human being, but God removed every sin from her in order to make her a dwelling place for himself; cf. ST III 27,1–5.

Est 8.16]. About the joy of that rising, Solomon says in Prv 13.9: "The light of the just ones," that is, the Blessed Virgin, "rejoices; the lamp of the wicked goes out."

(1.7) Second, light is the way [cf. Jn 8.12, 14.6] and the leader of the people on the way [cf. Ex 13.21]. Similarly, the Blessed Virgin is the one who directs us on this way. It is said in Jn 12.35: "Walk, while you have the light, that the darkness may not seize you." Christ says: "Walk," by making progress in what is good. He does not say: "Stand unemployed," as those do about whom the Gospel according to Matthew 20.6 says: "Why do you stand here all day unemployed?" He does not say: "Sleep," but: "Walk, while you have the light,"—that is: the Blessed Virgin—"so that the darkness may not seize you." By "the darkness" the works of darkness or the angels of darkness, the demons, are meant; or darkness stands for the torments of hell. Hence it says in Prv 4.18: "The path of the just ones proceeds as a shining light, and it becomes brighter until full (*perfectus*) day." "The path of the just ones": it is the Blessed Virgin who is the path: narrow [cf. Mt 7.14] and clean;[22] the Blessed Virgin is clean through the purity of her virginity[23] and narrow through the meticulousness of her religiousness,[24] as well as upright through the rectitude[25] of her way of life (*via*). So the path of the just ones, the Blessed Virgin, is as a light: as such, shining, and in respect of others she proceeds from what is good to what is better and increases until full day, that is, until the joy of eternity.

(1.8) Third, light expels darkness. In a similar way vices are eradicated by the glorious Virgin's power. Is 9.2 reads: "The people that walks in darkness"—that is, the darkness of ignorance before the coming of Christ and the birth of the Blessed Virgin Mary—"sees a great light," namely, the Blessed Virgin. She was a great light because, just as her Son enlightens the whole world, so the Blessed Virgin enlightens the whole human race.

---

22. *Munditia*, necessary for living a God-centered life: ST II–II 81,8, 180,2,2.
23. A great virtue, the highest form of chastity (ST II–II 151), also for those who do not live a religious life: ST II–II 152; cf. 186,4.
24. *Religio*: ST II–II 81–91.
25. *Rectitudo*: necessary in order to become happy, ST I–II 4,4; cf. 21,1. Being *rectus* refers to a disposition: just, righteous, upright of heart.

About this light it says in Gn 1.3: "God said: 'Let there be light,' and light was made." Let there be light for the creation of the Blessed Virgin's soul, and light was made in her sanctification. For we read in Gn 1.4: "God separated the light from the darkness," since after [this] she has not committed a sin.[26] In Gn 32.27 we read about this light: "Let me go, the dawn is already ascending." At dawn darkness flees and light is brought in. In a similar way the Blessed Virgin flees from the darkness of sin and brings in the light of grace. It is even said that dawn is like the bedewing hour because in its rising the heavens were made flowing with honey.[27]

Furthermore, we say that the dawn is like a mild breeze [Gn 3.8, 1 Kgs 19.12], because then the birds are chirping and thus show in a way joy and gladness. In a similar way the Fathers in heaven[28] rejoiced in the rising of the Virgin.

Moreover, we call the dawn *Aurora*, which is a contraction of *aurea* and *aura*,[29] "golden air," because of its preciousness. As Bernard says: "Take away the sun which enlightens the whole world; where is the day? Take away Mary, the *Maris Stella*, the star of this great and wide sea which is the world; and what would remain except fog and thickest darkness? Then what? But if she is present, darkness flees. And if she is present, light begins to shine."

(1.9) Fourth, the light of its rays is wide and expansive. In a similar way the Blessed Virgin lets the rays of her grace shine on all and gives all a share in it. Hence we read in Sir 24.19–20: "Come over to me, all you who desire me, and you will be made full by the things which I bring forth: for my spirit is sweet, more than honey," et cetera. "Come over," namely, from the emptiness of the world, "to me," that is: who is full of grace.[30] Or: "Come

---

26. And in this respect Mary was unique; cf. ST III 27,6,1.

27. A responsory from the First Nocturn of Christmas.

28. The Patriarchs of the Old Testament who believed, the first of whom was Abraham; cf. ST I–II 102,5,1.

29. It is more likely that the Latin word *Aurora* is derived from the Greek αὖσος [ausos], Ionic ηFως [æwoes]: "daybreak"; "the goddess of the red morning sky"; "the East."

30. Cf. *Ave Maria, gratia plena:* "Hail Mary, full of grace."

over" from the error of the world "to me," because I have virtue. Or: "Come over" from the pleasures "to me," because I love (*amo*) chastity.[31] And "you will be made full by the things which I bring forth," namely, by the spiritual gifts of graces: you will not receive too little, but evidently much, for it says: "My spirit is sweet, more than honey," because the Blessed Virgin is kind and merciful to all. Thus Bernard says: "The Blessed Virgin opens her bosom of mercy to all, and all people receive from her abundance: the sick receive care; the sad, consolation; the sinner, pardon; the just, grace.[32] Even more, God's Son receives the substance of the flesh, so that there would be no one who would hide away from her warmth."

(1.10) Fifth, light is the gracious mother of colors.[33] In the same way the Blessed Virgin is the mother of virtues. Just as colors make the body beautiful, so virtues the soul, because the mother of virtues is the Blessed Virgin. We read in Sir 24.18: "I am the mother of beautiful love (*dilectio*)," of God, that is. Love (*dilectio*) is a bond of two: it connects us with God and with fear, through which we flee from sin.[34] Solomon says: "The just one fears and turns away from evil" [Prv 14.16]. And elsewhere it says, in Sir 1.21: "The fear of the Lord drives out sin. And [she is the mother of] acknowledgment," of holy faith,[35] that is, "as well as of holy hope,"[36] that is, of hope of future happiness. Hence Bernard says: "If we have any virtue, if we have any salvation and grace, we know that we are completely satiated by her who overflows with delights. For here is that enclosed garden through which the Auster, the divine wind,[37] blows, and the odors of it flow into the spiritual gifts of the graces" [cf. Song 4.12–16].

31. See note 23.   32. See note 17.
33. Sunlight that breaks apart shows that it contains all colors; at night we do not see colors, not even in the moonlight.
34. Cf. ST II–II 7,1, 19, 22,2. Thomas distinguishes between fear as a virtue (fear of God) and as a vice (fear of worldly things, of losing your life: ST II–II 125).
35. Cf. ST II–II 7.
36. Cf. ST I–II 72,7,2; II–II 35,4,2.
37. In the Roman mythology it was the Southern wind (Scirocco). It could bring dark clouds and fog as well as scourging heat.

(1.11) Sixth, light is the most shining of the creatures. In a similar way the Blessed Virgin Mary is. Hence we read in the Book of Wisdom 7.29: "She is more shining than the sun"—meaning: than a just man who shines in the Church Militant[38]—and "above every constellation of stars"—that is: the saints in the Church Triumphant—"compared to light," compared to an angelic creature, that is, "she is found greater" in dignity and beauty [Wis 7.29].

(1.12) Seventh and last, light is a delight and a consolation to the eyes. In a similar way the Blessed Virgin is a consolation to humankind.[39] Hence it says in the Book of Wisdom 7.10: "(I loved [*diligo*] her) more than health," through which infirmity flees, "and more than the splendor of the body," through which deformation is purified; "and I have chosen and resolved to have her rather than the light" of a good life.

Evil ones, like the demons, hate this light, whereas it is delightful for good ones. Hence St. Augustine says that bread is bitter to the taste of someone who is ill, whereas it is sweet for someone who is healthy; and sick eyes hate light, whereas pure eyes love (*amo*) it. This light is amiable (*amabilis*) for the intellect that is made healthy by faith, and for our affections that are made healthy by love (*caritas*). And it is no wonder that the Blessed Virgin is amiable, because about her it says in Est 2.15 (Vg): "For she was very finely formed and of an incredible beauty, and the eyes of all saw her as gracious and amiable." Prv 11.16 says of her: "A gracious woman will find glory," that is, eternal glory,

to which we are led by the One who with the Father and the Holy Spirit lives, et cetera.

---

38. Here Mary appears as Lady Wisdom (see also note 17). The Church Militant is the Church on earth, which is involved in a spiritual warfare against evil spirits and thoughts; she is fighting against the aberrations of heretics; she is trying to win non-Christians for Christ (see also the *Collatio in sero* of the Sermons 13 *Homo quidam fecit* and 14 *Attendite a falsis*). Cf. also Sermon 21 (part 3 section 2.1), where St. Martin is presented as the perfect soldier of Christ for the spiritual warfare. Cf. ST II–II 188,3 and 188,4,5.

39. See note 17.

PART 3: *Collatio in sero*

"A light has gone up for the just, and joy for the upright of heart" [Ps 97.11]. Today it was said in what way the Blessed Virgin in her rising is a brilliant light. It remains to see in what way she is joy for [righteous or] upright people, since it is written in this verse: "and joy for the upright of heart."

❖

Joy is promised in sacred Scripture not to just any kind of upright people, but to the upright of heart, that is, the perfectly upright.[40] So, we will expound how we understand Jb 1.1, where it says of Job: "That man was single-hearted and upright who feared God and avoided evil"; "single-hearted" in intention,[41] "upright" in what he did. "He feared God and avoided evil," that is, sin. Thus Solomon says in Prv 14.16: "A wise man fears and turns away from evil." And elsewhere, in Prv 15.28, we read: "Through fear every man turns away from evil." To such a righteous man joy is promised [cf. Ps 97.11].

❖

We must look at the fact that there are two sides to a man: (1) the interior and (2) the exterior. And according to this it is necessary that a perfectly upright man be upright inside and on the outside.[42]

❖

(1) The interior man consists of the soul. And the soul has two parts: the intellect and the affection.[43] And in accordance with this it is required that there be rectitude in the interior man: (1.1) First, in respect of the intellect, because rectitude is the knowledge of the truth. (1.2) Second, it is necessary that there be rectitude in respect of the affection, which is the delight in true goodness.[44] This ought to be the case, since the

---

40. Because our heart is where our interior movements (like love) begin: ST I 20,1,1; cf. I–II 45,3. See also note 25.

41. In other words: not being two-faced, as Thomas formulates it in view of Mt 6.22, at the end of section 2.3.

42. Cf. ST I–II 21,1.

43. Cf. ST I 14 intr., 77,1,4, 77,4 and 8, 78 intr.

44. In ST I 16,4 Thomas considers how goodness and truth are related.

knowledge of love (*caritas*) keeps the intellect upright, and love (*amor*) for true goodness keeps the affection upright.[45]

(1.1) First, I say that knowing the highest truth keeps the intellect upright.[46] Thence we read in Ps 73.1: "How good," that is, very good (*valde bonus*), "is Israel's God for these who are upright of heart." He is good, meaning that he is pouring out his goods,[47] for those who are upright of heart: those who have knowledge of the highest truth through faith,[48] because faith is a special light for getting to know the Lord and the things that concern the Lord.[49] Ps 125.4 reads: "Bless, O Lord, the good ones" as for their affection, "and the upright of heart" as for their intellect. It is obvious, now, that for man to be perfectly righteous, the interior light must be aimed in the right direction; in other words, the rectitude of the intellectual part of the soul is required.[50]

(1.2) Second, the rectitude of the interior man is required in respect of his affection. Concerning this rectitude Bernard says that the rectitude of a rational creature consists in conforming his will to the divine will. Well, this conformity consists in love (*caritas*), which transforms the one who loves (*amo*) into someone beloved (*amatus*), not in his substance, but by making the will congruent with God's will.[51]

---

45. For Thomas's terminology see Sermon 01 *Veniet desideratus*, note 39: *amor* can be a passion and a virtue, but *dilectio*, *caritas*, and *amicitia* can only be virtues; cf. also ST I–II 26. Passionate love, like all other passions, may—but does not necessarily—blur the distinction between good and evil; cf. ST I–II 59,1–2 and 5.

46. Ignorance leads to sin: ST I–II 76. Cf. ST I–II 93,1–2 (knowing the eternal Law) and 109 (the necessity of grace for knowing, willing, and doing what is true and good).

47. Thomas takes over Dionysius's definition, which says that it is characteristic of goodness to distribute goods. This applies to the highest extent to God, who is the highest good and whose essence is goodness itself: ST I 5,4, 6,1–4, 65,2; I–II 1,4,1.

48. Which is a gracious gift from God: ST I–II 63,1.

49. Cf. ST I 12,13. The virtue of faith itself is extensively contemplated in ST II–II 1–16.

50. ST I–II 4,3.

51. ST I–II 4,4, 104,4,2.

(2) Even more, it is also necessary that everything be upright [or righteous] in the exterior man.[52] For this, three things are required: (2.1) first, that he be upright in his sight, in what he looks at; (2.2) second, that he be upright in speech or affection; (2.3) third, that he be upright in his walking [cf. Prv 4.20–27].

(2.1) First, I say that it is required that the exterior man be upright in his sight, or in what he looks at, as Solomon says in Prv 4.25: "Let your eyes see upright things, and let your eyelids go before your steps." It says: "Let your eyes see upright things," not only internally, but externally the things that are allowed to be seen. For Gregory says: "It is not allowed to look at what is not allowed to be desired." Proverbs says, "Let them see upright things," namely, the examples of the saints and the good works of our neighbors. "And let your eyelids," et cetera: a man ought to cast down his eyes toward the inferior and low things.[53]

But some have their eyes lifted up in pride and haughtiness of heart. In Prv 6.16–19 we read about these people: "There are six things the Lord hates, and a seventh thing his soul detests: haughty eyes, a lying tongue, (and hands that shed innocent blood, a heart that plots wicked schemes, feet that run swiftly to evil, the false witness who utters lies, and the one who sows discord among brothers)." When a peacock vaunts its tail and sees its feet, it immediately puts its tail down.[54] In a similar way, when some good people are carried away by pride,[55] which I hope will not happen, may they take a look at their feet and be made humble. It says [in Prv 4.25] "eyes," plural, not just one eye; and "let them see up-right things (*recta*)," not "up-left" (*sinistra*), that is, bad things.

---

52. Cf. Ps 15. Therefore, an upright man acts in accordance with justice: ST I–II 55,4,4.

53. Cf. Ps 119.37, Is 33.15. After all, what we see affects the soul: ST I 97,2; II–II 154,4; cf. Ps 45.12, Mt 9.36. In ST II–II 53,4 Thomas connects seeing diligently with prudence: negligence, not being attentive to what you take in, may well lead to a wrong way of thinking and a wrong decision.

54. The peacock is a royal bird (cf. 1 Kgs 10.22) and a symbol of vanity and pride. Its feet, however, are nothing to be proud of. Looking at your feet is also looking "down" at yourself, as opposed to "haughty" eyes looking at others (cf. ST II–II 161,2,1 [citing Ps 131.1] and 161,6).

55. A most serious sin, also because other sins may follow from it: ST I–II 84,2; II–II 162.

(2.2) Second, the exterior man ought to be upright [or righteous] in speech in accordance with his affection.[56] For the Apostle says in 2 Tm 2.15: "Be careful that you present yourself to God as approved by him, as an irreproachable laborer, rightly treating the word of truth." He speaks primarily to the highly placed man and accordingly to all others. He says: "Be careful," by the pain of contrition, "that you present yourself to God as an upright, irreproachable laborer," namely, as someone who is not worthy of blame but of praise and reward. Such is the one who has said useful things.

But evil ones are worthy of blame. "Rightly treating the word of truth," [the Apostle says]. Some do not treat the word of truth in the right way, namely, those who preach for their own glory or in order to show the excellence of their good qualities or for their own ostentation.[57] But those treat the word of truth rightly who treat it in such a way that God is glorified and the neighbor is edified [cf. Mt 5.16, Eph 4.29]. I have heard about a certain *magister* in theology who was *magister* for 25 years, and during 20 years, as he confessed on his deathbed, he had done it more because of vainglory than because of giving honor to God and the edification of the neighbor.

A beautiful sword that is made for (*ordinatus ad*) cutting—if someone used it for digging up mud, he would use it in a bad way, because he does not use it for the aim for which it is meant (*ordinatus ad*). In a similar way the word of truth is meant for God's praise and the edification of the neighbor.[58] So someone who uses it in another way or for another end, uses it in an evil way. Because of this it is said in Sir 28.25: "You must make a pair of scales for your words," that is, consider whether your words are to the praise of God or not, or whether they are harmful for the neighbor or not; "and an upright bridle for your mouth." A bridle is upright, when it is not more on the one side than on the other. But when it is loose on one side and very tight on

---

56. Otherwise, he/she would be a wolf in sheep's clothing. See Sermon 14 *Attendite a falsis: Collatio in sero*.

57. Thus it is against the virtue of truth (ST II–II 112) and one of the daughters of empty glory (ST II–II 132,5).

58. Cf. ST I–II 101,2; II–II 109,2–3.

the other, then it is not upright. And sometimes someone keeps the bridle of his mouth upright when things go well for him, whereas in adversity he blasphemes and groans[59]—James says in his letter about such people: "If someone considers himself religious, but does not restrain his language," from evil words, so that he blasphemes, "his religiousness is empty" [Jas 1.26].

(2.3) Third, every exterior man ought to be upright in his intellect. Hence the Apostle says in Heb 12.13: "Take right steps with your feet," namely, with your mind as well as with your body, "so that the lame does not err" by unbelief in his intellect,[60] "but may rather be cured," namely, by divine grace.[61] Someone became in his affection lame in two parts, as we read in 1 Kgs 18.21: "How long do you remain lame in two parts [or: feet]? If he is the Lord, follow him." Others are lame in one foot: they have true faith in their intellect,[62] but they hate the good with their affection.[63] They who have the error of unbelief in their intellect and hatred of goodness in their affection, are lame in both feet; or they are the ones who are elated in time of prosperity, but groan in time of adversity. Because of this the Apostle says in Heb 12.13: "Take right steps with your feet," et cetera, so that you may have humble patience, true faith, and good love (*amor*).

So, if we have a righteous man, interior and exterior—to such people joy is promised [in Ps 97.11]. But you will say: "The one who has written 'the upright of heart,' why did he not in a similar way write 'the upright of body' or 'the upright of steps' or 'of

---

59. See esp. ST II–II 13,2,3; it can be a forgivable, but also an unforgivable, sin, i.e., against the Holy Spirit (ST II–II 14). In this section 2 Thomas connects it with our sight, as he does in the ST: II–II 15.

60. ST II–II 1,5,1: "The godless are ignorant of the things that belong to the faith, because they neither see nor know these as such, nor do they know that these are credible."

61. Cf. Ps 6.3–5, etc.; ST I–II 68,5,1; II–II 9,1,2; III 4,4.

62. ST II–II 1,5,1: "In this way believers have an acquaintance with the things that belong to the faith, not by way of proof, but insofar as through the light of faith it seems that these things are to be believed."

63. Thomas does not mean here "hating your father and mother" as a condition for following Christ (Lk 14.26; cf. ST II–II 26,7,1), but as in 1 Jn 4.20: one cannot hate his brother and sister and love God; cf. ST II–II 26,1,1.

sight'?" The reason is that when there is rectitude in the interior man, there is rectitude in the exterior man as well, because, as we read in Mt 6.22, "If your eye be single," that is, without a fold of being two-faced or erroneous,[64] "your whole body will be enlightened," meaning: the multitude of your works will be good and upright. Thus, since the exterior man depends on the interior man, he is only writing "upright of heart" and not also "of body." In this way it is clear who the upright [or righteous] are.

❖

(3) Do you know what these upright people do?[65] They render three things to the Lord: (3.1) first, they improve their life; (3.2) second, they love (*diligo*) the Lord; and (3.3) third, they bless the Lord and they give the Lord thanks in return for the blessings which they received from God.

(3.1) First, I say, they improve their life. Hence it says in Prv 21.29: "The godless," who neither holds the Lord in veneration nor has compassion toward his neighbor, "unbridles his face," meaning, does not furnish the seat of his thought with a bridle, "stubbornly," that is, imprudently and without reverence; "but someone who is upright improves his life" by means of foresight.[66] Such is the one who is righteous through rectitude of justice to his neighbor and through the rectitude of contemplation towards God. But the godless unbridles his face, so that he does not accept an order of God, or if he accepts it, he does not accomplish the work [cf. Mt 21.30].

(3.2) Second, the upright of heart cling to God through love (*dilectio*). Thus we read in Song 1.4: "The upright love (*diligo*) you." Ps 25.21: "The innocent and the upright have clung to me," namely, through zeal and the virtue of love (*caritas*) mastered by practice.[67]

---

64. Cf. ST I–II 12,1,1. *Simplicitas* is derived from *sine plica* ("without a fold"); cf. Caesarius Heisterbacensis, *Dialogus Miraculorum* Dist. VI c. 20.

65. First Thomas has focused on what an upright man *is:* (1) interior and (2) exterior. Next he discusses what an upright man *does:* practical instructions.

66. ST II–II 49,7,3: Thomas considers foresight (*praevidentia*) a part of prudence, the first of the four cardinal virtues (II–II 47–56). Here he strongly connects it with the second cardinal virtue: justice (II–II 57–122).

67. *Fervor*, zeal, refers to the intensity, whereas *habitus*, a virtue mastered by

(3.3) Third, the upright of heart give the Lord thanks in return for the blessings received.[68] Hence it says in Neh 8.5 that when "Ezra absolved the Law, all the upright stood." "When he absolved the Law" means that he read it all the way through and explained it [cf. Neh 8.8]. It is called "Law" since it is binding for us. "But he also blessed the Lord Most High," the almighty Lord of hosts; "and the whole people responded: 'Amen'" [Neh 8.6]. Then it proceeds: "and all came together into Jerusalem to celebrate with joy" [Neh 8.12],

to which, et cetera.

---

practice (rather than "habit"), to the constancy: ST I–II 48,2, respectively, I–II 49–89.

68. This is considered justice unto God, which is called *religio*. ST II–II 81–91.

SERMON 18
GERMINET TERRA

Sermon on the Feast of the Birth of the Blessed Virgin Mary, the Eighth of September[1]

Genesis 1.11: *Let the earth put forth the green plant that brings forth seed and the fruit-bearing tree that yields fruit.*

PART 1: *Prothema*

ET THE EARTH put forth the green plant that brings forth seed and the fruit-bearing tree that yields fruit" [Gn 1.11]. Isaiah says about Christ: "Who will tell of his generations?" [Is 53.8] The generation of Christ rests in a way on the generation of Mary—I speak here of Christ's generation in time.[2] Hence the human understanding is not enough for telling the whole story of the generation of Mary.[3] Let us, therefore, call upon the grace of the Holy Spirit, by which[4] Mary is

---

1. The *Sermo* is about the Nativity of the Blessed Virgin; it was preached within the octave of this feast. The *Collatio in sero* is about the Exaltation of the Cross, during the First Vespers of this feast. So this sermon was delivered on a 13th of September. It is clear that this sermon was given to university students. Since the 13th of September was usually not a *dies predicabilis*, a day on which a sermon was given, it is most probable that it was a Sunday. During Thomas's years in Paris the only year in which the 13th of September was a Sunday was 1271.

2. "In a way" (*quodammodo*), for not in an absolute way; God did not depend on her, but he had chosen her to be the mother of Christ. Cf. how Thomas distinguishes between different meanings of necessity: in ST III 46,1 in the context of the Passion in view of God's almightiness.

3. Although she is a human being born from an earthly father and an earthly mother, her birth is a mystery: ST III 27,1–5.

4. Latin: *quam*, the antecedent of which is "grace" (*graciam*).

sanctified, and let us ask the Lord himself that he may give me something to say.

PART 2: *Sermo*

"Let the earth," et cetera. These words reflect the divine disposition to provide for each and every thing according to what befits it. Hence God in his providence gave to man, because he is earthly, a remedy from the earth.[5] Hence it says in Sir 38.4: "The Most High has created a medicine from the earth." Now a twofold medicine is put forth from the earth: the green plant and the fruit-bearing tree. The green plant is the Blessed Virgin, whose birth the Church is celebrating these days. For she is called (1) "plant" because of her humility [cf. the Magnificat: Lk 1.48], (2) "green" because of her virginity, and (3) "bringing forth seed" because of her fruitfulness.[6]

❖

(1) Regarding the species of plants we can consider three things: (1.1) a plant is short in height, (1.2) pliant in slenderness, and (1.3) health-bringing through strength.

(1.1) First I say that a plant is short in height. If we compare a plant with a tree, we see that a plant grows upwards a little bit, whereas a tree grows very high. Now, by the height of the tree pride is signified [cf. Dn 4.1–24]. Thus the Psalmist says: "I have seen the godless exalted and lifted up like a cedar of Lebanon" [Ps 37.35]. "I have seen the godless," that is, the proud, because

---

5. The Latin word *humanus* is translated as "earthly" here; Thomas plays with the words which are derived from the Latin word *humus*, soil, earth: *homo* (human being, taken from the earth; cf. Gn 2.7), *humanus* (human, earthly), and later on in this homily *humilis/humilitas* (low/lowliness, humble/humility), as opposed to being exalted, elevated, proud.

The word *remedium* occurs only once in Scripture, in Tb 6.7 (Vg): in the fish—thus in creation—the remedy against evil is found. The fish is the oldest Christian symbol of Christ; the letters of the Greek word ΙΧΘΥΣ stand for "Jesus Christ God's Son Savior." Thomas, however, does not refer to this explicitly.

6. Thomas presents Mary implicitly as a great example for every vowed religious: she excelled in obedience (ST II–II 104) and humility (161), in chastity (151)/virginity (152), and in a fruitful, virtuous life (ST I–II 55–67); cf. ST II–II 186,4–5. See also note 8.

"pride is the origin of godlessness";[7] "exalted" in the prosperity of the world.[8] Against them the Apostle says: "Tell the rich of this age not to be wise in a lofty way" [1 Tm 6.17]. And "lifted up" in their thoughts, because a proud man elevates himself above himself in his thoughts. As we read in Jb 20.6: "If he ascends to heaven and his pride and his head touch the clouds, in the end he will be lost like a dunghill." Thus you see that "the godless" is "exalted" in the prosperity of the world and "lifted up" in his thoughts "like the cedars of Lebanon." Hence it says in Am 2.9: "The height of cedars is his height." So a plant does not grow very high, but is short, in which humility is signified. The Psalmist says: "He put forth a plant for the servitude of the people" [Ps 104.14]. By "servitude" humility is signified.[9]

It is amazing that a tree is highly elevated from the earth and yet most firmly fixed in the earth. A plant, however, only clings a little to the earth, and its roots are just under the surface. In a similar way a proud man's heart is pinned to the earth, and he cannot come loose from the earth, although he makes himself very big and is elevated high.[10] On the other hand, a [lowly or] humble man does not have anything on earth;[11] therefore, his heart is easily removed from the earth. So in this way Mary is compared with a plant in regard to her moderation.

In the Blessed Virgin there were many things because of which she is praiseworthy. She was full of grace, according to the testimony of the angel.[12] She was chosen to be the mother

7. Sir 10.12; cf. ST I–II 84,2, where Sir 10.12–18 forms the guideline of the discussion. In this sermon the imagery that follows seems to be inspired by Sir 10.15: the roots, the humble.

8. The Holy Family (including Mary, of course) is traditionally regarded as poor; cf. ST III 40,3, and Sermon 08 *Puer Jesus*, section 4.3. Thus Mary is also (see note 6, above) presented as an example of religious poverty: SCG 130–135; cf. ST II–II 186,3.

9. Latin: *servitudo;* cf. Lk 1.38: "Behold, I am the handmaid (*ancilla*) of the Lord," etc.; cf. ST III 30,1: Mary accepted it voluntarily.

10. Thomas is playing with words here: he contrasts the tree which *inheret* and *multum elevatur,* respectively: *elevetur in altum* (is much elevated, elevated high from the earth) with the plant which *adheret* and whose roots *breviter evelluntur* (a short distance loose from the earth).

11. Cf. ST I–II 69,3.

12. Lk 1.28; not as Jesus was (full, by nature), but in the way John the Bap-

of God; indeed, she was made the mother of God. And still she gloried only in her lowliness, saying: "Because he has looked upon the lowliness of his servant" [Lk 1.48]. The Lord sought a woman through whom he would save the human race,[13] and opposites would be cured by opposites. The human race was lost by pride, because "the origin of every sin is pride" [Sir 10.15]. So it was not becoming[14] that in a proud mother the humble Son would live who had to save the human race through humility.[15] Hence God had no eye but for humility. About St. Mary's humility Augustine says in a homily on her Assumption: "O, true humility of Mary, which gave birth to God for the people, gave life to mortals, renewed the heavens, purified the world, opened Paradise for humankind, and liberated the souls of the people." So in the littleness of a humble plant the humility of Mary is commended.

(1.2) Second, a plant is not hard, but pliant. Pliant is what gives in at a touch; a heart is called pliant when it easily gives in. But we must observe that there is a certain virtuous and natural pliability of the heart as well as a vicious and unnatural one. The natural order requires that a lower thing gives in to an action of a higher thing.[16] The will or the heart of a human being is set between two; it has something above itself and something underneath. If it easily gives in to what is below, like the concupiscence of the flesh or the cupidity of the world, it is an unnatural pliability.[17] About this we read in Prv 2.16: "in order to save you from an" evil and "foreign woman, who makes her words pliant." Jeremiah warns us: "Go out of her [that is, Babylon's] midst, so that your heart may not become pliant" [Jer 51.45–46]. This was not the pliability of this plant. Likewise, the

---

tist (Lk 1.15) and St. Stephen (Acts 6.8) were (full, i.e., filled by grace): ST III 7,10,1.

13. Thus Mary is an *instrument* of salvation, not the Savior, that is, not the one who uses the instrument; cf. ST III 48,5.

14. *Decens* indicates a certain beauty (the verb *deceo* is, for instance, also used for clothes that look good on someone), harmony, and order—instead of hard evidence. God in his wisdom orders the whole of creation and has planned (from eternity) our salvation history.

15. Phil 2.8; cf. ST III 19,3–4.   16. Cf. ST I 2,3, the first way.
17. Cf. ST I 63,4,2 and I-II 71,2.

will of a human being has God above itself. Hence it ought to bow for a divine movement, because "a hard heart will endure much on the Last Day" [Sir 3.27]. Concerning this pliability Job says: "God has made my heart pliant" [Jb 23.16].[18]

A young man is compared to a plant by the Psalmist: "Let him come early in the morning," that is, in his youth, "like a plant" [Ps 90.6]. Someone is easily led in his youth. The Blessed Virgin had this tenderness through obedience, for immediately at the word of the angel she yielded (*obedio*) and believed that she had conceived by the Holy Spirit, and she subjected herself immediately: "Behold the servant of the Lord; may it happen to me according to your word" [Lk 1.38]. Thus it is with the saints, that they cannot but teach as they live; and because the Blessed Virgin was most obedient, thus she taught obedience.[19] Among other things that are said of her in the Gospel, we read that she taught in particular the precept of obedience, saying: "Whatever he may say to you, do it" [Jn 2.5]. She says: "Do whatever he may say," not: "whatever he may order," because it belongs to immediate obedience that it yields readily to the mere word of someone or something higher. Hence the Apostle says in Ti 3.1: "to obey what is said."[20]

Obedience is a special virtue.[21] Thus Gregory speaks of it in his book *On Morals:* "It is the only virtue that plants the other virtues in the mind and protects the ones that have been planted."[22] Some whisper and say that it is better to be obedient with a spontaneous will than on the basis of a vow. This is not true.[23] Among other exterior goods there is no good as great as offer-

---

18. Since Job is a just man (Jb 1.1, 42.7–8), Thomas interprets it as virtuous pliability.

19. See note 6. Thomas, however, presents Mary as so perfect that she becomes almost super-human and thus difficult to identify with and apparently impossible to follow. On the other hand, religious and people in holy orders were said or supposed to live a perfect life (*status perfectionis*), even more perfect than secular priests and archdeacons (ST II–II 184,8).

20. Thus prompt or immediate obedience is primarily, but not only, in respect of God: ST II–II 104,1 and 2,2.

21. ST II–II 104,2.

22. ST II–II 186,8.

23. Thomas is defending the vowed religious life in ST II–II 186,6–7.

ing sacrifice,[24] and obedience is even better than sacrificial animals [cf. 1 Sm 15.22, Is 1.11–20]. Hence Gregory says: "Obedience is placed above the law of sacrificial animals, because in them something else's flesh is slaughtered; in obedience, however, one's own will is slaughtered." The Blessed Virgin has set this teaching of obedience before us in her deed and word.[25]

"By the disobedience of one man" we are all sinners [Rom 5.9].[26] So it was becoming that we would be saved by obedience and that, just as the obedience of the Son began in the mother,[27] so the Blessed Virgin was obedient.

(1.3) Third, a plant is health-bringing through strength. So it is able to cure weaknesses; only if a plant has medicinal strength does it make sense what is said in Wis 16.12: "Neither a plant nor a bandage has cured them (but your word, Lord, has cured them)." The human race was weak, as the Psalmist says: "Have mercy on me, Lord, because I am weak; cure me" [Ps 6.3]. This weakness is acquired by reason of sin,[28] and God wanted to apply the remedy of a medicine. He did it like a good doctor. When good doctors want to show [that] their medicine [works], they first apply it to serious weaknesses, so that they thus may become famous. The whole human race was feeble, and as for the woman it seemed that it was completely corrupted.[29] Hence Solomon says: "I found a woman more bitter than death" [Eccl 7.26]. And so the Lord, willing to show that his medicine was good, showed it in a woman first, in order to distribute it through a woman to others.[30]

24. Cf. ST I–II 101,4; II–II 85.
25. In ST III 27,5,3, however, Thomas explains why the Blessed Virgin Mary does/did not teach.
26. Cf. ST II–II 163.
27. Cf. ST III 34.
28. Sin causes weakness, ignorance, malice, and concupiscence (ST I–II 85,3), and these may cause someone to sin. As for weakness: ST I–II 77,3.
29. E.g., ST II–II 149,4, 163,4, 177,2; cf. also I–II 105,3,1 (concluding remark); II–II 124,4,2, 165,2,1.
30. By depicting the woman in such a negative way, Thomas underlines the splendor of Mary and the goodness of God. This negative view of women, brought on by Aristotle and an interpretation of Genesis 3 employed by Church Fathers, was common in those days (e.g., in Thomas's commentary on Aristotle's VII *Ethic.*, *lectio* 5, n.8, he mentions the *incontinentia* of women as if it is

Hence we read in Sir 43.22: "The medicine of all people is in the swiftness of a cloud." And Solomon says in his prayer: "The Lord has said that he abides in a cloud" [1 Kgs 8.12]. In this cloud, that is, in the Virgin, is the salvation of the human race, because it is cured through this cloud.[31] Thus it says in Sir 24.25 (Vg): "In me is every grace of life and truth, in me is every hope of life and strength (*virtus*)."[32] And therefore, since the medicine of all people is in this cloud, that is, in the Blessed Virgin, the Apostle says: "Let us approach with confidence the throne of his grace, in order to obtain mercy in timely help" [Heb 4.16].[33]

It says: "in the swiftness of a cloud," because the strength (*virtus*) of this medicine appeared swiftly. "Swift" is that someone in his adolescence obtains grace, and the Blessed Virgin obtained grace in the maternal womb because she was sanctified in the womb from original guilt, although she was conceived in it.[34] As the Psalmist says: "God will not be shaken up in her midst" [Ps 46.6], meaning: neither by mortal nor by venial sin.[35] Hence Augustine says: "When we speak about sins, I do not want to mention anything at all concerning the mother of the Lord." "God will come to her aid early in the morning at daybreak" [Ps 46.6], that is, in her rising. Hence Jerome wrote in his Psal-

---

common ground; cf. also Thomas's use of Prv 31.10–31 on the strong woman in Sermon 16 *Inueni Dauid*, in section 1.1), yet Thomas accentuates it strongly in this sermon (although he does not explain it in sexual terms, as, e.g., Chrysostom and Augustine do). See also in section 1.2 of this sermon where he inserts "evil" in the quotation of Prv 2.16. It should be noted, however, that at the same time Thomas underlines that Mary was a woman and that our salvation came through a woman: he stresses that this woman as a woman, namely, as a mother and a virgin, has a pivotal place in the salvation history. See also how Gal 3.28 ("in Christ there is no male or female") functions in, e.g., ST I 93,6,2, and III 36,3, 72,10,3.

31. See note 13.

32. *Virtus* can also be translated as "virtue."

33. The reason given in Heb 4.14–15 why we ought to approach with confidence is different; cf. also ST III 59,2.

34. ST III 27,1–3.

35. See for this distinction ST I–II 72–73. God and his plan of salvation are not hindered by any sin; cf. ST I 22,1,2 (eternal providence) and 22,3–4; also ST I 9,1 (God as the unmoveable Mover) and III 1,3 (would God have become incarnate if we had not sinned?).

ter: "God will help her in her rising in the early hours." Therefore, we celebrate her birth above the other saints, except the birth of Christ and of John the Baptist.[36]

Thus the Blessed Virgin was a plant because of her humility.

❖

(2) Likewise, she was a green plant because of her virginity. It says in Jer 12.4: "Every plant of the land will wither," but the Blessed Virgin was a green plant through her virginity. Hence it says in Lk 1.26–27: "The angel Gabriel was sent to the Virgin Mary." See that in the greenness we observe (1) moisture, (2) beauty, and (3) usefulness or necessity.

(2.1) First, I say, in the greenness we see moisture as a cause, since moisture is the cause of greenness. Thus we read in Sir 40.16: "Greenness on all waterfronts." And you should know that, just as every plant withers because of fire or the sun, so the concupiscence of the flesh makes the greenness of virginity wither. It says in Jb 31.12: "It is a devouring fire aimed at consummation."[37]

But by what is the greenness of virginity nurtured? Surely by heavenly love (*amor*),[38] for virginity is something heavenly. Hence Jerome says: "Living in the flesh beyond the flesh is not a worldly or human way of life, but heavenly." And the Apostle has said in his admonition about virginity: "Everyone has received a proper gift from God: someone this gift, someone else another" [1 Cor 7.7]. Virginity is the result of God's grace with the freedom of the free decision.[39] So a young man said: "I can-

---

36. Christmas, the feast of Christ's birth, is of course a greater feast. John the Baptist's birth (celebrated on the 24th of June) is as great a feast as Mary's. These are the only three people whose birthdays are celebrated by the Church. (Of other saints only the day of their dying, which is the day of birth to new life in Christ, is celebrated or commemorated.)

37. In ST Thomas also speaks of another fire: the fire of love (ST II–II 24,10), which excites us to devotion (ST II–II 82,2,2); excess leads to corruption: ST I–II 28,5.

38. All virtues in us come with love; cf. ST I–II 65,3. For Thomas's terminology of "love," see Sermon 01 *Veniet desideratus*, note 39.

39. The consequence is that candidates for religious life must not be forced, but helped in the process of discernment: is God calling me? Is he giving me this grace? Cf. ST II–II 189,1,3 and 189,5, where Thomas speaks of religious life in

not live celibately unless God has given it to me" [Wis 8.21].[40]

The moisture of grace was in the Blessed Virgin, wasn't it? It surely was. Thus the angel said to her: "Fear not, Mary; you have found grace with God" [Lk 1.30].[41] She had grace in a most abounding way. Thus the angel said to her: "Hail, full of grace" [Lk 1.28].[42] And because she had the fullness of the moisture of grace, it was not enough for her to live as a virgin only in the usual way, namely, by marital continence, but beyond the usual custom it was her strongest resolution to live as a virgin forever. Thus she said: "How will this come to pass, since I do not know a man?" [Lk 1.34] This means: I am resolute not to know.[43]

(2.2) Second, we see in the greenness a beauty that delights. It says in Sir 40.22: "The eye will long for grace and a beautiful appearance, but above these for green farmland." Purity of the flesh and virginity are a delight for the eyes of God and the saints. And why? Order, or the beauty of the order, is properly delightful.[44] Augustine says: "If someone saw windows that have been placed in a house arbitrarily, he would not delight in them." The natural order of humankind is that the flesh is subject to the spirit.[45] It is becoming when we live according to this order. But when this order is confused, someone is disgraceful. And it is, therefore, that carnal sins, although some are not as severe as others,[46] make someone even more shameful, because they are disgraceful and disturb the order in humankind; they make higher what is lower in humankind, and the other way round. But in the Blessed Virgin nothing was disordered, nei-

---

terms of process and of nurturing a vocation. See also Sermon 13 *Homo quidam fecit*, in the *Collatio in sero*.

40. Cf. ST I–II 63,2–4.

41. Theological aspects of the Annunciation in ST III 30.

42. See note 12.

43. Thomas concludes that Mary vowed virginity: ST III 29,4; Mary remains the great example for Thomas's religious audience. Texts like 1 Sm 2.5 and Is 54.1 on a childless woman (in Isaiah without a man) who will give birth several times are not discussed in this context by Thomas, in accordance with the tradition.

44. See note 14.

45. Cf. Rom 8.1–17. The soul is, after all, the *forma* of the body and thus more excellent: ST I 76,1.

46. Thomas distinguishes between them in ST II–II 154, on *luxuria*.

ther in action nor in affection, nor did she have the first movements leading to sin. Hence it says in Song 4.7: "You are totally beautiful, my friend, and no stain is in you." And because of this it is said to her: "The king will desire (*concupisco*) your (beautiful) appearance" [Ps 45.12].

(2.3) Likewise, we find in greenness what is useful. As long as a plant is green, there is hope that it will produce fruit. But when it begins to shrivel, there is no hope of her fruit any more. Is 15.6 says: "The plant has shriveled, the grass is dead, all greenness has passed away." On the contrary, when a plant is green, there is hope that it will produce fruit. Hence it says in Isaiah: "And its leaves will be green, and it will not cease to produce fruit" [Jer 17.8]. In a similar way someone who is green through virginity produces the fruit of love (*caritas*), but when he shrivels through concupiscence, his works are fruitless in view of eternal life.[47] The Apostle says: "Someone who sows in the flesh will reap corruption from the flesh" [Gal 6.8]. A dry plant is not useful for anything but to be thrown into the fire [cf. Jn 15.6]. In a similar way the ones who become dry through the fire of concupiscence are useful for nothing but to be thrown into the fire of hell.

But the Blessed Virgin was excellent in virginity; indeed, she is the queen of the virgins. And because she had the greenness of virginity in an excellent way, she produced an amazing fruit. Other virgins produce, since they are virgins, a spiritual fruit. The Apostle says of this fruit: "The fruits of the Spirit are love (*caritas*), joy, and peace" [Gal 5.22]. But since the Blessed Virgin had an abundance of greenness, she even produced the fruit of the womb. It is said to her: "Blessed are you among women, and blessed is the fruit of your womb" [Lk 1.42]. And Is 7.14 says about that: "Behold, the virgin will conceive and bear a son (and you will call his name Emanuel)." Hugo [of St. Victor] says: "Since the love (*caritas*) of the Holy Spirit burned in her heart in a marvelous way, he has done marvelous things in her flesh." Other virgins have produced spiritual fruit, but

---

47. For the theological virtues of faith, hope, and love order us towards the supernatural happiness; cf. ST I–II 62,3.

she even produced the fruit of her womb. Thus she has been a green plant.

(3) It says: "Let it put forth the plant that produces seed." Seed of what kind? I say (3.1) holy seed, (3.2) virtuous seed, and (3.3) necessary seed.

(3.1) First, I say, the Blessed Virgin produced a holy seed, [in conformity with] Is 6.13: "It will be a holy seed that is in her." And why holy? Because its origin will be holy:[48] first, the holiness of God, because he himself is the Holy One of the saints. "You [plural] will be holy," he says, "because I am holy" [1 Pt 1.16]. From such a Holy One the seed comes, and thus the seed is holy [cf. Mt 7.17]. "The seed is the Word of God" [Lk 8.11], and Christ is God's Word [cf. Jn 1.1–18]. It is characteristic of seed that it produces what is similar to that from which it comes forth. Thus the seed of God's Word brings forth what is similar to itself, because it produces gods. Hence we read in Jn 1.12: "He has given them the power to become sons and daughters of God." Abraham is praised for his holiness. Just as Christ is the seed of God according to the Spirit [cf. Lk 8.11], so he is the seed of Abraham according to the flesh [Rom 9.5; cf. Mt 1.1–17], and "to Abraham promises were made and to his seed" [Lk 1.55, 73]. "In your seed," the Lord said, "all peoples will be blessed" [Gn 12.3]. And therefore that seed is blessed. Likewise, children of God are brought about by the seed of God's Word, just as the children of Abraham by the seed of Abraham: blessed is the seed that brings us the Blessed One [cf. Jn 8.31–59, 10.31–39].

(3.2) Furthermore, that seed is virtuous. Hence it is compared in the Gospel with a mustard seed, which is the tiniest seed and produces a great tree, so that the birds of heaven make their nests in their branches [Mt 13.32]. The little seed is Christ, who was little on the Cross and grew so big that he filled heaven and earth: "He ascended above all the heavens, in order to make all things full" [Eph 4.10].

---

48. Cf. ST I 65,1: He who is good brings forth what is good, as in Mt 7.16–18 ("You will know them by their fruits"). See also the beginning of Eucharistic Prayer II: "Father, you are holy indeed, the fountain of all holiness."

(3.3) Furthermore, that seed is necessary. Hence Is 1.9 says: "Unless the Lord had left seed for us, we had become like Sodom."[49] And St. Peter says: "There is no salvation in anything else, and no other name is given to the people in which we are to be saved" [Acts 4.12]. Amazing is this plant, and amazing its offspring. This earth is the human nature destitute of the moisture of grace, as Jer 4.23 puts it: "I have looked at the earth, and behold: it was empty and for nothing." Then how could it bring forth a plant? Surely, in no way.[50]

Again, this earth was arid because of the concupiscence of sin. Hence it says in Sir 43.3: "At noon it scorches the earth."

In addition, this earth was the lowest, because God created heaven above and the earth underneath [Prv 25.3]. So how has he put it forth? In Gn 1.11 it says: "God said: 'Let the earth put forth the green plant.'" "He said" the word, meaning: He put forth the word that produced a fruit. Thus we read in Prv 9.1: "Wisdom has built a house for herself,"[51] namely, in the Blessed Virgin, and he caused her to produce a plant for himself. The Psalmist says: "A man is born in her, (the Most High himself has established her)" [Ps 87.5]. This very man has filled this earth, because it was empty, as the Psalmist says: "You have visited the earth and you have saturated it; you have multiplied its riches" [Ps 65.10].

Also, because it was arid, the Holy Spirit has made it moist, according to the Psalmist: "The one who puts forth will rejoice in his raindrops" [Ps 65.11].

Besides, because the earth was lowest, he gave himself to it and entered it, so as to make it the heavenly seed. Is 55.10 says: "Just as a heavy rain comes down from heaven and saturates the earth and causes it to bring forth, so my word will be."

---

49. I.e., extinct; cf. Is 13.19–20; Jer 49.18, 50.40; Rv 11.8.
50. In other words: we cannot save ourselves; we need God our Savior, who saves us through the seed of his Word: ST I–II 91,5,2; II–II 2,7. This realization makes salvation history even more *mirabilis* (marvelous, amazing) for us.
51. Cf. ST III 32,1: the conception is an act of the triune God, but it is attributed to the Holy Spirit.

Therefore, if someone is empty through sin, let him ask for this plant, and he will be filled with good things. The Psalmist says: "We will be filled with the good things of your house" [Ps 65.5]. Likewise, if someone is arid, let him take refuge with that Word, and he will be moistened. The Psalmist says: "My heart has hoped in him and I received help" [Ps 28.7]. Likewise, if someone is downhearted, let him take refuge with that Word, and he will be led back to the heavenly light. The Psalmist says: "Send out your light and your truth; they have led me back onto your holy mountain and into your tents" [Ps 43.3].

May he deem us worthy to stand before, et cetera.

PART 3: *Collatio in sero*

"Let the earth bring forth the green plant," et cetera. The Most High has raised from the earth two remedies for us: the green plant and the fruit-bearing tree. We have spoken about the plant, which is the Blessed Virgin. Now it remains to speak about the fruit-bearing tree, the tree of the Cross of our Lord, which is to be venerated. We have begun the solemn days of his Cross.[52] It is very suitable to connect these two remedies, because the green plant has brought forth our salvation, whereas the fruit-bearing tree has sustained the plant and has exalted it. For the Son of God "became obedient (to death, even death on a cross)" [Phil 2.8], and it follows: "Because of this he has exalted him" [Phil 2.9].[53] Hence it says in the Gospel that "Jesus' mother stood at the foot of the Cross" [Jn 19.25].[54] Let us look at this tree.

It seems that Moses[55] describes three things concerning that tree: (1) its appearance, (2) its adornment, and (3) its fruit. If you seek its appearance, it is wood; its adornment: it bears many fruits (*pomiferum*); what it produces: it produces fruit (*faciens fructum*).

---

52. See note 1. 53. ST III 49,6.
54. She (and other believers with her) wants to abide with him because he sustains her (us) during her (our) life on earth (cf. ST III 46,3) and will exalt her (us) in the end (cf. ST III 57,6).
55. As the reputed writer of Genesis.

(1) First, I say, if you seek the appearance of this wood, I say it is wood. That wood really befits our remedy, for three reasons: (1.1) it befits the wound, (1.2) it befits the healing of it, and (1.3) it befits the healer.

(1.1) First, the wood of the Cross befits our remedy, because it befits the wound. The human race is wounded by wood, because the first man ate from the forbidden wood and therefore the divine Wisdom found the medicine from wood.[56] The human race is wounded because of disobedience, since the first man stole a fruit from the forbidden wood. The new man has placed himself, as a salutary fruit so to speak (*quasi*), back onto the wood. The Psalmist says: "Did I pay what I have not stolen?" [Ps 69.5][57] He has given himself back to the wood, so that he would recompense the injury and bring the remedy.[58] Hence we read in Wis 14.7: "Blessed the wood by which justice comes about."

See, we are going to compare wood with wood. Scripture says three things about the forbidden wood. "The woman, who saw that the wood was (1.1.1) good to eat from and (1.1.2) beautiful to the eyes and (1.1.3) delightful to look at, has taken from" the wood "and eaten it" [Gn 3.6].

(1.1.1) First, I say, that wood is good to eat from, and, because of this, it is suitable for being nourished. Contrary to this, the wood of the Cross teaches the mortification of the flesh. Hence it is said: "Your princes" have destroyed "it."[59]

---

56. Cf. Rom 5.18–19, 1 Cor 15.21–22. See also note 14. God is so wise that he takes the remedy from the thing that harmed us; things created can be abused but are not *therefore* intrinsically evil (cf. ST I 2,3,1, and 49,1).

57. The basis of this line of thought is Thomas's understanding of justice as "giving back what is due." The pride of the first human being was that he was not obedient to God but wanted to be like God (ST II–II 163,2). Only someone who was free of this sin, i.e., someone who had not "stolen" what properly belongs to God, could take away the guilt and the punishment by being more than obedient, by voluntarily "paying back" more than what was due, i.e., by abundance (ST III 46,4, 48,2).

58. It was salutary because it was an act of obedience that counteracted the disobedience of the first *homo*: Rom 5.19; cf. ST III 47,2.

59. It is not really clear from where this quotation has been drawn: probably from Jer 44.21, for here the words *principes vestri* ("your princes") are connected with sacrificing something, i.e., giving something up for God. The contexts of

Moreover, the former is the wood of death. The Apostle says: "If you live according to the flesh, you will die" [Rom 8.13]. But the wood of the Cross, on the contrary, has made us alive by mortifying the flesh. The Apostle says: "Christ has died once for our sins, the Just for the unjust, so as to offer us to God; made dead in the flesh, yet made alive in the Spirit" [1 Pt 3.18]. Likewise, the Apostle says: "If you made the flesh die in accordance with the Spirit, you will live" [Rom 8.13].[60]

(1.1.2) Second, there was worldly beauty in the forbidden wood. Thus it says in Gn 3.6: "She saw the wood, that it was beautiful to the eyes." But Is 40.6 [calls to our mind that]: "Every glory of it is like the flower of the field." A flower has the beauty and the glory of the world, but it is cursed, because through its beauty people are drawn to damnation. Jb 5.3 reads: "I have seen a foolish man with a strong root, and I have cursed his beauty." On the contrary, the wood of the Cross has shame. Hence it was written for that time in Dt 21.23: "Cursed by God is the one who hangs on the wood."

See that it says that it was beautiful to the eyes of Adam and Eve, and that it was praised for this. First, for the knowledge, of which the serpent said to them: "You will be like gods, knowing good and evil" [Gn 3.5]. Hence it was called "the tree (*lignum*) of the knowledge of good and evil" [Gn 2.17]. There are some goods which man does not use in an evil way, for instance, virtues. But having the skill of dealing with material things is not the same as having virtues.[61] Some have an abundance of goods of the world and often they use them in an evil way. That wood (*lignum*) had a visible beauty, whereas the wood (*lignum*) of the Cross had the disorder of foolishness. Hence the Apostle says: "We preach the crucified Christ: for Jews yet a scandal, for Gen-

---

Dt 29.10 and Acts 3.17 and of Ps 23.7 (Vg; in the version of the *Psalterium Romanum*) make it quite unlikely that Thomas refers to any of these verses here.

60. Thus mortification is nothing like suicide (ST II–II 64,5) or hatred of the body; it is training yourself to live a life in the Spirit of Jesus Christ for the sake of your well-being now and in the hereafter. So love of God and yourself, rather than hatred, is the motive. Fasting is a virtuous form of mortification of the body: it puts a check on our desires, makes our minds free to contemplate higher things, and is penance for our sins: ST II–II 147,1.

61. Cf. ST I–II 63,2–4.

tiles even foolishness" [1 Cor 1.23]. But the beauty of the first wood is completely changed into shame. Thus it says in Hos 4.7: "I will completely change their glory into shame." The shame of the Cross, however, is completely changed into glory. Thus it says in Ezek 17.24: "I, the Lord, have brought low the lofty wood and I have exalted the low wood."

See how the wood of the Cross is exalted.[62] Chosroes, king of the Persians, had taken that wood as a captive so to speak, from Jerusalem, and it was brought back to Jerusalem by Heraclius. And because of the memory of that glory we speak to the present day of the Feast of the Exaltation of the Holy Cross. The Cross is always exalted, because "the Lord strengthens the just ones" [Ps 37.17]. Augustine says in a commendation of the Holy Cross: "The Cross is not used to punish people any more, and yet it remains; we find it from those condemned (who make the sign of the cross when they pray), to the crowns of emperors." And Chrysostom says: "The Cross shines in crowns of kings everywhere, on the armor of soldiers,[63] on sacred altars, and kings receive a cross when they give up their crowns." Thus the wood of the Cross is exalted. The Lord will exalt it even more. Hence it says in Mt 24.29–30: "Sun and moon will be darkened, and they will see the sign of the Son of man in the sky," which is the wood of the Cross. And Chrysostom says that "the Son of man would never appear after the sun and the moon are darkened, if the Cross were not brighter than the rays of the sun."

(1.1.3) Moreover, that wood had delight. Thus it says in Gn 3.6: "It was delightful to look at." The delight of the flesh is not a true delight, since it is more about bitterness than about delight. Hence Solomon says: "I considered a laugh foolishness, and I said to joy: 'Why do you deceive yourself in vain?'" [Eccl 2.2] On the contrary, the wood of the Cross had the sting of bitterness, which is signified in 2 Sm 23.7 where it says: "He will

---

62. On the vigil of the Feast of the Exaltation of the Cross (the 14th of September) Thomas explains the origin of this Feast (cf. note 1).

63. St. John Chrysostom lived from about 349 to 407. Thus he is not referring to knights of the Cross, who were around in Thomas's time, but to soldiers of the Roman Empire who, since Emperor Constantine (after 325), were fighting for a Christian empire.

be armed with a sword and the wood of a lance." And the Apostle Peter: "Because Christ suffered in the flesh, you too must be armed with the same mindset" [1 Pt 4.1].

This sting of bitterness turns into sweetness, which is signified in Ex 15.23–24, where it is said that "the children of Israel arrived at bitter waters: the Lord ordered Moses to throw a piece of wood in, and the waters became sweet." If the just suffer adversities, the wood of the Cross makes these sweet [cf. Gal 2.19–20, Col 1.24]. The Cross even makes you glory in adversity, as the Apostle says: "I do not glory unless in the Cross of our Lord" [Gal 6.14]. And Jas 1.2 reads: "Brothers and sisters, consider it total joy when you fall into temptations of different kinds." And why? Because of the consideration of the Cross.[64] The Apostle says in Heb 12.3: "Reflect on him, who for us took upon himself such opposition (*contradictio*) from sinners," when he was counted among the robbers [cf. Is 53.9, Mt 27.38]. So, what should we consider evil, if he took contradictions on?

Thus the wood of the Cross befits the wound.

❖

(1.2) Furthermore, it befits the healing. Look in Sacred Scripture: where there was a danger, the remedy was given through wood. The first evil of man occurred when Adam was thrown out of Paradise [Gn 3.23–24]. What was the remedy? The wood of life [cf. Rv 22.2]. But, because he could not approach the wood of life [cf. Rv 2.7], he could not have the remedy. Thus the Lord has said: See "that he does not take from the wood of life" [Gn 3.22]—but Christ has taken up the wood for us. Hence it is written: "The wood of life, who would take hold of it?" [Prv 3.18][65]

Another danger was in the destructive flood [Gn 6–8]. The remedy came by means of the wood of the ark. If you are in a destructive flood, in the streams of this age, take refuge with the wood of the Cross. The Psalmist says: "If I walk in the midst of the shadow of death, (I fear no evil, for you are with me);

---

64. Cf. ST III 46–50. In ST III 46,3 Thomas expounds how abundant the fruit of this tree is for us.
65. Cf. ST I 102,5.

your rod and staff"—of the Cross that is—"(will console me)" [Ps 23.4]; by the Cross I am delivered and led to [the Lord's] guidance.

Again, the people of Israel was in danger when it was oppressed by the Egyptians [Ex 1.8–22]. The remedy came by means of wood, since Moses struck the Egyptians with a rod [Ex 7–12]; the rod divided the sea [Ex 14.21]. If you are attacked by hostile spirits, take refuge with the wood of the Cross.

It says in 1 Sm 4.7 that the children of Israel fought against the Philistines and that the Ark of the Lord was brought into the camp. And "the Philistines groaned, saying: 'Woe to us,'" because the Ark of God came into the camp. The Ark was made of wood that could not rot [cf. Is 40.20]. The Psalmist recalls: "Those who live in the borderlands became confused by your signs" [Ps 65.9].

Those who are overcome, fear the banner of their enemy, and since the demons are overcome by Christ,[66] they fear his banner, which is the wood of the Cross. Hence the Church sings: "Behold the wood of the Cross; flee, enemy parties."[67]

So the wood befits the wound and the healing.

(1.3) Third, it befits the Healer, because Christ is exalted by the wood of the Cross. Thus it is even written: "The Son of man must be exalted" [Jn 3.14]. But how is he exalted? Surely as a warrior. Hence what is said in Nm 24.17 befits him: "A rod will rise from Israel, and it will bring the kings of Moab to nought." The Apostle says: "He has thoroughly plundered the principalities and powers" [Col 2.15]. So the wood of the Cross is like a

---

66. Cf. ST III 49,2, referring to Jn 12.31.

67. Words taken from the so-called St. Antony's Brief (St. Anthony's Letter). A Portuguese woman tormented by evil spirits was determined to drown herself in a river. As she stopped for a last prayer at a shrine in honor of St. Antony, she received from him a piece of paper with a text (either during her prayer or after she had fallen asleep). As long as she had this text with her, she was cured. Copies of the text spread during the 13th century and it became very popular. The complete text, based on Rv 5.5, reads: *Ecce crucem Domini. Fugite, partes adversae. Vicit Leo de tribu Iuda, Radix David. Alleluia* ("Behold the cross of the Lord. Flee, enemy parties. The Lion from the tribe of Judah has conquered, the Root of David. Alleluia.").

triumphant chariot: it is the thing that elevates Christ. Thus it is like the sedan chair of Solomon [cf. Song 3.9]; it also is like the rod that guides the people, as the Psalmist says: "The rod of guidance, the rod of your Kingdom" [Ps 45.7]. Thus Christ is exalted like a warrior [cf. 1 Cor 15.54–57].

Moreover, he is exalted as a *magister* in his seat of instruction.[68] Concerning this exaltation he says: "When I am exalted from the earth, I will draw all things to myself" [Jn 12.32].[69]

We have seen now the appearance of the remedy.

(2) Let us take a look at the adornment of the wood. The adornment of a tree is that it be loaded with fruits.[70] And of this wood it is said that it is fruit-bearing. Well, then, which are his fruits? It says in Song 7.14: "I have served you all fruits, old and new." The old fruits are the prefigurations that refer to the wood. Hence we read in Hos 9.10 about these fruits: "I have seen" all "their fathers as the first fruits."[71] The new fruits, which are they? In Dt 33.13–15, in the blessing of Joseph, mention is made of three fruits: (2.1) the fruits of heaven, (2.2) the fruits of sun and moon, and (2.3) the fruits of eternal hills.

(2.1) Which are the fruits from heaven? The members of Christ are. The Cross was adorned with the members of Christ,[72] just as a tree is adorned with fruits; not only with the physical members of Christ's body, but with those of his mystical body,[73]

---

68. Christ teaches from the Cross, a metaphor derived from Augustine (cf. the *corpus* of ST III 46,4), obviously chosen in view of the academic audience.

69. Since the Cross coincides in this way with the Crucified, the Cross must be venerated as Christ himself: ST II–II 103,4,3; III 25,4.

70. Cf. the hymns for Lent *Vexilla regis prodeunt* and Thomas's own *Pange lingua gloriosi* (from the Vespers of the Feast of Corpus Christi).

71. Thus the old fruits are the believers of the Old Covenant: Abraham, Moses, David, et al.

72. The *Rhythmica oratorio* is attributed by some to St. Bernard of Clairvaux (12th century), by others to Arnulf of Louvain (13th century), both Cistercians. It contains seven meditations of Christ on the Cross, each one focusing on one member or pair of his members: the feet, knees, hands, side, breast, heart, and face. The text had already spread during Thomas's lifetime (cf. the *corpus* of ST III 25,4). It became very popular over the years. It has been set to music several times, e.g., by Dietrich Buxtehude (ca. 1637–1707): *Membra Jesu nostri*.

73. 1 Cor 12.12–27; cf. ST III 8,1.

of whom it is fitting to say: "With Christ I am crucified" [Gal 2.19]. About these fruits it is said in Song 4.16: "May my beloved enter his garden, in order to eat the yield of his fruits."

(2.2) Furthermore, the fruits of sun and moon are examples of virtue,[74] which Christ has shown on the Cross.[75] You have the example of love (*caritas*) from Christ on the Cross, because he loved (*diligo*) us and gave himself over for us [cf. Gal 2.20]. And in Jn 15.13 we read: "No one has a greater love (*caritas*) than someone who lays down his life for his friends."[76]

Again, he has shown us an example of humility, because "he has humbled himself" [Phil 2.8].

He has also given the example of obedience, "because he became obedient" [ibid.] to the Father.

And he has taught us the example of patience, for "when he was cursed, he did not curse" [1 Pt 2.23].

These are the fruits of the enclosed valleys, of which we read in the Song of Songs [6.11]: "I have come down into my garden, in order to see the fruits of the enclosed valleys."

(2.3) The fruits of the eternal hills, what are they? I say that they are the writings of the teachers who are imbued with wisdom. The Psalmist says: "Yet you (come) from the eternal mountains, shining in an amazing way" [Ps 76.5]. You will find some teachers who instruct you in the faith; and Christ on the Cross has taught us[77] faith, saying: "My God, my God, why have you abandoned me?" [Mt 27.46][78] He shows that the humanity has suffered, yet not because of powerlessness of the Divinity.[79]

Likewise, you will find teachers who show the way to hope;

---

74. Cf. Dn 12.3, Mt 13.43; 1 Cor 15.41–42.

75. Cf. ST III 46,3–4. The virtues mentioned in this section are discussed in ST II-II 23–27 (love), 161 (humility), 104 (obedience), and 136 (patience).

76. In section 2.3 we find how Christ on the Cross has taught us faith and hope as well: the three theological virtues.

77. In the *corpus* of ST III 46,4, Thomas cites Augustine, with reference to Eph 3.18.

78. It is an exclamation of faith, not of despair, according to Thomas: Christ is calling upon God, believing that God the Almighty can save him; cf. Thomas's commentary on Matthew: c.27 n.2.

79. Cf. ST III 46,12: Christ did not suffer insofar as he was God; divinity is incompatible with undergoing (*pati*) anything (such as change or suffering).

and Christ on the Cross showed the way to hope when he said to the criminal: "Today you will be with me in paradise" [Lk 23.43].

Likewise, you will find teachers who teach patience. Christ has done this on the Cross as he said: "Father, forgive those, for they do not know what they do" [Lk 23.34].

Likewise, you will find some teachers who incite to devotion; and Christ has done this on the Cross as he said: "Father, into your hands I commend my spirit" [Lk 23.46].[80]

Likewise, you will find some who give instructions on how to live a human life together; and Christ has done this on the Cross, because he has shown his mother what ought to be, and in a similar way the disciple, as he said: "'Woman, behold your son.' Then he said to the disciple: 'Behold your mother'" [Jn 19.26–27].

These are the fruits of the eternal hills which are mentioned in the Song of Songs [4.13]: "The things you are bringing forth are a paradise-garden of pomegranate trees bearing fruits." So it is the wood of fruits.

(3) Now, there are trees that have flowers and fruits all the time [cf. Ezek 47.12]. In a similar way the tree of the Cross has flowers all the time. See that the wood of the Cross has produced a triple fruit: (3.1) the fruit of cleansing, (3.2) the fruit of sanctification, and (3.3) the fruit of glorification.

(3.1) First, I say that the wood of the Cross has produced the fruit of cleansing, because through the Cross we are liberated from sins.[81] Hence St. Peter says: "He has borne our sins on the wood" [1 Pt 2.24]. Is 27.9 says about this fruit: "This is all the fruit, so that sin may be taken away."

(3.2) Second, the wood of the Cross has produced the fruit of sanctification, of which Rom 6.22 says: "You have fruit in sanctification." Of what does sanctification consist? It makes someone cling to the Cross. It is also true that man, alienated from God through sin, is reconciled through Christ.[82] Thus we read

80. Cf. ST II–II 82.   81. ST III 49,1.
82. ST III 61,3; cf. II–II 81,8; III 62,6,2, 63,6,2.

in Rom 5.10: "We are reconciled with God through the death of his Son." Jb 22.21 reads: "Be quiet for him and hold your peace; in this way you will have the best fruits," namely, "the fruits of the Spirit: love (*caritas*), peace, joy" [Gal 5.22]. And "Christ suffered outside the city walls in order to sanctify us" [Heb 13.12][83] by the wood. So the ministers of the Church use the sign of the Cross in any sanctification.

(3.3) The third fruit of the Cross is the fruit of glorification, about which we read in Jn 4.36: "He who reaps, gathers the fruit for eternal life." And in Wis 3.15 it says: "The fruit of good works is glorious." This fruit is gained through the Cross, as was said. Through sin humankind is excluded from paradise, and therefore Christ has suffered on the Cross, so that through the Cross the gate from the earthly things to the heavenly things would be open.[84] Hence the Cross of Christ is signified by the ladder that Jacob saw. As we read in Gn 28.12, Jacob saw the ladder, and its top touched the heavens, and he saw angels ascending and descending, and the Lord leaning on the ladder." All the saints go up to the heavens by the power of the Cross.[85] Hence the Apostle says: "By reason of the blood of the Cross we trust that the saints will go in" [Heb 10.19], et cetera.

We will ask the Lord, et cetera.

---

83. ST III 46,10: He suffered outside the Temple and outside the city walls, so that not only the Jews but all God's people in the whole world would be sanctified.
84. ST III 49,5.
85. ST III 57,6,2.

SERMON 19
BEATI QUI HABITANT

Sermon on the Feast of All Saints, the First of November

Psalm 84.5: *Happy those who live in your house, O Lord;
they will praise you forever and ever.*

Sermo

HERE IS NO ONE with a correct understanding who does not know that the community of God and angels and people is one community. The Apostle speaks of this in 2 Corinthians 1: "the faithful God by whom you are called into the community of his Son, our Lord Jesus Christ" [1 Cor 1.9]. And John 1 reads: "If we walk in the light, just as he also is in the light, we are in communion with one another" [1 Jn 1.7]. This is a community insofar as they share the same end, namely, happiness,[1] for God is happy, and angels attain happiness by effort, and people do, too. But God has it by essence, whereas the others have it by participation.[2] Therefore, it says in 1 Tm 6.15: "In his time the happy and only powerful (God will show us Jesus Christ)."

Now, people who live together, in the sense that they have the same end, must share with one another what they are doing in such a way that those who have not yet reached the end

---

1. Thus this community (*societas*) is one in the sense that we are one with God through the Son, one with the other people of God and with the angels, and one in the sense that we are directed towards the same goal: happiness (*beatitudo*). It is also one in the sense that there is no other community like it; it is unique. Cf. how Thomas explains "one" in ST I 11, on the oneness of God.

2. ST I 26 resp.; I–II 5,1 and 3, and 5,5–7.

are led to it. And therefore, we, the ones on the way (*viatores*) to happiness, are led into it by words and examples.[3] Whereas the ones who have already achieved the end help others to achieve it. And this is the reason why we celebrate the feasts of the saints who have already attained happiness,[4] so that we may be helped by their favors[5] and may be built up by their examples and stimulated by their rewards.

But since we cannot celebrate all the feasts of the individual saints, because their number is unknown to us [cf. Rv 7.9], and since in the solemnities that we do celebrate we neglect many things, the Church provides to our benefit that she celebrates the festivities of all the saints conjointly at the same time, so that what was not rendered to each individual saint would at least be rendered in his solemn feast, and everything that was neglected would be somehow replenished by it. Therefore, since we have come now to the festivities of the community of the saints, the happy ones,[6] we are to speak about happiness.

(1) So we must know that, although the affect of all people is directed towards happiness,[7] still there are some people with a different idea about happiness, very many of whom err. For some err concerning (1.1) the abode of happiness, (1.2) others concerning its duration, and (1.3) others again concerning the occupation or operation of the happy ones.

(1.1) Some err concerning the abode of happiness because they think that happiness is in this world: either in corporeal

---

3. Thomas says the same as for wisdom and knowledge; cf. Sermon 08 *Puer Jesus*, section 3.2.3. One Latin text reads *inducimus* ("we lead"): "We [Dominicans and Franciscans embarking upon preaching and teaching ministries] lead the ones on the way to happiness by words and examples." Another Latin version reads *inducimur* ("we are led"): "We, the ones on the way to happiness, are led into it by words and examples [of the saints]."

4. And we pray to them: ST II–II 83,4.

5. Through their prayers: ST II–II 83,11.

6. *Beatus* means "happy" as well as "saint," someone who attained the ultimate happiness *in patria*, in heaven; thus *societas beatorum* is synonymous with *societas sanctorum*.

7. This view was already formulated by Augustine. Cf. ST I–II 5,8; cf. I 19,3, 82,1, 94,1; I–II intr., 10,2, 13,6; III 18,1,3.

SERMON 19   283

things[8] or in virtues or in knowing things.[9] Against them the Lord says through Is 3.12: "My people, those who are calling you happy are deceiving you." And this is rightly spoken,[10] because

(1.1.1) this opinion is first of all at odds with the perfection of happiness. For, according to the Philosopher, happiness is the perfect good.[11] And since it is the ultimate end, it is absolutely necessary that it quiets desire. This would not be the case if, after these things have come into our possession, some desire would remain. In this life, however, neither can the perfection of the good be in the things of this world—because as people attain these things, they desire even more—nor can they be in virtues and knowing things, because for every man hitherto [the desire] remains to advance in virtue and knowledge.[12] The Psalmist says: "Your eyes have seen my imperfection" [Ps 139.16]. 2 Corinthians 13 reads: "For we know in part, (in part we prophesy)" [1 Cor 13.9].

(1.1.2) Second, this opinion is at odds with the purity of happiness. For, since happiness is the highest good, it cannot be mixed with evil.[13] For it is absolutely necessary that white be not at all mixed with black. Hence someone cannot be called happy who is subject to one or another misery, nor can someone at the same time be unhappy and happy.[14] Yet in this life no one can be found who is not subject to a particular misery, either insofar as it concerns discomfort as regards things or [insofar as it concerns discomfort as regards] friends or some person, through which also the realization of our virtue and knowledge is hindered.[15] Hence Job says about man that "he is filled with many miseries" [Jb 14.1].

8. ST I–II 2,1 and 2,5–6.
9. ST I–II 2,7.
10. ST I–II 2,8, 5,5; Thomas describes the group of people who think that true happiness is something created, and thus within creation, and therefore consider it possible to grasp it.
11. ST I–II 3,1,2.
12. Growth is a sign that one has not reached perfection yet; cf. the 4th way in ST I 2,3; also 4,1,1.
13. ST I 5,3,2.
14. At least, not concerning the same thing: ST III 46,8,1.
15. ST I–II 5,3, where Thomas cites the same text from Job. *Actus* is translat-

(1.1.3) Third, this opinion denies the stability of happiness. For happiness would not quiet our desire unless it were stable; the more we love (*amo*) the goods we possess, the more affliction they bring about as we fear losing them.[16] Therefore, according to the Philosopher, we must not think that a happy person is a chameleon which changes color at a glance; he must rather be unchangeable, something we cannot be in this life. For exterior things and the human body are subjected to various events, and no one is safeguarded against this, so that from experience we can learn that in this life there is no stability.[17] Thus it says in Jb 14.2 that man "never remains in the same state." And Prv 14.13 reads: "The ends of joy are taken up by grief."

Therefore, if you ask the Psalmist where the true abode of happiness is, he answers: "Happy those who live in your house, Lord" [Ps 84.5].

(1.2) Concerning the duration of happiness some people err, saying that the souls that have left the body attain happiness and that after a long course of years they return to a body and that they subsequently stop being happy because they are subjected [again] to the miseries of our present life.[18] And this is the error of Plato and his followers; even Origen fell into this error. What is said in Wis 2.22 can be applied to them: "They were of the opinion that the souls of the holy ones are not re-

---

ed here as "realization": the development of the virtue and knowledge which we have *in potentia*, so that it becomes full-grown, *in actu*, is hindered, because of the fact that we are acted upon (*passio*) by things that are harmful or not helpful.

16. In ST II–II 19,2 Thomas calls this type of fear "human" or "worldly," for it concerns what is worldly (*humanus, mundanus*). This fear is never a good (19,3); it is not a gift from the Holy Spirit (19,9); it diminishes our love (19,10) and will not remain in heaven (19,11), contrary to the holy fear of the Lord, which is a virtue: 19,7 and 9–12.

17. The idea that everything on earth changes all the time and nothing remains (the same)—as in the famous words πάντα ῥεῖ καὶ οὐδὲν μένει, attributed to Heraclitus—is based on our experience; cf. the first and third ways in ST I 2,3. God, however, who is not part of the creation but the Creator, is stable, unchangeable, and fully happy: ST I 4,1, 9,1, and 26,1 and 4.

18. The idea of reincarnation is not compatible with the Christian faith and is furthermore not appealing to Thomas: SCG IV 91.

warded." And in Mt 25.46 we read: "These will go into the eternal punishment, but the just ones will enter eternal life." Well, this idea of theirs seems to be reprehensible for three reasons:

(1.2.1) First, because it is at odds with the natural desire. For naturally there is in everything an appetite by which it conserves itself in being and in its perfection.[19] But there is a difference: things which lack the ability to consider [what perfection] in general [is], do not reach [for perfection]; their appetite is directed towards the here-and-now, so that their perfection is preserved.[20] Yet a rational nature which surmises [what perfection] in general [is],[21] naturally has the appetite to conserve its perfection all the time. So, if the soul has not reached everlasting happiness, it is not satisfied by natural desire. Nor would it be true happiness with the ignorance of a defect to come or with the foreknowledge of misfortune to come.[22] Well, in view of this natural desire the Apostle says in 2 Cor 5.2: "For we groan, longing to be clothed with our dwelling place from heaven," et cetera.

(1.2.2) Second, because it is at odds with the perfection of grace, for everything that is totally filled with its own perfection is immovably preserved in it.[23] Therefore, the first *materia* does not remain in the *forma* of air forever, since such a *forma* does not fill the total capacity of the *materia*.[24] The intellect truly remains immovable in its thinking according to the first principles, because through them the intellect is filled insofar as it concerns that truth. It is not, however, completely filled with probable chains of reasoning, and so it does not think in an

---

19. Cf. ST II–II 64,5 and 7. Although eventually it is God alone who conserves all things in being: ST I 9,2, 14,1–2, 46,1; III 13,2.

20. ST I 62,1, 63,3, and 75,6.

21. ST I 12,8,4. Therefore, Thomas approaches "perfection" from different angles, e.g., ST I 6,3 (in view of God), I 73,1 (in view of the substantial and accidental *forma*, the substance and the end), I–II 98,2,1 (in view of the nature of a thing and the time when it is/was).

22. Because the first is not stable and the second contains fear, which is incompatible with happiness. ST I 64,2; II–II 18,3; cf. I 102,2,1.

23. Cf. ST I 62,8; I–II 109,10,3; II–II 137,4.

24. ST I 66,1–2.

immovable way.²⁵ But a happy soul is totally filled with happiness; otherwise, happiness would not be a perfect good. Therefore, we read in a Psalm: "You will fill me completely with joy when I see your face" [Ps 16.11], et cetera. And because of this it continues: "Delights are in your right hand till the end" [ibid.]. And because the everlasting duration [of this] leads to such a fullness of grace, it says in Rv 3.12: "The one who will conquer, I will make him a pillar in the temple of my God, and he will not go out from it any more."²⁶

(1.2.3) Third, it goes against the equity of the divine justice, for through love (*caritas*) a human being clings to God with the intention never to recede from him.²⁷ Rom 8.35: "Who will separate us from the love (*caritas*) of Christ?" Hence it is not fully satisfying for love (*caritas*) if it is at times removed from the enjoyment of God. Because of this Jn 6.37 says: "I will not throw out who comes to me."²⁸

So if you ask the Psalmist what he thinks about this idea, he responds: "They will praise you for ever and ever" [Ps 84.5].

(1.3) Jews and Muslims (*Sarraceni*) err about the happy ones' occupation or what they do; they say that the happy people abandon themselves to excessive eating, drinking-bouts, and unions with women. The Lord rejects this in Matthew 25: "In the resurrection they neither marry nor are they given in marriage, (but they are as God's angels in heaven)" [Mt 22.30].²⁹ Indeed, their opinion is justly rejected, for it is,

(1.3.1) first of all, against the privilege of humankind. Because, if happiness were according to the use of food and sensual things that are found in other living creatures too, not only humankind, but even animals ought to have happiness—although this still is the privilege of humankind, that among the lower creatures only the human being is capable of happi-

25. ST I 17,3 85,6. So the principles may be clear, but as soon as our reasoning begins to depart from them, we may err.
26. SCG III 62; ST I–II 5,4.
27. ST II–II 25,1; I–II 49,2,3; the perfection of a Christian life consists in love (*caritas*): II–II 184,1.
28. Likewise, it is in accordance with the divine justice that sinners are punished, e.g., in ST I 49,2 and 113,7.
29. Cf. also ST I 98,2,1.

ness.[30] Hence the Psalmist says: "Lord, you will save people and yoked animals" [Ps 36.7], that is, through the salvation of the bodies; "yet" only "the children of the people will hope in the shelter of your wings" [Ps 36.8].

(1.3.2) Second, it goes against the nature of joy, for a higher nature is not made happy by something lower.[31] If, however, the happiness of humankind consisted in eating and drinking, then someone would also be made happy by the foods he eats, and thus these foods would be worth more than a human being. Humankind, however, is still placed above all other lower natures, according to the Psalmist: "You have laid all things under his feet, (sheep and cattle all over the world and furthermore the wild animals of the plain, the birds of the heaven, and the fish of the sea)" [Ps 8.7–9].

(1.3.3) Third, it goes against the concentration on the virtues. Because, for a human being, virtue consists in being torn away from pleasures.[32] Hence the virtues that concern pleasures are named by what restricts them, like abstinence, temperance, and the like. On the other hand, there are the virtues that concern wearisome and difficult things, as we clearly see in regard to strength and magnanimity and the like.[33] Now if the happiness of humankind consisted in the pleasures of the flesh, virtue, which is the way of happiness, would not tear us away from the pleasures of the flesh, but would imply the pleasures. This happens in those about whom Phil 3.19 says: "Their belly is their god," et cetera.

So, if we ask David[34] what he thinks that the occupation and action is of the happy ones, the saints, he would answer: "They will praise you" [Ps 84.5].

30. ST I–II 3,3–4. The lower creatures are the creatures on earth, as distinct from the creatures in the heavens, like the angels, who are happy too; cf. ST I 62,1.

31. Cf. ST I–II 4,5 and 7; a human being is made perfectly joyful only by God: ST I–II 5,6; II–II 28,1 esp. ad 2.

32. Virtues are certain perfections through which the reason is directed towards God, and all other powers in us are ordered in accordance with the reason: ST I 95,3; cf. I–II 55,1.

33. These virtues correspond with respectively the so-called *passiones concupiscibiles* (ST I–II 26–39) and *irascibiles* (ST I–II 40–48).

34. Psalm 84 is in fact attributed to the sons of Korah.

(2) Now it remains to see how we can arrive at this happiness. We must know then that there are three types of happiness.

(2.1) The first is worldly happiness, which consists in possessions and the enjoyment of worldly things. The Psalmist says: "They call the people that has these things happy" [Ps 144.15]. And indeed, this happiness consists primarily in honors, riches, and delightful things,[35] because, as it is said in 1 Jn 2.16: "all that is in the world: the concupiscence of the flesh," et cetera. Yet, under honor we understand dignity and a good name, so that in this way these three include those five in which, according to Boethius, earthly happiness consists.[36] Ambitious people strive after dignity by means of arrogance and money, as it is written in Eccl 10.19: "All things obey money," and in Prv 19.6: "Many honor a person" because of his riches. The Lord teaches [us], however, to arrive at dignity by the opposite way: by poverty and humility, because, as it says in Luke 2: "He has brought down the mighty from their seat" [Lk 1.52], and it is said in Mt 5.3: "Happy the poor in spirit, (for the kingdom of heaven is theirs)." It says "kingdom" because it is precious among the honors. Well, this happiness belongs foremost to Christ,[37] for, because the Old Fathers [Patriarchs] made use of riches,[38] he was the first who preached and taught this,[39] as we read in 2 Cor 8.9: "You know the gracious gift of our Lord Jesus Christ, (that, although he was rich, he became poor for your sake, so that by his poverty you might be rich)"; [compare] Matthew 2: "If you want to be perfect, go and sell (what you have and give

---

35. ST I–II 2,1–3 and 5–6.
36. "Those five . . . according to Boethius": In *The Consolation of Philosophy* Boethius names wealth, power, honor, fame, and desire. Even if someone had all five, he says, it would not be perfect happiness, i.e., the highest good, unless these were eternal.
37. ST III 40,3.
38. E.g., Abraham (Gn 24.34–35), Isaac (Gn 26.13–14), Jacob (Gn 32.6), David (2 Sm 12.30). King Solomon surpassed everyone: 2 Chr 9.22. Thomas frequently warns his pupils about riches, e.g., in ST I–II 30,4, 84,1; II–II 32,1,4, 118,4,3, 186,3,4, 188,7; and III 41,4,3. Since material goods are limited, excessive riches are a sin against the neighbor: ST II–II 118,1,2.
39. Cf. ST I–II 108,3,4. Although we find a similar teaching in Prv 16.19 ("It is better to be humble with the meek than to plunder with the proud").

to the poor, and you will have a treasure in heaven)" [Mt 19.21]. Yet people of this world often arrive at riches by quarrels or warfare or by somehow using violence in matters,[40] as it says in Jas 4.2: "You quarrel and wage war." But God teaches the opposite way,[41] namely, the way of mildness, by which no one either angers or becomes angry.[42] And this is not astonishing, because, as it says in Prv 3.34: the kingdom "will be given to the mild." And hence the Lord says, "Happy the meek (for they will inherit the earth)" [Mt 5.5]. And this happiness befits the martyrs, who were not angry with their persecutors, but rather prayed for them. Thus it says in Corinthians 8: "We are cursed, but we bless; (we are persecuted, but we endure)" [1 Cor 4.12]. Thus it is said about them: "no groaning resounds, no complaint,"[43] et cetera.

People strive to arrive at delights by various comforts. Thus it says in Isaiah 21: "They hold the tambourine (and the harp and rejoice at the sound of the flute)" [Jb 21.12]. But the Lord teaches the opposite way: mourning; he says: "Happy they who mourn (for they will be comforted)" [Mt 5.4]. And concerning this, Tb 3.22 (Vg) reads, "After lamentation and tears (you pour out exaltation)."[44] And this happiness befits the ones who confessed their faith, who under much sighing and mourning have lived their life on earth, in accordance with Lamentations 3: "For, many are our sighs" [Lam 1.22].

(2.2) The second happiness belongs to the political realm,[45]

---

40. ST II–II 118,1,2.

41. In what follows, Thomas presents the Beatitudes not only as a way to classify the saints in heaven, but also as the way to happiness for all people.

42. ST II–II 157–158. Mildness belongs to the virtue of temperance (II–II 143,1).

43. From the fourth stanza of the hymn *Sanctorum meritis inclyta gaudia*, sung at the First Vespers for feast days of the apostles: "Caeduntur gladiis more bidentium: *Non murmur resonat, non quaerimonia;* sed corde impavido mens bene conscia, conservat patientiam" (translated in the Breviary as: "Like sheep their blood they poured: and *without groan or tear*, they bent before the sword for that their King most dear: Their souls, serenely blest, in patience they possessed and looked in hope towards their rest").

44. These words are taken from Sarah's prayer to God for mercy after being falsely accused of murdering her seven husbands as they died each time during the wedding night: Tb 3.11–15.

45. ST I–II 2,4: Does the happiness of a person consist in power?

which consists in this: by acting with prudence someone governs his own actions well. The maximum of his ability is reached when he governs not only himself, but even a city and a kingdom. Hence this happiness befits in particular kings and princes. We read about this in Job 22: "The hearing ear blesses[46] me" [Jb 29.11].

Still, we must know that there is a difference between a king and a tyrant,[47]

(2.2.1) for a king is someone who is intent upon the good of the people by his reign. So, what a king issues is not discordant with the order of his wisdom [cf. Jer 23.5]. Prv 8.15 reads: "Kings reign by me." But a tyrant is by his own wish intent upon being discordant with the divine order of wisdom, for he aims rather at the satisfaction of his own desire, so that he accomplishes everything as he pleases and is intent to arrive at this through greed, by plundering others unjustly. Hence it says in Prv 28.15: "A godless prince over a poor people is a roaring lion and a hungry bear."[48] But the Lord teaches us to arrive [at happiness] by the contrary way: by justice.[49] Thus he says: "Happy they who hunger and thirst for justice, (for they will be filled)" [Mt 5.6]. And this is what is said in Prv 13.25: "The just eats and is satisfied." Now, this happiness befits the Old Fathers [Patriarchs], who with the greatest desire hungered for the perfect justice of Christ. We see this desire in Isaiah 58: "O, that you would rend the heavens (and come down)" [Is 63.19].

46. For Job in his misery this was history; Job refers to the past, when he was exceedingly wealthy (cf. Jb 29.2–10). Accordingly the Vulgate text reads *beatificabat*, in the imperfect tense. Thomas uses the present tense form *beatificat*; apparently he considers it reality for the rulers of his day.

47. Cf. Sermon 05 *Ecce rex tuus*, section 2.1.4.

48. Hence the title "King" (*Rex*) for Christ (or for God: SCG III 64) is not problematic for Thomas. But in our day we can no longer make the distinction that Thomas makes, because the term "tyrant" still is a negative term as Thomas explains it, but the term "king" has become a neutral term now; a king can be a tyrant. Thus the original Greek word τύραννος is synonymous with *our* word "king": the absolute sovereign. Since "power corrupts and absolute power corrupts absolutely," the Greek word soon had a negative undertone (as in Thomas's explanation). Cf. also ST I–II 105,1,2.

49. ST II–II 50,1,1: A king ought to be prudent (cf. section 2.2) and righteous (*iustus*).

SERMON 19

(2.2.2) Second, a tyrant is intent upon not being punished for the evils he has done; he does so by means of cruelty. He exerts himself to obtain this along this way, so that he may be feared so much that no one would contradict him.[50] The Psalmist says about these tyrants: "They have placed the dead bodies of your servants as bait for the birds of the sky" [Ps 79.2]. But the Lord teaches a contrary way, in order to obtain the way of mercy, saying: "Happy are the merciful, (for they will obtain mercy)" [Mt 5.7]. And he continues in Mt 6.14: "For if you forgive the people their sins (your heavenly Father will forgive you)." This happiness befits the angels, who, though they are without *passio*, appear so merciful to us,[51] as they come to our assistance in our miseries.[52] Thus we read in Is 33.7: "The angels of peace will cry bitterly."

(2.3) The third happiness is a contemplative happiness that is in particular proper to those who apply themselves to acquiring the truth and especially divine truth. Sir 14.20: "Happy the man who will abide in wisdom." Philosophers can only obtain this happiness if they are intent upon two things: learning the truth and obtaining authority.[53] They will only get to know the truth by studying. But God teaches a shorter way: by the cleanness of the heart,[54] saying: "Happy the clean of heart, (for they

---

50. Thomas is in favor of defending the common good and resisting evil, but he is not enthusiastic about a revolution against a tyrant or a tyrannical regime, even if he/it is unjust (ST II–II 42,2,3, 118,8,5). For a revolution may well lead to greater chaos and cruelty. Therefore, the tyrant(s) should be brought down, indeed, for the sake of the common good, yet it ought to be done under the direction of a righteous neighboring king: ST II–II 40,1, 42,2,3.

51. In human beings mercy (*misericordia*) is always with *passio* because we have a body (ST I 95,3; II–II 30,3,2); in God and in angels, who are without a material body, it must be without *passio*: ST I 21,3.

52. The term *compassio* is used by Thomas in the sense of "suffering with," whereas *misericordia* is more like what we call "compassion": being touched (*habens miserum cor*), so that you reach out to take away your neighbor's misery: ST I 21,3. Misery—not every weakness or suffering is misery—is contrary to happiness: ST I 21,4; II–II 30,1.

53. Thomas says this with irony (cf. below). Real authority is found in the teachings of Sacred Doctrine: Scripture and the tradition; cf. ST I 1,5.

54. Which is even necessary in order to focus on God: ST II–II 81,8; cf. 180,2,2. Living a holy life is a source of knowledge and insight about God. In

will see God)" [Mt 5.8].⁵⁵ Wis 1.4 reads: "Wisdom will not enter a malevolent soul, nor will she dwell (in a body subjected to sin)." And this happiness befits in particular the virgins who preserved a cleanness of mind and body.

Philosophers truly want to acquire authority by contentious debates. But, as it is said in 1 Cor 11.16: "If someone" wants "to be contentious" among you, "(we do not have such a custom and it is not proper to God's Church)."⁵⁶ Thus the Lord teaches us to arrive at divine authority through peace, as a man may be considered by others the one in authority, according to what he has said to Moses in Ex 7.1: "I have placed you as" lord "over Pharaoh." And therefore it is said: "Happy the peacemakers, (for they will be called the children of God)" [Mt 5.9]. Well, this happiness befits especially the apostles, about whom 2 Corinthians 6 reads: "He has placed in us the word of reconciliation" [2 Cor 5.19],⁵⁷ et cetera.

Now, the saying "Happy they who suffer persecution (for the sake of righteousness, for theirs is the kingdom of the heavens)" [Mt 5.10] does not mention another happiness, but is said in order to strengthen the ones mentioned before. For, if someone is pulled away from happiness because of persecution, he is not strong in poverty, in mildness, and in the other virtues. Therefore, all rewards mentioned before ought to be included in this happiness—and so he returns to what he said at the beginning [of the Beatitudes], saying: "for theirs is the kingdom of the heavens" [Mt 5.3, 10].⁵⁸ And in a similar way we should understand "because they will possess the earth" [Mt 5.5], and likewise the other sayings.

Thomas's view it would be impossible to study theology while living as an unbeliever. What you learn must be practiced; otherwise, it is meaningless.

55. Cf. ST II–II 8,7.

56. In view of the context it seems likely that Thomas quoted the whole verse.

57. Cf. ST I 43,7,6, 117,2 and III 64,2,3.

58. In ST II–II 124,1 and 5 Thomas cites this verse in the context of martyrdom.

So the happiness of the saints contains something of any of the sayings mentioned insofar as we find anything praiseworthy in them.

(ad 2.1) For, compared to earthly happiness, the happiness of the saints has an abundant abode. Hence it says: "Happy those who live in your house" [Ps 84.5]. This is the house of glory, about which the Psalmist says: "One thing I have asked from the Lord: (to live in the house of the Lord all the days of my life)" [Ps 27.4]. In this house he will obtain whatever he may desire, because: "We will be filled with the goods of your house" [Ps 65.5], as the Psalmist says. Revelation 1 reads: "You have made us (for our God) a kingdom and priests" [Rv 5.10]. There will be enough riches present there, as the Psalmist testifies: "Glory and riches are in his house" [Ps 112.3a]. There will be delights that refresh the total human being, according to the Psalmist: "They will be fed with the copiousness of your house (and you will slake them from the brook of your will)" [Ps 36.9].

(ad 2.2) Compared to the happiness that belongs to the political life, they have continuity, for the ruler of a city ought to apply himself to preserve the good of the city all the time. Hence it says: "(and his justice remains) for ever and ever" [Ps 112.3b]. For sure, this continuity comes forth from three things: first, from living together with good people. The Psalmist says: "I will be satisfied when your glory appears" [Ps 17.15].[59] Second, from the removal of condemnable behavior, for, although [people on earth] are satisfied, they still hunger always, as we read in Sirach 22: "Those who eat me will still be hungry, (and those who drink will still be thirsty)" [Sir 24.21]. Third, from the immunity to all evils and miseries, as in Rv 7.16: "They will no longer hunger or thirst, (nor will the sun or any heat strike them)."

(ad 2.3) Compared to the contemplative happiness, they will live in a way with the divine things, since contemplative happiness consists particularly in contemplation. And therefore it

---

59. Note that this is the final verse of a Psalm in which the Psalmist prays as he is persecuted by evil people. In ST I–II 69,2,3 Thomas explains that this verse applies not only to the hereafter, but even, albeit not to the full, to life on earth.

says: "They will praise you" [Ps 84.5], for they will see God without an intermediary and clearly, as it says in 1 Cor 13.12: "Now we see by means of a mirror, (veiled in mystery, yet then face to face; now we know in part, yet then I will know as I also am known)." And like sons and daughters they will love (*amo*) him incessantly, for according to the Greeks "son" is derived from "to love."[60] John 3 reads: "See what love (*caritas*) the Father has given to us, so that we may be called and are, indeed, God's sons and daughters" [1 Jn 3.1]. And as good sons and daughters they will honor God by praising him, in accordance with Is 35.10: "(The ones who are redeemed by the Lord will return and enter Zion with praise, and an everlasting joy will be over their head.) They will obtain joy and gaiety, (and pain and moaning will flee)."

Therefore, the Psalmist only mentions this[61] with the things that are said above in mind, because what is praised is known and loved (*amo*).[62] Hence Augustine says in Book 60[63] of *The City of God:* "This task, this affection, this realization,[64] is, just like eternal life, for all people."

May we be led to it by the Son, et cetera.

---

60. In Greek a word for "son" is φίλος (*philos*), "to love" is φιλέω (*phileo*).

61. "Happy those who live in your house, O Lord," Ps 84.5.

62. Cf. ST I–II 101,2.

63. The text reads LX, but it is in fact book 22: XXII, the last book. Chapter 30 is its last chapter: it discusses the eternal happiness of the City of God and the perpetual Sabbath. In Sermon 20 *Beata Gens,* section 2.3.3, Thomas refers to the same chapter.

64. *Actus:* see note 15.

SERMON 20
BEATA GENS

*Sermon on the Feast of All Saints,
the First of November*

Psalm 33.12: *Happy the nation whose lord is its God,
the people whom he has chosen for his heritage.*

PART 1: *Prothema*

"HAPPY THE nation whose lord is its God, the people whom he has chosen for his heritage" [Ps 33.12]. In many ways holy Mother the Church focuses her attention on challenging her sons and daughters to desire heavenly things [cf. Col 3.1]. And if you want to examine this correctly, you see that she is totally devoted to transforming us to desire heavenly things by showing contempt of earthly things. This is clear from the first Founder of the Church and our Savior[1] on, who, in his application to preaching and teaching, said, in Mt 3.2: "Repent," in order to remove us from earthly things. "The kingdom of heaven has come near": He says this in order to allure us to desire heavenly things.[2] Among other things that provoke a heavenly desire she reminds us and impresses in our hearts today the saints' glory for which we strive. God willing, we will ask God at the beginning that for the suitability of such

---

1. John the Baptist belongs to the New Testament (ST II–II 174,4,3). What he taught and did was preparatory: ST III 38,2,2, and 38,3; for instance, John's baptism of Christ, in ST III 27,6.

2. Thus conversion consists of a double movement: *aversio*, a turning away from what is evil or not worthwhile, and *adversio* or *conversio*, a turning towards God and the things that are God's; cf. ST II–II 20,1,1, 24,12,4, and 162,6.

a great celebration he may give me something valuable to say, which would be to his honor and to the honor of all the saints as well as to the salvation of our souls.

PART 2: *Sermo*

"Happy the nation" [Ps 33.12], et cetera. [This inspired saying] is meant for the souls of the people all together, so that they hear with delight the praises of their heavenly homeland (*patria*) and of their parents: the praises of their homeland, so that they hasten to return to it; the praises of their parents, so that they, by following their example, will not be lapsed.

But what is our homeland? The homeland for which we strive is the heavenly homeland. Thus the Apostle says in Heb 13.14: "Here we do not have a city that remains, but we seek a future city." Our parents are the spiritual men[3] who have taught us, instructed us, and who have given us the good example of living well.[4] These are the saints in the homeland, whose solemn feast we celebrate today, and therefore we ought to praise them continually with gladness. Thus we read in Sir 44.1: "Let us praise the glorious men, our parents in their generation."

See: by the mouth of David the Holy Spirit calls to mind this company of the saints in four ways: (1) first, on the ground of their dignity; (2) second, on the ground of their leader; (3) third, on the ground of how they are arranged; and (4) fourth, on the ground of their election. He calls that group of the saints to mind on the ground of their dignity where it says: "Happy the nation"; on the ground of their leader where it says: "whose

---

3. Thomas uses the word *viri*, "men," here. The use of this word is determined by Sir 44.1 (cited further on), which is the directive text for this part of the sermon. Besides, his audience consists of men only. By speaking of "men" here, Thomas might give the impression that "spiritual" women are not regarded as teachers and examples for his audience. But in view of, for instance, the *Sermo* of Sermon 17 *Lux orta*, on the feast of Mary's birth, we must say that such a conclusion would be drawn too quickly.

4. And lived examples are more convincing and moving than words: ST I–II 34,1.

lord is its God"; on the ground of how they are arranged he calls them a people when he says "people"; on the ground of their election when he says: "whom the Lord has chosen," et cetera.

❖

(1) First, I say, David calls to mind this company of the saints on the ground of their dignity, where we read: "Happy the nation." The dignity of this company is mentioned because (1.1) they have arrived at the place for which we strive. Furthermore, (1.2) they possess everything we desire. Moreover, (1.3) they are invested above what we can understand.

(1.1) First, I say, we look at the dignity of the saints, because they have arrived at the place for which we strive. Happiness (*beatitudo*) is the end of all our actions.[5] Hence the Apostle says in Rom 6.22: "You have your fruit in sanctification, but your end is eternal life." Look also at Augustine; he says in his book *The City of God:* "What else is the end of our desires than to arrive at the Kingdom where there is no end?"[6]

And see, in Sacred Scripture the end of humankind is compared to three things: (1.1.1) first, it is compared to a crown. Thus the Apostle says in 2 Tm 4.8: "What remains is that a crown of justice is reserved for me." (1.1.2) Sometimes it is compared to a prize, as the Apostle does in Phil 3.14: "I press on to the destination, to the prize of the heavenly call from above." (1.1.3) Likewise, it is compared sometimes to a reward. Thus we read in the Gospel according to Matthew 5.12: "Be glad and exult, for your reward is abundant in the heavens."

The Son of man has not made these three comparisons unjustly,[7] because every action of ours is reduced to these three:

(1.1.1) Some struggle (*certo*) when they act—this applies to the actives. Hence it says in Jb 7.1: "The life of a man on earth is

---

5. ST I–II 1,1–2 and 1,4–7.
6. There is no end for the ones *in patria*—in the homeland or heavenly homeland—for the ultimate end has been attained by them; cf. ST I 82,1.
7. The Son of man only made the third comparison directly; the other two are made by him indirectly, through the inspiration of Wisdom; cf. ST II–II 45,1.

warfare."[8] And those who have struggled according to the rules deserve a crown, because, as we read in 2 Tm 2.5: "no one will be crowned, unless he struggles according to the rules."

(1.1.2) Others, like the contemplatives, run. And these have nothing that slows them down; they run fast.[9] Ps 119.32 says about them: "I have run the way of your commandments." Well, those who compete in a race (*certo*) deserve a prize. The Apostle says in 1 Cor 9.24: "All run, but only one receives the prize."

(1.1.3) A third group are the workers, like the highly placed people, who bring about salutary works among the ordinary people. And these deserve a reward. Hence the Apostle says in 1 Cor 3.8: "Everyone will receive a proper reward in accordance with his work."[10]

But what is the glory of the saints in the homeland? I say that they have sought after a crown as good strugglers. They have pursued a prize as runners and have sought after a reward as good workers [cf. Lk 10.7]. People in the world work in order to have crowns, but that crown is corruptible. The crown of the saints is incorruptible.[11] Hence the Apostle continues in 1 Cor 9.25: "Those, indeed, in order to have a corruptible crown; but we, an incorruptible one." Thus is the dignity of the saints, because they have arrived at that place for which we strive.

(1.2) Furthermore, they have everything we desire and even more. Hence it says in Prv 10.24: "To the just he will give what they desire." Consider what you can desire among the pleasures and delights; all of that the saints have. But, I say, only as for

---

8. In the same way Thomas speaks of a "Church Militant" in Sermon 17 *Lux orta*, section 1.11, and in Sermon 21 *Beatus vir, Collatio in sero*, section 2.1.

9. Because no earthly things hinder them (cf. ST II–II 186,3,4); they have completely dedicated their lives to God in contemplation: ST II–II 180.

10. And merit is closely connected with God's gracious gift of love (*caritas*): ST I–II 114,4. See also how Thomas compares the merit of the active and of the contemplative religious, in ST II–II 182,2.

11. *Incorruptibilis* can be understood in different ways; cf. ST I 97,1. Here Thomas means incorruptible in the first sense, that it does not have *materia*. Cf. also Thomas's commentary on 2 Tm 4.8 in *lectio* 2 where he cites Is 28.5 ("the Lord will be a glorious crown and a brilliant diadem to the remnant of his people") and explains it as the joy concerning the truth and the aureole. Compare also how Thomas speaks of the immateriality of the food of the heavenly feast in Sermon 13 *Homo quidam fecit*.

spiritual delights, not the worldly and the foul things. Ps 16.11 reads: "Your delights are in your right hand."[12] If you desire riches, the saints are the wealthiest, for nothing is missing for those who fear the Lord, according to Prv 1.33: "They will thoroughly enjoy abundance."[13] Likewise, if you desire honors, the saints are invested with the greatest honor. Psalm 133: "Your honorable friends, O God, are honored beyond measure" [Ps 138.17 (Vg)]. If you seek knowledge, the saints have that perfection too, because they drink knowledge from the very fountain of wisdom [cf. Prv 18.4, Sir 1.5 (Vg)]. The saints have to the fullest extent everything that man can seek on earth either by sinning or by not sinning.

Thus it is clear what the dignity of the saints is: they have arrived at the place for which we strive, and they possess everything we can desire.

(1.3) Moreover, they are invested in the highest beyond our understanding, since the happiness of the saints[14] is beyond what you can understand.[15] Thus it says in Is 64.4: "Eye has not seen, O God; you alone have seen the things you have prepared for the ones who love (*diligo*) you." What is the reason why the saints are invested in the highest beyond what you can understand? Surely because the saints in the homeland have all their desires fulfilled. And how can they be filled with every good, unless they have come to the fountain of every good?[16] When a tree is heavy with fruits and you come to one branch,

---

12. The right hand is the powerful, giving hand (cf. ST III 58,1), the left hand the receiving hand.

13. Therefore, there is no hope in the inhabitants of the *patria*; hope is towards something good you do not (yet) have or experience: ST I–II 67,4. Likewise, fear of something evil: ST II–II 19,11.

14. *Beatus* means "happy" as well as "saint," someone who has attained the ultimate happiness *in patria*, i.e., in the heavenly homeland; *beatitudo beatorum* is translated as "happiness of the saints."

15. Cf. ST I–II 3,8 and 4,3.

16. Cf. Ps 42.2 and 23.1–6; cf. ST I 20,1,2. Whereas during our life on earth our desires will never be totally fulfilled; cf. ST I–II 5,3; II–II 28,3. Still Thomas speaks of a certain desire of the saints (and angels), yet not because of what they lack, but because of the bodily desires that are removed from them, in ST I–II 33,2 and 67,4,3, referring to 1 Pt 1.12: "It was revealed to them . . . things into which the angels long (*desiderant*) to look."

you cannot take them all. In a similar way if you go to another branch. But someone who cuts off the roots will take away all the fruits of the tree. In a similar way you cannot fully enjoy every good, unless you come to the fountain of every good, that is, as we read in Ps 103.5: "He who fulfills your desire with good things."[17] Hence the Lord has said to Moses in Ex 33.19: "I will show you every good," that is, myself [cf. Ex 33.20–23], in whom every good is. And since God is great and above every intellect, the saints who enjoy God are elevated so high that no one can reach [them]. Thus we read in Isaiah 53: "I will lift you up above every height of the earth" [Is 58.14], that is, above every high thing which an earthly man can understand. The Lord says in Psalm 149, "I will enrich you with the highness of your father,"[18] which applies to all his saints.

Thus it is clear what the dignity and the glory of the saints in the heavenly homeland is: since they have arrived at that place for which we strive, they have whatever we can desire; and they are invested on high, beyond what we can understand.

(2) Let us look at their leader.

(2.1) The whole dignity of the saints depends on their very leader. It is most miserable and degrading and terrible that a human being would be subordinate to someone inferior to himself or to a villain.[19] Hence the Lord utters a threat when he says through the Prophet: "I will hand Egypt over into the hands of cruel lords" [Is 19.4]. Someone who has a worthy master whom he serves, is happy. Thus it says in Sir 25.8: "Happy the one who has not served those unworthy of him." The unworthy are the demons. Yet we are God's children [cf. 1 Jn 3.1]. It is unworthy for children to serve the enemy of their father. So: happy are they who serve God. Thus it says in 1 Kgs 10.8: "Happy your servants." It is just to be subordinate to God, for

---

17. Cf. ST I–II 2,8; II–II 28,3.

18. The Latin text refers to Psalm 149, but in fact nowhere in Scripture is this text found. "Highness (*altitudo*) of the Father" may refer to Ps 132.11 and Lk 1.32 (where the term *sedes*, "throne," is used).

19. For this would go against the good order of creation: ST I 47,2; cf. I 109,4 and SCG III 17.

the highest perfection of a thing is that it is subordinate to what is more perfect than it.[20] *Materia* is not perfect unless it is subordinate to a *forma*,[21] and air is not beautiful unless it is subject to the sun, and so the soul is not perfect unless it is subordinate to God.[22] Therefore, our happiness lies in being subordinate to God. You could say: "Are we subjected to God, then?" Yes we are, but in a mediated way:[23] by mediating angels, highly placed people, and those who educate us,[24] who guide us where we ought to go in order to arrive at happiness.

But the saints in the homeland are not subjected to educators. Hence the Apostle says in 1 Cor 15.24: "Then the end comes, when Christ hands over the reign to God the Father and when he makes every dominion empty."[25] Therefore, he[26] says: "Happy the nation, whose lord is its God" [Ps 33.12].

(2.2) See also that there were and are some people who have said that bliss and happiness are in earthly things;[27] their opinion is expressed in Psalm 142: "Their storehouses are chockfull, bulging out from here to there. Their sheep are bearing (abundantly in their pastures; their cattle are fat)" [Ps 143.13–14 (Vg)]—and then: "They have called 'happy' the people that has these things" [ibid., verse 15a]. This is how the general public has spoken, but this opinion is false, because all things pass like a shadow [cf. Eccl 6.12].

---

20. Something is perfect insofar as it is perfect in its being, as it has things/characteristics needed for a perfect operation, and—to this point Thomas refers in this homily—as it has reached the end to which it is ordered. In ST I 6,3 Thomas points out that as such this applies to God alone.

21. Cf. ST I 7,1 and 44,2.

22. For God is all people's ultimate end, as it is said in Heb 2.10; cf. ST I 2 intr.; I–II 3,7,2.

23. ST I 22,3 (providence and God's reign); cf. III 20,1: in what way was the man Christ subordinate to the Father?

24. Respectively ST I 110,1–2, 111,1–4, 112,1–7 and II–II 45,5. A lower person, however, is still bound to criticize a higher person in terms of the fraternal correction: ST II–II 33,3–4.

25. In ST I 108,7,1 Thomas explains this verse by saying that the saints in the homeland serve the ones on the way; they guide others towards this ultimate end.

26. I.e., Christ, who speaks through the Psalms, as, e.g., in Heb 2.12.

27. ST I–II 2,1–6.

Moreover, they do not fill [themselves], because "the greedy will never have enough money" [Eccl 5.9].[28] You may think of earthly things that they remain, that they meet your desire, but I am telling you: yes, there is happiness, but it is not found there. So they are wrong, thinking that there is happiness in earthly things. Where then is happiness? The Psalmist answers in Ps 144.15b, saying that his God is his happiness.

Likewise there are or were some, like the Stoics, who said that happiness and bliss are found in internal goods. They held that having virtues and knowledge is the highest good.[29] Their opinion is rejected in Jer 9.23: "The wise will not take pride in his wisdom," says the Lord, "nor will the strong take pride in his strength." Why? Because everything that is within you is subordinate to your nature, but what makes you happy ought to be above you, not subjected to you. Because of this the text continues: "But he will take pride in this: knowing me and being acquainted with me" [Jer 9.24].[30]

There are others who say that happiness is found in these things that are [not above or within us, but] next to us. Such people put their trust in humankind.[31] Against them Ps 146.3 says: "Do not put your trust in princes."

Even in angels we must not put our trust; some have said that seeing angels is our end,[32] but our intellect is made for the vision of the Highest Cause.[33] Anselm says: "For we are not happy by seeing angels, but by seeing the virtue through which we love (*diligo*)[34] angels."

(2.3) "Happy the nation whose lord is its God." And how are we to understand this "its"? I say that it means that (2.3.1) God is to be known, (2.3.2) possessed, and (2.3.3) enjoyed.

---

28. ST I–II 46,6,1; cf. 30,4.
29. Cf. ST I–II 2,7.
30. Cf. ST I–II 2,8 (our happiness is not in created things) and 3,1–8 (it is in seeing the divine essence).
31. In ST I–II 4,8 Thomas is more nuanced, i.e., positive, about the value of fellow human beings or friends for our happiness (on earth).
32. Cf. ST I 88,1 and I–II 115,6,3.
33. So God has created us in order to be happy: ST III 9,2,3.
34. For Thomas's terminology of "love": see Sermon 01 *Veniet desideratus*, note 39.

SERMON 20

(2.3.1) First, I say that their God is to be known. The perfect happiness of the saints in the heavenly homeland consists in knowing God. Augustine says so in *Confessions*, Book IV, chapter 4: "For a man is unhappy who knows all those things, but does not know you; happy is the one who knows you, even if he does not know all those things. Someone, however, who knows you and also those things, is not happier because of those things, but he is happy only because of you." Happiness is that we may know God, or that we may have God to know.[35] But the saints in the heavenly homeland know God, don't they? They certainly do.[36] Thus we read in Jer 31.34: "A man will not need to teach his brother and his neighbor, saying: 'Know the Lord,' for all will know me, from the least of them to the greatest."

But in what way do the saints have God to know? I say that two things accompany this knowledge: (a) a clear and direct vision and (b) a perfect similarity with God.

(a) First, I say that this knowledge follows from a clear and direct vision.[37] For we see God only through things remote from him, through a similarity of the creatures and in things that we cannot explain.[38] Hence it says in Jb 36.25: "All people see him; everyone looks up to him from afar." The Apostle [formulates it in this way] in Rom 1.20: "The invisible things of God are observed as we understand them, through the things that are made." But in the heavenly home the saints see God clearly, not in a mirror or in an enigmatic way [cf. 1 Cor 13.12].

Well, in order to see God clearly we must have pure eyes. If eyes have darkness or if they are turbid, they are not sufficient to see the clarity with your mind; it is proper to the fire of concupiscence, to the fire of anger, or to the fire of desiring evil things, that you are prevented from the vision of God,[39] as we read in Psalm 68: "Fire," that is, the fire of concupiscence, "had

---

35. After all, in this life we cannot fully know God as he is; cf. ST I 1,1, 1,9,3, 2,1,1, 3 intr., 13,2,3, 13,11–12. Yet we can live with him and thus get to know him better.

36. ST I 12,1 and 5; I–II 69,2,3.

37. Cf. ST I 12,7. The following text breathes 1 Jn 3.2, cited further down, in (b).

38. Cf. ST I 12,11–12.

39. Respectively, ST I–II 77,5 and 82,3; 48,3; 33,3, and II–II 15,3.

overpowered them, and they could not see the sun" [Ps 58.9], that is, God.[40] So this knowledge is accompanied by a clear and direct vision.

(b) In the same way, this knowledge is accompanied by a perfect similarity with God, since knowledge does not come about unless through an assimilation of the one who knows with the thing known, as the Philosopher puts it.[41] Well, the saints in the heavenly homeland have a perfect similarity with God. As we read in 1 Jn 3.2: "When he appears, we will be similar to him, and we will see him as he is."[42]

If you want to arrive at similarity with God in the homeland, you ought to apply yourself to becoming similar to him in good works here, [on earth].[43] Christ came to give peace to the world. Eph 2.14 reads: "He himself is our peace, who has made both one." So do not sow strife, but bring disagreements back to peace if you want to be similar to Christ here on earth [cf. Eph 4.11–16]. Hence it says in the Gospel according to Matthew 5.9: "Happy the peacemakers, because they will be called children of God." A son bears a perfect likeness to his father. Thus in the heavenly homeland we will have God to know and to see. Therefore, Augustine says in his commentary on Psalm 119: "That vision (*contemplatio*) is promised as the end of all our actions."

(2.3.2) It is written in Dt 10.9 that the sons of Levi did not have a portion [of the land] among the brethren, since the Lord was their possession. The saints have God in their possession, and that is enough for them. Ps 16.6: "The ropes (that bound me) have fallen for me (when I saw) the very bright things, for my heritage is very bright to me." [Ps 16.5:] "The Lord is the portion of my heritage and my cup; (you are the one who returns my heritage to me)."

But in what way do the saints possess God? I say that they are happy in possessing God, since Jn 4.14 reads: "Happy the one who fears him."[44] And how have they arrived at possessing him?

---

40. Cf. ST I–II 36,2.   41. ST I 14,2,2, 85,5,3, and 88,1,2.
42. Throughout ST I 12 Thomas is explaining this text. He cites it explicitly in 12,1sc, 12,2,1, 12,5, and 12,6,1.
43. Mt 5.48 (cf. ST I–II 61,5; II–II 184,2), 1 Pt 1.16; Eph 5.1.
44. Cf. Ps 112.1. Thomas distinguishes between fearing God as God's gra-

I say through love (*dilectio*). Thus we read in 1 Jn 4.16: "Someone who remains in love (*caritas*), remains in God, and God in him." And in Tb 13.18: "Happy all who love (*diligo*) you."[45]

But what do you possess in possessing God? I say that by possessing God you possess what is in God [cf. Mt 23.20–22]. And what is in God? Glory and riches, as we read in Ps 112.3: "Glory and riches are in his house." The saints in the heavenly homeland have glory and honor. All are kings, as we read in Rv 5.10: "You have made us" kings, "a kingdom for our God." This glory is promised to the humble, because it says in Jb 22.29 (Vg): "The one who is humbled will be in glory." And in the Gospel according to Matthew 5.3 we read: "Blessed the poor (in spirit), because theirs is the kingdom of the heavens." Again, the saints have infinite[46] riches, for they have anything that someone can desire.

But to whom is that possession given? To those who quarrel?[47] Surely not. In the world man acquires something at times by quarreling about earthly things, and through fraud. But the heavenly riches are acquired by mildness.[48] Hence we read in Jas 1.21: "Receive in mildness the word that was planted." And in the Gospel according to Matthew 5.5 it says: "Happy the meek, for they will possess the earth." Thus the saints have God to know and to possess.

(2.3.3) Third, the saints in the homeland have God to enjoy and to delight in. Jb 22.26 reads: "In the Almighty you will overflow with delights." The saints in the heavenly homeland do not delight in a temporal thing, but in God, the fountain of every good. Thus the Lord says in Lk 22.30: "that you may eat and drink at my table in my Kingdom."

What is eating at God's table? It is to delight in and to be re-

---

cious gift of a holy reverence for him, and fearing what is not God. The latter is not a virtue and not part of eternal life: ST I–II 67,4,2 and II–II 19,11.

45. In view of the Scripture texts cited here, we see that Thomas speaks of a union with God which is a union through love; cf. ST I–II 25,2,2, 26,2,2, and 68,4,3.

46. For Thomas's understanding of infinity: ST I 7 (God's infinity), 14,12 and 86,2 (knowledge), 25,2 (power).

47. Quarreling is a sin, opposed to friendship: ST II–II 116.

48. ST II–II 157 on clemency and mildness.

freshed by the same thing by which God is refreshed. And what is the thing by which God is refreshed? It is his goodness. When you are refreshed by the goodness of God, you eat at God's table—and this is the happiness of the saints. Hence it is said in Lk 14.15: "Happy the one who will eat bread in the kingdom of the saints."[49]

And see: this delight has three characteristics:[50]

(a) This joy gives consolation. Through that joy a man loses all sadness,[51] as we read in Is 65.16: "The earlier fears are relegated to oblivion; they are neither in the memory nor will they rise over the heart, because you will see and exult in these things that I have made." Augustine says in *The City of God*, Book 22, chapter 30, that in one way the learning and the teaching of pain is forgotten, and in another way its infliction and experience. The learning and the teaching of pain is forgotten when someone neglects it [cf. Is 2.4]; the infliction and experience of it, when the pain is transformed into joy. The saints also forget all pains because of joy. And so that joy brings consolation.[52]

(b) Furthermore, it [the joy] is complete. Why is it complete? Because it concerns the Creator, whereas concerning all creatures nothing will come to your mind that will not make you rejoice. For this joy will lead to the contemplation of the Divinity, and from there to a contemplation of the creatures, and thus it will find refreshment in God and creatures everywhere. Therefore, the joy is complete [cf. 1 Jn 1.3–4]. Hence we read in Jn 16.24: "Ask, so that your joy may be complete." And Augustine says: "No one can arrive at this satisfaction, except by hungering for justice," as we read in the Gospel according to Matthew 5.6: "Happy those who hunger and thirst for justice, for they will be satisfied."

---

49. God's goodness is for all people (ST I 19,4,1, 23,4,1); it is abundant (ST I 21,4, 25,5) and without end (ST II–II 24,8, 27,5; cf. III 23,1). For the theme of the refreshment at God's table, see also Sermon 13 *Homo quidam fecit*, the *Sermo*.

50. Cf. ST I–II 4,1–2, 31,3, 32,4–5, 34,1–3, 35,1–6.

51. According to ST III 84,9,3 consolation mitigates sadness, but does not take it away completely. At least, that is the case as long as we live on earth; in this sermon Thomas speaks of the hereafter.

52. Cf. ST II–II 9,4,1.

(c) Moreover, that pure joy is not mixed with mourning and anxiety,[53] as the joy of the world is.[54] Concerning this joy of the world Prv 14.13 says: "A laugh will be mixed with pain." In Is 35.10 [we read about the heavenly joy]: "They will obtain joy and gladness, and pain and sighing will flee from them." And in Prv 1.33: "He will thoroughly enjoy abundance, after the endurance of the fear of evil things."[55] The merciful will have that joy, because [it is promised] in Mt 5.7: "Happy the merciful, for they will receive mercy themselves." Augustine says: "He himself is our end, whom we will see without end, whom we will love (*amo*) without disgust, and whom we will praise without getting tired. But what will be in that end? We will become empty without end; by becoming empty we will see; by seeing we will love (*amo*); by loving we will praise. Happy the one who will be in that end," for Psalm 36 says: "Happy those who live in your house, Lord" [Ps 84.5].

May we be guided to that happiness by the One who lives and reigns with the Father and the Holy Spirit, et cetera.

PARS 3: *Collatio in sero*

"Happy the nation whose lord is its God" [Ps 33.12], et cetera. In view of that glorious company of the saints, whose feast we celebrate today, we spoke about (1) the dignity of the saints and about (2) their leader. Because of the shortness of the time, we must say just something about (3) how this group is arranged, which is signified by the term "people."[56]

---

53. In conformity with Rv 21.4; the inhabitants of the heavenly homeland will not experience sadness or anxiety, even not by reason of the people on earth for whom they care and who pray to God; cf. ST I 113,7 and II–II 83,11.

54. Even our spiritual joy, which comes forth from love (*caritas*), can be mixed with sadness, as we do not fully participate in it: ST II–II 28,2. Christ's spiritual joy, however, was always complete, even in his Passion; cf. ST III 46,7–8.

55. Cf. the references mentioned in note 13.

56. Thomas does not mention point 4, which he announced at the beginning of the *Sermo*. The election of the saints is discussed, however, together with their distinction, in 3.2.

(3) What is a people? Augustine introduces this definition of "people" in *The City of God*, Book 19, chapter 31:[57] "A people is a multitude of men and women together, united by a consensus of law and by a common purpose." So, according to this definition, three things can be observed in the term "people": (3.1) the great multitude, (3.2) the ordered distinction, and (3.3) the harmonious union.

❖

(3.1) First, I say that for a people a great number is required, because one or two do not make a people. Does this nation consist of a multitude? It certainly does. Hence it says in today's Epistle reading: "I saw a great crowd which no one could count" [Rv 7.9].

(3.1.1) It pertains to the dignity of a king, and especially of this king, that he has a great people. Hence it says in Proverbs 5: "The dignity of a king is found in the multitude of his people" [Prv 14.28]. And Boethius says that a king boasts of the multitude of his citizens. In comparison with heaven the earth is nothing [cf. Wis 11.22, Is 40.15–17]. Dionysius says in *The Heavenly Hierarchy*, chapter 14, that a multitude of material things is nothing in respect of a multitude of spiritual things. And it is said about the Lord: "Thousands of thousands serve him and ten thousands times hundred thousand stood by him" [Dn 7.10, Rv 5.11], and after that the multitude of all the saints [is mentioned] [Dn 7.27, Rv 7.4]. In 1 Samuel we find: "Israel and Judah, innumerable as the sand of the sea, eating and drinking and praising" [1 Kgs 4.20]. Only God knows how big the multitude of the saints is [Rv 7.9]. Thus it says in Ps 147.4: "Who would count the multitude of the stars?"[58] So the multitude of the people pertains to the dignity of the king.

(3.1.2) Furthermore, it pertains to joyfulness. A human being is of a corruptible nature. The multitude of the people pertains to the greatness of the joy.[59] Hence it says in Is 22.2: "crowded town, exulting city."

---

57. It is in fact chapter 24.

58. The inference of this rhetorical question follows in verse 5: "our Lord is great and mighty in power." In Jb 38.7 the stars are identified with the sons of God. Thomas refers to this explicitly in SCG IV 6.

59. For the more people there are in heaven, the more people are with-

SERMON 20 309

(3.1.3) Moreover, the great multitude pertains to our safety. Many are the saints who are with us.[60] Hence it says in Jgs 5.20: "The stars that remain in their path and in order fought against Sisera," that is, against the devil. And Elisha said to his servant in 2 Kgs 6.16: "Fear not, for there are many more with us than with them."[61]

Thus the multitude of the saints in the homeland brings joy to the saints (3.1.2), honor to God (3.1.1), and safety to us (3.1.3).

❖

(4)[62] We must speak about the election of the saints. (3.3) The distinction of the saints is handed down to us on the basis of the knowledge in the Epistle reading [Rv 7.5–8], but that diversity is in the world, not in heaven.[63] Hence the Apostle says in Col 3.11: "There is neither barbarian nor Scythian, neither Jew nor Gentile."[64] And St. Peter says in Acts 10.35: "In every nation someone who fears God and does justice is received by him."

(3.2) Therefore, we hear in the Gospel about a difference between the saints that will be in the homeland in the glorious people.

(3.2.1) It has been handed down to us that some will be

---

drawn from corruption; cf. ST I 75,6. In death the corruptible body is separated from the incorruptible soul; cf. SCG II 57.

60. The saints *in patria* are concerned with people on the way, *in via, viatores*; they pray with us and for us (ST II–II 83,11) and help and protect us (cf. ST II–II 17,4)—whence we speak of guardian angels (I 113) and patron saints.

61. In verse 17 it shows that this refers to the heavenly hosts.

62. Apparently Thomas had very little time (maybe because of other festivities that were planned): this *Collatio in sero* is relatively very brief; point 4 is only mentioned (and in a way incorporated in 3.2); point 3.3 is reduced to a preliminary—although not unimportant—remark of 3.2.

63. So we make the distinctions for our sake, in order to know them better, whereas these distinctions are as such not in heaven: it is "a harmonious union." In other words: these distinctions are not *in re* (in the thing itself), but *in ratione tantum* (in our thinking only); they are made on the basis of their lives on earth; that is why these people are "elected."

64. Cf. ST III 36,3. Even on earth there is not such a distinction as for man and woman, Thomas says; both are image of God insofar as they are rational creatures; cf. ST I 93,6,2 (where he refers to Col 3.10–11, but cites in fact Gal 3.28); cf. also III 67,4: also, women can baptize as a servant of Christ, under specific circumstances.

kings. It is true that all the saints reign with God [cf. Dn 7.27], but the apostles reign in a special way. Thus it is said in Lk 22.29: "I prepare a kingdom for you, just as the Father has prepared it for me"; and just as they were leaders of the Church, so they have in the homeland a regal dignity. And how have they acquired that reign? Surely through their poverty. Others acquire a kingdom through riches. Let us hear Peter, who says in Mt 19.27 about the acquisition of the kingdom: "Behold, we left everything behind." And the Lord says in Mt 5.3: "Happy the poor in spirit, for theirs is the kingdom of the heavens."

There are newfangled debaters who do not know what they say. They say that virtue consists in keeping the middle and in such a way that every renunciation, even virginity, does not belong to the virtues, because renunciation does not keep the middle. The Philosopher says: "Those who have a smattering of things, because they turn their eyes only to a few things, speak out easily." Virtues should not keep the middle according to quantity, but according to a right (*rectus*) way of reasoning. The Philosopher says in Book 4 of *Ethics* that in extraordinary situations someone is magnanimous through extreme greatness, but in such a way that he must keep the middle—because he is magnanimous—where he ought to, in accordance with what ought to be and because of what ought to be.[65] Philosophers have laid aside all their belongings, so that they can make themselves free for the philosophy and live moderately. If this was the case with the Gentiles, it well ought to be the case with Christians. But if a man wanted to renounce when his wife asks him for what he owes her, renunciation would be a vice, even though we find the highest virtue in virginity.[66]

---

65. Cf. ST I–II 64. It is as such remarkable that a Christian preacher explicitly refers to a pagan philosopher in a sermon (so, in the liturgy) in order to make something clear about Christian virtuosity; cf. ST I–II 55,4. See also Sermon 06 *Celum et terra*. Thomas's point of departure for explaining what a virtue is, is Peter Lombard's definition (which is based on Augustine's). In this sermon Thomas refers to Aristotle as he reacts against a movement that rejects the pursuit of perfection in virtue and that calls for this upon Aristotle, unjustly, as Thomas contends.

66. Cf. ST II–II 152,4.

Thus the apostles have acquired the kingdom through poverty.[67]

(3.2.2) We find victorious martyrs, who, as Heb 11.33 [formulates it], "conquered kingdoms by faith,"[68] and those are happy, meek people, because "no groaning resounds (from their lips), no complaint."[69] About them the Gospel according to Matthew 5.5 says: "Happy the meek, for they will possess the earth."[70]

(3.2.3) Likewise, we find some who live in solace, like the holy confessors who mourned while they were in the world and did great penance. You have seen Anthony [of Egypt] and Benedict, who lived in tears and great, austere penance, and who now experience joy and consolation. Thus it says in the Gospel that they will be consoled [Mt 5.4].[71]

(3.2.4) Likewise, we find in heaven most righteous judges, namely, the prophets who preached justice; these were the ones hungering for justice, and therefore they are satisfied now. Thus it says in the Gospel: "Happy those who hunger and thirst after justice, for they will be satisfied" [Mt 5.6].[72]

(3.2.5) Likewise, we find in the homeland a group of patriarchs who fervently applied themselves to the works of mercy; the dignity of receiving others is now kept for them in heaven. Hence Abraham, who received everybody in his hospitality—

---

67. In this way Thomas has interpreted Mt 5.3 ("Blessed are the poor in spirit") in the light of Lk 6.20 ("Blessed are the poor"), as he does in ST I–II 69,3.

68. Cf. ST II–II 124,5.

69. From the hymn *Sanctorum meritis inclyta gaudia*, sung at the office of the feasts of martyrs. (For the complete text of the stanza quoted, see Sermon 19 *Beati qui habitant*, note 42). This phrase also occurs twice in the *Legenda sanctae Clarae virginis*. This may indicate that (also) Franciscans were present as Thomas preached this sermon.

70. In ST II–II 121,2 Thomas links meekness with God's gracious gift of devotion (*pietas*), on the basis of Augustine's exposition on the Sermon on the Mount.

71. In ST II–II 9,4 this beatitude is linked with the gift of knowledge, also on the basis of what Augustine says in his exposition on the Sermon on the Mount: "Knowledge befits those who mourn, because they have learned through the evil things that overcame them what they will endeavor to achieve as good things."

72. In ST II–II 58,7 Thomas cites Chrysostom, who sees justice as especially opposed to greed; in 58,1 Thomas defines justice as "the constant and lasting will to give to everyone his/her due."

even angels, according to Gn 18.3—has the dignity in heaven that all are received in his bosom [cf. Lk 16.22]. And therefore it says in Heb 13.2: "Do not forget hospitality." Abraham receives at his bosom all who are chosen. Thus it is said in Mt 8.11: "They will come from the East and the West, and they will recline at the bosom of Abraham, Isaac, and Jacob." About these it is said in Sir 44.10: "These are the men of mercy, who were always living devoutly" [cf. Mt 5.7, Lk 6.38].

(3.2.6) Likewise, we find in the homeland the group of virgins, who preserved their cleanness. This is the chaste nation. About these the Gospel says: "Blessed are the clean of heart, for they will see God" [Mt 5.8].[73]

(3.2.7) Likewise, we find in the homeland the choir of angels who strive for peace. And about them we read in the Gospel according to Matthew 5.9: "Happy the peacemakers, for they will be called children of God."[74]

It is clear now how the poor have acquired the kingdom; the meek, the earth; the mourning, consolation; those who hunger after justice received satisfaction; the merciful gained mercy; the clean, the vision of God; and the peacemakers are called children of God.[75]

May we be led to that community by him who with the Father, et cetera.

---

73. In the ST Thomas does not exclusively connect this beatitude with virginity, but with the good disposition of the will which is required for attaining happiness (ST I–II 4,4), with the gift of understanding (*intellectus*, in ST II–II 8,7), and with cleanness (*mundicia*: of body and mind), in particular for those who live a contemplative life (ST II–II 180,2).

74. In ST II–II 19,12, Thomas connects this beatitude with the gift of fear of God, and in II–II 45,6 with the gift of wisdom, both on the basis of the same text of Augustine. Cf. Sir 1.16 (a text not cited in the ST).

75. For Thomas's numeration of the Beatitudes, see ST I–II 69,3.

SERMON 21
BEATUS VIR

Sermon on the Feast of St. Martin,
the Eleventh of November

Psalm 83.6–7 (Vg): *Happy the man whose help is from you: he has set his heart on ascending while in the valley of tears, in the place which he has built.*

PART 1: *Prothema*

"HAPPY THE man whose help is from you: he has set his heart on ascending while in the valley of tears, in the place which he has built" [Ps 83.6–7 (Vg)]. The proclaimed words show explicitly enough that St. Martin has arrived at the glory of highness through divine help. That help is ready for all people. And just as St. Martin needed divine help in order to arrive at the glory of highness, so we, too, need divine help so that we can arrive at glory.[1] Therefore, in accordance with the exhortation of the Apostle in Heb 4.16: "Let us approach with confidence to the throne of his grace, that we may receive mercy and obtain grace in the favorable time," so that he may give me something to say, et cetera.

PART 2: *Sermo*

"Happy the man" [Ps 83.6–7 (Vg)], et cetera. It is a custom that when someone is promoted to a great status or to a great dignity, he and his relatives and friends commemorate this ex-

---

1. ST I 73,1,1; cf. I–II 3,1.

altation. This day St. Martin is promoted to the highest dignity and the highest place, namely, to the kingdom of the heavens. Therefore, Mother Church commemorates his happiness.

Concerning his happiness three things come up that we must consider on the ground of the words proclaimed. First, we can consider the beginning of his happiness [in this part, the *Sermo*]; second, the progress [in the *Collatio in sero*]; and third, the endpoint of his happiness [touched upon in the final sentence]. The origin or cause of his happiness was divine help, which is mentioned when it is said: "Happy the man (whose help is from you)." He has made progress in ascents: he advanced from one virtue to another, which is mentioned when it says: "He has set his heart on ascending." The endpoint of his happiness is the gain of eternal happiness, which is mentioned when it says: "in the place which he has built." Why? The Psalmist explains immediately[2] what he has said, as he adds: "The Giver of the Law will also give a blessing"; see: the divine help. [He continues:] "They will go from one virtue to another"; behold: the ascent from one virtue to another. "The God of gods will be seen in Zion" [Ps 83.8 (Vg)];[3] lo: the place that he has built.

First, I say that the origin or the cause of arriving at a particular dignity is divine help. With our reason we find in creatures that when something reaches something by its own nature, it is the cause of it. As for those things that it does not reach by its own nature—like fire: it is warm by its own nature, and therefore it is the cause of the heating in those things which it does not reach by its own nature.[4] Well, God is happy by his own nature, and thus he is the cause of happiness in others.[5] Hence the Apostle says in 1 Tm 6.16: "(our Lord Jesus Christ,) whom the happy and only powerful King of kings and Lord of lord-

---

2. In verse 8, not in verse 3 as the Latin text says.
3. Zion is the mountain on which Jerusalem, the city of God, is built, whence the use of the verb *ascendere*, to ascend, to go up (cf. Is 2.3, for example).
4. ST I 108,5,5 (*Secundo*...); III 7,9.
5. ST I 26,1–4, resp., I–II 2,8; others are not happy by nature, but participate in God's happiness insofar as he gives us a share in it. In this context Thomas refers to Ps 103.5.

ships will show." So no one can arrive at happiness unless by divine help.

Let us see what help the Lord grants us, so that humankind may arrive at happiness. I mention a triple help: (1) first, God chides mankind; (2) second, he teaches us; and (3) third, he takes us up.[6]

⁂

(1) That God chides us is a way to happiness. Jb 5.17 reads: "Happy the man who is chided by God." This correction pertains to being called.[7] Humankind is chided only because of sin. Being called happens from afar; through sin it happens that someone is far from God, as it says in Is 59.2: "Your sins cause a division between you and your God."[8] The Apostle shows us the blessing of being called when he says in Rom 8.30: "The ones he has predestined he has also called."[9] And St. Martin was called by the Lord and was chided, that is, removed from original sin and preserved from actual sin.[10]

Is 41.2: "Who has raised the just one from the East and called him to follow him?" Those who are raised from sin are raised by God. Some are converted in the East—that is, in their boyhood[11]—just like St. Martin; when he was ten years of age, he became a catechumen, against his parents' will. When he was twelve he thought of how he could become a hermit.

See that help: it is necessary for man that God chides him [cf. Heb 12.7]. You should know that no matter how often you are chided by a human being, this correction is not worth anything, unless you become more intimate with God's grace, which is calling you. Thus it says in Eccl 7.13: "Consider God's works: no

6. In what follows Thomas expounds these three steps in view of Rom 8.30.

7. *Vocatio*: ST I 113,1,3. *Correctio* is etymologically connected with *rectus:* right, upright, righteous.

8. Cf. ST I 48,4.

9. Cf. ST I 23,2.

10. ST I–II 113,1,3: "Being called" means that through God's help our mind is moved and excited to refrain from sinning. This is not the same as the forgiveness of sins; it is its cause.

11. The East, from where the day (life) begins. See also Sermon 08 *Puer Jesus, Prothema* and under 1.3 of the *Sermo,* and Sermon 09 *Exiit qui seminat,* under 2.2 and 2.3 of the *Sermo.*

one can correct someone whom he has despised." So it is not worth anything that someone be chided by highly placed people or by others, unless God works in him through his grace.[12]

God's chiding of man is a sign of his love (*dilectio*).[13] Thus we read in Prv 3.12: "The Lord chides whom he loves (*diligo*)."[14]

God chides man in three ways:

(1.1) first, by inspiring fear. Hence we read in Sir 1.27: "Who is without fear cannot be justified; fear of the Lord belongs to wisdom." So we must apply ourselves to having fear [of God]. This is the first step to happiness.[15]

(1.2) Second, God chides someone by forgiving him his sins. God is the only one who can forgive sins, according to Mk 2.7.[16] And in Psalm 27 we read: "Happy the ones whose iniquities are forgiven (and whose sins are covered)" [Ps 32.1].

(1.3) Third, God chides someone by pulling him away from sins. Isn't it a divine blessing that, just as God forgives a man his sins, he also preserves him from sinning?[17] Augustine says this in *Confessions*, Book II, chapter 7: "I ascribe it to your grace and your mercy that you have melted away my sins like ice. Also, the many evil things I did not do I ascribe to your grace, because I was not able to do them." Ps 1.1 touches upon this happiness, saying: "Happy the man who did not go astray following the advice of the godless (and did not come to a standstill on the way of sinners)." St. Martin did not need this grace of the removal of sins, since we do not read about actual sins committed by him. But God chided him in this respect: that he preserved him from sinning.[18]

❖

12. Cf. Is 26.12, Phil 2.13, Heb 13.21; we are just instruments (*instrumenta separata*, as distinct from *instrumenta coniuncta*: ST III 62,5) of his grace; we cannot do anything apart from him, as in Jn 15.4–5.

13. For Thomas's terminology of "love," see Sermon 01 *Veniet desideratus*, note 39.

14. This love is not only love out of justice (ST III 59,1), but also like the love of a father for his son, as Prv 3.12 continues. Cf. ST I–II 69,3,4 (where Thomas cites Jb 5.17: see note 7), 109,8,2; II–II 33,3,3; and III 59,1.

15. Cf. ST I–II 113,4,1; II–II 19,2 and 4–11: this fear of and reverence for God is a gracious gift of the Holy Spirit.

16. ST III 3,8,3, 89,1; cf. I–II 113,1–2.

17. ST III 88,1.

18. Thus—and in what follows—St. Martin, just like the Blessed Virgin (Ser-

(2) Second, God offers his help to a man by teaching him. In Ps 94.12 we read: "Happy the man whom you teach, Lord, and whom you instruct in your Law." This is not a teaching that would only enlighten the intellect; it moves the affection as well.[19] The art of oratory has an effect on a judge's affection. If this is the effect of human pleas, the effect of divine pleas[20] must be much stronger. Hence we read in Jn 6.45: "Everyone who has listened to my Father and has learned, comes to me." Someone listens to the Father when he is inspired with a good thing; someone who rejects inspired things does not learn. Isaiah has not acted in the latter way; he says in 1.5: "God has opened my ear, and I have not objected; I have not recoiled," that I may listen to him as to a *magister*. Someone who subjects his heart to the divine inspiration learns. This pertains to justification.[21] The Apostle says in Rom 8.30: "Those whom he has called, he has also justified."

There are three stages in the divine teaching [cf. 1 Cor 13.13].

(2.1) First, he enlightens the intellect through faith.[22] This is the greatest teaching. Having a little bit of faith is more than knowing everything that all philosophers in the world have known.[23] Hence it says in Dt 4.6: "(Show) that wisdom and understanding of yours before the peoples." And in Jn 20.29 it reads: "Happy those who have not seen and yet believe."

(2.2) Second, this teaching raises up the mind through hope. When the mind believes through faith, it is then elevated by hope.[24] This is the second stage of happiness. Ps 40.5: "Hap-

---

mons 17 and 18) and St. Nicholas (Sermon 16), is idealized in accordance with the customs of that time. But since he is depicted as almost superhuman, it becomes almost impossible for him to be an example for people who are not as "perfect."

19. God as well as creatures can enlighten and change a person's intellect and affection, but in different ways: ST I 111,1–2; cf.107,2 and I–II 79,3.

20. Cf. Ps 4.2, 43.1, 119.154; also Rom 8.26.

21. ST I–II 100,2,1, 111,2,2: God does not justify a human being without his/her co-operation and obedience (II–II 104).

22. ST I–II 62,4 (in *quaestio* 62 Thomas distinguishes the theological virtues of faith, hope, and love); cf. ST I 12,5; II–II 2,1, 6,1–2, 8,2 and 4.

23. See also homily 14 *Attendite a falsis*, under 1.2.2 of the *Sermo*.

24. For the relation between faith and hope, see ST II–II 17,7.

py the man whose hope is the name of the Lord and who has not looked at vain and unhealthy things that are false." Some do not trust in God, but in vain things. Which are vain things? Temporal goods, riches, honors, and the like.[25] Ps 39.6 says: "But still total vanity is the living man."[26] So you should not put your trust in those things.[27] Some, and that is worse, trust in unhealthy things; they turn to the interpretations of omens, predictions, and the superstitions of black magic.[28]

(2.3) The third stage of this teaching is that it changes the affection through love (*dilectio*), because it says in Tb 13.17: "Happy all who love (*diligo*) you." St. Martin's father and mother were pagans, yet still his soul did not sense anything but spiritual things [cf. 1 Cor 14.1], and he was so erudite that he has written a book on the Trinity.[29]

(3) The third divine help is that God takes us up [cf. Ex 19.4]. Ps 65.5 reads: "Happy the one whom you have chosen and taken up; he will live in your forecourts." This action of taking someone up pertains to the third blessing of God, namely, magnification. The Apostle says in Rom 8.30: "The ones whom he has justified, he has also magnified."

And how has the Lord magnified St. Martin? Surely with a triple step.

(3.1) First, through the holiness of his works. If someone reads St. Martin's biography, he will discover how grand he has been: how great his virtue, his abstinence, and his chastity have been. Gn 26.13 says of such a magnitude that "Isaac advanced and increased until the effect was great." St. (*Beatus*) Martin has been great in the observance of the Commandments. Thus

---

25. ST I–II 2,1–7.

26. Cf. ST I–II 4,8.

27. *Fiducia, confidere*: deeply rooted belief that precedes knowledge in someone or something who/that can and will help you (ST I–II 40,2,2). Eventually only God is to be trusted in this way, according to Psalms 49 and 146; cf. ST II–II 129,6,1.

28. All these are to be repudiated: ST II–II 92–96, 122,2,3, and 122,3.

29. Together with St. Hilary of Poitiers he strongly opposed Arianism, a popular heresy in early Christianity which denies the divinity of Christ.

we read in Proverbs 28: "Happy (*beatus*) those who hear your Law and guard it in their whole heart."[30]

(3.2) Second, St. Martin has been great because of the greatness of [his] miracles. (a) He has raised up three dead people. (b) His garments [cf. Acts 19.12] and the letters he sent cured those who were ill. About this magnification we read in Sir 45.2: "He has made him great in the fear of enemies,"[31] (c) that is: of his enemies, the pagans [Sir 45.2 (Vg)], "and by his words he has tamed monsters." For once there was a tree cut down, and he had placed himself in the path of its fall, and the tree fell over to the other side.[32] (d) Likewise, he wanted to penetrate the troops of the enemies unarmed, and subsequently he tamed the monsters, because his enemies sent peace negotiators. Because of these miracles St. Martin must be magnified, like the Blessed Virgin, who has said: "Because he has done great things for me" [Lk 1.49], namely, the greatest miracle of the miracles: that in her womb God became man and that she gave birth and yet she remained a virgin.[33] Also for St. Martin he has done many great things. Because of this he must be magnified by all people.

(3.3) The third step is proper to the magnification of the happiness of St. Martin, found in the spreading of his fame, all over the earth. For which is the devotion and which is the city where the name and the fame of St. Martin are not renowned? Ps 137.2 (Vg): "You have magnified your holy name above every name." Although a gloss relates this to Christ, still it could be said of St. Martin. Think about the miracles he has done. So many kings, so many emperors have applied themselves to

---

30. This quotation is from Prv 29.18 (= Ps 119.1–2, Prv 8.32).

31. It is God who made him great, for it was through grace that Martin could work these miracles: ST I 43,3,4, 104,4, 117,3,1.

32. Here Thomas refers to the event when druids whom St. Martin tried to convert offered to cut down their sacred fir or pine tree, if he stood in the path of its fall. He agreed. The tree was cut. But as it was about to crush St. Martin, he held up his hand and made the sign of the cross. Subsequently it fell the opposite way (according to the dramatic account of Sulpitius Severus in his biography of St. Martin, chapter 13).

33. ST III 28,1–3.

making a name for themselves on earth: some have built triumphal arches; others, houses and castles; and still "their memory has perished with their sound" [Ps 9.7]. There are only a few who know who Trajan and Octavian were.³⁴ But St. Martin, who was lowly on earth—the effect [of his life] is great. It says in Tobit 29: "Upon hearing (my name) the ear has blessed me" [Jb 29.11]. All who hear the story of St. Martin bless him.

The first point is clear now, namely, the beginning of how he became happy, which is the divine help, and how God chides and teaches man and takes him up.

PART 3: *Collatio in sero*

We continue with the progress of St. Martin to happiness, where it says [in the Psalm]: "He has set his heart on ascending."

Whoever wants to ascend to some high state must ascend little by little. Because St. Martin realized that he ought to ascend from the low state of misery to a high state, he prepared for himself the upward steps towards happiness. Well, in regard to St. Martin, we can consider a threefold ascent. (1) The first is by means of the sacrament of regeneration; (2) the second is according to the state; and (3) the third is according to merit.

(1) First, I say that St. Martin has prepared for himself the ascent by means of the sacrament of regeneration.³⁵ And anyone on whom this benefaction of being regenerated in Christ is conferred, does not go up a little step. The Apostle says in Gal 3.27: "All who are baptized in Christ, you are clothed with Christ." It is not a little thing to be clothed with Christ and to be strengthened by him.³⁶ Song 4.2 says about this ascent: "Your teeth are

---

34. Trajan was a mighty Roman emperor at the beginning of the second century CE who extended the boundaries of the empire, undertook an enormous building project in Rome, and enlarged social welfare. Octavian is the name of the first Roman emperor, Augustus, who ruled from 23 BCE until 14 CE. So both were very famous and great in the eyes of the people there and then.

35. Which is baptism: Jn 3.3–5. ST III 66,1,1, 66,3, 67,3, 68,2,1.

36. The effects of baptism: ST III 69,1–8.

SERMON 21   321

like a shorn flock." Hairs are sins:[37] the shorn flock that ascends from the bath consists of those who have been cleansed from sin through Baptism, and these ascend. This is signified in Mt 3.16, where it says that Christ after being baptized ascended from the waters. St. Martin has thought much about how he could arrive at that benefaction, and later on he has carefully thought about how he could keep himself clean, free from sin.

(2) The second ascent pertains to the state. Hence it says in Ex 24.1: "The Lord said to Moses: 'Go up the mountain, you and the seventy elders of the house of Israel.'" The Lord said that the others should stay down and that only Moses should ascend; ordinary people do not ascend, because they do not reach for the state of highness. The elders ascended a little bit, but only Moses went up [all the way] onto the mountain [Ex 24.1–2].

There are different states. If we consider the ascent of St. Martin in this respect, I say that he has ascended in three ways: (2.1) first, from the military to the clerical state; (2.2) second, from the clerical to the religious state; and (2.3) third, from the religious to the pontifical state.

(2.1) First, I say that St. Martin ascended from the military state to the clerical state, because the clerical military force[38] is higher than the worldly one. For worldly soldiers wage wars against enemies of flesh; we, however, wage the Lord's wars against spiritual enemies. Hence the Apostle says in 2 Cor 10.4: "The weapons of our military force are not of the flesh," but spiritual,[39] given by God for the destruction of errors, vices, and sins. About this ascent Is 2.3 says: "Come, let us ascend to the

---

37. Note that we still associate a baby's skin with innocence and that in cartoons "the bad guys" are often the unshaven: a villain's face.

38. *Militia clericalis, militia saecularis.* This imagery is also found in texts like 2 Cor 10.4 (quoted in the text) and in 1 Tm 1.18–19 and 2 Tm 2.3–4 where the Apostle Paul addresses Timothy, a cleric or bishop (to say it anachronistically), as a soldier of Christ. Cf. the image of the Church Militant in Sermon 17 *Lux orta*, under 1.11 of the *Sermo*, and in Sermon 19 *Beati qui habitant*, under 1.1.1.

39. Cf. ST II–II 40,2. See also, however, how Thomas defends the existence of religious orders whose members are Crusaders, in ST II–II 188,3.

mountain of the Lord and to the house of Jacob's God, and he will teach us his ways, and we will walk in his ways." The clerical state is a certain mountain.[40] We ought to ascend to the Lord's house and serve there and be taught in the teachings (*dogmata*) of the Church [cf. Mt 5.1–2]. Hence it says: "He will teach us his way,"[41] and we should not allow a contrary way. The Apostle says in Eph 5.3: "Let it not be mentioned among you"; and that we ought to walk in the way of the Lord [cf. Eph 5.2, 8, 15]. Someone who goes up onto the mountain of the Lord is chosen in the Lord's rank [cf. Wis 5.5]. So St. Martin ascended, because he was taught by St. Hilary, and was made a cleric by him.

(2.2) Second, St. Martin ascended from the clerical state to the religious state, since he became a monk in Italy. "Someone who strives to win a match abstains from all things" [1 Cor 9.25]. How much further does someone go in abstaining from things that hinder his duties? He would go as much further as his strife is more legitimate. Secular clerics have temporal goods, but religious do not have these, that they may not hinder them.[42] About this ascent Gn 35.3 says: "Let us ascend to Bethel[43] and live there, (abiding)." "Abiding" is added, meaning: in no way going out of there. Religious ought to stay in the religious life and not leave it, unless for reasons that pertain to the salvation of souls.[44]

(2.3) Third, St. Martin ascended from the religious state to the pontifical state. This is the right ascent.[45] For what did he ascend? Surely for the service of the altar and for administering the sacraments of the Church. Concerning this ascent Sirach 1

---

40. In Scripture the mountain is a place where people meet God; someone who lives in the clerical state wants or is to live in a closer relationship with God; cf. ST I–II 98,5,2.

41. Is 2.3 reads "ways," *vias* (not singular: *viam*).

42. ST II–II 186,3: possessions can be an obstacle, especially for perfect love.

43. The Hebrew name Bethel means "house of God."

44. Cf. ST II–II 189,4 (where Thomas does not explicitly mention this exception). Cf. also 185,4: whether a bishop could step down and become a religious.

45. It was the right (*rectus*) thing to leave the religious life in order to become bishop: ST II–II 184,7.

says: "In ascending to the holy altar, he has made his garment of sanctity glorious" [Sir 50.11]. Has the Lord magnified St. Martin in this way? Yes, he surely has, when a fiery ball appeared above him while he offered the sacrament of the altar.

Furthermore, he ascended for the salvation of the peoples. Thus we read in Prv 28.42: "There is much glory in the exaltation of the just ones, whereas the reign of the godless will ruin the people." One bad bishop, for sure, means ruin in many [people and things]. It is said in Obadiah 27: "As the saviors ascend the mountains (in order to administer justice)" [Obadiah 21], meaning: prelates ought to ascend for the salvation of souls. But the Lord complains about the evil ones in Ezek 13.5, saying: "You have not ascended, away from the enemy; you have not placed yourselves upon the wall to defend the Lord's house," namely, against the heretics and all who are evil.

So St. Martin ascended in a threefold way according to his state.

※

(3) But ascending according to one's state would not be worth anything, unless someone ascends according to merit.[46] Therefore, St. Martin ascended three times according to merit. Thus says Pope Symmachus: "Someone who is more important in dignity must be considered most worthless unless he excels in knowledge and holiness. Being a cleric does not amount to much if that man does not surpass a layman in virtue. In a similar way it does not amount to much being a monk or a bishop, unless one surpasses others in holiness of life."[47] So it is necessary that someone who ascends according to the state also ascends in merit. About this ascent it is said in Song 3.6: "Who is she who ascends through the desert, like a little twig of smoke from the scents of myrrh and frankincense and every powder of the merchant?" "Who goes up like a twig of smoke," not of terrifying smoke, but of fragrant smoke. But whence does that smoke come? Certainly "from the scents of myrrh," that is, the

---

46. Cf. ST II–II 185,3. Good works that establish justice for a fellow human being are meritorious: ST I–II 21,3–4.

47. ST I–II 98,5, respectively, II–II 186,1.

mortification of the flesh [cf. Mt 2.11, Jn 19.39], "and of frankincense," that is, devotion [cf. Ps 141.2, etc.], "and of every powder of the merchant," namely, all virtues.

(3.1) In every state whatsoever someone ought to apply himself to advance. We will consider how St. Martin applied himself to advance in every state.

(3.1.1) In his military state he applied himself to advance in mercy and devotion.[48] He also applied himself to advance in a reasonable way, because soldiers are eager to plunder.[49] By doing so he wanted to show that he was immune to this offense in his military state, and therefore he applied himself to mercy and devotion. Hence it is said in Lk 3.14 to soldiers: "Do not ransack anyone; make no false accusation against anyone (and be satisfied with your wages)."

(3.1.2) Likewise, in the state of a cleric he applied himself to obedience.[50] He was most obedient: he gave up everything at a nod of St. Hilary. Hence it befits him what is said in Sir 3.1 (Vg): "The children of wisdom form the Church of the just ones."

(3.1.3) Likewise, in the religious life he excelled in poverty and austerity.[51]

(3.1.4) Likewise, in the pontifical state he excelled in humility;[52] thus he has maintained the same humility in the pontifical state as he had maintained before, in accordance with Sir 3.18: "No matter how great you are, be humble in everything." Sir 32.1 reads: "They have made you the leader; do not want to be exalted; but be among them as one of them."

(3.2) See how St. Martin ascended [from state to state]. I say that he ascended with (3.2.1) prudence, (3.2.2) humility, and (3.2.3) fervor.

48. Resp., ST II–II 30 and 101. All the virtues Thomas mentions in this section 3 are central in religious life too; cf. ST II–II 186,1–2.

49. This is a very grave sin: ST II–II 68,8–9. Even among the gentiles plundering is not allowed according to Thomas in I–II 103,4,3; and Christians are supposed to give the good example.

50. ST II–II 104, 186,5 and 8.

51. ST II–II 186,3 and more elaborately in *Summa Contra Gentiles* III 130–135. As for Christ's poverty during his life on earth, see also ST III 40,2.

52. Cupidity, ambition, and being presumptuous do not befit a bishop: ST II–II 185,1; cf. 143, 160,2, 161.

(3.2.1) First, I say, he ascended with prudence[53] from the military to the clerical state; a war is initiated with preparation [cf. Lk 14.31]. And he prepared this ascent well. Still, it was pleasing to him not to ascend on high; when St. Hilary wanted to make him a deacon, he did not want this, but he remained an acolyte.

Likewise, he ascended from the clerical state and became a religious. Also he prepared this ascent well in his heart. But the ascent from the religious to the pontifical state he did not prepare in his heart, because he was promoted to be a bishop while he himself resisted. I say this with emphasis, because the pontifical state, although it is great, still must not be aspired to.[54] If someone said: "I want to apply myself so that I can govern the Church well later on," he has not spoken well.[55] Thus Augustine says in Book 19 of *The City of God*, chapter 19: "The higher place, without which a people cannot be governed, even though it serves the Church as it is proper, is yet indecently sought after." He continues: "And if no one put on this burden to acquire and examine the truth, it must remain vacant."

(3.2.2) Likewise, St. Martin ascended with humility. Thus it says: "in the valley of tears" [Ps 83.7 (Vg)]. In the Gospel according to Luke 14.11 we read: "If someone humbles himself, he will be exalted."

(3.2.3) Likewise, he has made that ascent with fervor.[56] Hence it says: "of tears"; because of the greatness of the desire, he applied himself to shedding tears. Thus he could say with Ps 42.2, 4: "Just as a deer desires the fountains of the waters (so my soul desires you, O God)"; "my tears have been my bread day and night," et cetera.[57]

---

53. The first of the cardinal virtues: ST I–II 61; II–II 47–51 (–56).
54. ST II–II 185,1.
55. For the conditions that make an act right or wrong: ST I–II 18–20; and what the consequences of this are: I–II 21.
56. In ST I–II 28,5 and 48,2,1–2, Thomas sees such fervor connected with love.
57. Cf. ST I–II 32,4 and 38,2.

So, because the saint we celebrate today has well prepared his ascent in the progress of happiness, he has arrived at the endpoint of happiness,[58] which is eternal glory,[59]

to which may we be led by him who with the Father and the Holy Spirit, et cetera.

---

58. Here Thomas just mentions the endpoint of his happiness, announced at the beginning of the *Sermo*.
59. It is perfect happiness: ST I 73,1.

APPENDIX

BEHIND THE NAMES

ST. AMBROSE (ca. 340–397): one of the four Western Doctors of the Church in Thomas's time. He was Bishop of Milan from 374 to 397, when the heresy of Arianism (the denial of the divinity of the Son) was rampant, although not really popular in Milan itself. He was known as an able administrator and an erudite theologian who was able to translate wisdom into practical advice in his writings and his sermons, as well as for his devout and very simple life style. The influence of his writings was and is enormous.

ST. ANSELM (1033–1109): Doctor of the Church since 1720 (Pope Clement VII). He was a Benedictine monk (1060) and abbot (1063) and became Archbishop of Canterbury in 1093. He did not have the authority of Augustine or Peter Lombard in Thomas's time, but he was an important precursor of scholastic theology. His so-called satisfaction theory and his proof of God's existence are revised by Thomas (cf. respectively ST I 2,1–3, and III 46,1–4).

ARISTOTLE (in these sermons referred to as "the Philosopher"): Aristotle's approach and ideas entered the Christian world in three phases. The initial entry was through Boethius, who translated two of his logical works (*On the Categories* and *On Interpretation*). In the 12th century other logical works, known through contact with Arab culture, were translated. These two groups of formal works were called the *logica vetus* ("the old logic") and the *logica nova* ("the new logic"). The question for Christian theologians and philosophers was whether Aristotle's *approach* could be used: a formal question. But in the 13th century, when the *content* of Aristotle's ideas became known, the problems were quite different, since the content of some of Aristotle's views concerning god and the world were incompatible with the Christian view of God and creation.

ARIUS: see Sermon 14, note 15.

ST. AUGUSTINE (354–430): one of the four Western Doctors of the Church in Thomas's time. For Thomas, Augustine was the highest authority after Scripture. He became the Bishop of Hippo in 396. As such he promoted religious life (by writing a rule and living according to it) and dedicated his life to building up the Church by preaching, writing letters, taking part in councils, and fighting all kinds of errors concerning the Catholic faith, such as Manichaeism (a syncretistic, dualistic religion), Donatism (which held that efficacy of the sacraments depended on the holiness of the minister: *ex opere operantis* instead of the Catholic *ex opere operato*), Pelagianism (which overreacted against the determinism of Manichaeism by promoting so much confidence in human ability that it denied the necessity of grace in order to live a Christian life), and Arianism (which denied the divinity of the Son).

ST. BASIL THE GREAT (ca. 329–379): one of the three Eastern Doctors of the Church in Thomas's time and one of "the three Cappadocians" (the other two are his brother St. Gregory of Nyssa and his friend St. Gregory Nazianzus). He lived as an ascetic monk and wrote, together with St. Gregory Nazianzus, two rules aimed at a life in union with God. In 370 he became the Bishop of Caesarea. He fought the Arians, and sought and found the support of the Pope. One of his great achievements is that he clearly described the terms "nature" and "person" *in divinis*.

ST. BERNARD OF CLAIRVAUX (1090–1153): Doctor of the Church since 1830 (Pope Pius VIII). As the founder-abbot of Clairvaux (1115) he became a leading figure in spiritual as well as political matters, not only within but also outside the Cistercian order and even outside the Church. He laid the foundations of the Order of the Knights Templar and took the initiative for the Second Crusade. He was involved in two controversies (the first about the Trinity) with Abelard, who advocated a rationalism in theology through which the Catholic faith would not be the norm. St. Bernard had a special devotion to the Blessed Virgin Mary and the Child Jesus. Thomas quotes him frequently in Sermon 02 (on Advent) and elaborately in his sermons on the Feast of the Birth of the Blessed Virgin and also in Sermon 09 in regard to the Trinity.

BOETHIUS, Anicius Manlius Severinus (ca. 480–524 or 525): a well-educated Roman statesman. He translated Aristotle's logical works *On the Categories* and *On Interpretation,* and thus prepared the way for scholastic theology. The two quotations from him in Thomas's sermons (19 and 20) have been drawn from his *On the Consolation of Philosophy,* his most famous work, which he wrote while he was imprisoned: in view of the instability of the favor of princes and the inconstancy of friends, he contemplated the value of wisdom and the nature of true happiness. It is remarkable that Christ is not mentioned in this work. It is not certain that Boethius was or became a Christian, yet in Thomas's time Boethius was regarded as a martyr in the Arian controversy.

ST. JOHN CHRYSOSTOM (347/349–407): generally considered the greatest of the three Eastern Doctors of the Church in Thomas's time. Thomas quotes him frequently. He led an ascetic life and became Bishop of Constantinople in 398. He disputed with Jews and all kinds of Christian heretics, but he also took action against abuses and wrongs within the Church, especially excessive luxury. By reason of his eloquence he has been called "golden-mouthed" since the 6th century. Already during the Council of Ephesus (431) Chrysostom was commonly looked upon as an authority.

ST. DIONYSIUS: see PSEUDO-DIONYSIUS.

POPE ST. GREGORY I, "the Great" (540–604): one of the four Western Doctors of the Church in Thomas's time. He was a Benedictine monk. In 590 he became Pope. Because of his teachings and the way in which he governed and organized the Church (clergy, episcopate, liturgy), he is regarded as the one who led the Catholic Church into the Middle Ages. Thomas cites him in ten of the sermons, usually concerning the moral life.

ST. HILARY OF POITIERS (d. 368): Doctor of the Church since 1851 (Pope Pius IX); Bishop of Poitiers since about 350. He was famous as a devout and erudite bishop and theologian who opposed Arianism (a popular and widespread heresy in the early Church that denied the divinity of the Son). After baptism St. Martin went to Poitiers to become a disciple of his. In 361 Hilary gave permission to Martin to live a solitary life. The legendary incident of Martin sharing his cloak with a beggar by cutting it in half took place before he met Hilary; according to the story, Martin was still a catechumen then.

IOVINIANUS: see JOVINIANUS.

ST. ISIDORE OF SEVILLE (ca. 560–636): Doctor of the Church since 1722 (Pope Innocent XIII). He was a source of inspiration in the Middle Ages because he had given the order to compile a *summa* of universal knowledge. Already in his time he promoted the study of Aristotle.

ST. JEROME (ca. 340/342–420): one of the four Western Doctors of the Church in Thomas's time. His commentaries on the Scriptures were quoted frequently in the Middle Ages; he was known as an ascetic and erudite hermit. He corrected the Latin version of the Psalms and of the New Testament (382–390), and he translated the Hebrew Scriptures into Latin (390–405). Jerome was involved in many conflicts with Arians, Pelagians, and others. He defended the life-long virginity of the Blessed Virgin Mary and promoted celibacy as a state of life preferable to marriage—issues at stake also in some of Thomas's sermons.

JOVINIANUS or IOVINIANUS: a monk of the 4th century, condemned as a heretic in 390 for his anti-ascetical preaching. Almost all we know about him comes to us through the writings of St. Jerome. Jovinianus held that married life is not inferior to virginity, that abstinence is not better than eating and drinking (with the right disposition), that someone baptized in the Spirit and with water cannot sin, that all sins are equal, that after this life there will be only one punishment and one reward, and that Mary did not remain a virgin after Christ's birth.

MANICHAEUS or MANI (ca. 216–ca. 277): The Persian prophet Mani taught that everything originated from two eternal principles: a good god and an evil god; light and darkness. His movement, Manichaeism, was able to become popular among Christians because he not only derived his ideas from Zoroaster and Buddhism among others, but also incorporated a version of Christian teachings on original sin and Christ (having only a virtual body) as the light. In the Middle Ages a form of these dualistic ideas appeared again among Albigenses (Cathari).

ST. MARTIN OF TOURS (ca. 316–ca. 397): after the Blessed Virgin Mary the most popular saint in the Middle Ages in France. There are many reasons for his popularity, as Sermon 21 shows. He, a pagan soldier, was converted to Christianity and eventually became a wise and devout bishop. He was zealous in converting pagans and in fighting heresies within Christianity (in particular, Arianism). Through the story according to which he cut his cloak in two and gave half to a semi-naked beggar, he became the example *par excellence* of Christian love (*caritas*). He is depicted as such in many churches and on many altars dedicated to him (and in churches and on altars dedicated to other saints as well). In medieval Italy, 143 villages were named after him; in France, more than 500. Also many miracles were ascribed to his intercession. (See also above: ST. HILARY OF POITIERS.)

ST. NICHOLAS (d. 345 or 352): Bishop of Myra. More legends than facts color his biography. Sailors spread his popularity throughout the centuries. Many miracles are ascribed to his intercession. His relics are preserved in the San Nicola church, Bari (Italy). Up to the present time oil flows from them; Thomas refers to this in Sermon 16. St. Nicholas, mentioned several times in Thomas's later theological writings, was a very popular saint in the Dominican order; in fact, the second priory, at Bologna, was attached to the church dedicated to San Nicolò delle Vigne.

ORIGEN (185–253/254): theologian of Alexandria, Egypt, who settled in Caesarea, Palestine, where he was ordained a priest. Although he was condemned posthumously by a synod in 403, he was still well respected in the Middle Ages. In Sermon 19 Thomas points out one of Origen's errors in view of a platonic theory. The controversies around Origen's teachings as well as teachings attributed to him are very complicated (e.g., on the allegorical interpretation of Scripture, subordination of the divine Persons, the eternity of creation), because his ideas were often used and abused in personal rivalries.

"THE PHILOSOPHER": see ARISTOTLE.

PSEUDO-DIONYSIUS (probably 5th or 6th century): The writings of this unknown author were very influential in the Middle Ages because he was identified as the Dionysius mentioned in Acts 17.34, who was converted on hearing Paul's speech at the Areopagus. In Paris he was even more popular, because some identified him in the 9th century as the Dionysius who came around 250 from Rome to (what is now called) France and became the first Bishop of Paris. His writings are influenced by Neo-Platonism (which includes an emphasis on the ecstatic union with God), and his Christology by Monophysitism (according to which there is only one nature, not two natures, in Christ).

POPE ST. SYMMACHUS (d. 514): became Pope in 498. He is reputed to be a defender of Christian orthodoxy during the Acacian or Laurentian schism (498–506). He built asylums for the poor near the three churches outside the city walls of Rome.

VIGILANTIUS, or VIGILANCIUS (d. ca. 400): a priest of Gaul (now France) whose ideas we know through St. Jerome's *Against Vigilantius*. He allegedly denied the efficacy of relics and of prayers to the saints and did not consider almsgiving, celibacy of the clergy (promoted since the 5th century by Pope Leo I and others, but only obligatory since the Second Lateran Council, in 1139), and the religious life to be virtuous.

INDICES

GENERAL INDEX

Abraham, 249n28, 269, 277n71, 288n38, 311–12
abundance, 61, 102, 127, 132, 181, 184, 211, 214, 220, 228, 250, 268, 272n57, 273, 299, 307
accountability, 94, 225–26
active and contemplative, 50, 246, 298. *See also* religious life
adultery, 115, 204
Agnes, St., 55
almsgiving, 55, 113, 133, 137, 207–8, 221n39, 229n72, 231–32
Andrew, St., 62n1, 78
angels, 25n6, 27, 29, 36–37, 41, 72–75, 85–86, 106, 109–10, 112, 133, 141, 169, 184, 196, 197n4, 199n13, 206, 216n12, 223–25, 237n21, 243, 245, 251, 261, 263, 280–81, 286, 287n30; of darkness, 248; defects in, 164–66; food of the, 53, 175–76
Anthony of Egypt, St., 311
Anthony of Padua, St., 276n67
apostles, 50–52, 110, 138–39, 149, 156–57, 160–62, 224n54, 245, 292, 310–11
Arianism, Arians, Arius, 68, 166, 199, 200n16, 330, 332
ascension, ascent, 33, 129, 155, 269, 313–26; improper, 261, 321. *See also* Gn 28.12 (Index of Holy Scripture)
Augustine, St., 97
Augustine's mother. *See* Monica, St.
attribution, 60, 164–66, 270n51
Aurora, 243n4, 249

Auster, 250
awe, 24n4, 39, 62, 233

Benedict, St, 117, 311
benefit of the doubt, 54
bishop, 72, 124, 136, 203, 238, 241, 322n44, 323–25
Blessed Virgin. *See* Mary
body, care of the, 90, 124–25, 172, 198, 220–21, 242, 292
brother, 74, 136, 149, 167. *See also* neighbor

called, being, 27, 181, 183–85, 189–94, 225, 315; to the religious life, 119, 122–24
celibacy, 266–67
chastity, 55, 96n33, 113n15, 125, 151–52, 248n23, 250, 260n6, 312, 318
Christ, the four comings of, 63–65, 66; the divinity of, 25–26, 39–41, 59, 62–63, 173, 215–16, 269; as doctor, 30, 91n16, 239, 272; as example, 87–88, 112, 117, 278; as friend, 30, 41, 68, 71, 217–18, 278; generation of, 25–26, 40; generosity of, 131–32, 171; grace of, 173; humanity of, 23–107, 171–73, 215–16, 269; image of God, 60, 62, 71–72; king, 27, 68–74, 193, 217–18, 231, 308; knowledge of, 40–41, 88–90, 166; lowliness of, 24, 56, 59; mercy of, 38; mission/sending of, 29, 42, 72, 114–15, 145–46, 161; the name of Jesus Christ, 46, 59;

Christ *(cont.)*
  necessity of his coming, 23–30, 46–57, 74, 145, 270; Passion of, 30, 64, 67n22, 75n61, 78, 115, 240, 272–80; poverty of, 107, 113, 288; power of, 40, 59–61, 68–69, 174; reconciliation brought by, 43, 45, 75, 279–80, 292; sanctification by, 37n9, 64, 74, 238, 279–80; Savior, 23–24, 30, 34, 39, 46–50, 80, 85, 120, 130, 133, 196, 219, 262n13, 270n50; teaching from the Cross, 278–79; unity of, 26, 36, 62, 66n16, 147; warrior, 38, 58, 276–77
Christian faith, 159
Church, 32, 97, 108, 113, 123, 177, 192, 210, 236, 251, 281–82, 295, 324; Militant, 32, 251, 298n8, 321n38
conscience, 48, 84, 95, 106, 124, 154, 230
consolation, 36, 203, 250–51, 276, 306, 311
contemplation, 35–36, 50, 61, 99–100, 102, 113, 120, 243–46, 257, 291, 293, 306
contemplative life, 50, 120n46, 246, 298, 312n73
courage, 50–51
covenant, 122–23, 227
creation, 62, 71–72, 103, 109n3, 119n36, 138, 140–41, 148, 168–69, 178–79, 233, 283n10
Cross, exaltation of the, 274
crucifix, 216
custom, 97, 206–7, 267

David, the image of Christ, 27, 32, 46, 57–59, 118n35
desire, of Christ's coming, 23, 30–31, 34; fulfilled by God alone, 48–49, 74–75, 143, 146, 184, 220, 249, 273, 284–85, 288, 290, 293, 298–99; to be saved, 31, 56
desires, earthly, 82–84, 96, 101, 111, 125–26, 136, 151–52, 172, 186–89, 195–96, 302
despair, 93–94, 222n44, 278n78
devil, 30, 37, 38, 45, 49, 58n46, 67n22, 92, 187, 193, 201, 229, 309. *See also* Satan
devotion, 48–49, 81, 105–6, 137, 154n76, 180, 206n43, 219, 236, 238, 240, 279, 295, 319, 324
distinction, between the divine Persons, 60, 169–70; between people, 53, 80–84, 96–97, 185; between pride and cupidity and lustfulness, 189; between the saints, 309
dogma, 178, 322

enlightenment, 43, 45, 143, 196n4, 248–49, 257, 317
example, the good, 53–54, 55, 57, 86, 87, 104, 112–13, 117, 122, 202, 211n63, 243n5, 260n6, 261n8, 278, 296

faith, 23, 27, 52, 54n34, 75, 122, 126, 135, 140, 159, 177, 188, 202–3, 251, 253, 278, 317; faith, hope, and love, 317–18
fasting, 96–97
fear, 48, 84, 94, 116, 137, 144, 177, 250, 252, 276, 284, 299, 307, 309, 316, 319
figures, in the Old Testament, 58n45, 131–32, 155n82, 174n14, 192, 198n11, 243–45, 247, 277
Filioque, 147n48, 161
foolishness, 84, 104, 118, 166, 273–74
Francis, St., 224, 240
freedom, 23, 64, 67, 75, 147, 157, 169, 200, 225, 227, 266, 310
friendship, 30, 32n39, 41, 68, 71, 98, 101, 132, 150–51, 175, 179, 185, 217–18, 278, 305n47

God, anger of, 76–77, 189; as doctor, 23, 47, 220–21, 260, 264–65, 272;

GENERAL INDEX

freedom of, 23, 118, 140, 149; generosity of, 32, 133, 221–23; happiness of, 281, 314; help of, 37, 63n6, 136, 157n92, 240–41, 271, 313–20; immutability of, 60n54, 119n36, 146–47, 164–65, 284; justice of, 28–29, 39, 228–29, 286; knowledge of, 40–41, 145–46; mercy of, 29–30, 39, 41, 49, 94, 132, 137, 220–22, 237, 316; power of, 169–70, 174, 179, 222, 225, 240–41; recognized in creation, 170 (*see also* Rom 1.20, Index of Holy Scripture); special love of, 49, 72–73, 140–41, 217–19; Triune, 25, 68, 109, 126, 159–70 (*see also* distinction); wisdom of, 79–80, 102, 111, 178, 219, 222, 272, 290, 299; word of, 66, 104, 110–14, 160, 166, 170, 269 (*see also* Jn 1.14, Index of Holy Scripture)

good works, 76, 92–93, 97–98, 109, 149–50, 205, 239–40, 280, 304, 323n46

grace, 26, 32–33, 36–37, 45, 76, 94–99, 119, 164, 177, 181, 214, 228–29, 242, 259, 315–16. See also Holy Spirit

grace, full of, 37, 89, 173, 249, 261, 267

grace, justifying, 64, 154, 233

Hail Mary, 129, 249
happiness, 33, 78, 100, 106, 123, 159n2, 164, 176, 178, 181–82, 221n40, 245n11, 248n25, 268n47, 281–94, 295–312, 313–26. See also Mt 5.1–12, Jn 20.29 (Index of Holy Scripture)
heaven, 81–82
heavenly bodies, 27, 72, 164, 244
heavenly homeland, 32, 42, 60–61, 106, 224, 296–312
heretics, 52, 56n39, 113, 147, 192–93, 323, 331. See also Arius, Jovinian, Mani, Vigilantius

highly placed people, 105–7, 187, 192, 255, 298, 301, 316. See also prelates
holiness, 82, 140, 163–68, 205, 269, 318, 323
Holy Spirit, 138–58; effects of the, 37, 45, 94, 139, 148–156, 162, 243, 317n20; freedom of the, 147, 162; gifts of the, 32n36, 33, 37, 45, 113n17, 156, 187, 225n56, 250; inspiration of the, 121, 144, 156, 179, 184n54, 201, 316–17; is love, 143, 268; mission/sending of the, 33, 37, 147–48, 151; sanctification by the, 143–44, 161, 238, 260, 265; sin against the, 113, 256n59
hope, holy, 250
hospitality, 24, 39, 77, 175, 311–12
human, being (interior, exterior), 54, 155, 206, 208, 210, 247, 252–57; constancy, immutability, 45, 83, 98, 153, 156–58, 164, 234, 261, 285–86; knowledge, 28, 38, 45, 53, 74–75, 79–80, 145–46, 151, 165–66, 173, 178–79, 190, 227, 253, 282–83, 323; power, 28, 51, 68–69, 165, 225, 269, 289n45; privilege, 74, 168–69, 185, 216–19, 222, 225, 227, 286; thinking, 63, 91, 152, 201–2, 215, 227–28, 254n53, 282, 284–86, 302
humanity, 218–19
humility, 42, 56–57, 59, 91, 106, 187, 211–12, 260–62, 278, 288, 324, 325
hypocrisy, 97, 136, 205–13

idolatry, 156, 188, 201
ignorance, 74, 95, 113, 152, 157, 169n61, 195, 202n25, 248, 253n46, 264n28, 285
image, rational creatures as God's, 71–72, 168–69, 216–17, 223, 309n64
Incarnation, 33, 36, 47, 62–64, 66, 69n32, 90, 147, 172, 215–16

inferiority, feeling of, 114
iniquity, 31, 135, 200, 228, 231
intention, 153, 157, 189, 191, 203–4, 206–7, 208n54, 252, 286
irony, 291n53

Jews, 27, 51n21, 69, 122, 149, 192, 199, 247, 286, 309
John the Baptist, St., 67, 117, 266
joy, 34–39, 43, 108–9, 120, 129, 137, 177–78, 182, 211, 239, 247–49, 252, 256, 268, 275, 286–87, 294, 306–9, 311
judge, 28, 42, 65, 69, 73, 101, 311
judgment, 28, 40, 66, 69, 80, 94, 98n38, 102, 125, 178, 223, 225
justice, and mercy, 29–30, 38, 207, 219, 229n70, 290–91; as a virtue, 51–52, 108, 110, 154, 183, 207–8, 257–58, 309. *See also* uprightness

king, 27, 35, 50, 56, 58, 68–74, 131–32, 217–18, 274, 290–91, 308, 309–10, 314, 319–20
knowledge, 38, 40, 53, 74, 79–80, 88, 100n44, 103, 105, 111–12, 131, 145–46, 165–68, 173, 190, 219, 227, 230, 234, 252–53, 273, 283, 299, 302–4, 311n71, 323

Last Judgment. *See* judgment
Law, Old and New, 69n30, 119, 122, 159, 277
life, everlasting/eternal, 39, 73, 76, 93, 113, 123, 133–34, 136–37, 165, 178, 268, 280, 294, 297; of grace, 76, 149–56
listening, 84, 92, 100–101, 105, 135, 205, 317
living together, 105, 279
Lord's Prayer, the. *See* Our Father
love, 26, 28, 32, 41, 50, 52, 57, 72–73, 76n64, 81, 94, 110, 125, 131, 141–45, 149–53, 160n6, 167–68, 170, 177, 183, 186, 190, 211, 225, 250, 253, 257, 266, 268, 278, 284, 286, 294, 305, 307, 316, 318. *See also* Gal 5.22 (Index of Holy Scripture)

magister, 52, 101–2, 116, 199, 203, 255, 277, 317
mammon, 231
man. *See* human, humanity
manager, 222–25, 228
Mani, Manichaeans, 118
marriage, 53, 55, 127, 128n69, 205, 219, 286
Mary, as an example, 104, 211n63, 260n6, 261n8; help of, 230, 265; Maris Stella, 247n20, 249; mercy of, 249–50; prefigured in Old Testament, 243–45; sanctification of, 243, 249, 260; virginity of, 243–44, 260, 266–68, 319; without sin and ignorance, 247, 249, 268
meditation, 35, 104–5
mercy, 29–30, 38, 41, 49, 81, 94, 132, 136–37, 154, 207, 219–21, 237–41, 250, 291, 307, 311, 313, 316, 324
mildness, 58–59, 76–78, 218, 249, 289, 292, 305
miracles, 33, 193, 198–99, 233, 241, 319
Monica, St., 97
Muslims, 286
mystery, 50n15, 62n4, 145n37, 160–63, 182n46, 200n16, 214, 259n3

natural, 141, 145, 159, 165, 172, 218, 225, 262, 267, 285
negative theology, 163
neighbor, 98, 106, 112n11, 136–37, 153, 157, 211, 219, 247, 255, 257. *See also* brother

obedience, 48n9, 98, 106–7, 157, 263–64, 272, 278, 324
old age, 93, 117, 121, 193, 202–3, 236
open-heartedness, 100, 105
Our Father, 129

GENERAL INDEX

peace, 28–29, 42, 45, 62, 75, 94–98, 105, 110, 112, 148, 152–53, 167, 292, 304. *See also* Gal 5.22 (Index of Holy Scripture)
peace, sign of, 65–66
people, a, 308
perfection, 24–26, 35, 40, 53, 55, 57, 59, 60, 77, 81, 86, 89, 98, 116–17, 123, 126–28, 132, 139, 150, 163, 222, 238, 242, 251n38, 252–53, 263, 283, 285–90, 299, 301, 303–4, 316n18; of Christ, 72, 91, 117; of God, 119n36, 163n22, 219, 242
perseverance, 83n26, 97, 100, 118–19, 152n65, 153n72, 158, 207, 210
philosophers, 15, 81n7, 178–79, 188n72, 202–3, 291–92, 310, 317
philosophy, 15, 146n38, 179, 202–3, 310
Plato, platonic, 202, 284
poor, the, 50, 53–54, 130–31, 137, 183, 190, 193, 219, 229, 237, 312
power, as a gift of God, 51, 241
Praesentia realis, 177n25
praise, 35–39, 46, 49, 175, 183, 196, 255, 296, 307. *See also* Ps 84.5 (Index of Holy Scripture)
prayer, 31, 109, 120, 129–37, 192, 206–7, 210, 233, 236, 238, 243, 289
preachers, preaching, 35, 50, 53, 114–16, 120–22, 126n58, 185, 192, 199, 203, 223, 255
predestination, 93n20, 123, 184n54, 191, 315
prelates, 185, 323. *See also* highly placed people
pride, 29, 56, 59, 94, 106, 111, 186–87, 189, 211n65, 215, 222, 227, 254, 260–62, 302
prodigal, 226, 229
prophets, 40, 118, 156n85, 160, 197–99, 226, 239, 311; false prophets, 95, 195–213
providence, 32, 73, 168, 222n45, 224, 260

prudence, 44n2, 55, 57, 103–5, 257, 290, 325

re-creation, 138, 149–56
reincarnation, 284–86
religious life, 52–55, 93n25, 105–7, 116, 123–24, 185, 260n6, 322, 324. *See also* active and contemplative, vows
revelation, 146, 151, 159–62, 179n36, 197–99, 202n27, 214, 237
riches, 131–32, 183, 214, 219–22, 227–32, 236, 270, 288–89, 293, 299, 305, 310, 318
rich people, 53–55, 113, 131, 137, 190, 196, 219–22, 226, 228, 230, 261

Sacrament, of Baptism, 126n60, 154, 193, 206, 320–21; of the Eucharist, 108, 174–78, 181, 323; of Ordination, 238–40, 321–23; of the Unction, 239
sacraments, 322
saints, 57, 59, 61, 65, 93, 114, 154, 183, 224, 230, 232, 233–312; their knowledge of God, 303–7
salvation, 31, 47, 59–61, 73, 80, 88, 126, 130, 133, 143, 172, 223–24, 262n13, 270, 287, 296, 322–23; our need of, 47–57
Satan, 196, 229. *See also* devil
selfishness, 166–67, 187–88, 215, 226–28, 238, 290, 319–20
sharing, 103, 167, 192, 218, 228, 249, 281
sin, 23, 30, 38, 47, 49, 51, 72, 75, 83–84, 98, 110, 122, 124, 154, 189–90, 192, 195, 229, 250, 252, 262, 271, 279–80, 315, 321; against the Holy Spirit, 113, 256n59; mortal, 47, 131, 265; original, 23, 126, 154n73, 315, 321. *See also* Holy Spirit, Mary
slave, of the devil, 31, 38, 49, 92, 187–88; of idols, 188; of sin, 38, 75, 235

solidarity, 143n25. *See also* sharing
spiritual, goods, 73, 128, 221, 225; pleasures, 171
stewardship, 56, 214–32
stigmata, 240
Stoics, 302
study, 101, 107, 202–3, 239

tepidity, 34, 39
Testament, Old and New, 57, 174, 192, 243,
thanks, thanksgiving, 35, 39, 120, 187, 258
theft, thief, 52, 209, 226, 231
truth, 29, 44, 59–60, 74–75, 77, 88–90, 101, 110, 114, 138, 151, 172–73, 178–80, 192, 201–2, 252–53, 255, 285, 291

unbelief, 123, 256
unbelievers, 95, 191–92, 193, 198n9
union with God, 25, 26, 36, 144, 148, 167, 177, 183, 281, 305
unnatural, 262
uprightness, 157, 246–58

vainglory, 208, 255
virginity, 53, 55, 113, 127, 266–68, 310, 312
virtue, 54, 83–84, 89, 112–13, 131, 177, 190–91, 221, 227, 235, 250, 262–63, 273, 283, 287, 292, 302, 310, 314, 323
vocation, 123, 181, 183–94, 266n39, 315–17
vows, 113n15, 200–201, 263, 267n43. *See also* religious life

warfare, 128, 251n38, 289, 298
wealth. *See* riches
wisdom, of Christ, 79–81, 89–90, 99–105, 111–12, 173, 178; divine, 32, 111, 151–52, 155, 185, 272, 290; human, 44, 107, 111, 302, 316
woman, 104, 202–3, 234–35, 247, 262, 264, 309n64

youth, 92–93, 107, 116–19, 235, 263

Zacchaeus, 54

INDEX OF HOLY SCRIPTURE

Old Testament

Genesis (Gn)
1.1: 169
1.2: 62n2, 71, 82, 141, 169
1.3: 170, 245, 249
1.4: 249
1.10: 83
1.11: 111, 112, 113, 259–80
1.26: 62n2, 216, 223
1.28: 216, 225n54
1.31: 170
2.7: 156
2.17: 29, 273
2.18: 218
3: 111n9, 264n30
3.5: 273
3.6: 272, 273, 274
3.8: 249
3.17–18: 125
3.22: 275
3.23–24: 275
5.24: 155n81
6–8: 275
7.4–8: 139n6
9.13: 65
12.1: 116
12.3: 269
15.1: 169
18.3: 312
24.34–35: 288n38
26.12: 127
26.13: 318
26.13–14: 288n38

28.12: 85, 106, 280
32.2–3: 86n6
32.6: 288n38
32.27: 243, 249
35.3: 322
41.2–7: 197

Exodus (Ex)
1.8–22: 276
3.14: 40
4.13: 29
7–12: 276
7.1: 223, 292
13.21: 248
14.21: 276
15.1–2: 38
15.2: 47
15.23–24: 275
19.4: 318
21.24: 27n19
21.33–34: 202
23.2: 97
23.20: 193
24.1–2: 321
25.6: 238
28.41: 239
30.31–32: 238
33.19: 60, 220n33, 300
33.20–23: 300
35.9: 238
35.28: 238
40.9: 238

Leviticus (Lv)
19.12: 128
24.20: 27n19
25.36–37: 136

Numbers (Nm)
12.6: 198
15.30: 29
20.6 (Vg): 214
24.17: 244, 276

Deuteronomy (Dt)
4.6: 317
4.7: 177
5.5: 43
10.9: 304
17.12: 29n26
17.15: 73
19.21: 27n19
21.23: 273
32.7: 102
32.13: 240
33.13–15: 277
33.24: 240

Joshua (Jos)
5.14: 30, 42

Judges (Jgs)
5.20: 309
8.23: 52
17.6: 27
19.4: 42

345

1 Samuel (1 Sm)
    1.18: 157
    1.19: 157
    2.1: 61
    2.1–10: 157
    4.7: 276
    8.20: 28
    13.14: 58
    15.22: 264
    16: 58
    16.12: 236
    17.34–36: 236
    17.45: 119
    26.7–8: 119
    29.10: 115
    31.9–10: 119

2 Samuel (2 Sm)
    3.12–13: 218
    22.36: 78
    23.7: 274

1 Kings (1 Kgs)
    2.36–37: 98
    4.20: 308
    5.25: 238
    8.11: 33
    8.12: 265
    10.8: 300
    10.22: 254n54
    18.12: 144n32
    18.21: 191, 256
    19.5: 110
    19.7–8: 110
    19.8: 178
    19.12: 249
    22.30: 25

2 Kings (2 Kgs)
    2: 155n81
    5.8: 198
    5.10: 231
    6.8–10: 196
    6.16: 309
    13.21: 198

1 Chronicles (1 Chr)
    17.1: 32
    29.1: 32
    29.14: 227

2 Chronicles (2 Chr)
    2.4: 32
    2.9: 238
    6.4: 33
    6.41: 239n30
    13.11: 84n30
    35.15: 198

Nehemiah (Neh)
    4.10: 191
    8.5: 258
    8.6: 258
    8.8: 258
    8.12: 258

Tobit (Tb)
    3.12: 157
    3.22 (Vg): 289
    4.7: 157
    6.7 (Vg): 260n5
    13.17: 318
    13.18: 305

Judith (Jdt)
    8.17: 57
    9.12: 71
    16.14: 148

Esther (Est)
    1.7: 185
    2.15 (Vg): 251
    5.3: 132
    6.6–11: 56n42
    8.16: 247, 248
    13.9 (Vg): 69, 142

2 Maccabees (2 Mc)
    1.11: 38
    1.24: 29

Job (Jb)
    1.1: 252
    1.6: 109n4
    1.21: 230
    4.18: 164
    4.19: 232
    5.3: 273
    5.9: 62
    5.17: 315
    7.1: 297
    7.9: 66n15
    8.8: 102
    8.11: 31
    9.11: 63, 67
    11.6: 143
    11.12: 215
    11.15: 157
    12.7: 103
    12.11: 101
    14.1: 283
    14.2: 284
    14.14: 169
    14.15: 184
    15.2: 104
    15.11: 36n4
    15.15: 164
    15.27: 157
    17.3: 177
    20.6: 261
    21.12: 289
    21.15: 215, 227
    22.18: 227
    22.21: 280
    22.26: 182, 305
    22.29 (Vg): 305
    23.16: 263
    23.17: 157
    24.5: 215n5
    24.23: 94
    25.3: 169
    27.6: 97
    29.2–10:
    29.11: 290, 320
    29.14–16: 207
    29.20: 154

INDEX OF HOLY SCRIPTURE 347

30.2: 191
31.12: 266
31.31: 175
32.8: 155–56
32.22 (Vg): 66
35.5: 82n18
35.15: 76
36.12: 84
36.25: 303
37.5: 233
37.15: 66n15
38.7: 308n58
38.33: 82n15
38.37: 82
39.5: 215n5
39.21: 50–51
41.26: 111

Psalms (Ps)
1.1: 316
1.3: 114n20
2.7: 25n9
2.8: 70
4.3: 124
4.4: 241
4.7: 71
5.4: 116
5.12: 43
6.3: 264
6.5: 120n45
7.5: 58
7.10: 233, 241
8.6: 36
8.6–9: 216
8.7: 226
8.7–9: 287
8.8: 223
9.7: 320
9.21: 28
10.7 (Vg): 140
10.8: 196
11.5: 48
12.5: 227
15: 254
16.5: 304

16.6: 304
16.11: 182, 218, 286, 299
17.15: 293
19.7: 81n12
19.15: 104
21.7: 247
22.4: 166
22.27: 183
23.2–3: 171
23.4: 276
23.5: 177
24.1: 221
24.7: 50
24.9: 50
25.21: 257
27.4: 99, 123, 143, 218, 293
28.7: 271
31.20: 183
32.1: 316
32.9: 193
33.2: 120
33.11: 119
33.12: 295–312
33.16: 56
34.6: 220
34.19: 56
35.13: 57
35.28: 40
36.7: 59, 287
36.7–8: 73
36.8: 287
36.9: 61, 293
36.10: 142
37.17: 274
37.35: 260
39.6: 318
40.5: 317
40.9: 183
42.2: 31, 325
42.4: 325
42.6: 167n48
43.3: 271
43.4: 183

44.25: 83
45.5: 77, 81
45.7: 277
45.8: 239
45.11: 99
45.12: 268
45.17: 161
46.6: 265
47.8: 69
49.7: 221
49.11: 224
49.18: 230
50.8–13: 141n11
50.16: 116
51.12: 156
52.10: 49
55.22: 238
58.9: 304
60.5: 239n29
63.2: 36
63.6: 220n34, 236
63.9: 220
65.5: 271, 293, 318
65.9: 276
65.10: 270
65.11: 270
66.12: 84
66.18: 135
68.11: 160n4
68.36: 233
69.5: 30, 38, 272
69.11: 208
73.1: 253
73.20: 72
73.28: 107, 123, 143, 145
75.3: 40
76.5: 278
76.12: 200, 203
77.7: 105
77.8–9: 29
78.24: 175
79.2: 291
80.3: 31
80.4: 60

INDEX OF HOLY SCRIPTURE

Psalms (Ps) *(cont.)*
80.8: 60
80.20: 60
82.6: 173n7
83.6–7 (Vg): 313–26
83.8 (Vg): 314
84.5: 281–94
84.12: 66n14, 181, 242
85.6: 29
85.11: 29
87.5: 270
88.16: 107
89.9: 165
89.10 (Vg): 77
89.21: 58
89.21–22: 233–41
89.42: 125
89.48: 223
90.6: 263
94.12: 317
96.1: 155n83
97.11: 242–58
98.1: 155n83
99.3: 164
100.3: 223
102.27: 141
102.28: 165
103.5: 220n34, 300
103.20–21: 206
104.14: 216
104.15: 108, 178, 239
104.24: 222
104.28: 167
104.30: 138–58
106.1: 120
107.25: 140
107.30: 60
109.3 (Vg): 112
112.3: 33, 221, 293, 305
113.4: 88
115.3: 140
117.2: 88
118.8–9: 221

119.1–2: 319n30
119.7 (Vg): 58
119.32: 154, 298
119.37: 254n53
119.90: 88
119.99: 104
119.103: 180
119.130: 239
119.155: 47
119.160: 88
122.1: 37
122.3: 97
122.6–8: 48
122.7: 95
125.4: 253
130.6: 35, 247n20
131.1: 59
131.2: 52
132.1: 59
132.9: 239
132.11: 300n18
133.1: 67, 177
137.2 (Vg): 319
138.17 (Vg): 299
139.14: 62
139.16: 283
141.2: 324
143.10–11: 142, 144
143.13–15a (Vg)
143.13–14 (Vg): 301
144.1: 58
144.5: 31
144.7: 241
144.15: 288
144.15b: 302
145: 227
145.9: 49, 219, 237
145.18–19: 49
146.3: 56, 302
146.3–4: 221
146.4: 139
147: 227
147.4: 308
148.3: 27
149.1: 155n83

Proverbs (Prv)
1.5: 100
1.24: 185
1.33: 299, 307
2.4: 102, 234
2.9: 68
2.16: 262
3.5: 57
3.11–12: 168n59
3.12: 316
3.15: 101, 182n48
3.16: 127
3.18: 275
3.34: 289
4.18: 248
4.19: 192
4.20–27: 254
4.25: 254
5.9: 229
5.9–10: 92
6.16–19: 254
6.23: 45, 239
8.6: 179
8.8: 112
8.15: 290
8.21: 220
8.31: 73, 217, 236
8.32: 319n30
8.34: 100
9.1: 32n35, 270
9.1–6: 84
9.2: 178
9.5–6: 178
10.16: 212
10.20: 187n69
10.24: 298
11.16: 251
11.26: 227
12.12: 108
13.9: 108, 248
13.12: 30
13.25: 290
14.13: 284, 307
14.16: 84, 250, 252
14.28: 308
14.34: 131, 190

INDEX OF HOLY SCRIPTURE

15.6 (Vg): 212
15.28: 252
18.4: 299
18.10: 59
18.20: 211
19.6: 288
19.12: 76
20.3: 104
21.29: 257
22.6: 93, 117, 236
22.21: 103
23.23: 229n71
25.3: 270
25.4: 143
25.27 (Vg): 226
26.4: 104
26.5: 104
28.9: 137
28.15: 219, 290
28.25: 152
28.42: 323
29.4: 70
29.5: 122
29.18: 196, 319n30
29.21: 96
31.10: 234
31.10–31: 209n58, 264n30
31.15: 179
31.21: 205
31.25: 209

Ecclesiastes (Eccl)
1.4: 83
1.13: 102
1.16: 99
2.2: 274
5.4: 201
5.9: 302
6.12: 301
7.13: 315
7.26: 235, 264
9.8: 239
9.10: 230
10.19: 288
11.6: 121

11.9: 28n22, 94, 118, 225
11.10: (Vg): 118, 235
12.1: 118

Song of Songs (Song)
1.4: 257
1.8 (Vg): 114
1.14: 106
2.5 (Vg): 101
2.8: 39
2.10: 121
2.10b–13: 106
2.16: 120
3.6: 323
3.9: 277
3.11: 36
4.2: 320
4.7: 268
4.12–16: 250
4.13: 279
4.16: 278
5.1: 41n29, 181
5.15: 31
6.2: 106
6.11: 278
7.11: 120, 121
7.14: 277

Wisdom (Wis)
1.4: 292
1.5 (Vg): 120
1.7: 166
1.14: 149
2.22: 284
2.23: 62n2, 153
3.6: 238
3.15: 280
5.4–5: 114
5.5: 322
5.6: 114
7.8: 80, 101
7.9: 182n48
7.10: 251
7.11: 220
7.13: 103, 228

7.14: 218, 220
7.22: 142, 143
7.23: 143, 145
7.24–27: 143
7.27: 146, 147
7.29: 251
8.16: 218
8.18: 218
8.21: 267
9.10: 147
9.17: 138, 146
11.1: 204n35
11.22: 308
11.24: 141
11.25: 26n14, 167
12.1 (Vg): 168
12.13: 73
12.18: 73
14.3: 222n45
14.4: 222
14.7: 272
14.22: 95, 152
16.12: 264
16.20: 176
17.3: 44

Sirach (Sir)
1.5 (Vg): 80, 111, 219n30, 299
1.9: 102
1.14: 94
1.21: 250
1.27: 316
3.1 (Vg): 324
3.18: 324
3.19: 77
3.25: 179
3.27: 125, 263
4.8: 30
5.7: 115
5.12: 103
6.18–37: 187n68
6.33: 100
6.34: 100
7.15–17: 212n68
10.12: 261n7

INDEX OF HOLY SCRIPTURE

Sirach (Sir) *(cont.)*
10.15: 111n9, 261n7, 262
10.31 (Vg): 193
11.29: 196
12.4: 229
14.14: 92
14.20: 291
15.3: 181
15.5: 101
15.10 (Vg): 38
15.14: 225
18.30–31: 118
20.14: 132
21.1: 115
24.3: 40
24.4: 81
24.5 (Vg): 40, 81
24.11: 95
24.17: 106
24.18: 250
24.19–20: 249
24.21: 293
24.25 (Vg): 265
24.33: 198
25.8: 300
26.19: 84
26.28: 84, 97
27.9: 49
28.3: 136
28.25: 255
29.26: 84, 174
31.10: 238
31.28 (Vg): 237
32.1: 97, 324
36.6: 155
38.4: 260
40.16: 266
40.22: 267
43.1: 82
43.3: 270
43.22: 265
43.29: 38
44.1: 296
44.8: 237
44.10: 237
45.2: 319
47.2: 236
48.14: 198
48.23 (Vg): 204
50.5–11: 206n44
50.8: 106
50.11: 206, 323
51.11–12: 38
51.13–31: 93n21
51.17: 227

Isaiah (Is)
1.5: 317
1.6: 30, 51, 238
1.9: 270
1.11–20: 264
1.15: 135
1.19: 122, 159
2.3: 322n41
2.4: 306
3.8: 227
3.12: 283
6.2–3: 159–70
6.7: 160n7
6.13: 269
7.14: 268
8.11: 241
9.2: 248
9.3: 37
9.5: 89
10.1–13: 211n65
10.12: 211
11.1: 244
12.3: 240
12.3–4: 120
12.6: 43
14.3: 31
15.6: 268
16.1 (Vg): 29, 34
17.10: 110
19.4: 300
21.8: 35
21.10: 197
22.2: 308
22.12: 188
22.13: 188
24.4: 164
24.5: 227
25.4: 140
25.6: 179
25.9: 39
26.8: 31
26.9: 31
26.12: 59, 316
27.5: 96
27.6: 121
27.6 (Vg): 156
27.9: 279
28.5: 298n11
28.19: 193
29.13: 136
30.10: 200
30.27: 76
32.17: 48
32.20: 114
33.5: 33
33.7: 291
33.8: 192
33.15: 254n53
33.22: 28, 69
35.1: 36
35.2: 37
35.4: 58, 67
35.6: 138, 191
35.10: 37, 294, 307
40.3: 85
40.6: 273
40.15–17: 308
40.20: 276
40.31: 154
41.2: 315
42.2: 77
42.8: 52
43.19: 25, 39
44.23: 39
45.7: 40
45.14: 83
45.15: 46
45.17: 60
48.17: 180
48.22: 95
49.4: 94

INDEX OF HOLY SCRIPTURE 351

49.24: 49
50.4–5: 116
51.7: 116
51.23: 124
52.6: 40, 67
52.7: 35
53.2: 31
53.4: 30
53.7: 77, 78
53.8: 259
53.9: 275
55.8: 201
55.10: 270
56.7: 32n37
57.19: 157
58.7: 174
58.14: 300
59.2: 315
59.9: 42
59.19: 144
60.1: 48
60.18: 48
61.1: 239
61.3: 239
61.8: 231
61.11: 38
62.4: 37
62.11: 26, 36
63.1: 38, 40
63.13–14: 154
63.15: 72
63.19: 31, 34, 290
64.3: 145, 184
64.4: 299
65.13: 181
65.16: 306
65.17: 156
65.20: 94

Jeremiah (Jer)
2.8: 201
2.21: 109
4.3: 125
4.23: 270
5.5: 186
6.14: 95
6.16: 97
9.3: 98
9.23–24: 302
11.19: 78
12.4: 266
15.18: 31
16.13: 92
17.8: 268
17.9: 172
23.5: 57, 67, 290
23.11: 204
23.15: 197
23.16: 201
23.24: 63
23.28: 199
25.15–38: 239n29
29.23: 28
31.3: 167
31.20: 29
31.22: 26, 34, 89
31.33: 28, 227n61
31.34: 303
44.21: 272n59
51.45–46: 262

Lamentations (Lam)
1.22: 289
2.14: 200
2.16: 67
3.19: 176
3.24: 145
3.27: 93, 117, 235
3.42: 135
4.1: 190
4.21: 36

Baruch (Bar)
3.11: 94
3.24: 33
3.38: 42, 90, 217
4.22: 31n29
5.4: 48

Ezekiel (Ezek)
1.12: 142
1.25: 166
2.2: 153
3.14: 241
5.5: 36
10.3: 33
13.3: 201
13.5: 323
13.19: 204
16.15: 188
17.24: 274
22.27: 209
23.41: 84n30
28.12: 169
28.17: 186
33.31–32: 124
37.5: 144
37.22: 27, 68
37.23–24: 27
43.4: 33
43.5: 33
47.12: 114, 279

Daniel (Dn)
2.31: 197
2.35: 26n11
2.45: 26n11
4.1–24: 260
4.24: 231
7.10: 109n4, 308
7.13: 39
7.27: 308, 310
10.1: 197, 199
12.3: 81n12, 165, 278n74
14.33: 179

Hosea (Hos)
1.7: 59
2.8: 187
3.4: 27n18
4.7: 274
8.3: 31
8.5–6: 194
9.10: 235, 277
11.8: 29
12.5: 236, 243

Hosea (Hos) *(cont.)*
  14.4: 60n50
  14.9: 237

Joel (Jl)
  1.17: 228

Amos (Am)
  2.9: 261
  3.7: 197
  8.5–6: 227

Obadiah (Ob)
  17: 50
  21: 323

Jonah (Jon)
  3.8: 59

Micah (Mi)
  5.1: 32
  7.1: 235
  7.2: 191
  7.6: 98
  7.7: 31
  7.17: 31

Habakkuk (Hab)
  2.3: 66
  3.18: 27

Zephaniah (Zep)
  3.3: 210

Haggai (Hg)
  2.7: 23–33
  2.9: 33

Zechariah (Zec)
  2.10: 43n35
  2.14: 34–43
  4.9: 32
  4.14: 239
  5.4: 66
  9.9: 27, 35, 36, 39, 50, 63, 66, 67
  9.11: 58
  12.10: 32
  13.4: 208

Malachi (Mal)
  2.3: 63
  2.15: 111
  3.1: 39, 85
  3.20: 243n4

New Testament

Matthew (Mt)
  1.1–17: 269
  1.21: 46
  2.1–8, 16: 192
  2.1–11: 193n96
  2.3: 167n48
  2.6: 32n34
  2.11: 27, 324
  2.16: 167n48
  3.2: 28, 295
  3.10: 109
  3.16: 146n40, 321
  3.17: 58n47
  4.11: 86
  4.16: 243n4
  5.1–2: 322
  5.3: 132, 183, 288, 292, 310, 311n67
  5.4: 188, 289, 311
  5.5: 78, 289, 292, 305, 311
  5.6: 183, 290, 306, 311
  5.7: 291, 307, 312

  5.8: 216n15, 292, 312
  5.9: 292, 304, 312
  5.10: 292
  5.12: 297
  5.14: 245
  5.15–16: 228
  5.16: 109, 237, 255
  5.17: 69n30
  5.21–22: 69n30
  5.21–48: 126n63, 206n49
  5.24: 153n71
  5.34: 128
  5.38: 27n19
  5.48: 304
  6.1: 208, 238
  6.1–4: 97
  6.4: 206
  6.12: 136n16, 137
  6.14: 136, 291
  6.16: 97, 208
  6.17: 156
  6.18: 97

  6.19–20: 220n39
  6.22: 257
  6.33: 221
  7.6: 229
  7.14: 248
  7.15–16: 195–213
  7.16: 210
  7.16–18: 269n48
  7.17: 269
  7.21: 230n77
  8.7: 30, 41
  8.11: 312
  9.11: 78
  9.22: 47
  9.32–33: 138
  10.8: 51
  10.26: 230
  11.10: 85–86
  11.19: 54n34
  11.25: 151
  11.28: 151
  11.28–30: 92n18
  11.29: 56, 59, 77
  11.30: 119

INDEX OF HOLY SCRIPTURE 353

12.30: 210
12.31: 113n17
12.34: 211
12.39: 193
13.8: 127
13.10–11: 178n34
13.23: 114
13.25–30: 110
13.32: 269
13.43: 278n74
13.44: 220, 235
13.47: 124
16.4: 193
16.19: 51
17.5: 58n47
18.3: 91
18.20: 43n36
18.23: 94
18.32–35: 136
19.12: 55
19.14: 119
19.17: 126, 219n30
19.21: 55, 116, 221n39, 289
19.27: 310
19.29: 128
19.30: 190
20.1: 115, 121
20.6: 248
20.14: 123
20.16: 185, 190
20.22: 134
20.22–23: 135
20.28: 70, 210
21.1: 48, 49
21.2: 51
21.3: 52, 56
21.5: 35, 39, 50, 62–78
21.7: 52, 56
21.8: 57
21.9: 46–61
21.13: 32n37
21.23–27: 104
21.30: 257
21.33–36: 226

22.2–10: 189n80
22.4: 174
22.30: 286
22.39: 143n25
23.6: 211
23.13–14: 209
23.14: 207, 210
23.15: 121, 122
23.20–22: 305
23.23: 207n53
23.25: 209
23.27: 209
24.13: 158
24.29–30: 274
24.35: 233
24.42: 66n19
24.45: 224
25.1–13: 101n48
25.6: 39
25.10: 230
25.10–11: 133
25.14: 225
25.14–30: 185n29
25.21, 23: 238n24
25.29: 130
25.30: 223
25.31–46: 101n48
25.34: 132
25.46: 28, 285
26.20: 174n16
26.26: 174
26.41: 195
27.38: 275
27.45: 193n96
27.46: 278
27.54: 193n96
28.18: 40n24, 69, 174

Mark (Mk)
1.2–3: 85n4
1.33: 220
2.2: 220
2.7: 51, 316
3.27: 49
4.20: 127n65

10.40: 135
11.10: 59
11.17: 32n37
11.24: 135
16.15: 28, 121
16.15–16: 50
16.20: 51, 121n47

Luke (Lk)
1.4: 75
1.10–20: 85n3
1. 24–25: 85n3
1.26–27: 266
1.26–38: 85n2
1.28: 267
1.30: 267
1.32: 58, 300n18
1.34: 267
1.38: 261n9, 263
1.42: 268
1.46–55: 61n57, 211n63
1.47: 61
1.48: 260, 262
1.49: 319
1.52: 288
1.55: 269
1.70: 204
1.73: 269
1.78: 41,
1.78–79: 243n4
1.80: 117
2.7: 107
2.13–14: 27
2.14: 75
2.15–16: 27
2.41–43: 117
2.42: 93, 96, 97
2.43: 98
2.46: 100, 117
2.47: 103, 104
2.49: 107
2.51: 77n70, 104, 107
2.52: 87–107
3.14: 324

INDEX OF HOLY SCRIPTURE

Luke (Lk) *(cont.)*
3.21–22: 126
4.18: 11, 37, 239n29
5.11: 232
5.27: 114n19
6.20: 311n67
6.35: 168n59
6.36: 49
6.38: 312
7.16: 199
8.5: 108–28
8.5b–7: 109
8.7: 125
8.8: 126
8.11: 110, 269
8.15: 114
10.1: 50
10.5–9: 121
10.7: 298
10.17: 51
10.27: 50
10.28: 181, 231
10.33: 49
10.34: 239
10.38–42: 246n18
11.9: 130
11.13: 157
11.39–52: 115
11.46: 204
12.35–48: 66
12.47: 189
14.11: 325
14.15: 306
14.16: 171–94
14.17: 185
14.18: 186, 187
14.18–20: 183, 193
14.19: 188
14.20: 188
14.21: 189, 190
14.21–23: 181n45
14.22: 191
14.23 (Vg): 191, 192, 193
14.31: 325
15.3: 229

15.8–9: 234
15.10: 109
16.1: 214–32
16.2: 226, 230
16.3: 230
16.4: 232
16.9: 231, 232
16.10: 238
16.13: 57
16.19–26: 137, 190
16.22: 312
17.7–8: 57
17.20: 66
18.1–9: 101n48
18.3–8: 202n28
19.1–10: 54n32
19.2–10: 54
19.10: 41, 46, 75
19.13: 225
19.16: 92
20.36: 73
21.2–3: 202n28
21.33: 79–84
22.19: 176
22.29: 310
22.29–30: 182
22.30: 305
23.34: 279
23.42: 137
23.43: 279
23.46: 279
24.36: 43n36
24.39: 139

John (Jn)
1.1: 52n29, 53
1.1–18: 269
1.3: 174
1.5: 44
1.10: 174
1.11: 63
1.12: 269
1.13: 155
1.14: 25, 42, 52n29, 53, 64, 89, 112, 173, 217

1.16: 173n7
1.17: 88
1.26: 43, 174
1.29: 67
2.5: 263
3.3–5: 320
3.8: 118, 140, 147, 162
3.12: 160
3.14: 276
3.16: 41
3.17: 42
3.27: 187
4.10–15: 83
4.13: 96, 172
4.14: 172, 304
4.20–23: 27
4.24: 71n42, 216n13, 236
4.28–29: 115
4.34: 182n48
4.36: 280
4.48: 188n72
5.22: 69
5.25: 65
5.27: 28
5.35: 45
5.43: 42
6.35–51: 40n19
6.37: 151, 286
6.41: 175
6.45: 184, 317
6.50–51: 183
6.54: 176
6.57: 177
6.66: 123
6.68: 181
7.38: 214
8.12: 41, 243n4, 245, 248
8.31–59: 269
8.32: 75
8.34: 49, 75, 92n18
8.36: 75
8.42: 40
9.29: 174

INDEX OF HOLY SCRIPTURE 355

10.1: 52n26
10.10: 52n26, 64, 76
10.11: 40n19
10.12: 210
10.13: 80
10.16: 191
10.27: 205
10.30: 68
10.31–39: 269
10.35: 114
11.25–26: 198n11
11.34–44: 198n11
12.15: 39n16
12.31: 37, 276
12.32: 277
12.35: 192, 248
12.45: 62
12.46: 42
12.46–47: 60n55
13.15: 87
14.3: 64
14.6: 88, 110n5, 173n11
14.9: 60n55
14.23: 26n15, 64, 150, 218
14.24: 150
14.26: 148, 151
14.27: 152, 153
14.31: 142n20
15.1: 108
15.2: 109
15.4: 59
15.4–5: 316n12
15.5: 242
15.6: 268
15.9–10: 26n15
15.11: 35
15.13: 278
15.15: 151, 179
15.18: 51
15.19: 51
15.26: 148
16.12: 179
16.14: 161
16.23: 130
16.24: 129–37, 306
16.28: 115
17.3: 76
17.6: 59, 161
17.17: 29n24
17.22: 148
18.37: 75
18.37–38: 88n5
19.9–10: 103
19.25: 271
19.26–27: 279
19.39: 324
20.19: 43, 75
20.23: 51
20.26: 75
20.29: 188, 317
21.4: 181n44
21.11: 123
21.12: 181

Acts of the Apostles (Acts)
1.1: 204
1.4–5: 158
1.9: 66
2.1: 157
2.2: 140, 144
2.3: 146n40, 161
2.4: 33, 37, 138
2.13: 178
2.37: 156n89
2.41: 192
2.43: 33
4.12: 56, 270
4.30: 241
4.31: 37
4.32: 150n61
5.29: 107
5.32: 157
8.9–24: 123
8.32: 78
8.34: 49, 75, 92, 100
10.35: 309
10.38: 37
13.26: 224
13.47: 224
14.27: 37
15.10: 119
17.28: 142, 144
19.12: 319
20.29: 210

Romans (Rom)
1.4: 143, 162
1.7: 110n5
1.14: 162
1.20: 60n53, 102n55, 162n14, 179, 237, 303
2.5: 125
3.3: 123
3.8: 201
3.9: 51
3.23: 51
3.26: 80n5
4.15: 27
5.2: 29n23
5.5: 150
5.9: 264
5.10: 43, 75, 280
5.18–19: 272n56
6.4: 154
6.6: 115
6.22: 38, 106, 212, 279, 297
6.23: 165
8.1–17: 267n45
8.12: 196
8.13: 273
8.23: 161
8.26: 317n20
8.30: 154n74, 184, 315, 317, 318
8.35: 286
9.5: 269
11.33: 219
11.36: 169n60
12.8: 228
12.12: 130
12.16: 56
12.17 (Vg): 109
12.21: 201n22

INDEX OF HOLY SCRIPTURE

Romans (Rom) *(cont.)*
  13.1: 68
  13.12: 44–45, 119
  13.14: 72, 155
  14.8: 226
  16.18: 238
  16.19: 106

1 Corinthians (1 Cor)
  1.9: 281
  1.23: 274
  1.23–24: 111n7
  1.24: 178
  1.28: 190
  2.9: 42, 73, 92, 145, 159
  2.9–10: 184
  2.10: 146, 161
  2.10–13: 145n37
  3.1–2: 52n29, 162
  3.8: 298
  3.9: 223n49
  3.16: 48
  4.1: 224
  4.2: 237
  4.5: 28n21
  4.7: 131, 187
  4.12: 289
  7.7: 266
  7.25: 55
  8.5–6: 68
  8.6: 26n13, 30n30, 169n60
  9.9: 73, 225
  9.22: 143
  9.23–25: 224
  9.24: 298
  9.25: 55, 298, 322
  9.27: 125
  10.17: 177n27
  10.26: 141n11
  10.31: 227n61
  11.16: 292
  11.25: 176
  11.29: 178

  12.3: 138, 199
  12.4: 100, 173
  12.8–10: 198
  12.12–27: 277n73
  12.21–26: 228
  12.23: 91n16
  12.27: 177n27
  12.31: 156
  12.31–13.13: 32n39
  13.1–3: 149, 240
  13.9: 283
  13.11: 91
  13.12: 165, 294, 303
  13.13: 317
  14.1: 318
  14.13: 203
  14.20: 91
  14.29: 198
  14.32: 226
  14.33: 48, 152
  15.11: 162
  15.21–22: 272n56
  15.24: 301
  15.49: 72
  15.52: 65
  15.54–57: 277

2 Corinthians (2 Cor)
  1.10: 38
  2.17: 36n8, 204
  3.5: 63
  3.18: 157
  4.6: 45
  4.11: 237n22
  5.1: 33
  5.2: 285
  5.16: 42
  5.19: 43, 292
  6.1: 229n74
  6.2: 132
  6.17: 115
  7.1: 195
  8.9: 107n72, 113, 221, 288
  10.3–5: 92

  10.4: 321
  10.4–5: 119
  11.14: 196
  12.4: 162
  12.7: 125, 135
  12.19: 36n8
  13.11: 48

Galatians (Gal)
  2.19: 278
  2.19–20: 275
  2.20: 278
  3.3: 53
  3.11: 76
  3.17: 206
  3.19: 85
  3.27: 320
  3.28: 309n64
  4.4: 147n44
  4.5: 147
  4.6: 147
  4.8: 75
  4.26: 36
  5.2: 192
  5.17: 95, 189, 195
  5.22: 33, 94, 110n5, 211, 268, 280
  5.22–23: 45
  5.25: 144
  6.2: 122
  6.8: 268
  6.14: 275
  6.15: 122, 149

Ephesians (Eph)
  1.10: 27
  1.13–14: 156n87
  2.2: 58n46
  2.4: 220
  2.10: 150
  2.14: 30, 42, 304
  2.15–16: 30
  2.16: 43
  2.17: 42, 75
  2.19: 37, 93n19, 175

INDEX OF HOLY SCRIPTURE

3.8–9: 239n28
3.9: 140
3.15: 25n10
3.16: 153
4.3: 148, 152
4.7: 173n10
4.10: 269
4.11–16: 304
4.13: 39, 72, 91, 117
4.14: 209
4.21–31: 36
4.23: 205n42
4.23–24: 205
4.24: 72, 155
4.26–27: 211
4.29: 255
5.1: 177, 217n20, 304n43
5.2: 322
5.3: 322
5.8: 322
5.15: 322
5.20: 187
6.11: 205n37
6.17: 77n71

Philippians (Phil)
1.1: 237n27
2.5: 56
2.5–8: 237n22
2.6–7: 47, 172
2.7: 25, 39n18, 90
2.8: 56, 106, 262n15, 271, 278
2.9: 59, 271
2.13: 59, 151n63, 184n54, 316
2.21: 166
3.10: 57
3.14: 297
3.19: 287
4.4: 48
4.7: 38

Colossians (Col)
1.11–13: 39
1.15: 60
1.15–16: 30n30, 140
1.16: 30, 62
1.18: 203n31
1.19: 173
1.24: 115n25, 275
1.25–29: 223n49
1.28: 91
2.3: 112, 173, 214
2.4: 214n1
2.8: 203
2.15: 276
2.18: 56
2.18–19: 203
3.1: 36, 84, 295
3.1–17: 127
3.2: 82
3.4: 214
3.9–10: 217
3.9b–10: 155
3.11: 309
3.12: 155
3.15: 187

1 Thessalonians (1 Thes)
2.6: 52

2 Thessalonians (2 Thes)
2.3: 111
2.13: 160–61

1 Timothy (1 Tm)
1.15: 75
1.18–19: 321n38
2.4: 69, 70n33, 74n56
2.5: 43
3.2–13: 238
4.1–2: 205
4.8: 240
4.12: 115n23, 204
5.1: 193

6.15: 281
6.16: 314
6.17: 222, 228, 261

2 Timothy (2 Tm)
1.8: 224n51
1.9: 30n30
1.10: 38n13
2.3–4: 321n38
2.5: 298
2.13: 29
2.15: 255
2.21: 213n69
3.4: 190
4.7–8: 92
4.8: 297

Titus (Ti)
2.7–8: 204
2.7b: 115n23
3.1: 263
3.2: 218n26
3.4: 219
3.5: 49, 154

Hebrews (Heb)
1.5: 36
1.14: 74, 223
2.10: 26n13, 169n60, 301n22
2.11: 74
2.12: 74
2.16: 74
2.17: 47
4.10: 84
4.13: 230
4.16: 94n26, 221, 265, 313
5.4: 185n59
5.8–9: 106
5.12: 53
7.14: 36
7.19: 116, 117
7.26: 238
8.8: 36

INDEX OF HOLY SCRIPTURE

Hebrews (Heb) *(cont.)*
  9.15: 43
  10.19: 280
  10.35–38: 168n59
  11.1: 188n72
  11.3: 23, 140
  11.6: 52, 168n59
  11.26: 168n59
  11.16: 169
  11.33: 50, 311
  12.2: 56
  12.3: 275
  12.5–7: 168n59
  12.7: 315
  12.13: 256
  12.15: 229n74
  12.22: 36n6
  13.2: 312
  13.12: 280
  13.13: 115
  13.14: 296
  13.15: 211
  13.21: 316n12

James (Jas)
  1.2: 275
  1.5: 132, 220, 222
  1.6: 135
  1.7: 135
  1.17: 132, 242
  1.18: 149
  1.21: 76, 305
  1.22: 180n40
  1.26: 256
  2.10: 131
  3.15: 111
  3.17: 77, 112, 151
  4.1: 92n18
  4.2: 289
  4.3: 134
  4.7: 92
  4.8: 48
  4.12: 28
  5.1: 226
  5.2–3: 228
  5.9: 226
  5.14: 239

1 Peter (1 Pt)
  1.16: 269, 304n43
  1.19: 176n20
  1.23: 155
  2.2: 52n29
  2.5: 32, 190n81
  2.21: 56
  2.23: 78, 278
  2.24: 279
  3.18: 273
  4.1: 275
  4.10: 228
  5.4: 224

2 Peter (2 Pt)
  1.21: 201
  2.4: 37
  2.12: 75
  2.19: 49
  3.3–4: 66

1 John (1 Jn)
  1.3: 35
  1.3–4: 306
  1.7: 281
  2.1–2: 130
  2.14: 177n29
  2.15: 144, 186
  2.16: 186, 288
  2.27: 151
  3.1: 179, 294, 300
  3.2: 151, 182, 303n37, 304
  3.9: 110
  3.13: 51
  3.14: 76, 149
  3.16: 30n30
  3.17: 167
  3.22: 133
  4.1: 199
  4.12: 75
  4.16: 150, 305
  4.20: 153n70, 256n63
  5.4: 92
  5.11–12: 30n30

Jude (Jude)
  10: 152
  18: 66

Revelation (Rv)
  1.7: 34
  1.8: 162
  2.4: 98
  2.7: 275
  2.12: 98n38
  2.17: 171
  3.4: 57
  3.11: 93
  3.12: 286
  3.16: 34
  3.17: 131, 190
  3.20: 179, 218
  4.1: 37
  4.11: 140n10
  5.10: 293, 305
  5.11: 308
  7.4: 308
  7.5–8: 309
  7.9: 282, 308
  7.16: 293
  12.1: 247n19
  12.10: 37
  12.12: 37
  19.9: 181
  21.4: 307
  21.5: 25n7, 39n17
  21.6: 214
  22.2: 275
  22.11: 220
  22.13: 162
  22.20: 41

www.ingramcontent.com/pod-product-compliance
Lightning Source LLC
Chambersburg PA
CBHW020313010526
44107CB00054B/1827